A History of the Muslim World to 1405

The Making of a Civilization

VERNON O. EGGER

Georgia Southern University

PEARSON

Prentice Hall

Upper Saddle River, NJ 07458

Library of Congress Cataloging in Publication Data

Egger, Vernon
    A history of the Muslim world, to 1405 / Vernon Egger
       p. cm.
    Includes bibliographical references and index.
    ISBN 0-13-098389-6
    1. Civilization, Islamic.   2. Islam—History. I. Title

    DS36.85.E34 2004
    909'.097671—dc21

                                   2003052833

VP/Editorial Director: Charlyce Jones Owen
Senior Acquisitions Editor: Charles Cavalier
Associate Editor: Emsal Hasan
Managing Editor: Joanne Riker
Executive Marketing Manager: Heather Shelstad
Production Liaison: Randy Pettit
Manufacturing Manager: Nick Sklitsis
Manufacturing Buyer: Tricia Kenny
Cover Design: Jayne Conte
Image Permission Coordinator: Beth Brenzel
Production Supervision and Composition: Preparé Inc.
Printer/Binder: R.R. Donnelley
Cover Design: Karen Salzbach
Cover Art: A medieval library portrayed in a 13th century manuscript of al-Hariri's *Moqamat*
Cover Printer: Phoenix Color Corp.

Credits and acknowledgments borrowed from other sources and reproduced, with permission, in this textbook appear on page 327.

Pearson Education LTD.
Pearson Education Singapore, Pte. Ltd
Pearson Education, Canada, Ltd
Pearson Education–Japan

Pearson Education Australia PTY, Limited
Pearson Education North Asia Ltd
Pearson Educación de Mexico, S.A. de C.V.
Pearson Education Malaysia, Pte. Ltd

19 18 17 16 15 14 13 12
ISBN 0-13-098389-6

Contents

DOCUMENTS

MAPS

TABLES

Preface

This book is an introduction to the history of the Muslim world for readers with little or no knowledge of the subject. I use the term *Muslim* rather than *Islamic* because this is a study of the history made by the Muslim peoples rather than a history of the religion of Islam. It is important to make a distinction between *Muslim* and *Islamic*—properly speaking, *Islamic* should refer to elements of the religion, while *Muslim* relates to the adherents of the religion. Thus, not all customs followed by Muslims are Islamic, and although a mosque is an example of Islamic architecture, a palace is not. A generation ago, the great scholar Marshall Hodgson wrestled with this problem and coined the term *Islamicate* to describe the cultural features of Muslim societies that were not strictly religious, such as secular architecture. The term has not gained widespread acceptance, and this book will avoid it.

If the distinction between *Islamic* and *Muslim* seems strained, suppose that someone said that the White House is an example of Christian architecture because a Christian designed it, or that Bastille Day is a Christian holiday, since it is celebrated in a country with a Christian majority. No one is tempted to make such assertions, and yet they are equivalent to speaking of *Islamic* palaces or *Islamic* medicine, as many historians do. Much of the history related in this book is not directly related to Islam, and so it is more appropriately called Muslim history.

The phrase *Muslim world*, as used in this book, refers to regions ruled by Muslim-dominated governments, as well as areas in which the Muslim population is a majority or an influential minority. For several decades in the seventh century, the Muslim world was coterminous with the region often referred to today as the Middle East, but it soon expanded far beyond that heartland. By the tenth century, many of the most important cultural developments in the Muslim world were taking place outside the Middle East. The size of the Muslim world has alternately expanded and contracted over time, and we will be concerned to see how and why that has happened.

The themes of the book are tradition and adaptation. The history of any society is one of the preservation of core values and practices, but also one of adaptation to changing conditions. Muslims follow a religion that is strongly anchored in both scripture and authoritative codes of behavior and are conditioned to adhere closely to the canon of their religious tradition. On the other hand, from the very beginning of their history, Muslims have found ways to adapt elements of their faith to their culture, as well as to adapt their cultural values and practices to the core of their faith. Islam is no more of a homogeneous world religion than is Christianity or Judaism.

The themes of tradition and adaptation allow us to make sense of some important issues in Muslim history. By being aware of the premium placed on faithfulness to the scriptures, we can understand more clearly how Muslims were able to maintain a common sense of identity throughout the wide expanse of the world in which they settled. Further, we can more readily appreciate why Muslims have accepted certain features of alien cultures and rejected others. From the first century of the Islamic calendar, when Muslims were having to decide how to administer a huge majority of non-Muslims in the former Byzantine and Sasanian empires, until today, when many Muslims are concerned about the impact of a secular, global economy on their heritage, the tension between adherence to tradition on the one hand and adaptation to changing conditions on the other has been at the center of Muslim concerns.

This book treats economic, political, intellectual, and social developments over a wide area and across many centuries. Of these topics, the intellectual and political developments receive more attention than social and economic history. The study of the social history of the Muslim world is in its infancy. Therefore, it is not possible at this point to write the history of the daily lives of ordinary men and women in large areas of the Muslim world. Economic history tends to stress connections among areas of the world, which is why it is a popular theme in the field of world history. The motif of connections and of global integration that economic history can convey runs throughout this book as a powerful undercurrent. In the first decade of the twenty-first century, however, I am convinced that our awareness of connections in Muslim history needs to be balanced by an awareness of diversity and discontinuities. Troubling stereotypes of Islam and of Muslims loom large in our culture and can be modified only by our becoming aware of the diversity of religious and political expressions within the Muslim world.

A widely held assumption in our society is that Islam is a crystallized artifact from the seventh century—or, at best, from the tenth or eleventh century, when Islamic law is often said to have stopped developing. It is important to be aware of the important stages in the historical development of Islam and to realize that critical periods in history have encouraged Muslims to be either flexible or inflexible in their reception of new ideas. It is also important to be aware of the varieties of expression of Islam. Many generalizations about Islam are actually applicable only to Sunni Islam, and even then, to the Sunni Islam practiced in certain countries, not to regions in other parts of the world. The history of Shi'ite Islam is usually ignored—or recognized only in passing. Shi'ites have played a major role in history and should be recognized for having done so.

Another widely held stereotype is that Muslims form a monolithic, homogeneous mass that acts in concert on given issues. In recent years, this assumption has given rise to the notion that "Islam" and "the West" are on the eve of a "clash of civilizations." According to this theory, when Muslims in one area have a grievance against "the West," other Muslim groups will come to their aid on the basis of their civilizational "kin." The impression of a monolithic Muslim world is reinforced by the fact that many world history books discuss the Abbasid caliphate (750–1258) as though it were an empire that united the great majority of the world's Muslims of that age, leaving the impression that Muslims have a history of political unity. Even the textbook discussions of the sixteenth- and seventeenth-century empires of the Ottomans, Safavids, and Mughals rarely note their great differences. The fact is that Muslim political unity was shattered in the third decade after the Prophet's death. There have been numerous Muslim political entities ever since then. Not only have conflicting interests divided them, but Muslim states have also frequently allied with Christian, Hindu, or other states against fellow Muslims.

Just as intellectuals prior to the seventeenth century thought that the universe possessed different physical properties from those on earth, so have historians and political theorists often treated Muslim history as different in kind from the history of the rest of the world. This book attempts to show through an examination of their history that Muslims are an integral part of the world community and have functioned as other human beings have under similar conditions.

Acknowledgments

This project has taken much longer than I anticipated when I began it with a naive expectation that it would require a couple of years to fill in the gaps in my lecture notes. Gaps, indeed. The book relies almost entirely on the work of other scholars. I have listed the sources that I have found most valuable—and that I recommend to other readers—at the end of the relevant chapters. I wish to express my appreciation to the members of the staff of the Interlibrary Loan office of the Henderson Library at Georgia Southern University for their consistently excellent help, and to the Faculty Research Committee and the Faculty Development Committee for making it possible for me to devote several months to full-time research and writing on this project.

I am also grateful for the comments, insights, and corrections that I received on the manuscript from Herbert Bodman, Donald Reid, David Commins, Gladys Frantz-Murphy, Erik Gilbert, John Parcels, Kenneth Perkins, and two reviewers who wished to be anonymous. They saved me from several egregious errors, although I obstinately persisted in certain interpretations despite their best efforts (but never when they agreed on a criticism). I invite readers to send me their own suggestions on how to improve this book—I have been known to yield in the face of overwhelming odds.

Finally, anyone who works on a major project within the context of a family knows that an author's acknowledgment of a family's support and patience is not a perfunctory gesture: The writing of a book inevitably disrupts family life. I welcome the opportunity to thank Mary, Krista, and Rachel for their good-humored patience and encouragement throughout this endeavor.

Vernon O. Egger

Note on Transliteration and Dating

Any work that deals with the Muslim world faces the challenge of the transliteration of words from one alphabet to another. Scholars need a comprehensive system that represents in the Latin alphabet all the vowels and consonants of other alphabets, but nonspecialists can find such a system more confusing and alien than useful. The problem is a serious one when transliterating only one language; in this book, we have to deal with several. I have tried to compromise between accuracy and ease of use.

Geographic place names are spelled in this book as they appear on modern English-language atlas maps (Khorasan, Baghdad, Cairo). In some cases, no consensus exists among cartographers on the spelling of place names, and so this book occasionally provides alternate spellings (Zaragoza/Saragossa, Qayrawan/Kairouan). In a few cases, this book uses names that are more easily understood by English-speakers than some that are more culturally authentic. An example is the Greek-based "Transoxiana" for the Arabic phrase *ma wara' al-nahr.*

In the interest of trying to make transliterated words less of an obstacle to the task of understanding the material, I have also used the more popular spellings for some words, even when doing so seems inconsistent with the practice of the book as a whole. Thus, I discuss "Sunnis and Shi'ites" rather than "Sunnis and Shi'is" or "Sunnites and Shi'ites."

For personal names and technical words in the Arabic, Persian, and Turkish languages, a simplified version of the Library of Congress system is used. No distinction is indicated in this book between long and short vowels, nor are diacritical marks provided for the vowels of words from any language. For the Arabic language, no attempt is made to indicate the so-called velarized consonants, and no distinction is made between the forms of the letter *h*, which should be sounded or aspirated. The combination *dh* represents the sound of the *th* in the English word *then*; *kh* is similar to the *ch* in the Scottish *loch*; *gh* is best described as the sound made when gargling. The *q* is pronounced farther back in the throat than the *k*. The symbol ' represents a glottal stop, the sound that begins each syllable of the English expression *uh-oh*. The symbol ' represents an Arabic consonant with no English equivalent, but it is important in words such as 'Ali or Shi'ite. Phonetically, it is a "voiced guttural stop" produced in the very back of the throat, by constricting the larynx to stop the flow of air. An approximation may be achieved by making a glottal stop as far back in the throat as possible.

The prefix *al-* is the definite article in Arabic, meaning *the*. Before most letters in the alphabet, the prefix sounds the way it is spelled, but it assumes the sound of certain letters when it precedes them (*t, th, d, dh, r, z, s, sh, n*). Thus, al-Rahman is pronounced ar-Rahman.

Notes regarding the significance of names containing 'Abd, Abu, and Ibn may be found in the glossary. Understanding these terms makes the learning of Arabic-based names easier and more meaningful.

This book uses the abbreviations B.C.E. (Before the Common Era) and C.E. (Common Era). The abbreviations refer to the same dates that are designated as B.C. (Before Christ) and A.D. (*anno Domini*), respectively, on the Gregorian calendar, but they are an attempt to use religiously neutral nomenclature. They have almost totally replaced the B.C./A.D. designations in books on world history because of the latter's Christian-specific nature. In a book on Muslim history, the most logical (and considerate) way of dating would be to use the A.H. (*anno hejirae*) system, which is based on the Islamic calendar. The first year of this system began in July 622 on the Gregorian calendar. Most readers of this book, however, are non-Muslim citizens of the United States, who, in my experience, are usually confused rather than helped by the use of the A.H. dating system. It is explained in the glossary.

PART ONE

The Formative Period, 610–950

Islam arose in the early seventh century as a religio-social reform movement in the small, hot, and dusty town of Mecca in the western Arabian peninsula. During its first decade, the movement appeared to be highly vulnerable, attracting only a few dozen followers. Many observers expected it to fail miserably. If those same skeptics could have used a time machine to travel one century into the future, they would have found Muslims ruling an empire from the Atlantic to the Indus River valley in modern Pakistan—a region that stretched across 5000 miles. Other groups before and after this period also conquered huge territories in a very short time, but their rule proved ephemeral. The Muslims, by contrast, created a new civilization in this vast area. Their achievement may well be the closest approximation to the cosmological theory of the "Big Bang" that human history has to offer.

The period of Muslim conquests was necessarily followed by an extended period of consolidation. Muslims shared a common set of beliefs and practices, but they lived in dramatically different cultures, had access to a wide range of resources, and were confronted with challenges specific to their region. As they worked out the implications of their faith, they found that their solutions differed from those of their fellow Muslims in other parts of the world. One of the most fascinating features of Muslim history is the continuity of Islamic identity in the absence of a central religious authority such as a pope, patriarch, or synod. The important developments in religious doctrine and practice were the products of pious individuals who communicated with each other across vast distances. As a result, differences arose among those who called themselves Muslims. In a few cases, such differences were irreconcilable and even deadly. In general, however, the story of Muslim history is that devotion to the Qur'an and the example of the Prophet have enabled Muslims across a wide spectrum of societies to recognize that they belong to the same community of faith.

Chapter 1 provides a broad overview of the areas in which Muslim societies first developed: the regions of what had been the eastern Byzantine Empire, the former Sasanian Empire, and the Arabian Peninsula. Muhammad's career was confined almost exclusively to the peninsula, but his immediate successors as leaders of the Muslim community were preoccupied with the areas they were conquering in the Byzantine and Sasanian empires. It was here that Islam in the post-prophetic period largely developed, and it is important to understand the pre-Islamic history of these territories. Chapter 2 discusses the conquests of the first century of Muslim history and the development of administrative structures in the newly conquered areas. It shows that this first Muslim state created after the death of the Prophet was an "Arab empire" that failed to live up to the ideals of Islamic equality and justice. Chapter 3 examines the first major divisions within the Muslim community. It traces the rise of a movement known as Kharijism and explores the early history of Shi'ism. It shows how the history of Shi'ism was linked to the revolutionary Abbasid movement that overthrew the Arab empire. Chapter 4 examines the political fragmentation of Muslim society after the eighth century and its organization into three caliphates. The apparent disunity of these political systems was balanced by the development of a highly integrated and sophisticated economic system that linked all of the regions under Muslim control. Chapter 5 surveys the religious and intellectual developments of the era. It is here that we can see more clearly the correlation between the cessation of the conquests on the one hand and the establishment of the foundations of religious institutions on the other.

The period from 600 to 950 is called "formative" not because Islam assumed its permanent form during this time, but because its possibilities for future development were narrowed into specific directions. For nearly three centuries after the conquest of the Pyrenees Mountains and the Indus valley, the frontiers of Muslim-ruled territory remained essentially stable. During this time, the methodology for determining Islamic law was developed, Islamic mysticism and theology developed their frameworks, science and philosophy were introduced as fields of study, and the distinctions between the terms *Sunni* and *Shi'ite* became well defined. As we shall see in Part Two, the subsequent three centuries saw further elaborations on Islamic traditions, but they were channeled by the developments of the period to 950.

CHRONOLOGY

570	Traditional date for the birth of Muhammad
602–628	Last Byzantine–Sasanian war
610	Traditional date for the first revelation to Muhammad
622	Hijra
632	Death of Muhammad; Abu Bakr becomes caliph
633	Muslim army crushes Ridda
634	Muslim conquests begin; 'Umar becomes caliph
637	Muslim armies conquer Syria
638	Muslim armies conquer Iraq
642	Muslim armies conquer Egypt
644	Slave murders 'Umar; 'Uthman becomes caliph

651	Muslim armies conquer Iran
656	Muslim soldiers murder 'Uthman; 'Ali becomes caliph
661	Kharijite murders 'Ali; Mu'awiya becomes caliph in Damascus; Umayyad dynasty begins
680	Battle of Karbala
685–705	Caliphate of 'Abd al-Malik, who makes Arabic the official language of the empire, mints coins with Islamic details and builds Dome of the Rock as symbol of Islamic supremacy
705–715	Muslim armies conquer Central Asia and Sind
711–720	Muslim armies conquer Iberian peninsula
740	Berber revolt in North Africa and Iberia
750	Abbasids overthrow Umayyads
756	'Abd al-Rahman establishes the Umayyad amirate of Cordoba
762	Al-Mansur founds Baghdad
765	Death of Ja'far al-Sadiq
768–814	Reign of Charlemagne in western Europe
813–833	Caliphate of al-Ma'mun creates the Bayt al-Hikma and provokes a storm of criticism for his attempt to enforce Mu'tazilism
860s	Anarchy in Baghdad, provinces become autonomous; Isma'ilis become active in Iran, Iraq, and Syria
874	Imami twelfth Imam goes into Lesser Concealment
850–900	Feudalism emerges in western Europe
909	Fatimids declare a caliphate in Ifriqiya
900–950	Acceptance of Shafi'i synthesis for jurisprudence
929	'Abd al-Rahman III declares a caliphate in Cordoba
936	Abbasid caliph cedes power to Turkish general
941	Imami twelfth Imam goes into Greater Concealment
945	Buyids seize power in Baghdad

CHAPTER 1

Origins

Islam arose in the Arabian Peninsula in the early seventh century. Arabia is surrounded on three sides by ocean and on the north by the Fertile Crescent, the arc formed by the life-giving rivers of Iraq and the green plains and mountains of western Syria. A remarkably arid region of almost one million square miles, the interior of Arabia attracted little interest from its neighbors. On the other hand, the era's superpowers—the Byzantine Empire and the Sasanian Empire—were keenly interested in Arabia's coastline and its frontiers with the Fertile Crescent. The traditional Byzantine–Sasanian rivalry entailed a competition for control both of those coasts and the desert frontiers. Thus, when a highly destructive conflict between the two imperial powers took place throughout the first quarter of the seventh century, the entire region was affected.

The inhabitants of Arabia followed the conflict closely, for they knew that its conclusion would determine which of the powers controlled their frontiers. What they— and the superpowers themselves—could not know was that during the war the balance of power in the region had completely changed. The two combatants were exhausted by 628, when the Byzantines appeared to have won the war. Meanwhile, however, a prophet named Muhammad was in the final stage of consolidating his political and religious authority in the peninsula and was creating a dynamic and seemingly irresistible force. Only a decade after the Byzantine triumph, Arab armies fighting in the name of the movement created by Muhammad would seize the greater part of the Byzantine Empire and utterly destroy the Sasanian Empire.

Southwestern Asia in the Seventh Century

The Arabs would conquer their two imperial neighbors in the name of a monotheistic faith that bore striking similarities to Judaism and Christianity. Like these two other faiths, Islam would take centuries to develop many of the institutions and doctrines that are most characteristic of it today. Many such developments would take place in the territories formerly under Byzantine and Sasanian rule. Thus, before we examine the career of Muhammad, it will be useful to survey certain features of the Byzantine and Sasanian empires, as well as of the Arabian Peninsula.

4

The Byzantine Empire

The Byzantine Empire owed a large debt to Alexander the Great, whose bloody campaigns between the Mediterranean Sea and the Himalayas during the late fourth century B.C.E. introduced Greek culture into southwestern Asia and northeastern Africa. In the centuries after Alexander's death in 323 B.C.E., the Macedonians and Greeks who came into this area as soldiers, merchants, craftsmen, and rulers brought with them their language, architecture, and social institutions. The result was a synthesis of Greek and indigenous cultures that is called Hellenistic civilization. Urban life along the eastern Mediterranean seaboard experienced a cultural transformation. Newly established cities, such as Alexandria in Egypt and Antioch in Syria, became the dominant economic and cultural centers, and the architecture of older cities received new inspiration with the advent of Greek styles for theaters, gymnasia, and temples. Greek became the language of learning and of politics. The era was remarkable for its scientific, artistic, philosophical, and economic achievements. This was the period when such philosophical schools as Stoicism, Epicureanism, Skepticism, and Cynicism flourished; Aristarchus devised his seemingly audacious theory that the sun, rather than the earth, occupied the center of the universe; Archimedes introduced the concept of *pi* and developed theories of the properties of the lever and of the specific gravity of water; and Eratosthenes became the first man known to have measured with remarkable accuracy the circumference of the earth.

The chief threat to the Hellenistic kingdoms was the Roman Republic, which began flexing its military muscle in the mid-third century B.C.E. by challenging Carthage for control of the western Mediterranean. Soon its ambitions extended to the eastern Mediterranean as well, and between 146 B.C.E. and 30 B.C.E. it absorbed its Hellenistic neighbors. The last of the Hellenistic rulers was Cleopatra of Egypt. She might have been as little known to most of us as the other Hellenistic rulers had it not been for her tragic affairs with the Roman leaders Julius Caesar and Mark Antony.

With the defeat of Mark Antony and Cleopatra, Octavian assumed the title of Augustus Caesar, and the Roman Republic became the Roman Empire. The empire's eastern half was in effect the Hellenized region. When Rome took over this area, the language of governmental administration changed to Latin, but the power of the Hellenistic legacy is revealed in the fact that Greek remained the most influential language of culture in the eastern Mediterranean until the Arabs came, six centuries later. The Romans themselves continued to look to Greek sources for the inspiration of much of their own cultural production.

Even during the famous *Pax Romana* of the two centuries during and after the reign of Augustus (the period 27 B.C.E.–180 C.E.), the former Hellenistic areas remained the most populous and wealthy sections of the empire. The emperor Constantine's decision to establish an eastern capital (Constantinople, or "Constantine's City") on the site of the ancient Greek colony of Byzantium, at the mouth of the Black Sea, reflected the importance that the East had for the Roman Empire. The dedication of the new capital in 330 C.E. is a convenient point to identify as the beginning of Byzantine history. It is important to remember, however, that the Byzantines always regarded themselves as "Romanoi" and that a distinctive Byzantine culture required at least two centuries to emerge.

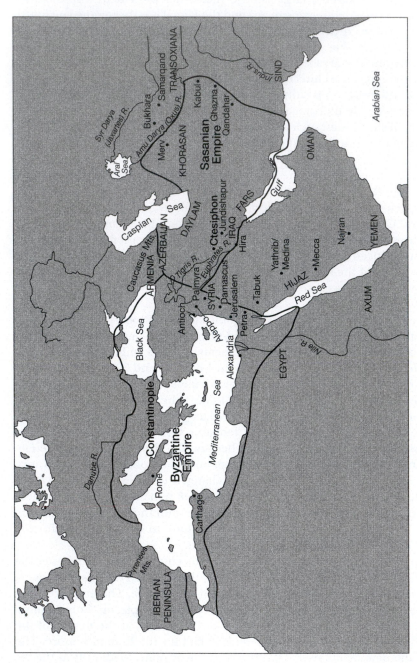

MAP 1.1   Western Asia and the Mediterranean on the Eve of Islam

The eastern half of the Roman Empire remained stable and even flourished over the next two centuries while the western half succumbed to the attacks of Germanic invaders in the fourth and fifth centuries. By 410, Germanic tribes controlled Europe west of the Adriatic Sea and North Africa west of modern Tunisia. Constantinople ruled over an area that extended across southeastern Europe to the Adriatic, into Asia to a frontier just west of the Euphrates River, and into North Africa as far as modern Tunisia.

The Mediterranean climate of the coastal areas produced long, hot, and dry summers and temperate, rainy winters. The agriculture of these regions usually specialized in the production of grapes, olives, and grain. Away from the coast, agriculture was much more limited. Topography was one factor. Rugged mountains and narrow valleys are the dominant feature of the Balkans (southeastern Europe) and characterize all but the narrow coastal plains and central plateau of Anatolia (the bulk of modern Turkey). Spotty rainfall was another factor. The Anatolian plateau typically receives just enough rainfall to make growing wheat worthwhile, but the interior of Syria, Egypt, and North Africa are arid, making agriculture impossible without irrigation. Irrigation had made Egypt one of the earliest centers of civilization, and the centrality of irrigation to the life of Egypt had prompted the ancient Greek historian Herodotus to call Egypt "the gift of the Nile." In Syria, the Euphrates and Orontes rivers and numerous oases provided water for irrigation. The river valleys and oases were the most densely populated regions of both Syria and Egypt. Because of their grain-producing potential, the two regions were invaluable "breadbaskets" for the empire, and were more important than ever after the loss to the Germanic invaders of grain-growing areas in the western Mediterranean.

The inhabitants of the eastern Mediterranean and the Black Sea engaged in a flourishing commerce in order to exchange the cash crops of one area for those of another. The Byzantine Empire possessed a remarkably long coastline relative to its land area. This geographical fact was a great benefit to its economy and to its government's ability to remain in communication with outlying areas. Goods could be shipped much more rapidly and cheaply by ships and boats than by carts and pack animals. Since most of the empire's hinterlands were within a short overland trip from water routes, travel between the geographic extremities of the empire was remarkably efficient. The huge city of Constantinople could safely outgrow the ability of its own region to produce food and rely instead upon Syria and Egypt to ship much of the grain that fed its people.

The region's foodstuffs were also valued commodities in other parts of the world. Grain traveled well without further processing, and it was ground into flour by either the wholesale or retail customer. Olives and grapes, however, spoiled quickly in their natural state and needed to be processed prior to shipment. Olives were pressed for their oil, which was used as food, lamp oil, and a soap substitute; grapes were fermented into wine. The Byzantines traded these products for furs, timber, amber, spices, and other items that they needed. They had access to Russia by way of the great rivers that drain into the Black Sea, and they were able to trade for the gold of Nubia (in the northern part of the modern country of Sudan) by sailing up the Nile.

The middle half of the sixth century may well have been the period of the empire's greatest triumph and influence. By that time, the areas that had composed the western Roman Empire were divided into feuding Germanic kingdoms, whereas the Byzantine half witnessed the emperor Justinian's rise to power (r. 527–565). Justinian aspired to reunite the entire Mediterranean under "Roman" rule (he spoke Latin and regarded himself to be the Roman emperor) and led military campaigns that regained large areas of the Italian Peninsula, the southern Iberian Peninsula, and North Africa. He codified Roman law in the *Corpus Juris Civilis*, which influenced both canon and civil law in Europe over the next several centuries. Justinian also wanted his city to reflect imperial brilliance, so he embarked on a huge construction program that included the Church of Holy Wisdom, or Hagia Sophia. During his reign, Constantinople became the largest city west of China, and numbered perhaps half a million people.

The empire remained a formidable presence for many centuries, but already by the sixth century it was clear that the state was having problems retaining the allegiance of all the different peoples of its complex society. Despite the brilliance of its culture and of the achievements of Justinian, the Byzantine Empire experienced several devastating blows during the sixth century. The bubonic plague struck in 541 and recurred frequently over the next several decades; earthquakes caused great damage to several important cities in Lebanon; the Sasanians sacked the great city of Antioch in 540 while Justinian's armies were engaged in campaigns in the western Mediterranean; the Avars and Slavs devastated the Balkans; and the Lombards seized large areas in Italy that Justinian had won at great cost. Justinian's successors were forced to raise taxes to pay for the great emperor's ambitious projects and campaigns, and they revoked the financial and political autonomy of the empire's cities in order to expropriate their surpluses more effectively.

Egyptians and Syrians, in particular, resented the these new measures. Egypt and Syria had been Hellenized since the time of Alexander, and the cities of Alexandria and Antioch were awe-inspiring centers of Greek culture centuries before Constantinople's foundations had been laid. It was precisely their increasingly secondary status that rankled the pride of the Hellenized provincial elites. They were acutely aware of their vulnerability to economic and political exploitation by Constantinople, and they were resentful of the loss of their religious leadership to the rising power of the patriarch in the capital city. Non-Greek-speaking inhabitants of these provinces had even less reason to be loyal to the capital.

Political opposition to the Byzantine government's policies often took the form of religious dissent. This is a phenomenon that we shall see replicated many times in the history of Muslim societies in which the government derives much of its legitimacy from its support of, and identification with, an official state religion. Advocating a different religious expression from that of the ruler in effect challenges the legitimacy of the ruler's religion and thereby indirectly challenges his political legitimacy. Religious dissent in the Byzantine Empire often took the form of arguments over the nature of Christ. From the beginning of the Christian movement, the followers of Jesus had wrestled with the issue of defining his nature as man *and* divine being. In the fifth and sixth centuries, the question had developed serious political repercussions, and the disputes over the issue later played a role in the spread of Islam into the area. It is useful, therefore, to note the distinctions among the terms *Orthodox, Nestorian,* and *Monophysite.*

The official interpretation of the state (Orthodox) church was defined at the Council of Chalcedon in 451, which stated that Christ had two "natures" (human and divine), perfect and perfectly distinct, which were united in one "person" (or being). Two major dissenting views existed, with special strength in Egypt and Syria. Their differences from the Orthodox position seem quite subtle and innocuous today, but in the fifth century, social and religious tensions were so great that any deviation from the official view was considered a threat to the civil order and to the integrity of Christianity itself. The group the Orthodox persecuted the most were the Nestorians, who derived their name from Nestorius, bishop of Antioch, the greatest city in Syria. Nestorians were accused of holding a heretical view of Christ's "person." It is not clear what Nestorius' actual position was, but his political enemies insisted that he taught that the presence of the divine and human in Christ was such that there were in him two distinct persons, as opposed to the Orthodox doctrine of two natures concurring in one person. To many of us today, that sounds like hairsplitting, but in those days, to hold the Nestorian position was to court imprisonment or even execution.

The other major dissenting group, the Monophysites, clashed with the Orthodox position over the subject of Christ's "nature" rather than over his "person." They rejected the Orthodox doctrine that Christ's divine and human natures were separate. In practice, they usually even went further and stated that Christ had a single, divine nature. Monophysitism became the doctrine of the Coptic Church in Egypt, which made up the vast majority of Egyptians. Monophysitism was also widespread in Syria, where its adherents formed the Syrian Orthodox Church, whose members are commonly known as Jacobites. A third group, the Armenian Church, formally adopted Monophysitism in 506, and by doing so, planted Monophysitism strongly in eastern Anatolia. Both Monophysites and Nestorians suffered persecution from the Orthodox Church, and Nestorians suffered persecution even from the Monophysite group in Syria. In the late fifth century, thousands of Nestorians migrated to the east, taking refuge in the Sasanian Empire. Although subject to periodic persecution from the Sasanian religious establishment, in general, Nestorians found a welcome refuge among the Sasanians. Intensely evangelistic as well as involved in international commerce, they spread as far as India and China and were present in considerable numbers along the Eurasian trade routes until the late fourteenth century.

Language was another factor that played a role in shaping social identities in the Byzantine Empire. Like any major society, it was multilingual. Latin remained the language of administration until the early seventh century, while Greek was the dominant spoken and written language in the basin of the Aegean Sea and was employed by elites in the large cities throughout the empire. The most widely used spoken languages in the Byzantine provinces of the eastern Mediterranean, however, belonged to the Afroasiatic language family: Coptic, Aramaic, and Arabic. Coptic was the primary spoken and written language in Egypt. Aramaic had been the lingua franca of southwestern Asia and the eastern Mediterranean since at least the fourth century B.C.E. It had displaced Hebrew as the language of the Jews. It was the language of Jesus and the apostles in the first century, and Jewish rabbis had used it to write the Babylonian and Jerusalem Talmuds. Aramaic was the language of commerce between the Mediterranean and the Indus River and was the majority language in both

Byzantine Syria and in Sasanian Iraq. One of its dialects, Syriac, became the most prestigious written form of Aramaic from the third through the seventh centuries. It was used for Christian liturgies as well as for philosophical and scientific treatises.

Substantial minorities in Syrian cities spoke Arabic, as did nomads and peasants in the frontier areas of eastern and southern Syria. Arabs had been a significant presence in the eastern Roman–Byzantine provinces for centuries, particularly in the semiarid central region and the desert region of the east and south. In northern Syria, the predominantly Arab city of Palmyra had arisen by the first century B.C.E. as a trading center between Rome and the Parthian kingdom that lay to the east. Over the years, it came under increasing Roman influence. A major caravan center, Palmyra reached its zenith of wealth and cultural development between 130 and 270 C.E., becoming the seat of Roman control over Asia Minor, Egypt, and Syria. It was during Palmyra's golden age that Philip the Arab became the Roman emperor (244–249). Important economically and politically, Palmyra was remembered in the popular imagination most for the "Arab queen" Zenobia who rose in revolt against Rome when her husband, Odenathus, was assassinated in 266. Rome regained control only with great difficulty in 272.

As the sixth century came to a close, the population of Arabs was increasing in Damascus, Aleppo, and other cities in Syria. The reasons for this demographic surge are not clear, but much of the increase in numbers may have been the result of migration from the northern Arabian Peninsula, where a sustained drought had led to a palpable "desertification" of the area. Arabs were not regarded as aliens within Byzantine society. Like the majority of the population in the area, they spoke Aramaic as well as their native tongue, and many knew Greek. Most of the Arabs of the Byzantine Empire, even the nomads of eastern Syria, seem to have been Monophysite Christians.

The Ghassanids are the most well-known Arab tribal confederation of the eastern section of the Byzantine Empire during the sixth and early seventh centuries. Based between Palmyra and Damascus, they had begun serving the Byzantines as a buffer against the nomads from the Arabian Peninsula and the Sasanians to the east. Their performance against the Sasanians in the sixth century was so valuable that Justinian rewarded their chief with the titles of patrician, phylarch, and king— the highest honors that he could bestow on anyone. Their service was important, since the regular Byzantine units were concentrated on the northern borders of the empire.

By the beginning of the seventh century, however, the Ghassanids and the Byzantine court were suspicious of each other. Despite their service to the Orthodox emperor, the Ghassanids had been Monophysites since at least 540. By 584, they had become so ardent in their faith that the Byzantines stopped paying regular subsidies to them. Since the government did not send additional regular army units to the frontier in order to compensate for the loss of dependable service by its Arab clients, the security of the area was henceforth in jeopardy.

By the end of the sixth century, the Byzantine Empire was the preeminent power of the Mediterranean and the worthy heir of both Alexander and Augustus. As the seventh century dawned, its leaders could be sanguine about the future. There were, in fact, serious disputes within the royal family and sporadic attacks on its frontiers, but because feuds among the ruling elite and war with neighboring states were the norm rather than the exception in the empire's history, no leading figure saw reason for alarm.

The Sasanian Empire

To the east, the Byzantine Empire faced its only major rival in the Sasanian Empire. The Sasanians were Iranians who seized power in 226 C.E. Iranians of various dynasties had dominated the Iranian plateau for most of the period after Cyrus the Great (ca. 550 B.C.E.). Their Persian culture and dialects had become the standard for a huge area whose eastern frontiers extended to the Syr Darya River in the northeast, the cities of Ghazna (modern Ghazni) and Qandahar in the east, and the Indus River in the southeast. After quickly conquering all of that area, the Sasanians soon lost the area between the Amu Darya River and the Syr Darya to outside invaders, but the region would remain culturally Persian for centuries. Because the Greek name for the Amu Darya was the Oxus River, Europeans have usually referred to the region between it and the Syr Darya as Transoxiana (or Transoxania), "that which lies beyond the Oxus." It was the area known later by the Arabs as *ma wara' al-nahr*, or "that which lies beyond the river."

By contrast with the Byzantine Empire, the Sasanian realm was a great interior land mass that relied more on transport by land than by water. The great majority of the region was in a desert setting. The Iranian plateau itself is ringed by mountains. In the west, the Zagros range extends from modern Azerbaijan in the northwest to the Persian Gulf, and then eastward toward modern Pakistan. The Elburz chain runs along the south shore of the Caspian Sea to meet the border ranges of Khorasan to the east. The arid interior plateau is distinguished by the remarkable Dasht-e Kavir, an impenetrable, salt-encrusted, muddy waste covering 20,000 square miles. Even the inhabitable areas of the plateau average less than ten inches of rainfall annually (comparable to Phoenix, Arizona). Cities of any size on the plateau had to be located within a short distance of the mountains in order to benefit from the spring runoff from melting snow. Otherwise, only small settlements could survive, relying on springs or a remarkable system of underground irrigation canals. These canals, or *qanat*s, brought water to villages from highland water sources. They were usually one-half mile to three miles long, but could extend as far as thirty miles, and were often intermeshed in networks of astonishing complexity.

Transoxiana was also a desert region, but it was bounded by the rich agricultural valleys of the Amu Darya and Syr Darya and was dotted with many large and small oases. The cities of Samarqand and Bukhara were the largest and wealthiest in Transoxiana. Both were situated on the Zeravshan River, which rises in the mountains that border China and flows west until it disappears in the desert west of Bukhara, well short of the Amu Darya.

The region south of the Caspian Sea is little known outside Iran, but merits attention here. The southwestern coastal plain of the sea is known as Gilan, and to the east is Mazandaran. In the period covered by this book, the coastal plains and the mountains south of them were usually referred to as Daylam. Some areas of Gilan receive up to seventy-eight inches of rainfall per year, with Mazandaran receiving somewhat less than half of that amount. (By comparison, New Orleans, Louisiana, receives an average annual rainfall of sixty-two inches.) Unlike most of the arid regions of southwestern Asia, rainfall here falls throughout the year, rather than only in the short winter. Gilan and Mazandaran were, consequently, the most densely populated regions of Iran and grew a wide variety of crops. They were distinguished by a reliance upon rice rather than wheat or barley for their principal grain.

While Gilan and Mazandaran were the most densely populated areas of the empire, the region with the largest total population was Iraq. Iraq contained the two largest rivers in the empire, the Euphrates and the Tigris. Like the Nile, they had given birth to civilization in a desert environment as early as the fourth millennium B.C.E., when local farmers began constructing ground-level canals to bring water to their parched fields. Both rivers were also navigable for hundreds of miles of their length and thus encouraged commerce. Iraq was the empire's wealthiest province, generating forty percent of the imperial revenues. Of all the regions of the empire, Iraq was the most alien to the ruling elite. It lay west of the rugged Zagros range and was not culturally Iranian. Nevertheless, its wealth was essential to the imperial economy, and as a result, the Sasanians placed a priority on protecting it from Byzantine encroachment.

Thus, despite its extensive desert regions, the Sasanian Empire enjoyed an adequate supply of agricultural production, and it was strategically located for long-distance commerce. Its position allowed it to control both the land route to China and India and the approaches to Persian Gulf ports. Because of the activity of its merchants, Iranian culture became influential along the central Eurasian trade routes for centuries to come. Overland transport was slow: Large caravans or armies could expect to travel only fifteen miles per day. The government made great efforts to provide security for major routes, to maintain roads and bridges, and to provide hostels and caravanserais.

The wealth derived from both agriculture and trade is reflected in the art of the Sasanian period. Enormous rock sculptures were carved into the limestone cliffs that are found in many parts of Iran. Architecturally, the most celebrated achievement of the period is the vast palace at Ctesiphon, near modern Baghdad. Built by Justinian's contemporary, Khusrow I (531–579), part of it still stands. Its open frontal arch is the largest brick vault ever known to have been constructed, and it was the inspiration for much later architecture in Iran during the Islamic period. Metalwork and gem engraving attained high levels of technique and artistry, with particularly striking examples in jewelry, body armor, and tableware. Iran's central geographic position enabled its artists and craftsmen to benefit from foreign ideas and techniques. These are particularly apparent in the pottery and silk sectors, in which Chinese styles and techniques were influential.

The dominant religion of the Iranian plateau since at least the sixth century B.C.E. had been Zoroastrianism. Although its presence in the world today is limited to the small group of Parsis, most of whom live in India, Zoroastrianism played a major role in history. It shaped many features of Iranian cultural identity, and it apparently bequeathed to Judaism (and, consequently, to Christianity) the concepts of a bodily resurrection, last judgment, heaven and hell, and Satan. Those ideas cannot be found in Judaism prior to the conquest of Babylon by the Iranian Cyrus the Great, who allowed the Jews to return to Jerusalem from Babylon and to set up an autonomous province within the Iranian empire from the sixth to fourth centuries B.C.E. Zoroastrianism focused on the

Great Hall of the Sasanian royal palace in Ctesiphon.

worship of Ahura Mazda (Ormazd), who was challenged by the evil principle Ahriman. Zoroaster (who lived sometime between 1000 B.C.E. and 600 B.C.E.) had clearly battled polytheism, but by the Sasanian period many of the old gods whose worship he had attacked were members of the pantheon again. The Sasanian version of Zoroastrianism is usually referred to as Mazdaism.

In Iraq, the westernmost territory of the Sasanian Empire, Zoroastrianism was a minority religion and had to coexist, sometimes uneasily, with other faiths. The Sasanian policy of granting refuge to non-Orthodox Christians from Byzantine territories affected the demography of the empire. So many Christians emigrated to Iraq that by the early seventh century Christians may have formed the largest single religious community in Iraq. Many Nestorian merchants based in Iraq made their way along the trading routes to China and the Indian Ocean basin, establishing Nestorian communities in Central Asia and India. By the late sixth century, even some members of the Sasanian royal family were converting to Nestorianism.

Judaism also flourished in Iraq, and it was probably the second largest religious community there. Jews formed the majority of the population in central Iraq, where they had lived since the time of the Babylonian Captivity of the sixth century B.C.E. During the late fourth and early fifth centuries C.E., Jewish scholars in Iraq compiled the famous Babylonian Talmud. For the most part, Sasanian rulers did not interfere unduly with their subjects' religious lives, but periodically the Zoroastrian priesthood, the Magi, persuaded them to persecute Christians and Jews.

The various Iranian peoples within the empire spoke different dialects of Persian, and those on opposite ends of the region found each other's language almost unintelligible. Nevertheless, the Sasanians found the culture of even distant fellow Iranians more congenial than that of Iraq, where the majority of the people spoke Aramaic. The Persian language is a member of the Indo-European family of languages and, as a result, is structurally more similar to Greek and Latin than to Semitic languages such as Aramaic, Arabic, and Hebrew. Little remains of Sasanian literature other than Zoroastrian religious texts or translations from other cultures, especially the Byzantine.

Iran did have great centers of learning, however. One was Merv, which was also the primary military garrison in the east, and the most famous in the west was Jundishapur (Gondeshapur) in Iraq, some one hundred miles east of modern Baghdad. At Jundishapur, Nestorian scholars worked with pagan philosophers from Athens who sought refuge from Byzantine persecution, and the school became particularly famous for its medical instruction. At these cities and at other, less important, intellectual centers, many books were translated from Greek, Sanskrit, and Syriac into Persian.

The empire struggled to maintain stability in a context of greater cultural diversity than the Byzantines faced. The Iranian peoples themselves, who inhabited the vast area between the Persian Gulf and the Syr Darya, were divided not only by a wide range of dialects, but also by means of subsistence: They included nomads, peasants, and wealthy urban dwellers. The diverse nature of the empire's subjects became more pronounced in Iraq, where Semitic culture predominated. Iraq was an ancient urban society whose wealth the court needed, a fact that the dynasty acknowledged only late in its history by constructing Ctesiphon as the empire's chief administrative city. Most of the ruling elite preferred the province of Fars, in the vicinity of modern Shiraz, and left Ctesiphon for vacations in Shiraz whenever they could.

Arabs were an important segment of the empire's population along and west of the lower Euphrates River in southern Iraq and between the Tigris and Euphrates in northern Iraq. Like their Byzantine counterparts, the Arabs of the Sasanian Empire included nomads, seminomads, peasants, and townsmen. Some Iraqi Arabs followed traditional polytheistic religions and a few seem to have followed Judaism, but most appear to have been Christian, another parallel with the Byzantine Arabs. Among the Christian Arabs, the nomads tended to follow Monophysitism and the urban dwellers tended to be Nestorian. The city of Hira was the largest Arab town in the empire. It contained a sufficient number of Nestorians to qualify as the seat of a bishopric as early as 410, even though the ruling Lakhmid tribe converted to Nestorianism only in the 580s.

The Lakhmids led a sophisticated community. The Arabs of southern Iraq developed an influential poetic tradition as well as the so-called Kufic script for their dialect of the Arabic language. The Kufic script under Islam would become important not only for writing, but also for the decorative arts. The poetic vocabulary of this tradition, as well as the script, would contribute to the development of a common Arabic language in the early Islamic period. The Lakhmids were important enough for the Sasanians to rely upon them for the same purpose that the Byzantines used the Ghassanids. They were responsible for warding off raids by nomads from the Arabian Peninsula and for serving as auxiliaries against their imperial Byzantine enemy.

Perhaps in response to Justinian's own assertion of power, Khusrow I initiated a new, aggressive policy toward the Byzantines, symbolized by the establishment of Ctesiphon in Iraq as the imperial capital. The economic importance of Iraqi agriculture could not be ignored, and a new urgency developed regarding competition with the Byzantines for control of international trade routes. Not all of the interaction with the Byzantines was hostile. In the sixth century, Byzantine architects helped to build the palace at Ctesiphon, and Aristotelian concepts were borrowed to redefine points of Zoroastrian ethics. It was during this period, moreover, that much of the translation work of Byzantine medicine, philosophy, and courtier literature into Persian was commissioned at Jundishapur. Nevertheless, diplomatic and military conflicts with the Byzantines dominated the last century of Sasanian history. In addition to establishing control of ports on the western coast of the Persian Gulf, the empire began diplomatic and military initiatives in the Red Sea in order to control the trade routes to the Mediterranean from the Indian Ocean. From 570 to 630, the Sasanians succeeded in controlling most of the coastline of the Arabian Peninsula.

In 540, major warfare broke out between the Sasanians and the Byzantines, and the former were able to control Aleppo temporarily. Fighting continued until 561, and then broke out again in 572, lasting for another twenty-year period, to 591. Only a decade of peace followed before the final war between the two powers began. Neither empire was prepared for the conflict. The Byzantines had lost the trust of the Ghassanids, and the Sasanians terminated their relationship with the Lakhmids in 602. In that same year, skirmishing began between the two great powers after a Byzantine emperor was overthrown in one of the many episodes of dynastic instability that characterized Byzantine history. Even the accession of a new emperor, Heraclius, in 610 did not end the plotting, and the Sasanians took advantage of the disunity in Constantinople. They inflicted a series of military disasters on the Byzantines, taking Antioch in 613, Jerusalem in 614, and the Nile delta in 619. By 620, Sasanian troops stood on the banks of the Bosporus and taunted the watchmen atop the walls of Constantinople. Heraclius was finally able to begin a counterattack in 622, and with help from Khazar tribesmen from north of the Black Sea, he waged a major campaign from the Caucasus, penetrating behind Sasanian lines into the heart of Iraq. By 628, all the Sasanian troops had been expelled from Byzantine territory.

The two empires were exhausted. Byzantine agriculture and town life in Anatolia, Syria, and Iraq were devastated, and the assassination of the Iranian emperor in 628 left the Sasanians in confusion and fear. Monophysites in Syria and Egypt, having been under Sasanian rule for a decade, were anxiously waiting to see if Byzantine policy would be more sensitive to provincial needs than it had been before the war. Jews in both empires were desperate, having been punished during the war for suspicion of helping the enemy. Arab nomads in the desert south of the traditional frontiers were probing the imperial defenses and discovering that the Ghassanids and Lakhmids no longer provided a barrier to plunder. Had the political elite in both empires not been so preoccupied with rebuilding, they might have been able to realize their precarious position and to take steps to prevent disaster. Instead, in less than a decade, the Byzantines would lose their territories in Syria and Egypt forever, and the world of the Sasanians would utterly collapse.

The Arabian Peninsula

Despite the proximity of the Arabian Peninsula to the Byzantines and Sasanians, imperial officials in neither empire regarded it as major security threat. Militarily, the
vast, northern plains normally represented only a nuisance, as small bands of tribesmen would occasionally raid border settlements in southern Syria and Iraq. Throughout the centuries, an occasional, temporary, tribal confederation would arise that
each empire then confronted with a massive show of force, but the confederation
would collapse after a few years due to internal conflicts. On the whole, however, the
peninsula was of more importance to both empires for its strategic position. The
Sasanians depended on the Persian Gulf for access to African and South Asian ports,
and the Byzantines relied on the Red Sea basin for its southern trade routes. Both
empires carefully monitored the security of those trade routes.

Arabia is almost a million square miles of largely arid to semiarid terrain, but
both its climate and topography reveal surprising variety. In the west, a highlands
area, the Hijaz, intersperses barren valleys and sheer crags with numerous lush oases.
It slopes to the east, where pebbly plains can spring to life with seasonal grass and flowers after the winter rains. The famous Empty Quarter of the south central region
cannot support human or large-animal life. Its tens of thousands of square miles of
sand dunes receive only a trace of rain, and temperatures can exceed 130 degrees.
In Yemen, however, peasants laboriously carved out terraces on the slopes of mountains that soar to over 12,000 feet above the narrow Red Sea coast. The terraces
trapped the rainfall from monsoons and produced grains, vegetables, and fruits without irrigation. Some of the valleys made lush for a few months by the monsoons grew
semitropical fruits and boasted of waterfalls. For at least three millennia, until the last
quarter of the twentieth century, Yemen's agriculture sustained by far the largest
population in the peninsula.

The wide variety of climate and topography in Arabia resulted in a corresponding
variety of means of subsistence. In Yemen, the agricultural and commercial economy
supported royal dynasties for much of the first millennium B.C.E. These governments
had been able to mobilize their populations to construct impressive monuments,
such as temples, palaces, and dams. International trade supplemented the agricultural
wealth of Yemen and other South Arabian kingdoms. Several cities, some on the coast
and some in the interior, thrived on the trade of luxury goods from the Indian Ocean
bases to the Mediterranean. The most famous of the products from Yemen itself was
frankincense, an aromatic tree sap. Frankincense was a luxury product, much in demand throughout the Mediterranean. All the major pre-Christian religions of southwestern Asia and northeastern Africa—as well as Christianity itself—required the
incense in their rituals, and families used it as an air freshener in their homes during the centuries before soap, toilets, and garbage disposals came into use. The legendary Queen of Sheba, famous in both the Bible and in Arab lore, is thought to
have ruled over Saba' in southwestern Yemen, which was famous for its frankincense.
Centuries later, Yemen was still so identified with the valuable aromatic that the Romans
called it Arabia Felix, or Happy Arabia.

Outside Yemen, most farmers in the peninsula depended on irrigation from underground wells. Usually the water sources were artesian wells, whose natural pressure sent water to the surface without pumping. Numerous oases lay scattered about

the peninsula except within the Empty Quarter. Some were tiny, but others could be surprisingly large. Yathrib (later known as Medina), for example, in the Hijaz, was a cluster of hamlets located in an oasis that was several miles across. An oasis located in the middle of a desert was a refreshing delight for a traveler. It would present the visual appearance of a thick forest of date palms, but would typically also support citrus trees, banana trees, and the essential grains. Cool water was almost always flowing from one part of the oasis to another, and the combination of the water and the dense shade yielded a dramatic contrast in temperature with that of the surrounding desert.

Every town and city had to rest on an economy whose base was agriculture, but a few cities obtained the bulk of their surplus wealth from the profits derived from the transit trade. Some cities in southeastern Yemen appear to fit that model, and so did Petra. Petra was founded by an Arabic-speaking people known as the Nabateans, who migrated to the northwestern fringe of the peninsula as early as the sixth century B.C.E. By 200 B.C.E., they had established Petra as an entrepot for the overland transit trade. A century before Jesus was born, Petra controlled the area as far north as Damascus, and Nabateans continued to exercise local authority even after the Romans annexed their domain: The apostle Paul escaped over the walls of Damascus in the first century C.E. under the rule of a Nabatean governor. Petra's rulers were sufficiently wealthy to hire Greek architects to design the facades of monumental structures carved into the sheer cliffs of the gorge into which Petra was fitted.

The appearance of Petra marks a watershed in the history of the area, for it was the first of the great caravan cities that were to play an important role in the history of southwestern Asia for the next millennium and more. The evidence suggests that, sometime between 500 B.C.E. and 100 B.C.E., the Arabs of the northern half of the peninsula developed a new saddle that provided two improvements over the old. For military purposes, the new saddle provided a secure perch from which to use a long sword and lance with devastating effect; and when used as a pack saddle, it allowed a larger load to be mounted on the camel. In the wake of this new development, the camel breeders of the northern part of the peninsula became prominent in regional trade, and thereby, became a formidable military force. The camel became such an important means of transport that it displaced wheeled vehicles from the region. As one historian has written, "the North Arabian saddle made possible new weaponry, which made possible a shift in the balance of military power in the desert, which made possible the seizure of control of the caravan trade by the camel breeders, which made possible the social and economic integration of camel-breeding tribes into settled Middle Eastern society, which made possible the replacement of the wheel by the pack camel."[1] As the economic and military advantages of the camel became apparent, caravans and caravan cities became more numerous.

The camel breeders of Petra were urban merchants who maintained relationships with the bedouin, or Arab nomads. The bedouin were of two basic types, the camel tenders and the seminomads. The most famous are the camel-tending bedouin, whose use of the camel provided them with remarkable mobility and independence from settled authority. In terms of material wealth, the camel-tending bedouin might appear to be very poor compared with those who dwelt in settled communities and with the seminomads. Because they grew no crops, their diet was restricted to camel milk and dates for most of the year, and they were also dependent on agricultural settlements and towns for tools, weapons, and food supplements. On the other hand, their martial skills, speed, and ability to escape into the waste lands enabled them to steal such items with near impunity from oases and towns, even within imperial territories. They were also able to extract "protection money" from settlements and caravans, contracting to protect their clients in return for tribute money (and attacking anyone who failed to agree to the offer). For this reason, the leaders of all caravan cities attempted to maintain peaceful relationships with the bedouin through whose grazing territory their caravans passed.

Contrary to a popular image, camel-herding bedouin appear never to have formed the majority of the population of Arabia. They have been present in almost all areas of the peninsula, but the agricultural settlements have always been able to support more families than has camel tending. Among the bedouin themselves, semi-nomads were more numerous than the camel tenders. As in other arid and semiarid regions of the world, most of the bedouin herded sheep and goats and kept a few camels on the side as pack animals. They spent the summers in the higher and cooler plateaus to allow their herds to graze and then moved to the lowlands during the winter in order to plant crops. Sheep herders occupied areas in which they had access to plentiful sources of water for their animals. Because of this dependence on reliable water sources, they were forced to maintain amicable relations with both agriculturalists and any state authorities in their area.

At their height, the agriculture-based South Arabian kingdoms of Yemen had the wealth to organize states that boasted institutions of commerce, law, and justice. Elsewhere in the peninsula, societies of oasis dwellers, camel tenders and sheep herders were too small or too poor to organize states. Instead they were organized by a set of relationships for which we use the inadequate term *tribe*. A tribe was a grouping of people who usually claimed to be descended from a common ancestor, but whose kinship ties might have been quite vague and uncertain. Nevertheless, they found it mutually advantageous to claim family ties, particularly for security. In the absence of a state, there were no written law codes, courts, or police. There appears not to have been even the concept of a law that transcended the limits of the tribe. In such circumstances, tribal ties protected individual life and property. Violence and theft were discouraged by the knowledge that a tribe would retaliate for the harm inflicted on one of its members. The more powerful the tribe, the less likely its members were to be violated. But weaker tribes felt compelled to retaliate against stronger tribes if only to preserve their honor. Retaliation itself demanded retaliation, spawning vendettas that could last for generations. Thus, tribalism did in fact deter individual violence, but exacerbated relationships among tribes themselves, and often led to chronic communal violence or the threat of violence.

Tribes were also important for economic reasons. Marriages took place within closely related families so that the two families' assets would not be dissipated, and when any family lost its assets due to drought or theft, the tribe would try to replace at least the animals. Generosity was a major virtue among tribesmen, symbolizing the dependence that each individual had on the group as a whole. Being part of a tribe was important for survival: One's identity was tribal, and one had nothing if he rejected the tribe. Not to have tribal protection was to be at the mercy of potentially hostile individuals and groups, as well as of nature. Because life outside the tribe was practically impossible, each individual felt an overwhelming pressure to conform to tribal norms.

The vast majority of the inhabitants of the peninsula spoke one or more dialects of the Arabic language. By the sixth century, a widely used dialect had come into common use in the northern half of Arabia, primarily in the service of poetry—the primary artistic production of the Arabs at the time. Through this poetic language, Arabs were beginning to share a common vocabulary and legendary tradition, thus gaining a semblance of a common identity. Poetry was not written down, for it was valued in its oral form, but an alphabet was developing at the time, based on the Aramaic one. The earliest Arabic inscription found to date is from the first half of the fourth century. It evolved into the so-called Kufic script that became dominant among the Lakhmids at Hira. It later came to be used for the text of the Qur'an and for official documents and monuments of the early Islamic state.

Arabs in the interior of the peninsula were overwhelmingly followers of traditional tribal gods and goddesses, but large numbers of Christians and Jews lived in settlements on the periphery. As we have seen, many Arabs on the Byzantine and Sasanian frontiers were Christian, and large numbers of Arab Christians lived in the southern part of the peninsula, as well. Najran, a refuge for Syriac Monophysites, became the most important Christian settlement in Arabia. Christian communities existed in Oman, and the religion seems to have come into Yemen from the Kingdom of Axum, on the coast of what is today Ethiopia. South Arabia and Axum had much in common: They were similar in climate and terrain; both were centers of frankincense production; and they shared Red Sea routes to the Mediterranean world. Christianity had penetrated Axum by the fourth century, and it showed up on the southwestern coast of Arabia perhaps as early as the fifth century.

Judaism became well established in oases in the Hijaz and in South Arabia after the fall of Jerusalem in 70 C.E. Jews eventually made up a large minority at the oasis of Yathrib (later known as Medina), and the royal house of Yemen was Jewish perhaps as early as the fifth century. A Jewish ruler in Yemen, Dhu Nuwas, began persecuting Christians in his realm, apparently out of fear of a growing Byzantine influence in the Red Sea. Massacres at Najran in 523, however, provoked the Christians across the Red Sea, and Axum, with Byzantine help, invaded Yemen. For the next fifty years, Yemen was to be under Axumite Christian occupation, until the Sasanians invaded in the 570s.

In the sixth century, Arabia was undergoing changes that would have profound implications for the future. Economically, Arabian agricultural societies in general were deteriorating. Yemen had experienced a slow decrease in wealth and power since the first century, and other areas of the peninsula offer evidence of a sustained drought. Many peasants were forced into a seminomadic life, and some former seminomads became pure nomads, harassing caravans and raiding settlements. Large numbers of Arabs were migrating to the north, settling on the frontiers of Iraq and Syria.

The northward migration of Arabs coincided with a new determination on the part of the Byzantines and Sasanians to intervene in the affairs of the peninsula. The invasion of Yemen both by the Byzantine–Axumite alliance and by the Sasanians within a span of half a century suggests that the fortunes of Arabia were becoming intertwined in an unprecedented way with those of its imperial neighbors to the north. Large areas of the eastern, southern, and western coasts of the peninsula were under direct or indirect Sasanian control after 575, and economic contacts were increasing between the peninsula and the Iranian empire.

The apparent superiority of the empires over the people of the peninsula was deceiving. The migration of peninsular Arabs was beginning to affect the demographic balance of the area between the Euphrates and the Jordan rivers. Combined with the fact that the Ghassanids and the Lakhmids were no longer serving to restrain the aggression of nomads on imperial borders, the two great empires were more vulnerable to attack from the desert than they had been in two centuries. In their obsession with each other's ambitions, they neglected their desert frontiers.

The Rise of Islam

During the first decade of the seventh century, the Byzantines and the Sasanians began their titanic struggle for dominance in western Asia. During the second decade, their armies fought in Syria and Egypt, and their navies clashed in the Red Sea. Meanwhile, the economic and demographic changes occurring in the Arabian Peninsula were beginning to have social consequences. It was in this context that the town of Mecca gave birth to a religiosocial movement that would transform large parts of the world for centuries to come.

The Meccan Environment

According to Muslim tradition, Muhammad was born about the year 570 in the Hijazi city of Mecca. Visitors to Mecca in the sixth century must have been surprised to find a town there at all. It lay in a dry gorge, surrounded by barren mountains, some of which thrust into the air more than a thousand feet above the town's mud-brick houses. Mecca was devoid of green plants, and its inhabitants had to import much of their food. The town possessed a spring that yielded slightly brackish water, but otherwise had little to commend itself as a place of human habitation. Perhaps because of the unlikely presence of the spring in that stony, barren wilderness, the site had been a holy place, apparently for centuries. The town itself, however, was little more than a century old when Muhammad was born.

Mecca was built around the Ka'ba, the shrine that made the place a cultic center for local tribes. Although it has been restored several times, it seems always to have been in the shape of a cube, some fifty feet on each side. Its corners roughly correspond to the four points of the compass. Embedded in the eastern corner are two stones—one of which is the famous Black Stone—that serve ritual, rather than structural, purposes.

Two different traditions exist regarding the function of the shrine, but they may be complementary. According to one tradition, the Ka'ba was unusual among the shrines in Arabia in that it housed many (perhaps as many as 360) representations, or idols, of gods, instead of just one. On the other hand, Meccans are said to have considered the Ka'ba the house of Allah, a deity worshiped widely among the Arabs of Syria and the Hijaz as the creator god and supreme god. He did not have an idol to represent him, a feature that conforms to the experience of many other cultures in which the supreme creator- or sky-god becomes removed from the everyday concerns of the people, but is still revered as the god with the highest status. The content of

The Ka'ba in Mecca.

the worship at the Ka'ba is not known, but evidence exists that some individuals had come together as a group and practiced what the Qur'an calls the "religion of Ibrahim (Abraham)." Apparently, an oral tradition already was strong that linked Abraham with the site of the Ka'ba, a tradition echoed in the Qur'an's assertion that he and his son Isma'il (Ishmael) constructed it.

Within several miles of Mecca were other sites considered holy by Arabs all over the Hijaz. Dedicated to various gods and goddesses, in pre-Islamic times, they were much more important and better known than the Meccan shrine. During three holy months of the year, tribesmen came on pilgrimage from a wide area to these other sites to trade and then perform their rituals. The most important such ritual acts took place at Mina and Arafat and made up the bulk of the rituals later included within the Islamic pilgrimage.

The dominant tribe at Mecca, the Quraysh, made money from serving as custodians of the shrine in their town, but there is no evidence that any of the great trade fairs associated with the pre-Islamic pilgrimages took place there. Mecca's chief source of wealth was its regional trade, which had begun in the second half of the fifth century C.E. Meccan merchants bought Hijazi agricultural products (especially raisins), hides, skins, and leather goods, as well as Yemeni perfumes, and traded them in southern Syria for products that were prized in the Hijaz and Yemen, such as textiles, weapons, olive oil, and Syrian perfumes. Mecca was not the commercial heir to Petra or Palmyra. There is no evidence that it possessed the wealth that had produced the impressive architecture of those two centers of international trade, and Mecca seems to have been practically unknown outside the peninsula. The international trade in luxury goods did not pass through the town, and even the trade in Yemeni incense seems to have been negligible. Nevertheless, Mecca had become a bustling center of regional trade at the end of the sixth century, and its merchants were confident and knowledgeable about the world outside their narrow, rocky valley. Trade with the southern districts of the Byzantine Empire was regular and lucrative, and travelers were constantly coming in from Hira. The Meccans were well informed about developments in the two empires to the north and had become familiar with the dominant economic, political, and religious characteristics of both empires.

Muhammad

Muhammad was born into a family stricken with tragedy: His father had died by the time he was born, and his mother died when he was six years old. He found a home first in the household of his grandfather and then of an uncle. As a young man, he became involved in the caravan trade and made trips into Syria. To all appearances, Muhammad was a man with remarkable personality gifts. He became known for his empathy, his mediating abilities, and his patience. Having grown up an impoverished orphan, he was acutely aware of how precarious life can be and of the need for mutual support.

When Muhammad was about twenty-five years old, he attracted the attention of a wealthy widow and business woman by the name of Khadijah, and they married. Suddenly his life changed, for he no longer had to worry about making ends meet. But rather than indulging in conspicuous consumption, he began a quest for a deeper religious experience. Muhammad began frequenting a local cave to meditate, and he made a habit of helping the poor. His increasing impatience with the dominant religious tradition in the Hijaz is mirrored in developments elsewhere in the region, suggesting that social conditions had begun to make the old religious traditions of the peninsula inadequate.

Muslim tradition remembers numerous other individuals in the Hijaz who were monotheistic in the era just before the coming of Islam. These *hanif*s are associated with the "religion of Abraham" in the Qur'an and in the Muslim traditions that arose later. In the interior of the peninsula, as well, near present-day Riyadh, the tribe of the Banu Hanifa was led by a Christian who was a contemporary of Muhammad. When the Christian leader died in 630, he was replaced by a prophet named Musaylima. Musaylima taught about a god named al-Rahman who demanded of his followers an ascetic lifestyle. Although there are legends about Muhammad's contacts with Syrian Christians in his work in the caravans, we do not know how familiar he was with the doctrines and rituals of Christianity or Judaism, nor the extent of his contacts with Christians and Jews in Arabia.

About the year 610, Muhammad began experiencing visions and trances in which he received messages that he understood to be the words of God. A figure, whom he later identified as the archangel Gabriel, was the channel through whom God provided His message to Muhammad. The experience was physical as well as spiritual, and Muhammad was afraid and even embarrassed, for his symptoms were similar to those of the *kahin*s, or pagan diviners and soothsayers of the region. With the support of Khadija and her cousin, however, he continued to be receptive to the visions and soon came to the conviction that he had been chosen for the role of prophet to deliver God's revelation to the Arabs. He identified it with the revelation originally sent through Abraham, the Hebrew prophets, and Jesus. Muhammad shared his revelations with his friends and family for about three years and then began preaching publicly. He gained a small band of followers, but most of them were of a distinctly common origin; his themes did not gain widespread acceptance among the Meccan elite.

The concepts and symbols of Muhammad's teaching bear a striking similarity to those of Judaism and Christianity. Muslims, in fact, have often pointed out that the expression, "the Judaeo–Christian tradition," should be revised to "the Judaeo–Christian–Islamic tradition." Muhammad taught that his message was the one that the Jewish prophets, including Jesus, had brought earlier, but that in the course of time, their teachings had been distorted. With Muhammad, God was once again bringing the pristine message, this time directly to the Arabs. Muslims believe that God's message came through Muhammad in two important ways. One was through the episodic revelations that Gabriel conveyed to Muhammad from God. The Prophet's followers wrote these down and eventually collected them together in the book known as the Qur'an (Koran). It would eventually be divided into 114 *suras*, or chapters. Apart from the formal revelations, however, were the Prophet's commentary on daily issues and his own example of the upright life. His charismatic personality and his stature as the Prophet were both compelling reasons for people to look to him for guidance on a multitude of issues as they tried to live in conformity to the will of God. The recollections of his followers regarding his sayings and his behavior under certain circumstances were later recorded as *hadith,* or Traditions, a topic that is treated in detail in Chapter 3.

At the center of Muhammad's teaching was the majesty of Allah. The word *Allah* derives from the Arabic word for *deity* or *god,* which is *ilah.* Allah is simply *ilah* with the definite article *al-* in front of it, rendering the same effect as in English: the supreme or the only god, or God. *Allah* is not a word specific to Muslims. Because of the meaning of the word, Christian Arabs refer to the focus of their worship as Allah, just as Muslims do. Worshipers of Allah in pre-Islamic Mecca probably recognized Him as the supreme deity within a pantheon of many gods and goddesses, whereas Muslims understand the term to mean the only deity at all. What appear to be the earliest passages in the Qur'an stress God's majestic power, His compassion for His creatures, and His justice. Gradually, the theme of the unity or oneness of God became prominent, leading to a clash between Muhammad and the polytheism of his environment. Many verses in the Qur'an refer to Allah as al-Rahman al-Rahim, usually translated as *the Merciful and the Compassionate.* God is a loving God who wants the best for those whom He has created and who is quick to forgive those who err.

God's mercy is required, however, because of His justice. He demands a high standard of behavior, which is predicated on obedience to His commands. The term most often associated with obedience to God in the Islamic tradition is the verb *aslama,* which means to submit or to surrender. The noun form, *islam,* thus means submission or surrender (to God). Submission entails acceptance of the legitimacy of the Prophet's mission and obedience to God's will as revealed through revelation.

The Qur'an contains numerous specific injunctions that are elements of the path of obedience, but the righteous life is exemplified most clearly in two major categories of attitude and action. The first is recognition and affirmation of the unity of God. The Qur'an makes it clear that to associate any being or object with God is the greatest sin that a person can commit. *Shirk*, or the compromising of God's sole claim to worship, is the unforgivable sin.

The emphasis on God's oneness and on His sole claim to worship led quickly to the frequent use by Muslims of the phrase "Allahu Akbar." This phrase is often translated into English as "God is Greatest," but more correctly it has the meaning, "God is Greater"—that whatever one can think of or be tempted to worship or give ultimate allegiance to, God is greater and more worthy of worship, loyalty, and commitment than that.

The other primary indicator of obedience to God is the conscientious use of wealth. The insistence on generosity to the poor, the orphan, and the widow runs as a leitmotiv throughout the Qur'an in a manner strikingly similar to the words of Hosea, Amos, Jesus, and other figures in the Bible. The Prophet himself was reminded of his humble origins and of God's concern for him, obliging him to be generous in turn to those who were on the margins of society:

> Did He not find you an orphan, and shelter you?
> Did He not find you straying, and guide you?
> Did He not find you needy, and enrich you?
> As for the orphan, do not oppress him,
> And as for the beggar, do not drive him away,
> And as for the grace of your Lord, declare it. (93:6–11)

The Qur'an portrays the greedy and stingy individual as doomed to a miserable end:

> As for him who gives and is God-fearing
> And affirms goodness,
> We shall "ease him to the Easing."
> But as for the miser and the self-absorbed,
> Who declares the Good to be a lie,
> We shall "ease him to the Hardship,"
> And his wealth will be of no use to him when he perishes. (92:5–11)

The pious believers, by contrast, show a concern for a relationship with both God and with the poor:

> They would sleep but little at night,
> And as dawn broke, they would seek forgiveness,
> And they shared their belongings with the beggar and the dispossessed. (51:17–19)

Those who persist in disobedience by refusing to worship Allah and to recognize His Prophet are subject to punishment in this world and in the life to come. Muhammad asserted that at the Last Judgment the fate of the wicked will be a fiery torment. On the other hand, those who submit to God will enjoy His favor in this world and will be generously rewarded at the Last Judgment. The imagery used to describe the bliss of paradise is as vivid as that of hell. In both cases, it is calculated to resonate with populations acquainted with the desert. The hellish fire and blasts of wind are contrasted with the gardens, cool water, and pampered service by young men and women that await the righteous in paradise.

It is clear from the wording of the Qur'an that the doctrine of the physical resurrection of the dead was incomprehensible and even ludicrous to many of Muhammad's audience, who raised many of the same objections to it as skeptics in other religious traditions have throughout the ages. Many in Mecca also objected to Muhammad's insistence that the basis for one's eternal fate at the Last Judgment would be merit and not status as a member of a particular tribe. That membership in a tribe with high status would not avail a person when it mattered most was inconceivable to members of the elite tribes. When skeptics challenged the doctrine of the Last Judgment and asked about the fate of revered ancestors of the current generation, Muhammad replied that, because of their polytheism, they were now in hell. Muhammad's teachings were thus particularly galling to the aristocrats of Mecca. On the one hand, he used the traditional value of generosity against them and exposed the fact that they had betrayed those values by becoming greedy and stingy; on the other hand, he turned upside down the traditional criterion for status, which was a prominent position in a powerful tribe. According to him, individuals from undistinguished backgrounds who submitted to God and His Prophet would fare better in eternity than would the most revered tribal leader who rejected the new teaching. Given the prevailing values of the period, it is clear why his message was welcomed by some groups, detested by others, and simply not comprehended by many.

The leaders of the dominant Quraysh tribe in Mecca were bitter critics of Muhammad's mission. Only the protection of Muhammad's uncle, Abu Talib, prevented him and his followers from being persecuted, rather than merely harassed. In 619, however, the Prophet's circumstances changed for the worse. In that year, both Khadija and Abu Talib died, leaving him without psychological support and social protection. The leaders of the Quraysh were free to impose an economic boycott on the small Muslim community, and individual Muslims became the target of physical beatings. With tensions growing between the leaders of the Quraysh and the Muslims, it became clear that Muhammad and his followers would have to find another setting in which to practice their faith. Muhammad investigated the possibilities at several nearby towns, but was unable to elicit any interest.

Then, unexpectedly, in 620, a group from the oasis of Yathrib, some 240 miles to the north, converted to Islam when they heard him preaching. The next year, another group from Yathrib came to Mecca and embraced Islam. Members of the group invited Muhammad to come to their oasis in order to mediate quarrels among tribal factions there. In 622 C.E., Muhammad and his followers emigrated to Yathrib, which later in Islamic history became known as The City (madina) of the Prophet, or Medina. This trek of hundreds of Muslims is known as the hijra. Years later, Muslims came to see that the Hijra was the decisive moment in Islamic history, and they accepted the year in which it occurred as the beginning of the new Islamic calendar. Year One of the Muslim era had begun.

Hijra has often been translated into English as "flight," but doing so misses an important element of Islamic history. It is true that the account of Muhammad's transfer to Medina points out the danger that he and his followers were exposed to, and that Muhammad left Mecca just in time to avoid an attempt on his life. On the other hand, Muslims have always seen the Hijra as a rejection of Meccan unbelief, rather than a flight to escape danger. Throughout history, many Muslims have been convinced that, should they come under non-Muslim rule, they should "perform hijra" by moving to an area ruled by pious Muslims.

Medina was not a compact city, but rather a large oasis that contained several hamlets. It was the home of thousands of Jews, some of whom were descendants of refugees from the great Jewish revolt against Rome in the second century. They formed at least three tribes. Two Arab tribes had come into the oasis later than the Jews, but had become the dominant forces there. The two Arab tribes were engaged in continual warfare with each other and had almost destroyed the community. The delegation that invited Muhammad to the oasis had done so in the hope that he could bring stability to the community. In a series of documents that have come to be called the Constitution of Medina, the inhabitants of the oasis recognized Muhammad as the community's political leader. As such, he was able to influence more people than ever before. His undeniable talents as a negotiator and arbiter reinforced his prophetic claims, and the number of his followers began to grow rapidly.

For the next eight years, Muhammad sought to implement Islamic principles in Medina and to build up the economic and military resources of his city. His responsibilities were entirely different from what they had been in Mecca, and the revelations that continued to come to him reflect the new circumstances. Compared with the earlier revelations, these new messages are more concerned with legislative matters, rules for communal living, and challenges to his message from Jews and Christians.

A major concern of his was to provide a means of support for the Muslims who had accompanied him to Medina. Opportunities for the employment of recent immigrants were limited in the oasis economy, so Muhammad resorted to raiding caravans that carried the Meccan trade. The attacks began to wreak economic damage on the Meccan economy, and so, in 624, the Quraysh attempted to intercept and defeat Muhammad's forces at a caravan watering hole called Badr. The Battle of Badr was a shocking loss for the Meccans and a corresponding boost to the prestige of Muhammad throughout the Hijaz. The next year, the Meccans attacked Medina itself, and this time, the Quraysh won a decisive victory at the Battle of Uhud. Inexplicably, they failed to follow up on their victory, allowing the Muslim community an opportunity to recover.

The subsequent period of self-doubt and reflection led to the emergence of a maturity and seriousness of purpose that the Muslims had not before possessed. The results were manifested when, in 627, Mecca launched the largest attack yet. Greatly outnumbering the Muslim forces, the Meccans and their allies were confident of victory, but Muhammad had anticipated the attack and inspired the Medinans to work hard to prepare their city's defenses. Hills and large boulders presented obstacles to any attack on three sides of the city. The northern approach was the only one that was level and unobstructed. There, the Medinans dug a large moat, or ditch, which rendered the Meccan cavalry useless. After several days of frustration, the attackers were forced to retreat. The "Battle of the Ditch" convinced Muhammad's followers that their cause was poised for imminent victory.

The battle was, in fact, a turning point in Muhammad's career. Throughout the five years of struggle with Mecca, Muhammad had already developed a reputation throughout the Hijaz as a leader who had to be taken seriously. He had sent out emissaries to oases and nomadic tribes, attempting to gain allies. Several communities agreed to help him in the event of clashes with Mecca, and some of them accepted his religious teachings—he did not force his allies to become Muslims. Other communities, however, feared his growing power and allied with Mecca instead.

In the year following the Battle of the Ditch, Muhammad felt strong enough to begin testing the military power of his new community. In 628, he captured at least two oases in the northern Hijaz, and then he led a group of followers toward Mecca, declaring that the Muslims wished to perform the rites of pilgrimage at the city. Although his group was deliberately *not* heavily armed, the Meccan leaders asked to negotiate. Muhammad, realizing that they had lost their nerve and would no longer be a serious threat to him, agreed to do so. The two groups signed a treaty that postponed the pilgrimage for one year. Although some of the Muslims thought the concession was a humiliation, Muhammad realized that the Meccans had recognized him as a legitimate and equal power and had conceded his right to enter their city.

During the next two years, Muhammad's military forces captured several oases in the northern tier of the peninsula and made an unsuccessful raid into Byzantine territory in southern Syria. In 630, he forced the issue of supremacy with Mecca by leading an army against the city. The Quraysh capitulated with almost no resistance. Muhammad entered Mecca, cleansed the Ka'ba, and dedicated it solely to Allah. Most Meccans made their submission to Muhammad's cause, and Muhammad immediately named several of the most talented of them to be high-level administrators and advisors. Some of his longtime followers, who had been persecuted by these same people, were bewildered and angered by the appointments, but Muhammad continued to reveal his keen political instincts and his astute assessment of personalities by co-opting the talent and ultimate loyalty of his former enemies.

From his base in Medina, Muhammad ordered a campaign to the far north of the peninsula that resulted in the capture of the oasis of Tabuk and three Byzantine towns near the Gulf of Aqaba. Numerous tribes in the peninsula now began sending delegations to Muhammad, seeking terms of understanding with this formidable new ruler. Muhammad was content to make alliances with some of the more powerful ones; with others, he secured agreements to submit to Islam and to pay a tax. By 632, he dominated western Arabia, and Muslim communities could be found from the Persian Gulf to Yemen. In March of that year, Muhammad's health began to fail. His condition deteriorated rapidly into June, when he died.

A Framework for a New Community

Muhammad's sudden death in 632 was a shock to those who had been caught up in the dramatic developments of the previous decade. The course of events after the Battle of the Ditch had been particularly riveting and had seemed to be the prelude to a new order in the region. With the Prophet's death, however, what would become of his religiomoral movement and the nascent state that he headed? Few were aware of it at the time, but Muhammad had transformed the Hijaz irrevocably, and his career has become one of the turning points of world history.

Confronting the Death of the Prophet

The Prophet died in the arms of his favorite wife, the young 'A'isha. The passage that follows, which comes from the earliest extant biography of Muhammad, captures the shock of the community in Medina when the news of his death spread. It also emphasizes the centrality of the tenet of strict monotheism in Islam. The two major figures mentioned here, Abu Bakr and 'Umar, were among the first converts to Islam, were fathers-in-law of the Prophet (Abu Bakr was 'A'isha's father), and became the first two leaders of the Muslim community after the Prophet's death.

When the apostle was dead 'Umar got up and said: "Some of the disaffected will allege that the apostle is dead, but by God he is not dead: he has gone to his Lord as Moses b. 'Imran went and was hidden from his people for forty days, returning to them after it was said that he had died. By God, the apostle will return as Moses returned and will cut off the hands and feet of men who allege that the apostle is dead." When Abu Bakr heard what was happening he came to the door of the mosque as 'Umar was speaking to the people. He paid no attention but went in to 'A'isha's house to the apostle, who was lying covered by a mantle of Yamani cloth. He went and uncovered his face and kissed him, saying, "You are dearer than my father and mother. You have tasted the death which God had decreed: a second death will never overtake you." Then he replaced the mantle on the apostle's face and went out. 'Umar was still speaking and he said, "Gently, 'Umar, be quiet." But 'Umar went on talking, and when Abu Bakr saw that he would not be silent he went forward to the people who, when they heard his words, came to him and left 'Umar. Giving thanks and praise to God he said: "O men, if anyone worships Muhammad, Muhammad is dead: if anyone worships God, God is alive, immortal." Then he recited this verse (3:138): "Muhammad is nothing but an apostle. Apostles have passed away before him. Can it be that if he were to die or be killed you would turn back on your heels? He who turns back does no harm to God and God will reward the grateful." By God, it was as though the people did not know that this verse . . . had come down until Abu Bakr recited it that day. The people took it from him and it was (constantly) in their mouths. 'Umar said, "By God, when I heard Abu Bakr recite these words I was dumbfounded so that my legs would not bear me and I fell to the ground knowing that the apostle was indeed dead."

SOURCE: Ibn Ishaq. *The Life of Muhammad. A Translation of Ibn Ishaq's Sirat Rasul Allah.* Translated with introduction and notes by A. Guillaume. Lahore and Karachi, Pakistan Branch: Oxford University Press, 1967, 682–683.

Muhammad lived in Arabia at a time when the inhabitants of the towns there seem to have been experiencing a crisis of faith similar to that of the citizens of the Roman Empire in the second century, when the so-called mystery religions began to challenge the traditional state-sponsored pantheon of Roman gods and goddesses. For reasons not clear to us in either case, the old gods and goddesses began to lose their ability to hold the faith of the masses, and many individuals went in quest of a more substantial religion. We do know that Judaism and Christianity were the dominant religions of Syria and Iraq to the north of Arabia and were also well established in the northern and southern extremes of the peninsula. As religions of settled communities and of a literate, cultured tradition, they were respected by the polytheistic Arabs. At first, Muhammad seems to have thought of Jews and Christians as natural allies in the struggle against polytheism. As we have seen, he taught that his message was the same as that preached by the Jewish prophets, including Jesus. Following the Jewish example, Muhammad initially ordered his followers to face towards Jerusalem while performing their prayers, and while in Mecca, he seems to have followed the Jewish example in several other points of ritual and doctrine.

No later than the early period in Medina, however, it became clear that Islam would have to define itself apart from each of these other two religions. After the Hijra, Muhammad's relations with the Jews deteriorated rapidly. The Qur'an suggests that certain Jews in Medina challenged the Prophet's versions of several narratives because they did not conform to the biblical renderings. Muhammad also had reason to suspect certain Jews of complicity with the enemy during the three battles with Mecca. After each of the first two battles, he exiled a Jewish tribe, and after the Battle of the Ditch, he executed the adult males of the remaining Jewish tribe, a number that amounted to several hundred individuals. He then sold the women and children into slavery.

It also seems to be the Medinan period when criticisms of Christians became more commonplace. Christians claimed to follow the teachings of Jesus, but the Jesus of the Qur'an is quite different from the one whom the Christians worshiped. According to the Qur'an, Jesus was indeed born of a virgin named Mary (although the birth took place at the base of a palm tree instead of in a stable), performed miracles, and brought a message from God. Contrary to the account in the Bible, however, the Qur'an teaches that the plans to crucify Jesus were thwarted and that God delivered him from execution. More important, the Qur'an denies that Jesus is the incarnation of God, as the Christians claimed. In one passage (5:116–120) it portrays a conversation between God and Jesus in which God asks Jesus if he ever claimed that he and Mary were divinities worthy of worship. Jesus emphatically denies having done so, reinforcing a passage earlier in the chapter that rejects the concept of the Trinity and emphasizes Jesus's status as a mortal prophet (5:72–75).

Because of the clashes between Muhammad on the one hand and Jews and Christians on the other, certain passages in the Qur'an are highly critical of those two religious groups. Chapter 5 is particularly harsh, calling Christians "unbelievers" whose fate is the fire of hell because of their concept of the Trinity (5:72–73); Jews are linked with the polytheists in their hostility to Islam (5:82); and Muslims are warned not to take Jews or Christians as friends because of their mockery of Islam and their unfaithfulness (5:51, 57). On the other hand, the Qur'an more often refers to Jews and Christians as "People of the Book"—that is, as having a version (albeit distorted) of the revelation from God. In some passages (2:62, among others), the Qur'an seems to state explicitly that Jews and Christians should be recognized as spiritual kinsmen to Muslims. Many of them, it points out, are clearly God-fearing and righteous. Despite the political tensions and the doctrinal differences separating Jews and Christians from Muslims, the Qur'an's overall evaluation of the Jews and Christians was that, as People of the Book, they deserved to be allowed to practice their religion. As we shall see in subsequent chapters, the Muslims who conquered the vast areas from the Atlantic to the Indus River would regard the People of the Book as protected peoples.

The controversies that swirled between Muhammad and the established communities of Jews and Christians helped to establish the identity of Islam, which was in the tradition of Judaism and Christianity, but it was God's original revelation, without the distortions that accumulated in those two communities. The doctrine emerged that the Prophet had brought the original version of both Judaism and Christianity—the version held by Abraham, revered by both Jews and Christians—and this time the Arabs would be the first to hear it. The new faith was vehement in its rejection of polytheism, and its uncompromising monotheism would force even Christians, who considered themselves to be monotheists, to rethink their doctrines and practices in the face of Islamic criticism of the doctrine of the Trinity and the use of icons and statuary. If differences existed between the Qur'an on the one hand and the Torah and the Gospel on the other, it was because Jews and Christians had distorted the revelation. This sense of having completed the revelation and of having corrected the errors of previous generations would be an inspirational force that would generate a profound sense of self-confidence to the new Islamic community. Arab Muslims were no longer Arab polytheists who lived on the periphery of superior civilizations. They were bearers of the original and authentic revelation from the one true God, and their neighbors could only benefit from their counsel.

Conclusion

The sense of mission that the Arabs of the Hijaz gained from Islam would have dissipated rapidly without an institution to channel it. Muhammad's monumental political achievement was to create a polity in western Arabia that served in effect as a substitute for tribal membership. Just as the Monophysites and Nestorians of the Byzantine Empire had expressed their dissatisfaction with the economic, political, and theological developments within their society through the medium of divergent religious claims, so Muhammad's critique of his society took a religious form. When Muhammad donned the prophetic mantle in the streets of Mecca, criticizing the polytheism, greed, and selfishness of the people of his hometown, his opponents perceived an implicit claim for political and religious leadership of the community. Unlike the Monophysites and Nestorians, Muhammad was able to overthrow the old order and establish both a new religion and a new polity in Arabia.

As we have seen, no state had existed in northern Arabia before Muhammad's time, and yet his success seems to have filled a yearning felt by tribesmen scattered over a vast area. Over the centuries, northern Arabia had witnessed the rise of impressive, but ephemeral, tribal confederations. Only in Yemen had there existed a political and revenue system such as Muhammad created. In Medina, Muhammad had created an *umma*, or a community that agreed on certain standards of behavior and certain fundamentals of governance. In his original agreement with the inhabitants of Medina, Muhammad had meant by *umma* everyone in the city, not just the Muslims, but by the end of his career, he had restricted the use of the term to Muslims only. Perhaps the most novel feature that the Umma entailed was the concept of a law to which all members of the polity were bound. As we shall see, Islamic law later developed into a complex science, but even during the early years of Islamic history, the standards of behavior and the obligatory acts that are detailed in the Qur'an constituted a concept of law that, at least in theory, transcended tribal custom and tribal competition. All who called themselves Muslims were expected to obey God's revealed standards. Tribal loyalties and customs were clearly secondary in this understanding. As subsequent history shows all too clearly, tribal identities and antagonisms did not fade away. But the idea that one's ultimate loyalty was to God, rather than to one's tribe, contained powerful latent possibilities. Oppression no longer had to be viewed as simply a fact of life in a cruel world; it was an affront to God and a violation of his law against which his community should take a stand. Tribal, regional, and ethnic obligations had now become, at least theoretically, subject to the greater claims of a divine and universal law. The foundations had been laid for a new human community. The superstructure would be built by subsequent generations of Muslims.

NOTES

1. Bulliet, Richard. *The Camel and the Wheel.* Cambridge, Massachusetts: Harvard University Press, 1975, 110.

FURTHER READING

Southwestern Asia in the Seventh Century

Bulliet, Richard. *The Camel and the Wheel.* Cambridge, Massachusetts: Harvard University Press, 1975.

Cameron, Averil. *The Mediterranean World in Late Antiquity: A.D. 395–600.* London and New York: Routledge, 1993.

Crone, Patricia. *Meccan Trade and the Rise of Islam.* Princeton, New Jersey: Princeton University Press, 1987.

Frye, Richard N. *The Golden Age of Persia.* New York: Barnes & Noble, 1975.

Jenkins, Romilly, James Heald. *Byzantium: The Imperial Centuries, AD 610–1071.* Toronto: Published by the University of Toronto Press in association with the Medieval Academy of America, 1987.

Hoyland, Robert G. *Arabia and the Arabs from the Bronze Age to the Coming of Islam.* New York and London: Routledge, 2001.

Morony, Michael G. *Iraq After the Muslim Conquest.* Princeton, New Jersey: Princeton University Press, 1984.

Shahid, Irfan. *Byzantium and the Arabs in the Sixth Century.* Washington, D.C.: Dumbarton Oaks Research Library and Collection, 1995.

Whittow, Mark. *The Making of Byzantium, 600–1025.* Berkeley, California: University of California Press, 1996.

Yarshater, Ehsan, ed. *The Cambridge History of Iran,* vol. 3, *The Seleucid, Parthian and Sasanian Periods.* Cambridge, New York: Cambridge University Press, 1983.

The Rise of Islam

Denny, Frederick Mathewson. *An Introduction to Islam,* 2d ed. New York: Macmillan Publishing Company, 1994.

Kennedy, Hugh. *The Prophet and the Age of the Caliphates.* London and New York: Longman, 1986.

Peters, F.E. *Muhammad and the Origins of Islam.* Albany, New York: State University of New York Press, 1994.

Ruthven, Malise. *Islam in the World,* 2d ed. New York: Oxford University Press, 2000.

Watt, W. Montgomery. *Muhammad at Mecca.* Oxford: Oxford University Press, 1953.

Watt, W. Montgomery. *Muhammad at Medina.* Oxford: Oxford University Press, 1956.

There are several good English translations of the Qur'an. It is important to understand that, unlike the Bible, the Qur'an in any language other than the original is not considered to be the Qur'an itself, but only a translated version: The Qur'an is to be found only in the Arabic language. As is the case with translations of the Bible, however, one can choose from a wide variety of prose styles. The following are two popular styles:

Ali, Ahmed, tr. *Al-Qur'ān: A Contemporary Translation.* Princeton, New Jersey: Princeton University Press, 1984.

Dawood, N.J. tr. *The Koran.* London: Penguin Books, 2000.

Many features of the early history of Islam are controversial. This chapter is based on the work of scholars who try to discover the historical events behind the (often problematic) traditional Muslim accounts. Another, quite different, approach of the past twenty-five years has been to consider the traditional accounts to be of almost no historical value and to suggest new chronological and geographical frameworks within which to understand the origins of Islam. Some scholars suggest that Islam did not arise in Mecca and Medina, but that it arose within a dominant monotheistic—rather than polytheistic—society, and that the Qur'an was collected over the course of a century, rather than two decades. For an introduction into this line of historical revisionism, consult the following works:

Crone, Patricia, and Michael Cook. *Hagarism: The Making of the Islamic World.* Cambridge, New York: Cambridge University Press, 1977.

Hawting, G.R. *The Idea of Idolatry and the Emergence of Islam: From Polemic to History.* Cambridge, New York: Cambridge University Press, 1999.

Wansbrough, John. *Qur'anic Studies: Sources and Methods of Scriptural Interpretation.* Oxford: Oxford University Press, 1977.

For a thoughtful critique of this revisionist approach, consult the following text:

Donner, Fred M. *Narratives of Islamic Origins: The Beginnings of Islamic Historical Writing.* Princeton, New Jersey: The Darwin Press, Inc., 1998.

CHAPTER 2

Arab Imperialism

Islam bestowed on the inhabitants of the Arabian Peninsula an irresistible dynamism just at the moment that the two great civilizations to the north had exhausted each other. In less than a decade after Muhammad's death, the Arabs came into possession of the territories of what had been the Sasanian Empire and took over the wealthy Syrian and Egyptian provinces of the Byzantine Empire. Within the lifetime of some of the children who had met Muhammad and sat on the Prophet's knees, Arab armies controlled the land mass that extended from the Pyrenees Mountains in Europe to the Indus River valley in South Asia. In less than a century, Arabs had come to rule over an area that spanned five thousand miles.

The leaders of this unprecedented achievement included some men of remarkable ability, but, on the whole, their effectiveness was handicapped by their inability to transcend their provincial attitudes. Because their Arab identity was so strong, they could rarely see the conquered territories as the arena for the continued expansion of a universal Islamic society; instead, they saw it as a cash cow to be exploited. When the pace of conquest slowed and the revenues from the pillaging began to dry up, they were unable to prevent tribal factionalism from developing as their followers began to compete for scarce resources. Perhaps an even greater failure was their refusal to receive into their society the non-Arabs who converted to Islam. The discrimination the new Muslims experienced contrasted sharply with the ideals of justice and equality that had attracted the converts in the first place, and opened the Arabs to charges of hypocrisy and oppression. The inability of the leadership to resolve these problems led to a revolution that overthrew the Arab empire after only a century of spectacular expansion.

Arab Conquests

During the last few years of his life, the Prophet gradually expanded his sphere of influence within the Arabian Peninsula by means of military campaigns and peaceful alliances. In the aftermath of his death, the Muslim leadership at Medina began a series of conquests that still have the power to amaze the observer. Taking place over

33

a period of ninety years, these conquests swept away the imperial forces of the Arabs' proud neighbors to the north and resulted in a permanent cultural transformation of the societies that came under Muslim control.

Arabia and the Fertile Crescent

The Prophet's sudden death in 632 was a stunning and disorienting experience for his followers. Having become dependent upon him to serve as both the channel of God's revelation and the political and military leader of the new state, the community was bereft of its religious and political leadership at a stroke. That the despair and confusion in the wake of his death did not cause the collapse of his nascent movement is a testimony to the strength of the institutions and the ideals that Muhammad had left behind and to the quality of the leadership that succeeded him.

According to the most commonly accepted version of events, several factions emerged among the Muslims, each advocating its own solution to the leadership vacancy. The three primary groups were the original Muslim migrants to Medina, the natives of Medina who converted to Islam, and the Meccans who converted after the conquest of their city in 630. Two of the first converts to Islam, 'Umar ibn al-Khattab and Abu Bakr, played leading roles during the decision-making days after the Prophet's death. In the heat of the debate over the course of action to be taken, 'Umar made a passionate speech that convinced those present to accept Abu Bakr as the leader of the Umma. Abu Bakr was a pious, highly respected confidant of Muhammad who was famous for his knowledge of the genealogy of the region's tribes, a valuable asset for the politics of the day. He and the Prophet had solidified their relationship by Muhammad's marriage to Abu Bakr's nine-year-old daughter, 'A'isha, soon after the Hijra. The young wife became Muhammad's favorite, and he died in her arms. The title of the position that Abu Bakr now held came to be known as that of the caliph, although as we shall see later, it is not clear whether Abu Bakr himself was addressed by this title. There is evidence, in fact, that 'Umar and Abu Bakr worked together closely during the latter's short administration.

With the loss of the Prophet, the new leader's most pressing challenge was that many of the tribes that had subjected themselves to Medina no longer considered themselves under Medina's control. Interpreting the situation in traditional fashion, they felt that the terms that they had contracted with Muhammad had been of a personal nature, and that it was incumbent upon his successor to renegotiate the terms. They failed to pay their tax and waited for Medina to react. A reversion to paganism does not appear to have played a major role in this challenge to Medina's authority. There were, indeed, certain "false prophets" leading challenges to Islam's dominance among tribes in central and northeastern Arabia, but these were not areas within Medina's sphere of influence. In most cases, the revolt represented a residual tribal antipathy toward unfamiliar centralized control, and it is clear that in some cases the affected tribes were divided, with significant factions wishing not to break with the Umma. Abu Bakr's stature as a leader, however, lay in his recognition that to allow tribes to secede from the union would doom the newly emerging society and allow a relapse into the polytheistic and violent tribalism of the recent past. He perceived that Muhammad's polity inextricably combined religious expression with political authority. Islam was not a religion that could recognize a difference between what belonged to God and what belonged to Caesar. In the Prophet's vision, any distinction between the "religious" and the "political" was fatuous. Political infidelity would result in religious infidelity.

The military campaign that Abu Bakr ordered to bring the recalcitrant tribes back under Medina's control is known in Islamic history as the *ridda* wars, or the Wars of Apostasy. The campaign is important historically because it marks the transition to the Arab wars of conquest outside the peninsula. The campaign to coerce rebel groups to resubmit to Medinan hegemony made two seamless shifts in policy. The first was a transition from pacification of the rebellious tribes to one of subduing Arabian communities that had never had a treaty with the Prophet. The subjugation of the rebels was a short affair, which may be explained in part by evidence that many of the secessionist tribes and settlements were experiencing internal divisions over the issue of rebellion and put up only a half-hearted resistance. In the process of coercing rebel groups back under Medinan hegemony, the Muslim army at some point began to subdue the Arabian tribes that had not made submission. Despite fierce resistance from a handful of tribes, Medina won an overwhelming victory and was master of the peninsula by 634. Augmented by the manpower of the forces that it had conquered in the Ridda wars, the Muslim army was large and confident, whereas its opponents could never unite against Medina. The decisive victory by the diverse coalition that made up the Islamic state made a deep impression on many Arabs regarding the inadequacy of a purely tribal identity.

Just as the Ridda wars are impossible to distinguish from the war for the conquest of the peninsula, so the latter evolved imperceptibly into invasions of the Byzantine and Sasanian empires. The specific reasons for this evolution into major international military expeditions are lost to history, but scholars have suggested three factors that may have converged precisely when the two empires were at their weakest. The first was a geopolitical motivation on the part of the Muslim leadership. As Medina's campaign moved into the northern part of the peninsula, the objectives of the Muslim elite may well have expanded. Muhammad himself had already attempted to gain control of the Arabian tribes and settlements on the route from the Hijaz to Syria; now Abu Bakr seems to have been concerned about the threat posed to the Umma by nomads and rival settlements situated on important trade routes. He was concerned with bringing under his control any potential security threat to the trade of the new state, and he used a combination of force, cajolery, and material incentives to do so.

The second factor was the inspiration of religion itself. Many of the soldiers who fought for Medina throughout the Arabian campaigns were genuinely motivated by religious concerns. The Qur'an repeatedly enjoins believers to engage in a struggle (*jihad*) against unbelievers until God's rule is established on this earth. Muslims who refuse to help either by fighting, or by helping the cause by contributing to it financially, are called hypocrites. On the other hand, those who fight are rewarded not only spiritually (in the afterlife), but also materially (the troops are to share four-fifths of the loot captured in fighting the infidels). The scriptures, the promise of material reward, and social pressure all combined to create a polity that offered powerful ideological motivations for participation in warfare.

Which of these motivations was most important to the typical rank-and-file soldier? It would be interesting to know. Few of the fighters could have been knowledgeable regarding the nature of societies beyond their own, and no doubt initially envisioned fighting and converting only pagan Arabs. As it turned out, they chose to tolerate the existence of the huge number of Christians and Jews in the lands west of Iran, and nowhere did they welcome non-Arab converts to Islam. What, then, was the nature of God's rule that they hoped to establish as a result of their efforts? Unfortunately, it is as impossible to know the answer to this question as it is to know the exact motivations of the Frankish crusaders who went off to Palestine or of the *conquistadores* with Cortes who claimed to be engaging in a mission for God against the Aztecs.

A third factor in the unexpected irruption of the Islamic movement into regions outside the peninsula was one that we shall see repeated many times over the next eight centuries when nomads were recruited into armies in the Afro-Asiatic land mass: Although the nomads were supposed to be instruments of the policy of political leaders, their own needs and expectations often dictated policy. The irony facing the Medinan and Meccan elites was that a majority of their troops were of necessity the very bedouin who historically had depended on raiding settlements for the acquisition of their surplus. In a sense, the Muslim leadership was riding a tiger by depending on armies made up of the social group that posed a perpetual threat to the personal, political, and economic security of town dwellers.

It would have been extremely difficult, if not impossible, to have escaped the dilemma. Muslims expected the raids and battles to yield plunder as well as strategic or religious gains. The Qur'an stipulated that the Prophet would retain one-fifth of the captured property from such battles for distribution among the community, and the remainder would be divided among the warriors who participated in the fighting. The wars under the first caliphs continued that policy, with one-fifth of the captured property going to the caliph. Each Muslim victory yielded plunder and recruits from the ranks of the vanquished. The additional warriors made the next stage of conquest easier, but they also made the next stage imperative. Further conquests were needed to satisfy the demand and expectation of plunder. The conquest of neighboring tribes within the peninsula, then of settlements outside the peninsula, and then of contiguous areas beyond, proved to be a way of providing the nomads with loot, which kept their minds on new enemies and opportunities, rather than on the central government. Controlling the forces that made their very success possible, however, would be a continuing challenge for the Muslim leadership.

The Arabian Peninsula merges imperceptibly with the land mass of southwest Asia. So, too, did the presence of Arabs extend from the peninsula into the Fertile Crescent. From the Medinan perspective, the Syrian and Iraqi Arabs were obvious candidates for incorporation into the Umma. The Syrian portion of the Fertile Crescent received priority. As we have seen, Muhammad had already sent more than one army in its direction. Its oases and green hills were known to those who plied the caravan trade, and it was the setting for many of the important religious figures mentioned in the Qur'an. Populated by numerous Arabs, it attracted Muslims for both religious and economic reasons.

In the autumn of 633, four Arab armies entered southern Syria and were soon joined by a fifth army that Abu Bakr transferred to Syria from its location on the southern Euphrates in Iraq, where it had been engaged in raiding and reconnaissance. The total manpower of the Muslim forces probably amounted to about 24,000 troops, including both infantry and cavalry. Abu Bakr died a few months later and was succeeded by his friend 'Umar by the same process of deliberation that had brought Abu Bakr into the leadership role a mere two years earlier. Reflecting the common vision of the two men, the Syrian conquest proceeded without interruption.

Whereas the Muslim conquest of Syria proceeded seamlessly despite the death of the first caliph, the Byzantine defense of the region never became coherent. Plague and sustained warfare had reduced the population of the area by twenty to forty percent over the previous century, and adequate provision had not been made for the loss of the Ghassanid auxiliaries. Byzantine armies, forced to move at the rate of their infantry, might travel twenty miles per day at best and by this time had developed a reputation for preferring a defensive rather than an offensive posture. They had also lost much of their discipline and combat readiness. The best of the regular imperial troops were concentrated near Constantinople, and those in Syria were outnumbered by their own, friendly, Arab forces by a ratio of at least two to one, and perhaps five to one. The populace was sullen. The numerous Monophysite Christians had no reason to feel loyalty to distant Constantinople, and the Jews were suffering severe persecution in retaliation for their active support of the Sasanian occupation that had just ended.

The first objective of the Muslims was to establish dominance over the Arabic-speaking areas of southern and eastern Syria. Many of these tribes put up stiff resistance against what they thought was another raid from desert dwellers, but many local Arabs, including Christians, joined the conquering armies. With these reinforcements, the invaders developed a numerical advantage over the local defenders. Syrian cities in the interior began to fall, and Damascus surrendered in 636. At that point, Heraclius realized that the invasion was a serious threat and sent in a huge Byzantine army that was reinforced by Arab and Armenian mercenaries. At the Yarmuk River, a tributary of the Jordan River just south of Lake Tiberias (the Sea of Galilee), the Muslims and their local allies decisively defeated the Byzantine coalition, effectively sealing the fate of Syria. The only question would be how long the sieges of the remaining cities would take. Over the next few months, Antioch and Aleppo fell, and Jerusalem capitulated in 637. The seaport of Caesarea was the last Byzantine city to fall, in 640. The Muslim Arabs now ruled the coastal plains and the interior, although they never gained effective control of the remote and rugged Lebanese mountainous areas.

Although the chronology is not certain, it appears that after the battle of Yarmuk, 'Umar felt that he could send troops into Iraq. When the Muslims began their attacks on Iraq, local Arab nomads and the Aramaic towns fought to protect themselves. Soon, however, the primary Muslim army devastated a much larger Sasanian force at Qadisiya, northwest of Hira. It then moved on to capture Ctesiphon. From that point, the largely Nestorian and Jewish population of central Iraq put up little resistance. Meanwhile, a second Muslim army captured southern Iraq. The young Sasanian emperor, Yazdagird, fled east, and, by 638, the Muslims had secured almost all of the Tigris and Euphrates valleys. The conquerors established military settlements to serve as garrison cities that could ensure security, serve as supply points, and keep the Arab troops from mixing with the local people. Kufa and Basra were the biggest of these new settlements, and within a short time, each of these new towns was thronged with tens of thousands of Arabs from the peninsula.

Meanwhile, in 639, the Arab commander 'Amr ibn al-'As requested permission from 'Umar to lead a force into the Nile valley. 'Umar, whose clearly stated focus had been the subjugation of Arab populations rather than conquest in general, initially refused. After further consideration, 'Umar gave his reluctant consent, perhaps being persuaded by the security threat posed by the Byzantine army and navy that were based in Alexandria. Muslim armies now entered a new phase of their conquests. From that point, they would spread the hegemony of Islam wherever their power enabled them to overcome local resistance. 'Amr's army benefitted from the policies of the Orthodox patriarch, Cyrus. After the Byzantines retook Egypt from the Sasanians in 628, Cyrus had begun a savage repression of Monophysitism, with the result that Copts provided no support to their hated Byzantine overlords. 'Amr's army won control of Egypt by 641, and he created a military garrison and capital, calling it Fustat. Significantly, it was near the old Roman settlement of Babylon, on the southern fringe of the Nile delta, rather than at the traditional seaside capital, Alexandria. Whereas Alexandria was Greek in culture and faced the Byzantine-dominated Mediterranean, Fustat—like Kufa and Basra—was for Arab troops, and was oriented toward Medina.

Iran

Seven years of campaigning won the Fertile Crescent and Egypt for the Muslim armies. The flat terrain and arid and semiarid climate were familiar and congenial to the victors; the poor organization and morale of the imperial armies had allowed the traditional superiority of nomadic attackers to prevail over settled life; and after the initial shock, the population had reacted to the new administration with a mixture of relief and resignation. The momentum of the victories carried the Muslim armies to the east and to the west simultaneously, and they were continuously augmented by migrants from Arabia, new converts in the conquered territories, and even by warriors, such as former Sasanian troops, who were not required to convert as a condition of service in the Muslim army. The next stage of the conquests would prove to be no less remarkable than the first, but would be much more difficult.

The Sasanians had been defeated in Iraq, but Yazdagird's generals organized a large army on the Iranian plateau with the intention of driving out the invaders. 'Umar ordered a campaign to meet him that entailed having to advance through the Zagros Mountains, a terrain unfamiliar to the Arab army. The Zagros at that point are 125 miles wide. They run north and south and are arranged in parallel, rugged ridges that contain deep gorges. It was in the Zagros that the Arab army encountered Yazdagird at Nahavand in 642, the most difficult and costly of all the battles the Arabs had to fight against the Sasanian forces. The Arabs won, however, and Yazdagird once again fled to the east as a fugitive, with the Arabs in pursuit.

The Arab campaign to conquer Iran was well planned, but it faced formidable challenges. One was a change in leadership. In 644, 'Umar ibn al-Khattab was stabbed to death by an Iranian who had been captured during the conquest. His successor was 'Uthman ibn 'Affan, who had supported Muhammad from the beginning of his mission. Again reflecting the remarkable unity of the early leadership, the Iranian campaign continued without interruption under the new caliph.

The other challenges were the different terrain and the new level of resistance from the local inhabitants. In southwestern Iran, the Sasanian royal family's favorite province of Fars produced the fiercest resistance of all. Five years (645–650) of sustained, brutal fighting were required to reduce such opposition, during which time the Sasanian aristocracy was exterminated. The inhabitants of Fars resisted conversion to Islam for longer than any other group in Iran. In order to control the other Iranian cultural areas, an invader must master the Zagros Mountains, rugged Azerbaijan in the northwest, and the Elburz Mountains south of the Caspian Sea, as well as maintain a vigilant watch on the great deserts of the interior. Moreover, unlike Iraq, whose population had not defended the Sasanian regime, other provinces fought the invaders almost as fiercely as the inhabitants of Fars did. The Muslim army encountered bitter and prolonged fighting in Azerbaijan from the fiercely independent mountain peoples there. As a result, the province suffered extensive destruction. On the northern Iranian plateau itself, the Arabs also faced stiff resistance. The Arabs secured the southern slopes of the Elburz Mountains while following the trade route east through Rayy en route to Khorasan. They took Nishapur (Neyshabur) and Merv (near modern Mary) in 651, not long after Yazdagird was murdered in that region by his own companions. Due to its size and its resistance, Khorasan was not effectively under Arab control until 654.

In 656, the conquests suddenly stopped for a decade, due to a civil war that rocked the new community of Islam. This bloody conflict was a shock to the many Muslims who had assumed that the principles of religious unity, equality, and justice would bring an end to factionalism. (The civil war will be the subject of a detailed treatment in the next chapter.) At this point, it is sufficient to say that the conflict began when the third caliph, 'Uthman, was assassinated in 656 by disgruntled warriors from the garrison of Fustat in Egypt. These men then secured the selection of 'Ali ibn Talib as 'Uthman's successor. 'Ali was the Prophet's cousin and had been among the very earliest of the converts to Islam. He was widely admired, and a devoted group of followers had been demanding that he be selected caliph ever since the death of the Prophet. Now, however, because he took no steps to punish the murderers of his predecessor, 'Ali became the target of a vendetta by 'Uthman's kinsmen, who were known as the Umayyads.

The vendetta grew to such large proportions that it became a civil war. The leader of the Umayyad cause was 'Uthman's nephew, Mu'awiya, the talented governor of Syria. In 661, 'Ali became the third caliph in a row to be murdered, stabbed to death while at prayers in a mosque. Mu'awiya now claimed the right to succeed 'Ali as caliph. Because Mu'awiya remained in Syria, Damascus became the center of Muslim political and economic power, and Medina was relegated to the periphery of the Arab empire. Mu'awiya (661–680) proved to be a skillful and honest administrator, but one of his decisions won him enduring enmity among many Muslims. Rather than relying on a council to select the next caliph, he named his own son to be his successor. His family, the Umayyads, thus became the dynastic rulers who claimed the leadership of the Arab empire from 661 until they were overthrown in 750.

Under the Umayyads, the conquests resumed. Using Coptic sailors who had been in the Byzantine naval squadron based in Alexandria, the Arabs led several fruitless naval raids on Constantinople between 667 and 680. During these same

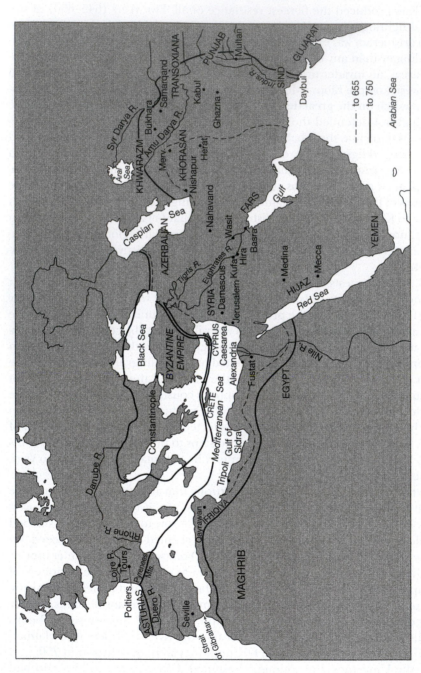

MAP 2.1 Arab Conquests, 632–750

campaigns, however, the Arabs captured Crete and established a presence on the island of Cyprus, which they used as a base to attack Byzantine shipping for the next three centuries. Arab armies could not secure a lasting foothold in the densely settled areas north of the Taurus Mountains. The Byzantines had lost Syria and Egypt, but still retained Anatolia and the Balkans. Anatolia's population was equal to that of Egypt and Syria combined, and by possessing it and the Balkans, Constantinople was sufficiently wealthy to remain the mighty capital of a powerful empire for centuries to come. The Sasanians had been destroyed, but the Byzantines would engage the Muslims in almost continuous warfare for centuries and present a difficult barrier against further Islamic expansion despite their notorious political instability.

North Africa and the Iberian Peninsula

North Africa did not lure the Arabs the way Syria and Iraq had. Arab troops occupied Tripoli in 643 during 'Amr's consolidation of his victory in Egypt, but he attempted no conquests further west. For several decades thereafter, North Africa provided an opportunity for local warriors and adventurers to make raids while the main theater of conquest lay to the east.

North Africa west of central Libya (the Gulf of Sidra) is usually referred to as the *Maghrib,* an Arabic word meaning "land of the west," or "land of sunset." The Maghribi coastal plain is fertile for most of its length, and the area comprising modern Algeria and Tunisia was a major source of wheat, wine, and olive oil for the Romans and Byzantines. Peasant villages dotted the coast and were found throughout the valleys and passes of the mountain ranges, which become progressively more imposing from Tunisia into Morocco. Most of the towns were ports along the coast, although some were located in fertile wheat-growing areas dozens of miles inland. Roman Carthage had attained a population of at least 100,000 at its peak, but it never fully recovered after having been sacked by the Vandals in 439.

In the seventh century, the Berbers were the dominant ethnic group throughout the 2000 miles from the Libyan plateau to the Atlantic coast. The Berber languages belong to the Afroasiatic language family, along with the Semitic, Chad, and ancient Egyptian languages. However, several of the major Berber dialects are almost mutually incomprehensible, and the result has been a long history of rivalry and conflict among the major groupings. Like the Arabs themselves, some Berbers were camel nomads, a greater number were seminomads, and the largest number were settled in villages and towns. The pastoral and village Berbers had always remained little touched by Roman and Byzantine culture, but urban Berbers had assimilated to it, especially in the beautiful and prosperous areas of northern Tunisia and eastern Algeria, the Roman province of "Africa." Under the Arabs, this province would become known as Ifriqiya.

The coastal areas of the Maghrib were largely Christian, and boasted hundreds of bishops in an age when each town had its own bishop. Luminaries such as Tertullian (c. 160–c. 220) and Augustine of Hippo (354–430) established North Africa as a major center of Christian activity. Carthage was one of the major churches in the Christian world during the third and fourth centuries. During the fourth and fifth centuries, however, a major controversy broke out within the North African Church that opened bitter ethnic and social cleavages, leaving the Christian community divided on the eve of Muslim expansion.

During the mid-seventh century, the Maghrib was a venue for raids by Arabs stationed in Egypt. Under Mu'awiya, the Umayyads launched larger raids into Byzantine North Africa in the 660s and 670s, coordinated with their attacks on Constantinople. A notable accomplishment of these raids was the creation in 668 of a headquarters at Qayrawan (Kairouan), which eventually became one of the most important cities in North Africa. However, the raiders were not able to capture Byzantine cities or subdue the Berber tribesmen.

The first major invasion did not take place until 693. Although the army captured Carthage, it was soon expelled by tribal forces. A second invasion in 698 was more successful. In that year, Carthage was destroyed, and during the period 705–714, the Maghribi governor Musa ibn Nusayr overran the areas to the west, all the way to the Atlantic. Musa owed much of his success to Berber tribesmen, many of whom converted to Islam during the 690s and joined his army. Unlike the sedentary Berbers, numerous nomadic Berbers from the coastal plains formally adopted Islam (albeit with a considerable admixture of folk religion) by the end of the seventh century. North Africa may well have been the most Islamized of the conquered areas by that time. Thousands of nomadic Berbers joined the conquering Muslim armies. Although they were not paid a stipend as the Arabs were, the Berber warriors were allowed to share in the distribution of the plunder of the conquests, unlike the non-Arabs in the Muslim armies of the east. Many Berbers became high-ranking civil and military officers in the new administrative system.

Before he had even consolidated his position in the Maghrib, Musa received an unexpected appeal from the Visigothic royal family of the Iberian Peninsula for support against a usurper named Roderick. The Visigoths had crossed the Pyrenees three hundred years earlier, but had not managed to subdue the whole peninsula until the 630s, when Muhammad was consolidating his position at Medina. They had long been influenced by Roman culture, and provided patronage to those who produced it. The great Latin scholar Isidore of Seville (c. 560–636) was a beneficiary of such cultural largesse. Initially maintaining a clear division between themselves and the much larger Hispano–Roman population, the Visigoths gradually adopted legal and religious policies during the seventh century that appeared to be creating a stable society. The economy, however, remained dangerously dependent on a weak agricultural sector that proved to be vulnerable to recurring droughts during the seventh and early eighth centuries. The famines and social unrest that resulted provoked the formation of factions within the military elite, leading to great instability within the regime. The Jews, who had already been persecuted by the Visigoths, now became scapegoats for the growing unrest, and were tortured, enslaved, and forced to convert to Christianity. The political crisis reached its peak in 710, when Roderick seized the throne and one faction within the royal family appealed to Musa for aid.

In 711, Musa sent an army across the Strait of Gibraltar and devastated Roderick's forces. Whatever Musa's intentions for the expedition might have been, the campaign rapidly became one of conquest. The largely Berber force swept across the disorganized peninsula with surprising ease, subjugating the bulk of it within five years. The invaders met little resistance from the inhabitants of most areas and were actively aided by members of the substantial Jewish population, some of whom served in garrisons that were assigned the responsibility to preserve order in captured cities. By 720, the Iberian Peninsula had been pacified, except for a small area in the mountainous north called Asturias.

Central Asia and the Indus River Valley

Some towns in Khorasan took advantage of the civil war between 'Ali and Mu'awiya (656–661) to assert their independence, but they were almost immediately recaptured. In order to secure its position, the Arab army in the region captured Herat in 660, extending the empire's frontier considerably eastward. Khorasan was a wealthy province and, as the Sasanians had known, it was the front line in the defense against Central Asian nomads. The new Umayyad dynasty placed a high value on securing control of the area, and in 671 Damascus ordered a massive colonization effort, which resulted in the settlement of 50,000 Arab warriors and their families in Merv. Merv thus reasserted the role it had played under the Sasanians, serving as the primary garrison city in the east. For the next thirty years, Arabs raided across the Amu Darya for the purpose of looting and keeping the area disorganized, but not of annexing it.

Transoxiana, the target of the looting, had long been a cultural melting pot. Most of the area is desert or semidesert, but it was densely settled in the many oases and along the Amu Darya and Syr Darya river valleys that bordered it on the south and north, respectively. The two most important cities were Samarqand and Bukhara. Because of the region's location, it was frequented by merchants from all over Asia, whose activities augmented the wealth derived from agriculture. As a result of its attraction to traders, Samarqand and Bukhara were cosmopolitan centers and numbered among their citizens Zoroastrians, Buddhists, shamanists, Nestorians, and Manichaeans, as well as adherents of other religious traditions. Intellectuals were attracted to the cities, and rich merchants were pleased to patronize them, so the two cities had a reputation for a rich intellectual life.

In 705, Qutayba ibn Muslim became the governor of Khorasan and began his spectacular, albeit destructive, ten-year career as the leader of Umayyad expansion into Central Asia. His task was quite different from that of the other Arab military commanders, who were leading bands of Arab or Berber warriors with nomadic backgrounds, and for whom constant movement was normal. By the early eighth century, tens of thousands of Arabs had assimilated into the local Iranian society in Khorasan, having bought farms or set up businesses. Although they were offered the normal stipend for military service, as well as a share in the loot, many of the Arabs were reluctant to set off on the campaigns. Qutayba was forced to supplement the local Arab contingents with Syrian soldiers and levies of non-Muslim Khorasanis. Qutayba's army captured Bukhara in 709 after a three-year siege. The ensuing sack of the city resulted in the deaths of thousands of people and the destruction of invaluable manuscripts. In 711–712, Qutayba annexed Khwarazm (the lower reaches of the Amu Darya) and Samarqand; and in 713, he subjugated Farghana, the upper valley of the Syr Darya, which today lies in the eastern extremity of Uzbekistan. According to the Arab chroniclers, the conquest of Central Asia was unusually brutal, and Qutayba's end was equally so: His own troops killed him. Tired of the endless campaigning, both the Arab and the Iranian Khorasanis wanted to return to their families and businesses.

About the time that Qutayba began his conquest of Transoxiana, the conquest of Sind began. Sind was the name Arabs gave to the valley of the Indus River and the territories lying to its east and west. It was one of the cradles of civilization. Like Egypt and Iraq, Sind is a desert in which riverine irrigation produces a large surplus of foodstuffs. The Indus allows a rich agricultural valley to extend for almost four hundred miles through this arid region and made possible the Mohenjo-daro civilization of ca. 2300 B.C.E. Because of the agricultural wealth to be derived from the area, it was contested by neighboring empires and had been controlled by the Sasanians. By the early eighth century, the majority of the population was Buddhist, but Hindus were engaged in an aggressive campaign to become the dominant community. During the first decade of the eighth century, an Arab merchant ship was beached during a storm near the town of Daybul, approximately where modern-day Karachi is located. Pirates plundered the passengers' possessions and enslaved the women and children. Al-Hajjaj, the governor of Iraq, demanded that the local ruler arrange for the release of the captives and the restoration of their property, but was rebuffed. Al-Hajjaj sent two unsuccessful expeditions against the city, but the third was commanded by his young son-in-law, Muhammad ibn Qasim, who became famous as the conqueror of Sind.

In 711, Muhammad ibn Qasim's well-equipped army captured Daybul after a fierce siege. Muhammad then moved north up the Indus. He captured the city of Multan in 713 after another arduous siege and overthrew the Hindu ruler there. Many of the local Buddhists, like those in other cities that he captured, welcomed him because they were anxious to be rid of their Hindu rulers, whom they viewed as usurpers. In fact, the bitter sieges of Daybul and Multan were the exceptions in a conquest that was characterized more by voluntary surrenders than by brutality. With the conquest of Multan, Muhammad became the ruler of all of Sind and part of the Punjab, the name given to the area through which five rivers flow to form the headwaters of the Indus. As Muslims were approaching the Pyrenees in Europe, Muhammad ibn Qasim had set up an Umayyad administration over the Indus valley, 5000 miles to the east.

Umayyad Administration

Neither Islam nor the Islamic state was fully formed when the Arab armies burst into the Fertile Crescent. Both the religion and the political administration were little more than statements of ideals that would become institutionalized later within a variety of social contexts. The first three caliphs, based in Medina, were in office during a remarkable period (632–656) of expansion out of the Arabian Peninsula. It is safe to say that, although at times they supervised the campaigns, at other times conquests took place so rapidly on remote frontiers that they learned about them long after the fact. They made policy, as well they could, at considerable remove from the new provinces of the emerging empire. When 'Ali became caliph in 656, a period of confusion set in because of his need to defend his position against his enemies. As a result, he spent most of the time in Iraq, leading his army.

Upon 'Ali's death in 661, Mu'awiya became the new caliph. Rather than moving to Medina, he remained in Damascus, where he had been governor and where his political and military support lay. Thus, Damascus served as the capital of the Umayyad Empire until the Abbasid revolution in 750. Because of the conquests, immense amounts of treasure flowed into the city, and much of it was invested in new palaces, mosques, fountains, and fortifications. Umayyad princes constructed palaces in the city and on the edge of the Syrian desert. Although the caliphs and their officials in Damascus attempted to impose uniform policies throughout the empire, the immense distances and the remarkable cultural differences that were involved forced them to allow many local practices to continue, although officials often tried to adapt local practices to Qur'anic prescriptions.

The Caliphate

As we have seen, the Prophet's death in 632 presented the Umma with a leadership crisis. Not only did his followers need a new leader, but they also had to confront the question of the nature of their future leadership. The Qur'an had made it clear that Muhammad was the last of the prophets. His teachings regarding any aspect of individual or collective behavior were accepted without question: His authority extended

The Great Mosque of Damascus, built 706–715. *Source:* Ashmolean Museum; Ashmolean Museum, Oxford, England, U.K.

from the prayer mat to the battlefield. What, then, would be the scope of authority of his successor, since he would not serve in the prophetic role? Moreover, what would be the process of succession? That is, how would his successor be identified, and how would the Prophet's followers acknowledge his authority?

Given the importance of the issues surrounding the new leadership, it is surprising how little we know about them. The account accepted by most Muslims relates that Muhammad himself did not name a successor, that his death brought about widespread confusion, and that three major factions of Muslims were prepared to go their separate ways by naming a member from their own group as the leader they would follow. This account suggests that Muslim identity had not yet replaced more particularistic ones, even for Muhammad's earliest converts. Nevertheless, they knew and trusted each other well enough that 'Umar was able to arrange the acceptance of a candidate acceptable to all three groups. The description of how Abu Bakr was selected echoes the mode of succession familiar to tribal society. Upon the death of the chieftain, the most influential members of the tribe would swear allegiance to the most admired and influential member of the tribe and signify their loyalty to him by clasping his hand. Similarly, 'Umar persuaded those present in the meeting in Medina to accept Abu Bakr by acclamation, and they offered him their handclasp (*bay'a*). This account is plausible, for it seems reasonable that the mode of selection in 632 would resemble the one with which the Muslims were already most familiar. As we shall discuss in detail in the next chapter, an important minority of Muslims—the Shi'ites—were to insist that Muhammad had, in fact, named a successor.

More baffling in the narratives of this crucial period is the silence regarding the nature of the authority that the Umma vested in the new leader. We do not even know for certain the title with which his followers addressed him. Abu Bakr is said to have been the first *caliph*, a word deriving from the Arabic word *khalifa*. The Arabic term, however, can connote both *deputy* and *successor*, which are clearly distinct meanings. Many histories of this period assume that the title of the caliphs was *khalifat rasul Allah*, or "successor of the Prophet of God." Many writers have stressed the political and military responsibilities of the caliph and downplay the spiritual side. No existing document dating from before the mid-eighth century, however, contains the title in question; it first appears only during the caliphate of the Abbasids, the dynasty that overthrew the Umayyads in 750.

On the other hand, it is certain that 'Uthman, the Umayyad caliphs, and the early Abbasid caliphs all used as their official title *khalifat Allah*. The latter term conveys the meaning "deputy of God," which suggests considerable spiritual authority. It is difficult to conclude other than that most Muslims of the first Islamic century considered the caliph to be "deputy of God" and to regard loyalty to him to be indispensable for salvation. His sanction validated the religious obligations that were incumbent upon every believer. The caliphate was a necessary institution for the purpose of defining religious obligations that related to ethics and the ritual of worship. Also, difficult cases that needed interpretation were taken to the caliph for adjudication.

The confusion over the nature of the early caliphate appears to be the result of two important developments in the nature of the institution. (We shall explore these developments in more detail later.) The first was the emergence of a schism within the Umma, clearly apparent by the mid-eighth century, over the nature of caliphal qualifications and authority that led to the distinction between Sunni Muslims and

Shi'ite Muslims. The second was the fact that, by the late ninth century, caliphs in fact no longer participated in making religious law. Sunni scholars writing after that time, whose accounts are our primary sources for learning about early Islamic history, wrote from a perspective that has shaped our understanding of the period. They had no experience of a caliph with spiritual authority, and they were hostile to the Shi'ites, who insisted on the need for one.

What does seem clear is that, from an early time, caliphs were addressed by the title *amir al-mu'minin*. This is variously translated as "Commander of the Faithful" or "Prince of the Believers." The title denotes no specific functions, but can imply supreme military and political power, as well as responsibility for the preservation of the integrity of the religious community. The vast majority of Sunni Muslims have been willing to concede that the first four caliphs fulfilled these functions in admirable form. They generally refer to them as the "rightly guided" caliphs, whose integrity should be the model for all subsequent Muslim leaders. As we shall see, the Umayyad caliphs gradually lost the support of important sectors of the Umma. Not only was their dynasty overthrown, but the role of the caliphate was altered, as well.

The Administration of Non-Muslims

Within a remarkably short time after Abu Bakr became the caliph in 632, the complexities of the caliphal office multiplied exponentially. Initially responsible for the welfare of a small Arab society, the caliph was suddenly governing a huge, heterogeneous, and complex empire. It is not unrealistic to assume that when Abu Bakr was the caliph, he knew personally a large proportion of the people for whom he was responsible. Within a handful of years, however, any new caliph was confronted with the need to provide security and justice for millions of people scattered over thousands of miles of territory. The conquest was in many ways as unexpected for the Arabs as for the conquered peoples, and the new rulers had to improvise policy. It turned out to be quite simple: Leave the normal routines of life undisturbed for the conquered peoples, collect the taxes, keep the Arab soldiers at a social and religious distance from the natives, and implement the teachings of the Qur'an as fully as possible.

As Abu Bakr's military campaigns consolidated Medina's control over the northern section of the peninsula and entered the frontier zones of neighboring empires, the Muslim armies increasingly confronted Christian Arabs. Deeper into Syria and Iraq, the armies found that the majority of both the settled and nomadic populations were Christian or Jewish. The accounts of the surrender of Syrian cities were written years after the events in question, and they contain much confusing and contradictory information. Accounts from both the Christian and Muslim chronicles suggest that the initial phase of the campaign was violent, entailing the pillaging and destruction of property (including orchards and livestock), indiscriminate killing, and the enslavement of considerable numbers of the local population. The visit of the caliph 'Umar ibn al-Khattab to Jerusalem in 638 seems to have marked a turning point in this regard. From this point on, a regularized administration and a more lenient policy characterized relations with the Christian and Jewish populations.

As the conquests became consolidated, the Arab rulers found that the administrative policies of the Byzantines and Sasanians offered them contrasting models of governing a multireligious society. Whereas the Byzantine authorities sought to enforce religious uniformity within their realm, the religious pluralism within the Sasanian domain had forced the rulers to develop a practical compromise with their subjects' religious communities. Occasionally, Jews and Christians had even asked the Sasanian government to intervene in quarrels within their communities in order to determine policy regarding doctrine and leadership. By the end of the sixth century, the government had recognized the highest-ranking rabbi in Iraq as the legitimate ruler of the Jewish community. He was responsible for the collection of taxes and for the administration of justice (according to Jewish law) within the Jewish community. The Nestorians and Monophysites were also organized as religious communities, and the Nestorians were beginning to administer church law to the entire community. The Sasanian government thus granted a certain degree of autonomy to religious communities and guaranteed them military protection. The quid pro quo was that the non-Iranian, non-Zoroastrian subjects were required to pay a head tax in return for security.

The Arabs found the Sasanian religious policy to be more relevant to their needs than the Byzantine model. The Qur'an could be adduced as evidence that people with their own scriptures should not be persecuted; Muslims were a tiny minority within their own empire and could hardly expect to emulate the Byzantine persecution of other faiths; and the Sasanian policy offered a welcome source of revenue from non-Muslims. The Arabs referred to Jews and Christians by the Prophet's term, "People of the Book," and they were allowed, and expected, to continue practicing their religion. They and other non-Muslims who possessed their own scriptures and who paid taxes to the Muslims for protection were called the *ahl al-dhimma*, meaning "protected peoples." A person who belonged to such a community was a *dhimmi*. Dhimmis were often retained as local officials in conquered areas, without regard to their religious affiliation. Even devotees of religions that might appear to be compromised by polytheism were often granted the status of protected peoples. The Zoroastrians of Iran, the Buddhists of Central Asia and Sind, and the Hindus of Sind were initially persecuted because of their polytheism, but most such communities became the beneficiaries of a laissez-faire religious policy.

The earliest treaties that the Muslims signed with cities in Syria and Iraq suggest that the entire city was responsible for paying a tribute to the central government. It was not long before these terms were revised so that dhimmis were assessed an individual head tax (*jizya*). Also, because they were initially the only land owners and Muslims were not, the dhimmis paid taxes on their land and other property. Policies towards dhimmis varied according to period and place across the huge empire. For example, despite the concept that non-Muslims were paying taxes in return for protection, they could, and did, serve in the army during the period of conquest. Their services in some cases were so critical that certain governors refused to allow them to return to civilian life. Policies never became fully standardized across the empire, and in general, life for dhimmis continued as before. Even on such issues as the drinking of wine or the eating of pork, both of which are forbidden to Muslims, the authorities rarely interfered with such practices as long as the dhimmis did not try to sell those items to Muslims.

On the whole, non-Muslims received much better treatment than Jews did in Europe from the medieval period on, although we shall see that circumstances arose that could make life difficult for them. Throughout history, the same factors have affected the relationship between Muslims and other religious groups as those affecting the relationship between religious and ethnic groups anywhere in the world: the health of the economy, the sense of personal security that people feel, the attitudes of the leading members of the regime, and the political and military relationship between the society in question and its neighbors.

The Administration of Muslims

From the beginning of the conquests, the Muslim Arabs differentiated themselves from their subjects both ethnically and religiously. They sought to institutionalize the differences through the enactment of regulations, while they simultaneously tried to implement the religious injunctions of the Qur'an into their own daily life.

Arab Warriors

One of the most pressing concerns for the Muslim leadership was that of regulating the movements of the Arabs who made up the bulk of the conquering army. On the one hand, it was essential to prevent them from assimilating into the conquered territories. If they became settled into the majority culture and economy, their military skills would be compromised and they would not be able to respond instantly to a mobilization order. On the other hand, their very unruliness needed to be controlled in order not to disturb the social order. It appears that 'Umar was the caliph who created the basic framework for dealing with the Arab troops. First, he created garrison towns—Kufa and Basra in Iraq, and Fustat in Egypt were the best known—that were designed to house Arab soldiers and their families to keep them from assimilating into the countryside. For several decades, Kufa and Basra were used as staging areas for regular campaigns into Iran to collect tribute and to enforce the terms of the treaties made with the cities there. The garrison cities were thus strategically located: They were easily accessible from Arabia in order to facilitate migration. They were also on the margins of the settled areas of the newly conquered territories in order to discourage interaction between the Arabs and the local inhabitants.

According to Muslim tradition, Muhammad's practice in his military campaigns had been to award four-fifths of the plunder captured in raids to the troops and to retain one-fifth for administrative purposes. The first caliphs continued this policy in the early conquests. But as the frontiers expanded, regular campaigning was more difficult to maintain, and the spoils of war could not be relied upon to provide a steady income. Another method of subsistence had to be devised to supplement the plunder and to keep the troops content. 'Umar seems to have been responsible for beginning the awarding of regular pay to the troops and promising them a share in the revenue of abandoned lands. The amount to be paid to an individual was determined by how long he had been involved in the campaigns. Those who fought for Medina in the Ridda wars and initial conquests received much more than those who began in the last stages of the Iraqi campaign. After the battle of Nahavand in 642, 'Umar equalized the stipends of the latecomers with those of the veterans. Reflecting Sasanian military policy, members of the cavalry were paid twice or even three times that of the infantry. The attraction of the share in the spoils of victory and the security of regular pay encouraged Arabs from the peninsula to migrate to the garrison cities.

Non-Arab Converts

The ruling elite of the Umayyad dynasty never fully came to terms with the fact that Islam might be attractive to non-Arabs. Islam had begun as a religion for the Arabs. It arose in Arabia, the revelation was delivered in the Arabic language, and it was Arabs who conquered in the cause of Islam. Many Arabs seemed surprised that non-Arabs began to convert to Islam, and they became annoyed when non-Arab Muslims insisted on being treated equally with the Arabs on the grounds of Islamic brotherhood. It was one thing to regard members of other Arab tribes as having a claim to equal treatment, but quite another for non-Arabs to claim such rights. The claims of the non-Arabs challenged not only the ethnic prejudice of the Arabs, but also the viability of the tax policy that had been devised for the new empire. To try to accommodate the non-Arab Muslims, the Arabs allowed them to become clients of Arab tribes, much as the bedouin had long done for the practitioners of low-status, but essential, occupations, such as metalworking and the tanning of leather.

Most of the converts during the early Umayyad period came from the huge number of prisoners of war captured during the conquests. Some of them became slaves of the conquerors, but most were freed. Some found that they could not return home, and others decided that the fastest route to social mobility was to assimilate into Arab culture and society. Despite their efforts to assimilate, the majority of Arabs would not accept them as social equals. Normally, even if they fought in the armies, they were given neither pay nor a share in the spoils of war, since their adopted tribe was supposed to support them. As we have seen, when the military campaigns became as distant as Transoxiana and North Africa, military commanders felt compelled to share the plunder with their soldiers who were non-Arab converts. The unequal treatment regarding pay and the constant humiliation of taunts and discriminatory behavior, however, caused their resentments to build.

Over the years, more and more rural individuals and families converted to Islam. In village societies where religion is the primary identity marker, conversion to another religion can be inferred by others as a rejection of one's family or heritage. It is not uncommon for families to disown, and for neighbors to shun, someone who has converted to an outside religion. This pattern seems to have been the case with particular relevance to Iraq and Khorasan. The social isolation of new converts to Islam in their villages could often be intolerable, and as a result, many migrated to cities where they could practice their religion in an environment in which Muslims predominated. Their departure from the village meant that the collective tax obligation fell more heavily on the remaining villagers, causing them considerable economic difficulty. In those areas where a significant percentage of the population converted, a tax crisis occurred. The remaining villagers could not pay the collective sum, and many more peasants fled the land, leaving lands uncultivated. By the last quarter of the seventh century, the large number of Iraqi peasants fleeing the villages and converting to Islam is said to have prompted the governor, al-Hajjaj, to send the new converts back to the land and to have forbidden further conversions.

Regulating Women's Roles

The development of Islamic norms for women has been a controversial issue. Little is known about the status of women in pre-Islamic Arabia or even in the Byzantine and Sasanian empires in the seventh century, making it difficult to assess the impact of Islam in any of those areas. Early Arabic chronicles provide little information regarding the roles and activities of women. When they are mentioned, only the activities of the women of the ruling class are described. At present, we have only tantalizing clues regarding the early expectations of women's roles and status.

From the evidence available to us, it appears that women in early seventh-century Arabia participated freely in public life. Khadija, the Prophet's first wife, owned property, sought out Muhammad for marriage, and was sufficiently influential in Mecca to serve as a protector for his early career. On the other hand, when she died, Muhammad was reduced to poverty, suggesting that her property reverted by custom to relatives, and was not hers to dispose of. Other women served as prophets and soothsayers, and in the battles between Mecca and Medina, women appeared on the battlefield to jeer the enemy, to mutilate the bodies of wounded and dead enemy soldiers, and even to use the sword and bow in combat. Female critics of the Prophet were not hesitant to belittle him publicly. Marriage and divorce practices varied considerably in the peninsula. Some tribes were matrilineal (descent was traced through the females) and others patrilineal; in some tribes, polygyny was practiced, whereas others practiced polyandry. Wives were referred to as the "property" of their husbands, and some scholars think that women had no right of divorce. Others point out that some women did divorce their husbands, and these scholars assume that women initiated divorce equally with men.[1]

The Qur'an includes some verses that appear to represent increased opportunities for women, whereas others seem to be curbs on activity that had been possible earlier. One famous Qur'anic teaching is that Muslim men are allowed to have up to four wives if they treat them equitably (4:3). Some commentators infer that the limit on the number of wives that a man may have represents a gain for women, assuming that in the pre-Islamic era, a man may have had an unlimited number of wives. Others argue that the verse is an exhortation to Muslim men after the battle of Uhud to marry more than one woman at a time of a surplus of women, while simultaneously limiting women to one husband at a time. The Qur'an specifies that a bridegroom must give his bride a dowry which she keeps with her, regardless of the fate of the marriage. The Qur'an also guarantees women a share of their family's inheritance equal to one-half that which would accrue to their brothers. Again, many commentators think that both developments represent an advance in the rights of women. The dowry served as an economic buffer in the event of divorce, and although the stipulated inheritance share is less than that of males, the guarantee of a specified amount of inherited property gave women an economic security that women in other societies, including Europe, did not have for many centuries to come.

The topic of relations between the sexes receives a significant amount of space in the Qur'an. Husbands are given guidance on how to deal with recalcitrant wives (4:34–35) and how, if necessary, to divorce them. When the Qur'an treats the topic of divorce, it addresses men only. (See 2:226–237, 241; 65:1–7.) It goes into some detail on the fair—and even generous—way to treat a divorced wife, but it does not address the issue of a woman who wishes to divorce her husband. The issue of sexual modesty is also addressed, and subsequent interpretations of those verses have had an important influence on Muslim life for centuries. The issue arose initially as a problem within the Prophet's own household. The Prophet's home in Medina became the gathering place of more and more people as the community grew. It had a large courtyard around which his wives' apartments were placed, and the courtyard itself served as Medina's first congregational mosque. Inevitably, some people began to treat the courtyard as public space, without consideration for the privacy of the family. Some would show up at the Prophet's door uninvited. Others, like guests throughout history, would fail to notice when it was time to go home after a dinner or wedding feast, with awkward consequences for the family. Still others would seek out the apartments of the Prophet's wives in order to deliver a petition, in the hope of having access to the Prophet himself. The revelation of 33:53–59 instructs the community to respect the privacy of the Prophet's house and to speak to his wives only from behind a curtain or screen. Another revelation (or perhaps a cluster of revelations) that seems to have been sent soon after this one is 24:27–32, which repeats the injunction to ask permission before entering a house. The passage adds that men and women alike must lower their eyes when encountering others and guard their private parts. Women were to cover their bosoms with veils and to refrain from showing off their beauty, except to close relatives.

The text of the Qur'an specifies that the Prophet's wives were to be veiled and secluded from the harassment that the celebrity status of their husband had brought upon them. On the other hand, the Prophet's favorite wife, 'A'isha, continued to play an active role in political life for several decades after his death. When and how veiling and seclusion became extended from the Prophet's wives to Muslim women in general is unknown, but it almost certainly required many decades to become normative.

Many historians suspect that the influence of Sasanian and Byzantine mores played an important role in the development of Islamic norms regarding women, but we know practically nothing about what was expected of Sasanian women. Byzantine women of the era were not secluded in their homes and were not subject to rigid dress codes. On the other hand, it was expected that women of the higher Byzantine social classes would wear a veil and not frequent the streets. Observers were shocked when they did happen to see a woman of high status without a veil. What is of importance in this regard is that such expectations were held of women among the elite social classes. It should be noted that the veiling and seclusion of women has never been universal among Muslims, either. Some (admittedly small) Muslim groups throughout history have rejected the practice outright, and it has always been more common among the wealthy urban social strata than among the poor and the rural population. Like the bound feet of aristocratic Chinese women, the wearing of a veil and seclusion within the home were declarations that a woman did not have to engage in manual labor. We shall see in later chapters how the development of Islamic law and the influx of new ethnic groups into the Umma affected the roles and status of women.

The Rationalization of Society

For the first half-century or more after the conquests, the subject peoples noticed very few changes in their lives. The ruling elites in the various territories were new, to be sure, they did not have a social blueprint that they wished to impose on their subjects. This was due in part to the fact that Islamic institutions were still not fully formed and in part to the fact that continued military expansion remained the top priority for the Arab leadership. In huge areas of the empire, the officials with whom the general public had to deal remained reassuringly familiar. The Iranian *dihqan*s,

Qasr al-Hayr East, an Umayyad palace in eastern Syria. *Source:* Ashmolean Museum; Ashmolean Museum, Oxford, England, U.K.

or lesser nobility, were the state's tax collectors in former Sasanian territories for the first half-century of Arab occupation. Christians and Jews continued to hold high administrative positions for many years in Iraq, and in Egypt the Coptic community maintained a monopoly on the accounting staff in the tax division until the late nineteenth century. In like manner, Persian was the language of administration in former Sasanian territories, while Greek was used in former Byzantine holdings.

A notable example of the appropriation of existing offices was that of the official that Muslims called the *muhtasib*. The first muhtasib appeared in Syria, but Muslim societies all the way to the Atlantic soon had one. The muhtasib clearly served the function of the Byzantine *agoranomos,* or market inspector, as well as the *astynomos,* a public health official whose primary function was to maintain streets in passable condition. The muhtasib's duties included the prohibition of the disposal of market and household refuse in the streets and the encroachment of buildings into public space. As the market inspector, he made sure that scales were accurate and that customers were not cheated by unscrupulous merchants. This official was so critical to the maintenance of a smoothly functioning urban society that the office remained active for over a thousand years.

Despite their own proud military tradition, the Arabs recognized advantages in the Sasanian military organization, supply, tactics, and arms, and borrowed directly from them. Likewise, the organization of the civilian government borrowed heavily from the Sasanians, first at the provincial level, and later (especially after the Umayyads) in the imperial administration. Sasanian royal traditions of justice, court procedure, control, and enforcement were to prove highly influential in shaping Islamic institutions.

Sasanian and Byzantine legacies would continue to shape Islamic history for many centuries to come, and in some ways the Sasanian influence on the army and the central government became even more important in the eighth and ninth centuries. On the other hand, the last decade of the seventh century marks an important milestone in the Umayyad government's development of its Arabic and Islamic identity. Until that time, not only had the Muslim authorities continued to use existing officials, policies, and official languages, but also they had not bothered to mint new coins, allowing the high-quality Byzantine and Sasanian coins to continue to circulate. The caliph 'Abd al-Malik (685–705) was determined to establish an explicitly Islamic and Arab identity for his regime. First, he began the construction of monumental mosques that symbolized the triumph of Islam over Judaism and Christianity. (The Dome of the Rock in Jerusalem is the most famous such mosque.) Second, he began the minting of gold coins that bore Arabic inscriptions to replace the Sasanian and Byzantine coins that had been used to that time. This innovation had great symbolic and ideological value, for the high-quality Umayyad coins would soon become prized all over the known world. Third, 'Abd al-Malik inaugurated a policy of converting the language of administration to Arabic.

'Abd al-Malik's process of Arabization took many years—it would be another fifty years before the chancelleries of Khorasan were transformed from the Persian language to the Arabic, and the Coptic accountants in the financial bureaus of Egypt maintained their arcane registry system into the late nineteenth century. But as a result of 'Abd al-Malik's policy, Arabic became the language of written communication in administration, literature, and religion over the vast region that the Arabs had conquered. It also became the majority language spoken west of the Iranian plateau. The Arabizing and Islamizing policies of 'Abd al-Malik's administration allow us to identify the 690s as a watershed in the cultural history of the area. From then on, visitors to the area knew that a new civilization was emerging.

Dissolution of the Arab Empire

In the early, heady, days of conquest, the Arabs could be forgiven for assuming that rapid expansion and the enormous inflow of plunder and taxes would continue indefinitely. The leadership had stumbled on what appeared to be the fulfillment of their goals: the extension of the dominion of God's rule, the acquisition of a steady source of revenue, and the channeling of the martial culture of the peninsula toward external enemies rather than allowing it to disrupt Muslim society. This euphoria soon faded as the frontiers moved farther away and as the issues of Muslim identity became more complicated.

As early as the battle of Nahavand (642), it became clear that further conquests would be less rewarding than the earlier ones. Syria, Iraq, and Egypt were wealthy, adjacent to Arabia, and relatively flat. As a result, their acquisition had provided a high return on the investment of troops and effort. Nahavand, however, was in the Zagros, and, like the remaining conquests to the east, north, and west, it was hundreds of miles from the Muslim capital. It was beginning to dawn on Muslim administrators that further conquests would be in mountainous areas or across vast deserts, and usually against peoples who were not as wealthy as the victims of the first wave of conquests. Inhabitable North Africa was a thin strip two thousand miles in length, but only a few miles wide; the Byzantines in Anatolia were Greek and much more loyal to the regime than the inhabitants of Syria and Egypt had been; the Iranian highlands had wealth, but the area was conquered only after terrible fighting. The great wave of expansion in the second decade of the eighth century—the conquest of Iberia, Sind, and Transoxiana—was lucrative, but it came and went very quickly. No more conquests of significance were made, and yet spending was lavish in order to support the court, irrigation projects, monumental building, and a huge army. As early as the caliphate of 'Umar II (717–720), the empire was facing major financial problems.

Another challenge facing the Umma by the early eighth century was the social tension arising from the accelerated pace of assimilation within the empire. As we have seen, the early Muslim leaders attempted to thwart assimilation by creating garrison cities for the Arab warriors. The creation of such settlements had been an ad hoc arrangement that served several purposes. The central government could confine the Arab warriors to a limited area where they were more easily controlled; by living in the cities, soldiers were less likely to be corrupted by the non-Islamic environment; control of the non-Muslim majority could be maintained with the threat of a large contingent of the occupation army located within an easy march of rebellious villages or towns; and the new cities were ideal staging points for further campaigns.

On the other hand, the policy proved to be unworkable for a number of reasons. First, ethnic segregation failed to achieve its goals. The clustering of thousands of troops in hastily constructed cities attracted large numbers of indigenous inhabitants who offered the troops needed goods and services. These new immigrants came from a variety of ethnic and religious backgrounds, and they mixed socially with the Arabs. Inevitably, some Arabs intermarried with them despite the strong social disapproval of most other Arabs. A slowly growing number of Muslims in these cities were, therefore, the offspring of unions between Arab Muslim fathers and mothers who were Christian, Jewish, or Zoroastrian. Multilingual and multicultural, this group of Muslims felt at ease with elements from both the local and the Arab cultures.

Far from the garrison cities, on the distant frontier province of Khorasan, the assimilation of Arabs into local society was even more evident. The mass Arab colonization of Khorasan in 671, discussed earlier, entailed the relocation of perhaps 50,000 Arab troops and their families from Basra. This enormous population transfer meant that, overnight, Khorasan acquired the third largest Arab population outside Arabia, after Iraq and Syria. Many of the settlers were already married, but many others now married Iranian women. Social assimilation progressed rapidly in the province as Iranians converted to Islam and Arabs adopted local customs. The Arabs of Khorasan became landowners and merchants, began dressing like Iranians, and learned to speak Persian dialects. An Arab landowning class came into being whose members were reluctant to assume the military duties their fathers and grandfathers had welcomed.

By the end of the seventh century, many Muslim Arabs were "going native," while increasing numbers of non-Arabs were becoming Muslims. By serving in the military on crucial fronts, the new Muslims diluted the Arab nature of what had originally been an all-Arab force. In Khorasan, Iranians made up a large proportion of the military units that engaged in the conquest and defense of the Amu Darya frontier, and in North Africa and in the Iberian Peninsula, Berbers constituted a majority of the military units. New converts were beginning to question the rationale for Arab social dominance as mixed communities containing Arabs and non-Arabs emerged in cities scattered all over the empire. With the passage of time, the ethnic slurs they received from some Arabs and the unequal distribution of revenue granted to non-Arabs became less tolerable.

The assimilation taking place in the garrison cities of Iraq and the Arab colonies in Khorasan was producing a new type of Muslim society that stood in stark relief to the Arab identity of the Muslims of Arabia and Syria. Arabia and Syria still lived by a tribal ethos, and the caliphs, with rare exceptions, were dependent on the loyalty of certain Arab tribes for their power. For the most part, the leadership seems to have failed to recognize the changes that were taking place, and only rarely did they make any attempts to address the new social realities. The first "Arab civil war" of 'Ali and Mu'awiya was followed by an even more destructive conflict from 685 to 692 that resulted from the development of tribal coalitions and a jockeying for power that ensued upon the death of Mu'awiya in 680. The caliph 'Abd al-Malik, who had to fight that civil war from the time of his accession in 685, relied on Arab immigrants to Syria for his support. For that reason, the Umayyad army developed a well-deserved reputation as a "Syrian" army. Tensions between the Syrians and the garrison cities became so great that in 701 'Abd al-Malik created Wasit, a garrison city located between Kufa and Basra. Staffed by Syrian soldiers, it was patently an effort to control and intimidate the Arabs of the two older Iraqi garrison cities, whose ideas and actions were becoming irksome to the ruling elite. Later Umayyad caliphs tended to rely on one or another Syrian tribe for military support, with the result that even the Syrian Arabs became splintered into factions.

The caliph 'Umar II (717–720) attempted to address the resentments of both the non-Arab Muslims and the assimilated Arabs towards the Syrian elites, as well as the growing financial problems of the empire. He ended the practice of having non-Arab Muslims pay the head tax, and he ordered that all Muslims serving in the army be paid an equal stipend, regardless of ethnicity. He also removed the Syrian garrisons from Iraq. To the dismay of non-Muslims, he ordered all religious images, including Jewish and Christian, to be destroyed, and he forbade non-Muslims from wearing silk clothing and turbans. He seems to have been the first Muslim ruler to have instituted social distinctions between Muslims and non-Muslims based on the style of dress. He also ordered a halt to the wars of conquest, apparently with the objective of saving money, and he reorganized the caliphal finances in an effort both to economize and to eradicate corruption.

Those who benefitted from the policies of 'Umar II had little time to rejoice. When he died in 720, all of his major policies were almost immediately reversed. Local governors resumed their raids and conquests, and some successes were

The Arrival of al-Hajjaj in Kufa (694–695)

The Arab garrison cities were notorious for their unruliness, but none was more troublesome to the Umayyad authorities than Kufa. In 656, 'Ali had found his base of support there, and after his murder, it remained a center of opposition to Mu'awiya's dynasty. In 694, the Umayyad caliph 'Abd al-Malik appointed al-Hajjaj (661–714) to be the governor of Iraq. Al-Hajjaj had won a reputation for absolute loyalty to the Umayyads and for great brutality in suppressing revolts against the dynasty. As governor of Iraq, he proved to be an administrator of great ability, implementing many policies that promoted economic prosperity and sending out the expedition that conquered Sind in 711–713. The selection that follows is from his first speech as governor. It is one of the most famous speeches in early Muslim history, and several versions of it survive, with only slight variations.

Al-Hajjaj set out for Iraq as governor, with 1200 men mounted on thoroughbred camels. He arrived in Kufa unannounced, early in the day. . . . Al-Hallaj went straight to the mosque, and with his face hidden by a red silk turban, he mounted the pulpit and said, "Here, people!" They thought that he and his companions were Kharijites and were concerned about them. When the people were assembled in the mosque he rose, bared his face, and said:

> *I am the son of splendor, the scaler of high places.*
> *When I take off my turban you know who I am.*

By God, I shall make evil bear its own burden; I shall shoe it with its own sandal and recompense it with its own like. I see heads before me that are ripe and ready for plucking, and I am the one to pluck them, and I see blood glistening between the turbans and the beards.

By God, O people of Iraq, people of discord and dissembling and evil character! I cannot be squeezed like a fig or scared like a camel with old water skins. My powers have been tested and my experience proved, and I pursue my aim to the end. The Commander of the Faithful emptied his quiver and bit his arrows and found me the bitterest and hardest of them all. Therefore he aimed me at you. For a long time now you have been swift to sedition; you have lain in the lairs of error and have made a rule of transgression. By God, I shall strip you like bark, I shall truss you like a bundle of twigs, I shall beat you like stray camels. Indeed, you are like the people of "a village which was safe and calm, its sustenance coming in plenty from every side, and they denied the grace of God, and God let them taste the garment of hunger and of fear for what they had done" (Qur'an, xvi, 112). By God, what I promise, I fulfill; what I purpose, I accomplish; what I measure, I cut off. Enough of these gatherings and this gossip and "he said" and "it is said!" What do you say? You are far away from that! I swear by God that you will keep strictly to the true path, or I shall punish every man of you in his body. . . .

And then he went to his house.

SOURCE: Lewis, Bernard, ed./tr. *Islam from the Prophet Muhammad to the Capture of Constantinople: I. Politics and War.* New York: Walker and Company, 1974, 23–24.

recorded: From Sind, the Arabs invaded India, and plundered the whole of Gujarat. These gains were rapidly lost, however, when Indian princes counterattacked. By 729, the Arab presence in Sind was threatened with extinction. In Europe, Muslims crossed the Pyrenees in the 720s and captured Narbonne, Carcassonne, and Nîmes, with the result that Muslims controlled the coast from the Pyrenees to the Rhone River. In the Iberian Peninsula, quarreling among the Arab factions precluded further expansion into Europe for half a decade, but the Muslim successes north of the Pyrenees had alarmed Eudo, the Duke of Aquitaine. He joined forces with a Berber rebel against the Muslim governor of the peninsula, 'Abd al-Rahman al-Ghafiqi. 'Abd al-Rahman defeated Eudo and began moving north, sacking churches and monasteries. Eudo called for aid from his former rival, the Frankish warrior Charles Martel, who met and defeated 'Abd al-Rahman between Tours and Poitiers, probably in October 733[2].

The Battle of Tours/Poitiers was an important achievement for Martel, but it was not, as many Europeans have claimed, the decisive blow that stopped Muslim expansion into Europe. Muslims continued to plunder the lower Rhone valley with impunity throughout the remainder of the decade, capturing Arles and other cities, until Martel intervened in 739, taking the area for his kingdom. It would be legitimate to argue that the Muslim conquests had always been a matter first of reconnoitering, and then of raids that, if successful, in turn resulted in expeditions of conquest. In that sense, Martel's accomplishment can be seen as slamming the door shut on raiding the interior of Frankish territory. However, it had been clear for almost a decade before Tours that the Muslims' supply and communications lines were overextended whenever they crossed the Pyrenees on a raid.

The conquest of "Frankland" was the farthest object from any Muslim's mind. Much more instrumental in the halt of the Muslim expansion process were internal factors. Factional fighting among the Arabs of the Iberian Peninsula in the 720s led to extended periods of anarchy there; after 734, Qayrawan was the regional capital of both the Maghrib and of Muslim Europe, and the officials in Qayrawan had no interest in dissipating their resources against the Franks; Berber revolts in the Iberian Peninsula and the Maghrib in the 740s ended Umayyad control in those areas; and the overthrow of the Umayyad dynasty itself in 750 led to a wholesale reordering of the administration of the western Muslim world. No one was surprised when Pepin the Short (son of Charles Martel and father of Charlemagne) recaptured Narbonne in 751, ending the Muslim presence in Provence. Muslims, however, continued to raid southern Europe for centuries to come, by land and by sea.

An almost frenetic pace of campaigning across the empire characterized the period 720–740, apparently in an effort to resolve the empire's financial crisis by plunder. Few gains were registered, and several catastrophic military failures occurred, particularly on the fronts in the Caucasus and in Transoxiana. Tens of thousands of Arabs lost their lives in ill-planned battles, and Muslim rulers lost control over large areas on those frontiers. By 741, the Caucasus, Transoxiana, and Sind were again securely in Muslim hands, but for reasons due more to the weakness of the Umayyads' opponents than to Umayyad policy. Rather than producing revenue, the campaigning was extremely expensive and resulted in even graver economic problems. During the administration of the caliph Hisham (724–743), the Umayyad army numbered perhaps 400,000 troops,[3] and the plunder with which to reward them had largely dried up. Periodically, soldiers on most of the major fronts—in Sind, the Caucasus, and Transoxiana—expressed their displeasure at the relentless campaigning, sometimes in the form of deposing and killing their commanders.

In addition to the deepening financial crisis, another problem for the Umayyads was that the non-Arab Muslims showed their anger at having had their financial disabilities reimposed. In Transoxiana and in North Africa, they rose in revolt almost immediately upon the death of 'Umar II. The simmering resentment broke out again a decade later in a major rebellion in Khorasan, in which both Iranians and Arabs participated. Twenty thousand Syrian troops had to be brought in to quell the uprising. The biggest outburst, however, began in 740 in North Africa, with the outbreak of the Great Berber Revolt. Policies toward the Berbers had varied from governor to governor, but after 720 these North Africans had more reasons to resent the Arabs than to appreciate them. They had never been paid military stipends, and now they were sometimes denied a share in the captured booty; Muslim Berbers (especially females) were often taken as slave tribute to the East; and Berber property was constantly threatened by seizure by unprincipled Arab generals and governors. The revolt of 740 took place simultaneously in several locations in North Africa, and it spread into the Iberian Peninsula. Thousands of Arab troops were sent to those two areas to try to suppress the rebellion, but the Umayyads lost the entire region west of Qayrawan. Qayrawan itself was retained by the Arab governor, but the rest of North Africa became a collection of quarreling Berber principalities.

When Hisham died in 743 after a caliphate of nineteen years, the empire entered a period of great instability. The expansionist policy was bankrupt both ideologically and financially. The majority non-Muslim population had no stake in it, and by now, many Muslims, as well, had no desire to make sacrifices for it. Many Arabs had lost confidence in expansionism as it had been practiced, and non-Arab converts chafed under a discriminatory policy. The Syrian army upon which the Umayyads had traditionally based their power was by now greatly reduced in size, having been scattered to trouble spots all over the empire, with thousands of its members having been killed. Intertribal Arab conflicts broke out in Syria, Iraq, and Khorasan, and by the end of the decade, one major Arab confederation seemed poised to seize the caliphate from the Umayyads. Before it was able to do so, however, it was thwarted by a well-organized revolutionary movement that transcended ethnic identities. Beginning in 747, an army marched from Khorasan into Syria, systematically defeating the armies of the last Umayyad caliph. When it overthrew the dynasty in 750, a new era in Muslim history had begun, that of the Abbasid caliphate.

Conclusion

The Umayyads carved out a vast empire that extended from South Asia to western Europe. This enormous area became the matrix within which the distinctive features of Islam would emerge over the next several centuries. The Arabs who created this empire were a proud and martial people. It may well be that Islam's survival in a new and hostile environment was due in large part to the Arabs' utter self-confidence and to their assumption that Islam was exclusively an Arab religion. As the religion of the Arabs, Islam became a feature of their cultural identity that they jealously protected and did not allow to become submerged in the face of challenges from the long-established religions in the vast new empire. The Arabic language, as well, became a vehicle for Arab cultural hegemony. It was the language of the Qur'an; it soon became the language of administration and the lingua franca of commerce; over the next several centuries it displaced most of the spoken languages between the Iranian plateau and the Atlantic Ocean; and its mesmerizing poetry, with its cadences and rich evocations of the independence and romance of the bedouin lifestyle, inspired subsequent literature, especially that of the Iranian peoples.

In this regard, the Umayyad achievement was monumental, but it was undermined by grave weaknesses that demanded radical solutions. The dynasty never developed a plan for administration other than constant conquest and the exploitation of non-Arabs for the benefit of Arabs. As a result, it failed to address the grievances that its subjects, Arabs and non-Arabs alike, were beginning to express. Tribal favoritism, the conscription of sedentary Arabs for campaigns of conquest, and the failure to develop policies that could accommodate non-Arab Muslims in the Umma became issues that eventually brought the dynasty to an end. Islamic principles of equality and justice became rallying cries against the Umayyad regime and demonstrated that the new religion was a powerful new force on the scene.

NOTES

1. For an indication of the ambiguity of the evidence, compare the differences in interpretation of the status of women in pre-Islamic Arabia found in the following works:

   Ahmed, Leila. *Women and Gender in Islam.* New Haven and London: Yale University Press, 1992, pp. 41–45.

   Esposito, John L. *Women in Muslim Family Law.* Syracuse, New York: Syracuse University Press, 1982, pp. 14–15, 28–30.

   Hoyland, Robert G. *Arabia and the Arabs from the Bronze Age to the Coming of Islam.* New York and London: Routledge, 2001, pp. 128–34.

   Levy, Reuben. *The Social Structure of Islam.* Cambridge U.K.: Cambridge University Press, 1971, pp. 91–97.

2. The date is usually given as 732, but see the discussion in Roger Collins, *The Arab Conquest of Spain, 710–797* (Oxford: Basil Blackwell, 1989), 89–91.

3. Blankinship, Khalid Yahya. *The End of the Jihād State: The Reign of Hishām ʿAbd al-Malik and the Collapse of the Umayyads.* Albany, New York: State University of New York Press, 82.

FURTHER READING

General

Hawting, G.R. *The First Dynasty of Islam: The Umayyad Caliphate, A.D. 661–750*, 2d edition. London and New York: Routledge, 2000.

Kennedy, Hugh. *The Prophet and the Age of the Caliphates: The Islamic Near East from the Sixth to the Eleventh Century.* London and New York: Longman, 1986.

Arab Conquests

Abun-Nasr, Jamil M. *A History of the Maghrib*, 2d ed. Cambridge, U.K.: Cambridge University Press, 1975.

Collins, Roger. *The Arab Conquest of Spain, 710–797.* Oxford: Basil Blackwell, 1989.

Donner, Fred. *The Early Islamic Conquests.* Princeton, New Jersey: Princeton University Press, 1981.

Gibb, H.A.R. *The Arab Conquests in Central Asia.* London: Royal Asiatic Society, 1923.

Ikram, S.M. *Muslim Civilization in India.* Ainslie T. Embree, ed. New York and London: Columbia University Press, 1964.

Kaegi, Walter E. *Byzantium and the Early Islamic Conquests.* Cambridge, U.K.: Cambridge University Press, 1992.

Administration

Crone, Patricia and Martin Hinds. *God's Caliph: Religious Authority in the First Centuries of Islam.* Cambridge, U.K.: Cambridge University Press, 1986.

Morony, Michael G. *Iraq After the Muslim Conquest.* Princeton, New Jersey: Princeton University Press, 1984.

Dissolution of the Arab Empire

Blankinship, Khalid Yahya. *The End of the Jihād State: The Reign of Hishām 'Abd al-Malik and the Collapse of the Umayyads.* Albany, New York: State University of New York Press, 1994.

CHAPTER 3

The Development of Sectarianism

The issue of legitimate leadership has been a central concern for Muslims since the death of Muhammad. The figure of the Prophet has cast a long shadow throughout history. Muslims have yearned to have a leader who embodied his qualities, but have usually had to settle for men whose ambition and weaknesses only accentuated the contrast with the ideal. The issue of the caliphate was not just a political question, but also one of maintaining the religious integrity of the community. Only fringe groups thought the caliph should have prophetic qualities, but most Muslims were convinced that in some sense he was responsible for continuing to provide religious guidance to the community in the absence of the Prophet.

Because no consensus existed regarding the nature of the caliphate, controversies swirled about the method of selecting the caliphs as well as about the adequacy of the men who were chosen. The quarrels ensured that the first century of Muslim history would be politically unstable. Three of the first four caliphs were murdered, a growing number of Muslims became convinced that the Prophet had chosen 'Ali as his successor and were angry that he was passed over in the selection process the first three times, and revolts began to break out more frequently against the Umayyads as their regime became increasingly identified with injustice and corruption.

The debate over the nature of the caliphate had many repercussions. This chapter will revisit the Umayyad period to explore two of them. One was the emergence of divisions within the Umma that eventually crystallized into three major branches of Islam: Shi'ism, Kharijism, and Sunnism. The other was the Abbasid revolution, which resulted in the overthrow of the Umayyads and began a new chapter in Muslim history.

'Ali and the Politics of Division

One of the most recognizable figures in Muslim history is 'Ali, the cousin and son-in-law of the Prophet. His martial skills, dedication to the Prophet's cause, and concern for justice were widely admired. His attempt to resolve some of the problems arising out of the rapid expansion of the Muslim state raised the expectations and hopes of many Muslims, but it also aroused the enmity of others. His short and tragic career as caliph left a lasting mark on the Umma.

Political Dissension

The Arabs conquered Syria, Iraq, and Egypt during the caliphate of 'Umar. During the decade of his administration (634–644), the task of administering the Umma became vastly more complex than it had been when Abu Bakr was caliph. Many issues became controversial, such as the distribution of plunder, the allocation of revenues from seized land, the awarding of contracts and administrative offices to family members and friends of the ruling elite, and the adherence to local customs in the numerous new lands in which Muslims found themselves. The pace of the conquests was so rapid, and the number of issues that everyone from the caliph on down had to deal with was so great, that none of the issues boiled to the surface during 'Umar's tenure. He was assassinated in 644, just as the more difficult and less remunerative phase of conquests was beginning. It was the ill fortune of his successor to confront the issues directly.

'Uthman, one of the Prophet's earliest converts, had been highly respected and was a popular choice for the caliphate at the time of 'Umar's murder. He was not unchallenged, however. Muhammad's cousin and son-in-law, 'Ali, let it be known that he wanted to be caliph and that he planned to change policies that many considered unfair. The council chose 'Uthman, who served as caliph during the period 644–656. Overall, he has been held in respect by most Muslims throughout history, particularly for his role in determining a standard version of the Qur'an. According to Islamic tradition, the Qur'an was not collected into its current form until after the Prophet's death, and when it was, several versions existed. 'Uthman reflected the concern of many Muslims that, since the Qur'an is in fact the word of God, its various written expressions should not differ. He is credited with having named a commission that agreed on a standard text.

In general, 'Uthman's administration was similar to that of 'Umar. Like his predecessor, he awarded lands abandoned by the Sasanian elite to individuals and tribes despite the official policy that such properties should be held in trust for the Umma; he maintained the garrison cities as permanent settlements despite their growing irrelevance as forward outposts and purely Arab enclaves; and he attempted to bring local affairs within the far-flung administrative units increasingly under the supervision of Medina.

Where 'Uthman's administration diverged from previous practice was in its transparent favoritism of Meccan elites. Most of the soldiers in the Muslim armies that conquered Iraq and Egypt were from tribes of lesser status than the Quraysh, but they had been Muslims longer than the Quraysh elite, who had converted after the fall of Mecca. 'Umar had consistently given precedence to warriors who had entered the Muslim armies from the earliest period, and they benefitted particularly in Iraq, where they were placed in charge of the revenues of many of the Sasanian royal lands and were named administrators of the province and of the cities. 'Uthman, by contrast, followed the time-honored tribal practice of naming his close relatives to be leaders of all the major provinces as well as the important garrison towns of Kufa and Basra.

These leaders, in turn, enacted measures and made appointments that favored the Umayyad clan and the merchants in Mecca who were linked financially with them. As a result, those tribesmen whose status and wealth had risen due to their having been charter members of the Umma now saw their position threatened by the politics of "business as usual." The Umayyad clan and their allies, whose members on the whole had resisted the Prophet as long as possible, were now displacing those who had been the earliest supporters of the Islamic movement.

'Uthman was not intentionally hurting the "older" Muslims. He probably viewed his nepotism as not merely customary—and even obligatory in light of traditional tribal values—but also as necessary in his quest to bring some coherence to the administration of the growing empire. Only by naming people whom he knew and trusted could he hope to bring about uniformity to policy in the same manner that he had brought about uniformity to the text of the Qur'an. Likewise, he felt compelled to make changes in the process of revenue collection, now that the flow of plunder from the conquests had slowed. The traditional one-fifth of the captured treasure that had come to the caliphal coffers for administrative expenses, pensions for widows and early Muslims, and the like, had been shrinking. 'Uthman ended 'Umar's practice of allowing the provinces a wide latitude in determining their tax policies and began channeling a larger fraction of the tax proceeds to Medina to make up for the lost revenue from plunder.

Despite 'Uthman's good intentions, by the early 650s important Arab families in Iraq and Egypt had become hostile to his policies, and Kufa, Basra, and Fustat had become centers of discontent. In 656, several hundred Arabs from Iraq and Egypt marched to Medina to protest the new policies before 'Uthman personally. The caliph made no secret of his impatience with the complaints, and some of the protesters interpreted his comments as an insult. With passions aroused, a few hotheads climbed the wall surrounding 'Uthman's home, broke through the door, and killed him while he was engaged in religious devotions.

'Ali's Caliphate: Shi'ites and Kharijites

Upon 'Uthman's death, the mutineers and others in Medina acclaimed 'Ali as their new caliph. Long critical of the policies that had benefitted the Quraysh at the expense of the common Muslim, 'Ali was popular among the insurgents as well as among many who had known and admired him all his life in the Hijaz. His lifelong loyalty to his cousin the Prophet, his courage and skill as a warrior, and his piety had caused many to hold him in high esteem. Over thirty years earlier, he had married Fatima, a daughter of the Prophet, and the couple's two sons were Muhammad's only surviving grandchildren. His selection as caliph at this time, however, was controversial and bitterly resented by some. 'A'isha, Muhammad's youngest and favorite wife, held an old grudge against 'Ali, and others among Muhammad's closest friends resented 'Ali's popularity and his threat to the interests of the Quraysh. They seized upon the fact that the mutineers had been responsible for 'Ali's elevation to the caliphate, and they pointed out that 'Ali had not only failed to make any effort to bring 'Uthman's murderers to justice—he had not even condemned 'Uthman's murder.

Passions on both sides were high. 'Ali's supporters were euphoric that he had finally become caliph and would now bring justice to the Islamic community, whereas his opponents were possessed by a deadly rage stemming from their suspicion that his ambition had pushed him into becoming an accomplice in 'Uthman's murder. It was clear that a major clash was imminent, and both 'Ali's supporters and his opponents immediately set out for the garrison cities of Iraq in order to recruit troops for the struggle. 'Ali marched to Kufa, where 'Uthman's policies were especially resented, while his opponents tried to rally the garrison in Basra in their favor. 'Ali's opponents included 'A'isha and several of the Prophet's oldest and most loyal followers, but they were unable to recruit as many soldiers in Basra as 'Ali was able to raise in Kufa. The ensuing Battle of the Camel (so named because 'A'isha sat upon one of the animals while she watched the conflict) resulted in a victory by 'Ali's forces.

Almost immediately, however, the legitimacy of his caliphate was challenged by a relative of 'Uthman named Mu'awiya, the governor of Syria. For the next five years, the attention of the Umma was focused on the grand struggle between these two men. The supporters of one side or the other were known as the partisans, or *shi'a*, of one or the other. Just as there had earlier been *shi'a 'Uthman* and *shi'a 'Ali* during the debate over 'Uthman's policies, so now the *shi'a Mu'awiya* were opposing the *shi'a 'Ali*. The term *shi'a* in this context had no specifically religious meaning; it simply connoted support for the legitimacy of the claim of one or the other man in the quarrel.

In 657, the two armies met at Siffin on the Euphrates River. After skirmishing for several months, it seemed that they were set for the decisive engagement. At that point, Mu'awiya's army asked for arbitration of the issues that divided the two men. 'Ali felt compelled to agree to the arbitration because of a widespread sentiment on both sides not to shed the blood of fellow Muslims, but one group of his followers regarded his concession as an act of irresoluteness uncharacteristic of a true caliph. They defected and became known as Kharijites (*khawarij*, from *kharaja*, meaning "to depart or leave").

The term Kharijism appears frequently in Muslim history in the centuries after the Battle of Siffin. In the early years, it usually referred to the belief that a leader who violated a Qur'anic prescription was a grave sinner and should be excluded from the community of believers. The sinner had, by virtue of his error, become an unbeliever and should be killed. In practice, the groups who were called Kharijites were rarely in a position to exclude anyone from the Umma; rather, they themselves were a minority that withdrew from the larger community on the grounds that the majority had fallen into error. Kharijism was a feared and hated movement, because most of its early adherents believed that they had the right—and even duty—to kill non-Kharijites. In the late seventh century, however, a group of Kharijite scholars in Iraq rejected violence and rebellion and began to wrestle with the issue of how to live among a majority whom one regarded to be impious. By the late ninth century, it was this group's nonviolent policy of withdrawing from society that was more characteristic of Kharijism than the earlier tactic of violent attack. Unfortunately, non-Kharijite chroniclers over the next few centuries often labeled any group that rebelled against the government as Kharijite, lumping togther a wide variety of movements and making it difficult to identify the actual beliefs of the groups.

Kharijite tendencies were particularly strong among nomads and peasants, who were suspicious of the motives and policies of urban leaders. The Great Berber Revolt of 740, discussed in the previous chapter, was raised under the banner of Kharijism, and the doctrine subsequently became highly popular among Berbers. Several

Kharijite Berber states established themselves in the wake of the revolt, setting themselves apart from the Umayyad dynasty and its successor, the Abbasid dynasty. They set out to follow what they considered to be authentic Islam. Kharijism gave religious sanction to the inclination of these marginal groups to live separately from the rest of society, and it enabled them to feel spiritually superior to the majority, even if they were economically inferior.

'Ali remained unaccountably inactive in Kufa even after Mu'awiya's followers began proclaiming that their leader was the genuine caliph. In 661, a Kharijite assassinated 'Ali as an act of judgment on his failure to do God's bidding. Mu'awiya then claimed the caliphate but stayed in Damascus, where his political and military support lay. 'Ali's ineffective caliphate and his violent death were a profound shock to his followers. For the previous quarter of a century, a growing number of Muslims had come to regard him as an advocate for the principle of equality and for a government dedicated to justice. Many of his followers believed that he had spiritual gifts not accessible to other mortals. The triumph of the Umayyad clan exacerbated the sense of loss, particularly in Kufa.

'Ali and his family came to be regarded as symbols of protest against the growing power of the Umayyads and their Syrian supporters. 'Ali's fate was viewed by many as a tragedy. He became a symbol of a great man who was caught in the vortex of evil forces and destroyed. More important, however, was the growing sense among some of his admirers that he had been a virtuous man who gave his life in God's cause. In this sense, his death was a sacrifice to be emulated. Those who protested injustice, or who sought a leader with great charisma, found him to be an attractive figure with which to identify. Many Muslims would come to agree that the Alids (members of 'Ali's family) had been blessed and chosen by God to lead the Umma.

Karbala

Despite the misgivings of many Muslims that 'Ali had failed to act with proper discretion in bringing the murderers of 'Uthman to justice, few could go so far as to believe that he had been involved in the plot. Thus, 'Ali's frustrated caliphate and his assassination were a loss felt by the Umma at large. Mu'awiya's hounding of 'Ali for the last five years of his life was viewed as unseemly, and although Mu'awiya ruled with tact and propriety, he was never quite able to rehabilitate his image with a growing number of Muslims. No doubt his abandonment of Medina was a major source of hostility, at least from the Hijazis, for the city slid rapidly into the status of a backwater, while Damascus became a glittering capital city by the end of the century. Pious Muslims who considered Medina and Mecca to be the center of the world became increasingly critical of the Umayyads over the years, as it became clear that the new rulers were not as pious as their forebears had been. Tales of sumptuous palaces, wine drinking, and a generally dissolute lifestyle among the princes became the stock of anti-Umayyad sentiment.

Mu'awiya's critics grudgingly acknowledged that he was not the profligate that many of his relatives seemed to be, and he managed to maintain a simple style of ruling in which he made himself accessible to petitioners. In this regard, he was continuing the tradition of Arab tribalism and of early Muslim leadership alike. He also treated 'Ali's sons by Fatima with great courtesy. According to Shi'ite tradition, the

The Rightful Caliph: The Shi'ite Version

Shi'ites rejected the conciliar selection process for caliph that resulted in the choice of Abu Bakr, 'Umar, and 'Uthman. They were convinced that the Prophet had declared 'Ali to be his successor at a small pool (ghadir) called Khumm (hence, Ghadir Khumm, or Ghadir al-Khumm) while returning to Medina after having performed his last pilgrimage (the "Farewell Pilgrimage") shortly before his death. The following account is from Muhammad Baqir Majlisi's The Life of Hearts, *which dates from about the year 1700, but it reflects an early tradition (note the wry reference in the last sentence to 'Umar, the second caliph):*

When the ceremonies of the pilgrimage were completed, the Prophet, attended by 'Ali and the Muslims, left Mecca for Medina. On reaching Ghadir Khumm he halted.... The reason for encampment in such a place was that illustrious verses of the Qur'an came powerfully upon him, enjoining him to establish 'Ali as his successor. He had previously received communications to the same effect, but not expressly appointing the time for 'Ali's inauguration, which, therefore, he had deferred lest opposition be excited and some forsake the faith. This was the message from the Most High in Sura 5:67: "O Messenger, publish that which has been sent down to you from your Lord, for if you do not, then you have not delivered His message. God will protect you from men; surely God guides not unbelieving people."

Being thus peremptorily commanded to appoint 'Ali his successor, and threatened with penalty if he delayed when God had become his surety, the Prophet therefore halted in this unusual place, and the Muslims dismounted around him.

... Having ordered all the camel-saddles to be piled up for a *minbar* [pulpit] or rostrum, he commanded his herald to summon the people around him. When all the people were assembled, the Prophet ascended the minbar of saddles, and calling unto him the Commander of the Believers ('Ali), he placed him on his right side. Muhammad now rendered thanksgiving to God, and then made an eloquent address to the people, in which he foretold his own death, and said, "I have been called to the gate of God, and the time is near when I shall depart to God, be concealed from you, and bid farewell to this vain world. I leave among you the Book of God, to which if you adhere, you shall never go astray. And I leave with you the members of my family who cannot be separated from the Book of God until both join me at the fountain of al-Kawthar."

He then demanded, "Am I not dearer to you than your own lives?" and was answered by the people in the affirmative. He then took the hands of 'Ali ... and said, "Whoever receives me as his [master or ally], then to him 'Ali is the same. O Lord, befriend every friend of 'Ali, and be the enemy of all his enemies; help those who aid him and abandon all that desert him."

It was now nearly noon, and the hottest part of the day. The Prophet and the Muslims made the noon prayers, after which he went to his tent, beside which he ordered a tent pitched for the Commander of the Believers. When 'Ali was rested Muhammad commanded the Muslims to wait upon 'Ali, congratulate him on his accession to the Imamate, and salute him as the *amir*, or commander. All this was done by both men and women, none appearing more joyful at the inauguration of 'Ali than did 'Umar.

SOURCE: Williams, John Alden, ed. *Themes of Islamic Civilization.* Berkeley, California: University of California Press, 1971, 63–64.

---

elder son, Hasan, was proclaimed caliph by pro-Alid supporters in Kufa, but abdicated when Mu'awiya threatened continued warfare. He returned to Mecca, where he lived comfortably on a generous financial settlement that Mu'awiya granted him, until his

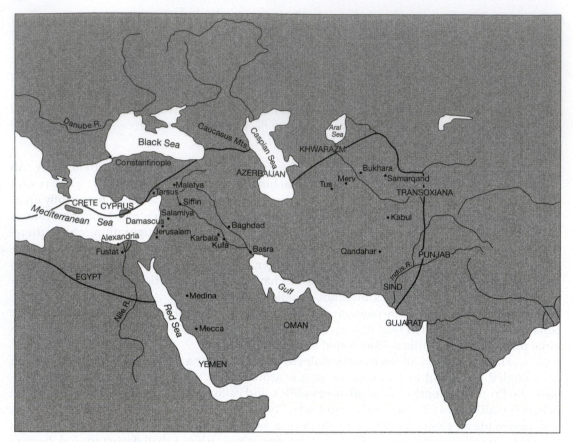

MAP 3.1 The Age of Sectarian Development, 650–950

death in 669. His younger brother Husayn became the head of the family at that point, and it was in him that many pro-Alid individuals now invested their hopes. Since Mu'awiya had won his conflict with 'Ali, there was no longer reason for a group called the *shi'a Mu'awiya,* but those who continued to regard 'Ali's family to be the source for legitimate caliphal leadership were still partisans and continued to be called the *shi'a 'Ali,* or Shi'ites.

At the end of his life, Mu'awiya's tact and political judgment abandoned him. In 680, he shocked many Muslims by insisting on the recognition of his son Yazid as his successor. The sudden imposition of the dynastic rule of an unpopular family provoked a severe reaction. The leaders of Medina refused to acknowledge Yazid, insisting that the new caliph be selected by consensus, as had been done previously. The deep-seated hostility in Iraq to the family of 'Uthman now erupted anew, especially in Kufa, which had maintained a strong sympathy for the memory of 'Ali. Leaders of that city invited Husayn to lead resistance to Yazid. Husayn set out for Kufa with several dozen armed followers and family members, but a military detachment sent by Yazid intercepted him on a plain called Karbala, not far from Kufa. There, on the tenth day of Muharram (the first month on the Islamic calendar), he and most of his followers were brutally killed.

The shrine for 'Ali in Najaf, Iraq. The original portion dates from the tenth century.

Before 680, Shi'ism had been the conviction that someone from 'Ali's family should exercise caliphal power. Before Karbala, this sentiment could be emotional and passionate, but we have no evidence that it had developed the characteristics of a religious movement. The negotiations between the Kufans and Husayn, for example, include no trace that support or lack of support for him was a matter of religious allegiance, but rather was predicated on the implementation of justice.

Karbala marked a transition in this respect. Although religious ritual would not be worked out for several decades, there is an unquestionably different tone to Shi'ite sentiment after 680. Kufans felt a profound sense of guilt at not having come to the aid of Husayn's little band, and for a growing number of followers, his death was interpreted as a sacrifice made on behalf of God's people. The narrative account of his death became elaborated and embellished as time passed, and many Muslims, as they heard it, felt that they participated vicariously in his suffering during those agonizing last hours before Husayn and his followers, abandoned and suffering from thirst, were finally cut down without mercy.

The Abbasid Revolution

In the aftermath of Karbala, the idea that an Alid was more qualified than an Umayyad to be the caliph took on unprecedented strength and widespread support. The fervent supporters of an Alid caliphate, however, were frustrated in their hopes that one of the sons or grandsons of Hasan or Husayn would take up the cause. For the next six decades, their families were known for producing more religious scholars than political activists.

The accession of Yazid in 680 brought forward an opportunity for an Alid challenge to the Umayyads, but it came from an unexpected quarter. From 682 to 692, four successive Umayyad caliphs had to contend with a revolt by 'Abdullah ibn al-Zubayr, a son of one of Muhammad's closest companions. Ibn al-Zubayr claimed to be caliph, and he had a strong base of support in his home in the Hijaz as well as in Iraq, both of which broke loose from Umayyad control for several years.

Meanwhile, in Kufa, a man named Mukhtar took advantage of the Umayyads' loss of control over Iraq to raise a separate revolt. He claimed to be advancing the cause of Ibn al-Hanafiya, a son of 'Ali and a half-brother to Hasan and Husayn. Ibn al-Hanafiya lived in Mecca, and was known as a gentle religious scholar. There is no evidence that he had any contact with Mukhtar, but the latter was able to take control of Kufa in 685–686.

Mukhtar claimed that Ibn al-Hanafiya was not merely the rightful caliph, but also the *mahdi*, a messiahlike figure who would bring justice in place of the oppression and wickedness that now prevailed in the world. *Mahdi* literally means "guided one," with the implication of "rightly guided one." Within the first few decades of Islam there arose informal traditions to the effect that the end of history would be heralded by a Muslim Mahdi and by Jesus. In some accounts, Jesus was predicted to precede the Mahdi, and in others the Mahdi came first. The influential Hasan al-Basri (d. 728), on the other hand, identified the Mahdi with Jesus himself. Some Muslims thought that the Mahdi was already present: The Umayyad caliph Sulayman (715–717) claimed to be the Mahdi, and 'Umar II (717–720) for several years was widely regarded by many pious scholars as the Mahdi. As we shall see, the doctrine of the Mahdi became an integral feature of Shi'ism, but only marginal to Sunni doctrine.

The Umayyads crushed Mukhtar's uprising in 687, but the depth of the religious evolution that was taking place in Shi'ite circles may be ascertained by the speculations that began to appear when Ibn al-Hanafiya died in 700. Some of his admirers claimed that in fact he had not died, but rather was in concealment on Mt. Radwa in the Arabian Peninsula, where he was nourished by springs of water and honey and protected by a lion and a leopard. In the fullness of time, he would return to put an end to the tyranny of the transgressors and to bring about a reign of righteousness. Other followers of Ibn al-Hanafiya desired to have a leader in the flesh instead of on a remote mountain, and they turned to his son Abu Hashim for spiritual leadership. This disagreement among Ibn al-Hanafiya's followers prefigured the complexity of the early history of Shi'ism, which is replete with numerous groups claiming one or another charismatic figure as their spiritual leader and the rightful caliph.

The movement that centered on Ibn al-Hanafiya and his son is important for two reasons: the evidence it provides that certain Alid leaders were beginning to be viewed as messianic figures and its connection with the revolutionary movement that eventually overthrew the Umayyad dynasty in 750. The potential that Shi'ite sentiment held for challenging the Umayyads was becoming clear to the dynasty's opponents, and early in the eighth century, one group—the Abbasids—began cultivating that sentiment in a remarkably astute way. As we have seen, some Muslims felt that the leadership of the Umma should reside in the descendants of 'Ali and

Fatima (and thus of the Prophet himself), while others were satisfied with leadership that lay in the hands of any of 'Ali's descendants (such as Ibn al-Hanafiya).

In addition to the relatively small group of people who held passionately to this "pro-Alid" sentiment was a much larger number of Muslims who were convinced that the ideal ruler should at least be a member of "the family of the Prophet." Defining the boundaries of "the family" was frequently a contentious enterprise, but all could agree that it was contained within the clan of Hashim and not of the clan of 'Abd Shams, from whom the Umayyads were descended. One of the families in the Hashimite clan was that of 'Abbas, an uncle of the Prophet. Its members are known as the Abbasids, and they became famous as the group that overthrew the Umayyads.

The Abbasids' success was due in no small part to the fact that they organized a sophisticated underground movement that was able to elude the best efforts of the Umayyads to ferret it out. Several Alids attempted ill-advised revolts against the Umayyads after 720, but the Abbasids patiently bided their time before challenging the might of the state. Because of the movement's secrecy, details about it are shrouded in obscurity, but the leaders exploited Alid sentiment by making two seemingly incompatible claims regarding their intentions. To those groups that had been attracted to the figures of Ibn al-Hanafiya and his son Abu Hashim, they claimed that the Abbasid family had inherited the mantle of spiritual leadership from them. The Abbasids claimed that when Abu Hashim died in Palestine in 716, he had designated Muhammad ibn 'Ali, a great-grandson of 'Abbas, to be his spiritual heir. By implication, Muhammad ibn 'Ali or his successor would be the caliph in the event of the overthrow of the Umayyads.

By the decade of the 740s, however, the leaders of the Abbasid movement were trying to make their cause attractive to an even wider spectrum of Muslims, and they broadened their propaganda by claiming that they would replace the Umayyads by "the accepted (agreed-upon) one from the family of Muhammad," the Prophet. The implication was that, once the Umayyads were overthrown, a consensus would determine the best-qualified member of the Prophet's clan to be the caliph. The ideal of having the leadership of the Umma once again in the hands of the family of the Prophet was one shared by a multitude of Muslims.

Muhammad ibn 'Ali lived in what is now southern Jordan, but the political activism that he directed was based in Iraq and Khorasan. Initially, Kufa was the actual base of operations. As a large urban center with a long history of antipathy towards the Umayyads, the city provided a warren of alleys in which Abbasid leaders and agents could operate for several years with relative security. On the other hand, the city's loyalty to 'Ali and Husayn was so pronounced that Umayyad police eventually placed the markets and public spaces under constant surveillance. Because of the increasing pressure from the government, the Abbasids estabilished a third base five hundred miles to the northeast, in Khorasan's capital of Merv.

Merv was a happy choice. It was remote from Damascus, it had a large Arab population as well as a rapidly growing non-Arab Muslim population, and it was a center of discontent against the Umayyads. As we saw in the previous chapter, the Arab settlers there had assimilated in many ways to Persian culture. Many of the Arabs bought land or became merchants in this entrepot that opened onto Central Asia. They resented being conscripted into the massive military campaigns of 705–715, which forced them to abandon their farms or businesses for most of the year.

Discontented with Umayyad policies, many Khorasani Arabs looked to the family of the Prophet for leadership. Merv's community of Persian-speaking Arabs produced many of the subsequent leaders of the Abbasid movement.

The decade of the 740s proved to be decisive for the crystallization of the Abbasid movement. The Great Berber Revolt shook the authority of the Umayyad government and forced it to shift thousands of troops into North Africa and the Iberian Peninsula. In 743, Muhammad ibn 'Ali died and was replaced by his son Ibrahim. In the same year, the caliph Hisham died. The Abbasid leadership soon moved to take advantage of the death of Hisham by sending a representative to Khorasan to begin the revolution. Almost nothing is known of this man's background except that he seems to have been a convert from Iraq. The name by which he was known from that time on, however, was Abu Muslim 'Abd al-Rahman ibn Muslim al-Khorasani, which literally means "Father of a Muslim, servant of the Merciful, son of a Muslim, from Khorasan." The name is a masterpiece of anti-Umayyad propaganda, suggesting to all who heard it that the Abbasid movement was interested not in tribal or ethnic identities, but only in the welfare of the Muslim community as a whole.

Abu Muslim assumed the leadership of the anti-Umayyad movement in Khorasan, and in 747, he raised the black banners of revolt. He sent an army westward while he stayed in Khorasan to secure the movement's base. The campaign was a stunning success. The Umayyads, discovering Ibrahim's link to the movement, arrested him and had him executed, but the revolutionary army continued its inexorable march, taking Kufa in September 749. A period of uncertainty regarding the leadership of the movement followed. Abbasid agents sent correspondence to the leading Alid figures from the peninsula, offering them the caliphate, but they could not negotiate an arrangement suitable to both sides. Abu Muslim's representatives in Kufa then selected a brother of Ibrahim named Abu al-'Abbas as caliph. During 750, the Abbasid army moved into Syria and Egypt and destroyed the last vestiges of Umayyad power. All but one of the members of the former royal family were murdered. The shedding of blood was so common an occurrence, in fact, that the new caliph's title, "al-Saffah" ("the blood shedder") seemed apt. The only Umayyad prince who survived—'Abd al-Rahman—escaped into the Iberian Peninsula, where we shall hear from him again in his capacity as the founder of the independent state of Andalus. The Abbasids quickly consolidated power and remained in Kufa for the next decade before establishing their permanent capital in the new city of Baghdad.

Shi'ite Identities

The new regime proved to be a profound disappointment to the pro-Alids. The Abbasid campaign had raised the hope that an inspired leader who combined both temporal and religious legitimacy would be installed as caliph. However, the leading Alids were not able to accept the terms on which leadership was offered to them by the Abbasids, and the new Abbasid caliph, al-Saffah (750–754), was hardly known outside his family. Some Alids were feted at court when the new dynasty established itself, but others rejected the new regime as illegitimate. Several of them revolted against the Abbasids. The most spectacular of the Alid revolts took place in 762–763, carried out by two brothers who were descendants of 'Ali's son Hasan. They planned simultaneous

The Early Alids and Abbasids

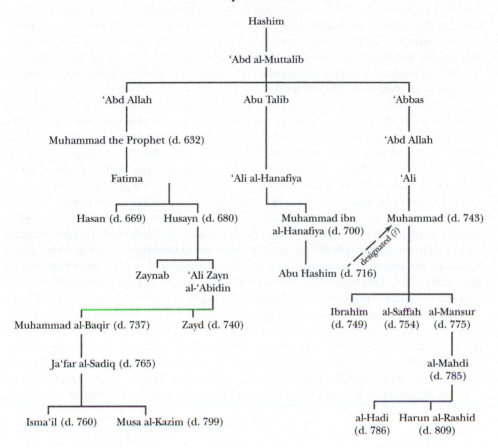

revolts against the newly established Abbasid court from Basra and Medina, but they failed to coordinate their efforts and both were killed. Many pro-Alids decided against outright revolts and instead began creating organizations to cultivate piety in an otherwise corrupt world; others recruited members into groups that were prepared to take over the leadership of the Muslim world when conditions were favorable. Thus, rather than resolving the demand of the pro-Alids, the Abbasid movement and revolution seem to have intensified the speculation and activity within such circles.

The *Ghulat* and the Zaydis

The middle decades of the eighth century witnessed a remarkable range of activities among the pro-Alids. On the one hand were the so-called *ghulat*, "those who exaggerate," or "the extremists." This term did not refer to a particular group, but rather to the members of numerous groups that championed the cause of individual Alids. They were lumped together under the label of "exaggerators" because of the claims for superhuman qualities that they made for their Alid leaders. Typically, they claimed that in some sense God had become incarnate in their leader, and many asserted that, through him, God was continuing to bring revelatory truths despite the insistence by the majority of Muslims that Muhammad was the last of the prophets. In order to give legitimacy to the successors of such great leaders, some of the ghulat began developing sophisticated theories of the transmigration of the soul, asserting that the former leader's soul had taken residence in the new leader's body. Others among the ghulat denied that ʻAli had died.

Often the term ghulat was applied to pro-Alids who substituted a reverence for their leader in the place of a concern for obeying the ritual requirements of Islam, such as the five daily prayers. When it is recalled that Muhammad was viewed by the majority of Muslims as a mortal who had been chosen for the divine purpose of bringing revelation and that ʻAli's supporters during his lifetime had typically claimed only the qualities of piety and wisdom for him, we can see why the ghulat were regarded by most Muslims as having exceeded sensible, and even acceptable, bounds.

In contrast to the fervid speculations of the ghulat were the Zaydis. Zayd, a grandson of Husayn, led an abortive revolt against the Umayyads in 740. Zayd asserted that the legitimate caliph was the man who combined descent from either Hasan or Husayn with learning, piety, and the political will to challenge the existing state authorities. This uncomplicated and activist program appealed to many Muslims, and several Zaydi ministates were set up in the highlands of the Elburz and in Yemen in the decades after the Abbasid revolution. Zaydism rapidly became identified as an Alid challenge to Abbasid legitimacy. However, even though its Alid sympathies place it technically within the movement known as Shiʻism, its aversion to speculative thought kept it from developing a doctrine of the leader's unique spiritual role in the way that the majority of Shiʻites did. Zaydis differ little from the Muslims who have come to be known as Sunnis except for their insistence that their leader be descended from Hasan or Husayn.

The Husayni Alids

When the term *Shiʻite* is used today, it usually refers to a tradition that falls between the fervid speculations of the ghulat and the doctrinal simplicity of the Zaydis. To understand the origins of the major branches of modern Shiʻism, we must turn to Medina, where, in the early eighth century, the descendants of Husayn were quietly developing a reputation for piety and spiritual leadership. Several generations of Husayn's descendants lived in Medina, collecting the extra-Qurʼanic sayings of Muhammad, as well as anecdotes about his life conveyed by his companions. These scholars responded to questions from pious individuals who inquired about the best way to live a holy life, and they wrote commentaries on the Qurʼan.

The Centrality of Muhammad al-Baqir and Jaʻfar al-Sadiq

The first of Husayn's descendants was his son ʻAli Zayn al-ʻAbidin, a survivor of Karbala. He in turn had two sons who became better known than he was. One was Zayd, for whom Zaydism was named; and the other was Muhammad al-Baqir, one of the most highly respected of the religious scholars in the first third of the eighth century.

He became the leader of the Husayni branch of the Alids about the year 713. Muhammad al-Baqir's son Ja'far al-Sadiq succeeded him as leader in 737 and became a major figure in the newly developing discipline of Islamic law. At the time of his death in 765, he was widely respected by Alids and non-Alids alike for his scholarship, wisdom, and generosity.

During the half century of leadership by Muhammad al-Baqir and Ja'far al-Sadiq, the self-conscious identity that we call Shi'ism can perhaps be seen for the first time. Both men won universal respect for their learning and wisdom, even among those who had no interest in the nascent Shi'ism of the day. Among a certain group of Alids, however, they were regarded as more than mere scholars of erudition and piety: They were spokesmen for God. With them, one of the most distinctive doctrines of Shi'ism began to take shape, that of the Imam.

The word *imam* in Arabic is a preposition that means "in front of" or "before." It soon became widely used to designate the man who stands in front of the congregation in the mosque to lead the prayers, and this has been the typical meaning of *imam* among non-Shi'ites. In villages, he is probably the most pious man or otherwise a respected personage, while in urban areas he has scholarly credentials as well as spiritual responsibilities. The members of the congregation, however, do not regard him as having anything like the spiritual authority that Shi'ites invest in their supreme leader. In this book, *Imam* will be used to designate the man whom Shi'ites view as their legitimate leader, and *imam* will denote the Sunni prayer leader.

According to Shi'ites, the prophetic age had come to an end with the Prophet Muhammad, but mankind was still in need of a divinely appointed and guided leader. The Prophet's heirs, the Imams, would continue the prophetic role in every respect except that they would explain the existing scripture, rather than introduce a new one. Each Imam was infallible and sinless and was the rightful leader of the entire Umma. The caliph, therefore, was illegitimate and a usurper. Shi'ites came to believe that the rejection or disobedience of any of the Imams was an act of infidelity and was a sin on the same level as the rejection of the Prophet. In later Shi'ite hagiography, 'Ali, Hasan, Husayn, and 'Ali Zayn al-'Abidin were regarded as having been recognized as Imams during their lifetimes. While there is no doubt that all of these individuals were regarded as leaders and sources of wisdom, the evidence suggests that it was the followers of Muhammad al-Baqir and Ja'far al-Sadiq who first constituted groups of disciples conscious of having an identity apart from other Muslims due to their allegiance to their Imam.

To be regarded as a challenge to the caliph's legitimacy, however, was clearly dangerous under either the Umayyads or the Abbasids. Muhammad al-Baqir and Ja'far managed to inspire a devoted following without appearing to threaten the political authorities. They developed three ideas that became characteristic of subsequent Shi'ite life and thought. First, they taught that an Imam was known by the fact that the previous Imam had designated him. This doctrine stood in sharp contrast to the Zaydi position, as well as to the belief that an Imam would simply be recognized by the quality of his teaching. Second, they confirmed that the Imam possessed spiritual knowledge that was different in kind, not just in degree, from other religious scholars. Learned and pious scholars were certainly useful in a community, but an Imam was indispensable. He had access to knowledge about God that was unavailable from any

other source. Third, they convinced their followers to develop the discipline needed to refrain from trying to seize political power, or acting in such a way as to bring
scandal upon the community. They lived in dangerous times, and their followers had
to act circumspectly.

The achievement of Muhammad al-Baqir and Ja'far al-Sadiq was to create a
self-conscious identity for the Shi'ite community and to make it possible for an individual to accept the authority of the Husayni Imams without engaging in a revolt
against the government. Shi'ites were convinced that it was God's will that the Imam
should also be caliph, but the majority recognized the political realities of the age.
The Umayyads had been overthrown in 750, only to be replaced with another dynasty that did not represent the Alid line, but God would rectify that situation in His
own good time. In the meantime, the Imam would be the channel that God would
use to provide the spiritual guidance required for living the godly life.

In 760, Ja'far designated his son Isma'il to be his successor upon his death,
which he believed was imminent. Soon thereafter, however, the one who died was
Isma'il, not Ja'far. The community was stunned. No one within Ja'far's circle could
believe that he had named the "wrong" successor, but they also could not fathom
the mystery of Isma'il's untimely death. No evidence exists that Ja'far himself attempted another designation of a successor or sought to interpret the conundrum
of his designated successor's having predeceased him.

At Ja'far's own death in 765, his followers had to decide on an Imam themselves. Dozens of different groups arose, distinguished from each other by their
choice of Imam or by doctrinal differences. It would have been impossible at the
time to know which sect would become the most influential, and it required more
than a century for two of them to become dominant. One claimed that Isma'il had
in fact been the seventh Imam and that his son Muhammad was the Imam upon
Ja'far's death. Because of their belief that Isma'il was the seventh Imam, they have been
known variously as *Isma'ilis* and as *Seveners*. The other major group of Ja'far's disciples recognized Isma'il's brother Musa al-Kazim as the rightful Imam after Ja'far.
They came to be known as the *Imamiya*, or *Imamis*. As we shall see, they are even
more widely known today as the *ithna' 'ashari* Shi'ites, or *Twelver* Shi'ites.

The Imamis

Our knowledge of the history of the Shi'ites during the two centuries following
the death of Ja'far is remarkably limited. In part, this is a testimony to the perilous
and secretive life that Shi'ites usually had to follow, and in part it is due to the fact
that many of the documents that we rely on from the period are hostile to Shi'ites.
At some point in their history, in fact, they developed the doctrine of *taqiya*, or religious dissimulation: When threatened with the loss of life or property and when
no danger to Islam itself is involved, Shi'ites are permitted to pretend to recant
their faith. What is clear is that a bewildering variety of factions arose over the
course of those two hundred years and that no one in that period could have predicted with confidence that the Imamis and the Isma'ilis would eventually become
the two dominant groups of Shi'ites. As a rule, the Imamis followed Ja'far's dic-
tum that a political challenge to the existing order would be counterproductive to
their spiritual goals, and they were content to practice their faith in a world whose
political order they despised.

Their quietism did not allow them to escape the suspicions of some of the Abbasid caliphs. The caliph Harun al-Rashid (786–809) persecuted them and allegedly poisoned Ja'far's son Musa al-Kazim. During a civil war between the sons of Harun al-Rashid, however, the central authority became so weak that several Shi'ite factions came out in open revolt in Iraq and in the Arabian Peninsula. Harun's son al-Ma'mun won the war in 813 and seems to have been keenly aware of the need to appeal to Shi'ite sensibilities. When he claimed the caliphate in 813, he also claimed the title of Imam, a title all subsequent Abbasid caliphs would take.

What al-Ma'mun meant to convey by his new designation is unclear, particularly in light of a stunning announcement that he made in 817. He had fought the civil war of 809–813 from his base in Merv and had not returned to Baghdad even after he claimed the titles of caliph and Imam. Now, in late 817, he surprised the empire by naming Musa al-Kazim's son, the Imam 'Ali al-Rida, his heir-apparent and son-in-law. His motive for doing so is still widely debated. What is clear, however, is that the rapidity of 'Ali al-Rida's rise to prominence was matched only by the suddenness of his decline. Soon after al-Ma'mun made his announcement, he began a march to Baghdad, which he had decided should be his capital after all. En route to the city, 'Ali al-Rida died suddenly in Tus (modern Mashhad). Shi'ites believe that he was poisoned, but cannot agree on who was responsible.

The Imamis enjoyed a respite from persecution under al-Ma'mun and his successor, but in 847, the new Abbasid caliph initiated a period of intense repression against them that lasted for the next twenty-five years. In 874, Hasan al-'Askari, the fifth Imam after Ja'far al-Sadiq, died, apparently without a son. As had been the case when Ja'far himself had died, the community was thrown into confusion. Numerous sects formed (some traditions assert as few as fourteen, but others name as many as twenty), and for several decades the Imamis were severely splintered.

Under the leadership of a man named 'Uthman al-'Amri, however, a radically new doctrine provided the core for the unification of most of the Imami Shi'ites. 'Uthman claimed that Hasan al-'Askari had been survived by a young son, who was now in hiding under God's protection. That Hasan had a son was news to most of the faithful, but under the capable leadership of 'Uthman and three of his successors, this belief became standard doctrine. The young boy was named Muhammad and acquired the title Muhammad al-Muntazar ("the looked-for," or "the anticipated"). In practice, he was usually referred to as the "Hidden Imam." 'Uthman and his three successors claimed to be intermediaries between the Imam and his followers, bringing to the faithful the religious guidance granted by the Hidden Imam.

In 941, however, the Imam sent word that he would no longer have a spokesman or intermediary, and Imami Shi'ism entered upon a new phase of history. The period from 874 to 941 soon came to be known as the Lesser Concealment (or Occultation), and the period after 941 came to be known as the Greater Concealment— "greater" in the sense that, without an intermediary, the Imam was even more concealed than before. The Hidden Imam was recognized as the twelfth in a line of Imams that began with 'Ali, and he was now designated as the Mahdi (as a result, he is sometimes referred to as Muhammad al-Mahdi as well as Muhammad al-Muntazar). From this time on, the Imamis have often been referred to as the Twelver Shi'ites.

The introduction of the doctrine of the Greater Concealment marked a surprising turn for a movement that had insisted on the need for constant spiritual guidance from an Imam. The Imami world view now became nostalgic and tragic, and Twelver Shi'ites longed for the time when they had had direct access to spiritual truth. Nevertheless, Twelvers continued to believe that the twelfth Imam was in control of history. Because of the new understanding of him as both the last Imam and as the Mahdi, the task for the next period of their history was to understand how he continued to give guidance to his community and what his role in history was. We shall explore this topic in more detail in Part Two.

The Isma'ilis

Both *Isma'ili* and *Sevener* seem to have originated as derogatory terms for the followers of Muhammad ibn Isma'il, but they have persisted because of their widespread use. The Isma'ilis themselves designated their movement simply as "the mission." We have no record of their activity between the death of Ja'far in the middle of the eighth century and the last third of the ninth century, when they emerged from obscurity. From evidence that exists from the time of their reemergence, it seems that they developed the doctrine that when Isma'il's son Muhammad appeared to die, he was instead hidden and protected by God. As the Mahdi/Imam, he was being prepared by God to return and bring justice and righteousness to the world at a time of God's choosing. In the meantime, the Imam communicated with his followers through designated spokesmen. Thus, from the late eighth to the late ninth centuries, the period when the Imamis relied upon a present, visible Imam, the Isma'ilis held a doctrine of a Hidden Imam.

The Isma'ilis also began to develop a theory of interpretation of the Qur'an that placed a premium on esoteric knowledge— that is, knowledge which, by virtue of its difficulty, was intended for a spiritual elite. We shall see that other Muslim groups also became preoccupied with esoterica during the same period, but the Isma'ilis became its outstanding practitioners. At the heart of the system was a distinction between the outer (*zahir*) and the inner (*batin*) meaning of the Qur'an, the religious law, and the ritual aspects of Islam. Religious laws and ritual prescriptions, it was asserted, change with every prophet that God has sent, but God's truths remain immutable and eternal. Thus, the revealed scriptures and the laws laid down therein must be understood as concealing a true, more spiritual meaning that is superior to their literal appearance. Only individuals with superior insight are able to interpret the hidden meanings.

The zahir/batin polarity undergirds the exalted status of the Imam and of the religious hierarchy that came to characterize Isma'ilism. The divinely guided, infallible Imam interpreted the true meaning of revelation to individuals who had proven their ability and integrity as bearers of the truth. Such intermediaries between the Imam and the ordinary proselyte became designated as a *hujjas*, or "proofs" of God's presence. These representatives of the Imam taught the spiritual truths by means of allegorical interpretations to students who had committed themselves through a formal initiation into the serious work of the organization. The masses, meanwhile, continued to know only the zahir meaning. Isma'ilis expected that, at the end of time, when the Imam returns as the Mahdi, he will abrogate the law of the Prophet. At that time, there will be no need for laws, because spiritual truth will be directly accessible to everyone.

After a century of underground activity, the Isma'ili movement suddenly reappeared in southwestern Iran and southern Iraq in the second half of the ninth century, just as the period of the Lesser Concealment began for the Imamis. The Isma'ili movement emerged as a highly disciplined organization engaged in intensive missionary activity, and its members were uncompromising in their determination to create a new Islamic society characterized by justice and righteousness. They made impressive gains in Iraq and Syria and sent out missionaries all the way to Khorasan, Sind, Yemen, and the Maghrib. By the last decade of the ninth century, the Isma'ilis had established their headquarters in Salamiya, Syria, and appeared to pose a formidable security threat to the Abbasids. In 902, however, 'Abd Allah, the leader of the headquarters at Salamiya, suddenly left his base of operations and began making his way westward. In 910, he appeared in Ifriqiya, some 1600 miles from Salamiya. There he was welcomed by a Berber army that had recently seized power in Qayrawan. His supporters recognized him not merely as the spokesman for the Imam, but the Imam-caliph and Mahdi himself, returning to take over the leadership of the entire Muslim world. A major challenge had been issued to the weakening Abbasid caliphate. 'Abd Allah's movement at this point became historically known as the Fatimid empire. Because its subsequent narrative belongs as much to imperial history as it does to religious history, we will resume its story in the next chapter.

The Shi'ite Movement

By the middle of the tenth century, Shi'ism had spawned two major groups: the Twelvers and the Isma'ilis. Several small Zaydi states continued in existence for many centuries, but they were always in remote, mountainous areas, quite removed from developments in the rest of the Muslim world. Ghulat sects continued to appear, but they discovered that they had to shed their extreme views if they wished to have an influence in the wider Umma.

The label *Shi'ism* slowly accumulated connotations that set Shi'ites apart from the majority of Muslims. Some were subtle differences, while others were quite striking. As we shall see later, the Sunnis tended to agree that religious truth was what the majority of pious scholars said that it was, whereas both Isma'ilis and Twelvers refused to admit that majority opinion is necessarily true or right. Because the two Shi'ite groups were, in fact, usually embattled minorities, both came to advocate the inherent virtue of belonging to a militant minority. Both of these groups of Shi'ites agreed that some truths can be known only by an elite and can be interpreted to the masses only by symbol and legend. Both groups tended to express emotion in their worship more than did the Sunnis. They focused on the persecutions they had suffered and the martyrdom of the heroes of the faith.

Both Isma'ilis and Twelvers believed that their respective Imams should be ruling the entire Muslim community. A latent corollary of that conviction was that all temporal authority in the absence of the Imam is illegitimate. The biggest difference between the Isma'ilis and Twelvers was the identity of the Imam. An intriguing contrast between the two groups is the fact that, from the death of Ja'far al-Sadiq to the late ninth century, the Imamis insisted on the need for a present, visible, Imam, but then accepted the doctrine of the Occultation after 874. The Isma'ilis, on the other hand, had been comfortable with the idea of a concealed Imam until the beginning of the tenth century, when the loyal followers of 'Abd Allah converted to the idea that he was the Imam. From the late ninth century until today, Twelvers have had a Hidden Imam, and the Isma'ilis usually have had a visible Imam.

The change in doctrine regarding the Imam had important political, as well as religious, consequences. As we shall see in the remainder of this volume, during the period from the ninth to the thirteenth centuries, various groups of Isma'ilis were active in attempting to achieve political power for their Imam. The Twelvers, on the other hand, were more ambivalent about the state during this period. There was no doubt that the Hidden Imam would soon be coming back to rule, but, in his absence, the practice of piety in this corrupt world was sufficient. God had His own plan for its purification, and any changes would be according to His timetable. As a result, Twelver Shi'ites were able to coexist with both the political and religious establishments much better than Isma'ilis or Zaydis did, and their persecution became a rare occurrence. The Isma'ilis, on the other hand, became the target of violent persecution.

The Sunni Consensus

As the Shi'ites were developing their characteristic doctrines and practices based on the conviction that the caliph should be a member of 'Ali's family, the majority of Muslims were also engaged in the process of developing their doctrines and institutions. We will examine this achievement in some detail in Chapter 5. At this point, it is useful to note that the Sunnis, as the majority are called, derive their name from their insistence on following the *sunna*, or *path*, of the Prophet. Whereas Shi'ites are convinced that Muslims need the guidance of an Imam in order to follow God's will correctly, Sunnis are satisfied that conscientious and pious Muslims can determine God's will by means of a careful reading of the Qur'an and of authenticated accounts (the Hadith) of the Prophet's behavior and teachings. In the eighth and ninth centuries, biographies of the Prophet were written and thousands of anecdotes of the Prophet's actions and sayings were collected together, all for the purpose of using the Prophet's life as a model of upright behavior. As we will see, enormous efforts were expended in order to develop reliable methods for obtaining spiritual guidance.

These efforts were made with the goal of developing a comprehensive guide for determining godly behavior under all circumstances. It was a complex and arduous enterprise that only qualified scholars could adequately perform. For most Muslims, however, knowing the basic ritual obligations was sufficient. These rituals are known as the "Five Pillars." The basis for all of them is to be found in the Qur'an, although many of the details as they are practiced today were elaborated over the course of many years. Their repetition cultivated in Muslims a sense of identity and purpose that gave believers the assurance that their cause was in accord with God's will. Moreover, the rituals reinforced in the minds of Muslims the fact that Islam is a collective, rather than merely an individual, enterprise, thereby providing emotional support to individuals when their faith or their physical strength faltered. The description of the rituals in the discussion that follows reflects Sunni practice; Kharijites and the various Shi'ite groups differ in some of the details.

Shahada, *or proclamation of faith.*   To become a Muslim, one recites, "There is no god but God, and Muhammad is His prophet." Muhammad's central teaching was that there is only one God, and that, therefore, the greatest sin is the denial of God's singularity and unity, and the placing of some other being to be equal to Him. God is all-powerful, and created all life; it is the duty of His human creatures to give thanks to God for life itself and to submit their will and their lives to God through daily obedience. In the Arabic language, the word *Islam* denotes submission, and a *Muslim* is one who submits. Muslims believe that people are responsible for their actions; at the end of time, each person will account for all of her or his deeds at the Last Judgment and go to paradise or to hell on the basis of the accounting.

Salat, *or ritual prayer.*   One of the most powerful rituals that reinforces the collective nature of Islam is the salat, or ritual prayer. The sight of others—perhaps even thousands of others—performing the prayer in unison reminds the believer that untold millions of others are performing the ritual all over the world at the appointed times. The frequent repetition of the prayer is a strong reinforcement of the conviction that one is participating in the most important enterprise in the world.

The salat is performed five times daily—dawn, noon, midafternoon, sunset, and evening—and the invocations and ritual movements are carefully prescribed. The salat can be performed at home, in a school or factory, or outdoors, but Muslims consider a mosque to be the most efficacious place for prayer. The mosque is explicitly designed for the salat. The English word *mosque* derives from the Arabic word *masjid*, which means "place of prostration," the name given to the pre-Islamic shrines. Mosques have always been constructed with the purpose of marking off space to consecrate for prayer. As a result, they do not have pews and they do not need to be tall or imposing, but simply large enough to serve the prayer needs of hundreds, or even thousands, of people.

The call to prayer (*idhan*) is issued by the *mu'adhdhin* (frequently rendered *muezzin*) from the one or more minarets, or towers, that became a characteristic feature of mosque architecture. Before performing the prayer, the believer must enter a state of ritual purity by washing the face, feet and ankles, and the arms to the elbows. He or she then determines the *qibla*, or direction of the Ka'ba in Mecca, which is marked in a mosque by the *mihrab*, a niche in the wall. After declaring to God the intention of making the prayer, the ritual begins. Of the thirty-five prayer times in the week, the Friday noon service is the one that Muslims make the most determined effort to perform at a mosque. That is the occasion when the *khutba*, or sermon, is delivered, and because of the large number of worshipers, it is the one that most effectively reinforces the sense of community.

Zakat, *or almsgiving.*   Concern for the poor, the widow, and the orphan is a constant refrain throughout the teachings of Muhammad. Since all humans are equally creatures of God, oppression of the poor and weak by the rich and powerful is therefore an affront to God himself. It is incumbent upon believers not merely to refrain from oppressing the poor, but to be active in sharing their wealth with them, as well. The zakat was the form of tax that Muhammad made mandatory upon new Muslims. In later centuries, Muslim jurists decided that the zakat should represent two percent of an individual's wealth. It came to be understood as a form of self-purification: By giving away part of one's property, one purifies the rest.

A mihrab, the niche in the wall of a mosque that indicates the qibla.

Sawm, *or fasting.*   Ramadan, the ninth month on the Islamic calendar, is the month of fasting. From before dawn until sunset, Muslims do not drink, eat, engage in sexual relations, or, in modern times, smoke. Prepubescent children, the sick and infirm, and the pregnant are exempted from the obligation, and travelers can postpone it. Most Muslims continue their regular work schedule during the day, but some sleep during the day and sit up all night; others engage in around-the-clock reading of the Qur'an. The breaking of the fast in the evening is a festive occasion, and some families spend more on food during Ramadan than during the entire remainder of the year. Because Muhammad stipulated that Muslims use a lunar, nonintercalated calendar, each of the months begins eleven solar days earlier the next year. The impact of Ramadan on individual lives varies accordingly: The fast is shorter and less stressful during the short periods of sunlight in winter than during the long ones of summer.

Ramadan is a month that mingles hardship with joy. Muslims have come to associate the month with the revealing of the Qur'an to Muhammad, and therefore it celebrates the beginning of Islam. It encourages reflection on human frailty and the believer's dependence on God. Like the other rituals, it reinforces the collective, communal aspect of Islam, as participants encourage each other through the experience and make a special effort throughout the month to help the poor and the hungry.

The **hajj,** *or pilgrimage.*   According to the traditional account, Muhammad developed the rituals of the hajj after his conquest of Mecca. He combined elements of the pre-

Islamic pilgrimage to the Ka'ba with others from surrounding shrines, such as Mina and Arafat, and sanctified them as an Islamic practice dedicated to God. The new hajj became a complex event spread over an area twelve miles in extent that took several days to complete. Muhammad enjoined believers to fulfill the pilgrimage at least once in their lifetime if at all possible. It is performed in the month of Dhu al-Hijja, the last month on the calendar. The event emphasizes the humility of the believer before God, and the equality of all humanity. Upon entering the sacred precinct, male pilgrims don two simple pieces of white cloth, and women dress in simple attire, as they dispense with all material goods that would establish ranks among them.

The pilgrimage has an awe-inspiring effect upon the participants. In part, this is due to being present in the place that sacred history was made. Muhammad taught that Abraham and his son Isma'il (Ishmael) built the Ka'ba, which was also the center of Muhammad's career; thus, pilgrims can imaginatively reenact momentous episodes in Islamic history. Another feature of the pilgrims' experience is that, as Islam spread across the world, Muslims representing a wide variety of ethnic groups and geographical regions began coming on the hajj. The varieties of skin color and languages spoken were vivid statements of the powerful appeal of Islam and of its triumphal march across the world, reassuring the believer that he or she was participating in God's plan. Precisely because Mecca was the meeting place for Muslims from all over the world, it soon became the logical site for scholars and travelers to meet and to exchange ideas. Throughout history it has served as a force for cosmopolitanism, the flow of ideas, and education.

Conclusion

The period between the Prophet's death in 632 and the Abbasid revolution in 750 witnessed momentous events that shaped the future direction of Muslim history. The frontiers of the Muslim world were established by the Umayyad conquests and would change very little for the next several centuries. The Abbasid revolution then transformed the "Arab empire" of the Umayyads into a cosmopolitan state that consciously attempted to incorporate a variety of ethnic groups not only into the community of believers, but also into the ruling elite itself. These positive developments were countered by the emergence of profound differences among Muslims that proved impossible to breach. The different assumptions that would eventually crystallize into Sh'ism, Kharijism, and Sunnism began making their appearance during the first century of Muslim history.

Central to the emergence of both Shi'ism and Kharijism was the figure of 'Ali, the Prophet's cousin and the husband of the Prophet's daughter Fatima. 'Ali's role in history is unusual. He must be regarded as one of the most important figures in Muslim history, and yet he led no major military campaigns, left no corpus of writings, and was totally preoccupied during his five years as caliph with defending his office—so much so that he was unable to accomplish any notable objectives. His importance lay in the perceptions and expectations that people had of him. He had many opponents among the Quraysh because of his criticism of the administrative practices of the new empire. On the other hand, the Muslims who would eventually become known as Shi'ites saw in him the rightful successor to Muhammad as leader of the

Umma, and they regarded the selection of Abu Bakr, 'Umar, and 'Uthman as the first three caliphs to have been a plot against the implementation of God's will. Still other Muslims enthusiastically cheered the beginning of 'Ali's caliphate, even though they did not regard him as having been divinely ordained as Muhammad's successor: They were expecting him to reverse the policies of 'Uthman and to implement justice. When he faltered, they felt betrayed and initiated the Kharijite movement.

Most Muslims fell in between these two groups. They did not see evidence that 'Ali had been chosen as the Prophet's immediate successor, and they did not believe that he had committed a grave offense in being willing to negotiate with an enemy when the alternative would be a bloodbath of Muslim against Muslim. Members of this third group—the Sunnis—regard 'Ali to have been one of the four "rightly guided" caliphs—that is, the four caliphs who preceded the Umayyad dynasty.

FURTHER READING

'Ali and the Politics of Division

Kennedy, Hugh. *The Prophet and the Age of the Caliphates: The Islamic Near East from the Sixth to the Eleventh Century.* London and New York: Longman, 1986.

Watt, W. Montgomery. *The Formative Period of Islamic Thought.* Edinburgh: Edinburgh University Press, 1973.

The Abbasid Revolution

Lassner, Jacob. *The Shaping of Abbasid Rule.* Princeton, New Jersey: Princeton University Press, 1980.

Sharon, Moshe. *Black Banners from the East: The Establishment of the 'Abbāsid State—Incubation of a Revolt.* Jerusalem: Magnes Press, and Leiden: E. J. Brill, 1983.

Sourdel, Dominique. "The Abbasid Caliphate." In *Cambridge History of Islam*, I, 1970, 104–139.

Shi'ite Sectarianism

Brett, Michael. *The Rise of the Fatimids: the World of the Mediterranean and the Middle East in the Fourth Century Hijra, Tenth Century C.E.* Leiden: E. J. Brill, 2001.

Brett, Michael. "The Mīm, the 'Ayn, and the Making of Ismā'īlism." *Bulletin of the School of Oriental and African Studies* 57, 1994, 25–39. Reprinted in Brett, Michael, *Ibn Khaldun and the Medieval West.* Ashgate/Variorum, 1999.

Daftary, Farhad. *The Isma'ilis: Their History and Doctrines.* Cambridge, U.K.: Cambridge University Press, 1990.

Ibn al-Haytham, Ja'far ibn Ahmad. *The Advent of the Fatimids: A Contemporary Shi'i Witness.* Translated and edited by Wilferd Madelung and Paul E. Walker. London and New York: I. B. Tauris, 2000.

Jafri, S. Husain M. *Origins and Early Development of Shi'a Islam.* London: Longman Group Ltd., 1979.

Momen, Moojan. *An Introduction to Shi'ism: The History and Doctrines of Twelver Shi'ism.* New Haven and London: Yale University Press, 1985.

Moosa, Matti. *Extremist Shiites: The Ghulāt Sects.* Syracuse, New York: Syracuse University Press, 1988.

The Sunni Consensus

Denny, Frederick Mathewson. *An Introduction to Islam*, 2d ed. New York: Macmillan Publishing Company, 1994.

Esposito, John L. *Islam: The Straight Path*, 3d ed. New York and Oxford: Oxford University Press, 1998.

CHAPTER 4

The Center Cannot Hold: Three Caliphates

The Abbasid victory over the Umayyads in 750 was a genuine revolution and not a mere change in dynasties. The old Sasanian cosmopolitan and imperial tradition had triumphed over Arab particularism, and the revolution signaled a shift from the Umayyad focus on conquest to one of institutional consolidation. The Abbasid period was the era during which the major Islamic institutions and doctrines took the forms that we know today. Abbasid patronage of the arts and sciences also contributed to a cultural efflorescence that would have a profound impact on Europe and, ultimately, other regions of the world.

On the other hand, the splendor of the Abbasid court, coupled with the five-hundred-year history of the dynasty, has sometimes left the impression that the state it headed was as powerful as its cultural impact. The state actually flourished for only a century. Even more significant, two competing caliphates arose in the first half of the tenth century to challenge the Abbasid caliph. The dream of a unified Muslim community in which God's law would be implemented uniformly and impartially and in which righteousness would be dominant seemed farther from fulfillment than ever, three hundred years after the career of the Prophet.

These political and religious divisions are the flashy, centrifugal forces of this period that tend to capture the attention of the observer. Just as important for the history of the area, however, are centripetal economic developments that were working to bind together the far-flung regions of the Muslim world despite these religious and political differences. Agricultural and manufacturing technologies, new crops, paper, precious metals, stylistic innovations for luxury goods such as ceramics and porcelains, and numerous other ideas and commodities were exchanged across thousands of miles, forever changing the means of production and the assumptions about everyday culture for Muslims and for those peoples who in turn borrowed from them.

The Abbasid Caliphate

The Abbasid revolt began a new age for the Umma. Many Muslims had high expectations of the new dynasty, for they regarded its members to be the representatives of the House of the Prophet. During the first several decades of its history, the new empire emitted occasional flashes of brilliance, and its subjects could feel justly proud of it. By the middle of the ninth century, however, it began to falter. It never attempted to regain the areas of the Maghrib and the Iberian Peninsula that had been lost by the Umayyads in the Great Berber Revolt, and in the ninth century it began losing effective control of its remaining provinces. By the middle of the tenth century, the Abbasid caliph was a figurehead for military officers who wielded effective power over a limited area.

The Early Period

The first Abbasid caliph, Abu al-'Abbas, assumed the title al-Saffah, or "the blood shedder." It was an apt title for two reasons. First, it was a name that had been associated with the idea of the Mahdi in the literature of the previous decades, and therefore the new ruler was asserting his divinely sanctioned status in accordance with the propaganda of the Abbasid movement. (All subsequent Abbasid caliphs would follow his example in assuming titles with a religious implication; the third Abbasid caliph even adopted the title al-Mahdi). Second, as in any revolution, the stakes were high, and much blood would have to be shed. Several long-time leaders of the Abbasid movement itself were executed for objecting to the selection of al-Saffah as caliph. Numerous Shi'ites who were regarded as potential threats to the new regime were also killed or otherwise persecuted.

When al-Saffah died in 754, his brother Abu Ja'far succeeded him and assumed the title al-Mansur ("the victor"). Al-Mansur (754–775) laid the foundations for the Abbasid empire. He began by choosing a site on the west bank of the Tigris River for the new capital city. Officially named *madinat al-salam*, or "City of Peace," it came to be known by the name of the village that lay next to it, Baghdad. The choice of the site was particularly astute: The Tigris and the Euphrates rivers came close together at this point and were connected by a navigable canal. Construction on the new capital began in 762, with 100,000 workers employed in the gargantuan project. It was a circular city some one and one-half miles in diameter that was designed for palaces, public buildings, and military barracks. Over the next few decades, the city grew into a large metropolis, and the original design was submerged in the welter of development. Extensive suburbs began springing up outside the circular walls to house those who flocked to the city to seek favors at the court or to participate in the city's flourishing international commerce. The wealthier neighborhoods boasted of sewers, courtyards, and pools lined with tiles. By the ninth century, the city was six miles long and four miles wide, a geographical area five times greater than that of Constantinople. With its population of close to half a million, it was certainly one of the two or three greatest cities in the world.[1]

The Abbasid revolution seems to have been a genuine attempt to make Islamic society more inclusive. The particularistic concerns of the Arab tribes that dominated the Umayyad government had led to policies that alienated other Arabs and non-Arabs alike. In North Africa and the Iberian Peninsula, the anger against such policies had expressed itself in the ferocity of the Berber Revolt of the 740s, which so shattered the edifice of central authority that the Abbasids themselves were not able to reassert effective control west of Ifriqiya. Even in Ifriqiya itself, they found it advantageous in 800 to concede autonomy to the province's governor, Ibrahim ibn al-Aghlab, a native of Khorasan. The Aghlabids went on to develop a regional power that extended its sway to Sicily.

In the rest of the former Umayyad territories, however, the Abbasid cause successfully appealed to a powerful current of piety by virtue of its demand for the abolition of the Umayyad dynasty and the installation of the Prophet's family as the leader of the Umma. As we have seen, the Abbasid era disappointed the pro-Alids, and it was also a bitter pill for the Arab elites who had benefitted from Umayyad policies. The latter immediately lost their privileged position at court and their centrality in the army and were replaced by the Khorasani guard. Over the next few years they also lost their tax exemptions for their property. Many Arabs, however, as well as most non-Arab Muslims, welcomed the new government because it did not favor any particular ethnic group. Its ideology was based on the spiritual and legal equality of all Muslims.

The Abbasid regime's more cosmopolitan and less parochial character was countered by its increasing remoteness from the ordinary citizen. It is easy to overdraw the contrast between the court ceremony of the early Abbasids and the late Umayyads, for Mu'awiya (d. 680) may have been the last of the caliphs who actually welcomed the common people to his presence with their petitions and appeals. But despite the increasing pomp of the later Umayyads, the Abbasid caliphs soon became much more removed from their subjects than even their immediate predecessors were. In Baghdad, the legacy of Sasanian ceremonial was revived, and the caliph became shielded from his public not only by monumental palaces, but also by a remarkably differentiated set of chamberlains and servants. Only the most important officials and foreign guests were allowed in the presence of the caliph. The new government quickly developed a complex bureaucracy, the members of which were recruited from throughout the empire. At the apex of the administration was the *wazir*, who served as the caliph's prime minister or chief executive officer. Reporting to him were ministries of the army, finance, posts and intelligence, and the chancery, among others.

The urbanity of the era is reflected in the poetry and prose that it produced. Poetry had been the greatest cultural expression of the Arabs. Although the Umayyad period had seen some development of poetic themes and styles, nostalgia for hunting parties and desert encampments remained dominant. Under the patronage of the Abbasid caliphs, new themes emerged. The most famous of the poets of the age was Abu Nuwas (d. ca. 813), who was of mixed Arab and Iranian origin. He spent time with bedouin in order to learn the venerated traditions of Arabic poetry, and then sought patronage in Baghdad. He was unsuccessful for several years and began developing new themes that reflected the worldly sophistication of the great metropolis. He gradually became famous for his wit, cynicism, and glorification of wine drinking and pederasty, and he finally gained a coveted position at court in the last few years of the reign of the great caliph Harun al-Rashid (r. 786–809).

Court poets such as Abu Nuwas were expected to demonstrate their command of one or more of the major genres of poetry popular at the time. Others rejected such conventions as being artificial and even dissolute. A stark contrast to the career of the social climber Abu Nuwas was Abu al-'Atahiya (d. 826), whose goal was to convey religious values and morality to the common people on the street. To do so, he discarded all the formal poetic conventions of his time, and used only the simplest language that would be comprehensible to anyone.

Arabic literature broadened its scope during this period. A prose style emerged that was employed to convey the traditions of courtly behavior (primarily Sasanian in origin) to bureaucrats and courtiers and to record the historical exploits of the Muslim community. Many outstanding prose writers made contributions in the period that spanned the eighth, ninth, and tenth centuries, but some must be mentioned. Sibawayh (d. ca. 793) was an Iranian, but composed the single most influential exposition of Arabic grammar. Ibn Ishaq (d. 768) was born in Medina but moved to Baghdad. He compiled the first major biography of the Prophet. His use of sources was criticized by some of his fellow scholars, and his work was revised by the Egyptian Ibn Hisham (d. ca. 833). The latter version has remained the major source for details of the Prophet's life. Al-Jahiz (d. 869), who was descended from an African slave, lived in Iraq. His mastery of style, and his combination of intellect, erudition, and wit made him a highly influential author. Al-Tabari (d. 923) wrote books on a wide variety of subjects, but is most famous for his huge *History of Prophets and Kings*, a compendium of history from creation until his own time. It is one of our most important sources for the first three centuries of Muslim history.

The labeling of certain historical periods as "golden ages" is often misleading, because economic, political, and cultural developments do not always coincide. In the Abbasid case, this caution is certainly justified. Culturally, its most productive period falls after the middle of the ninth century, but its political and economic high point was during the first few decades of the dynasty. The caliphate of Harun al-Rashid (786–809) is celebrated in the famous *One Thousand and One Nights* as the period of glory for the dynasty, even though to his contemporaries the caliph could boast of no special achievements. In retrospect, however, his reign of a quarter of a century was a halcyon period. The caliph was the unquestioned ruler of the realm, Baghdad had developed into a world capital, and a *pax Islamica* brought a sense of optimism and confidence that southwestern Asia has only rarely known.

Harun himself contributed to the undoing of that optimism. In 802, he designated his oldest son al-Amin to be his successor as caliph, but stipulated that a younger son, al-Ma'mun, should rule over an enlarged and autonomous Khorasan and succeed al-Amin as caliph at the latter's death. Soon after Harun died in 809, however, al-Amin demanded that al-Ma'mun cede the western parts of Khorasan to him and that the taxes from the remainder of the province be forwarded to Baghdad. Al-Ma'mun refused, and a long and destructive war between the brothers ensued. During 812–813, al-Ma'mun's army besieged Baghdad itself for a year, and al-Amin was killed.

Al-Ma'mun named himself caliph in 813, but he elected to set up his court in Merv, where his base of support lay. Near-anarchy reigned in Baghdad, and the city was heavily damaged in internecine fighting over the next six years. We saw in the previous chapter that al-Ma'mun finally decided in 817–818 to relocate to Baghdad (with fatal consequences for the Imam 'Ali al-Rida). Moving slowly, he arrived only in 819. Exhausted, the factions in the city surrendered with hardly a struggle.

Military and Economic Problems

The heart of the empire had suffered a decade of warfare from 809 to 819. Not only did Baghdad and other cities incur major damage, but ambitious local leaders in every province had tried to take advantage of the confusion to bolster their own power. When al-Ma'mun took up residence in Baghdad in 819, he began trying to restore the unity of the empire. He had remained in control of Iran during the war, and was now successful in regaining the areas as far west as Benghazi in eastern Libya and as far south as the Holy Cities. The area west of Benghazi, however, was permanently lost. The Aghlabids continued to rule in Ifriqiya, technically as Abbasid vassals, but in reality as an independent principality. As a result, the Maghrib and the Iberian Peninsula remained outside the Abbasid orbit.

In the field of culture, al-Ma'mun was more successful, and in that context he became one of the most influential caliphs in history, as we shall see in the next chapter. With the coming to power of al-Ma'mun's younger brother, al-Mu'tasim (833–842), however, the Abbasid dynasty entered a new and tragic era. On the one hand, the middle third of the ninth century probably represents the zenith of Abbasid political power if measured in terms of the control that the central government was able to exert over the provinces. On the other hand, certain developments set the stage for a precipitous decline in the prestige and power of the central government in general and of the caliph in particular.

Changes in the army played a major role in this process. Throughout the ninth century, the army became increasingly multiethnic in its composition. This was not a unique development for the time, as the Byzantine army itself became dependent on Slavs, Turks, Armenians, and eventually Normans. But just as the Arab forces that had achieved the spectacular conquests of the first decades of Islamic history were replaced by Khorasanis early in the Abbasid era, the Khorasanis became supplemented in the ninth century by Daylamis (from Daylam, the region south of the Caspian Sea), Armenians, Berbers, Sudanese, Turks from Central Asia, and other ethnic groups. What is striking is that the vast majority of the Abbasid troops were beginning to come from the border areas of the empire, or from outside it altogether—few Iraqis, west Iranians, Syrians, Egyptians, or peninsular Arabs were represented in it.

The new pattern of composition of the army had advantages for the caliph. By not having to rely on the local populace for troops, a ruler was freer to use troops against either external or internal enemies without having to negotiate with chieftains or notables for the use of their subjects. In addition, his troops did not hesitate to attack civilians on the streets, since they had no local families at risk. Furthermore, Muslim armies of the ninth century were becoming more professional in general and were intent on employing a variety of weaponry on the battlefield in an effort to gain the tactical edge over their opponents. The different ethnic groups represented a military division of labor that, when used well, made an army a formidable force against a less diversified force. The Turks specialized in mounted archery, the Berbers and Armenians were lance-bearing cavalry, the Daylamis were predominantly light infantry employing bows and javelins, and the black Sudanese served as heavy infantry.

The most notable ethnic group in the new army was that of the Turks. As early as the civil war between his older brothers, al-Mu'tasim had begun building a private army composed of slaves, and he continued to do so after he became the caliph. He eventually owned several thousand such soldiers, mostly Turks of Central Asian origin. These military slaves came to be referred to as *mamluk*s, from an Arabic term meaning "owned" or "belonging to." After a training regimen they were usually manumitted and became clients of their former masters. As free clients, they gained limited legal rights to property and marriage. Mamluks, then, were not servile and abject victims of a brutal system, but rather formed a proud and intimidating force who preferred the company of their own kind and regarded the civilian populace with contempt. They were answerable only to the caliph, and could attain the rank of general or minister of state, controlling the destinies of hundreds of thousands of people and owning vast estates. Thus, rather than being a subservient part of the army, they actually enjoyed important privileges.

The value to caliphs of an army composed of foreign ethnic groups lay in the soldiers' undivided loyalty. Free, indigenous soldiers could be torn between allegiance to the court they served and the local interests of the region from which they came. The irony is that the new pattern developed instabilities of its own, and caused even greater difficulties for the administration than the earlier system had. Two factors were prominent in the developing crisis. One was that the military was evolving into a *de facto* caste, separated by a wide cultural gulf from the rest of society. The martial values of the professional military had always set such a force apart from the rest of society, but now those differences were made all the greater by differences in language and customs. The other problem was that the economy upon which the caliphal government was based was growing weaker, making it more difficult to sustain the military at any acceptable standard of living. The rich province of Iraq was beginning to suffer a double blow to its agriculture: In some parts of the region, river channels were shifting, leaving irrigation works and fields without access to water, whereas in the region close to the Persian Gulf, many fields were suffering from salinization due to repeated irrigation by river water full of salts. To attempt to solve the latter problem, tens of thousands of slaves from East Africa were brought in to drain swamps and to remove the salinated soil in an effort to restore fertility.

Because of the economic strains, the government had difficulty paying its troops regularly. The soldiers became restive, and the various ethnic groups suspected each other of benefitting from favoritism. The mutual suspicions led to frequent clashes among the various units, and the Turks gained a reputation for initiating many of the fights. More disturbing still, the civilian population of Baghdad frequently fell victim to slights or outright injury from the arrogant soldiers, most of whom did not bother to learn Arabic. As early as 836, al-Mu'tasim felt compelled to separate the Turks from the other troops and from the general populace by moving his capital some eighty miles to the north, where he built the city of Samarra. The move was intended to be permanent: Samarra entailed a massive investment on a scale not less than the founding of Baghdad itself. The palace and mosque complexes were imperial

The Great Mosque of Samarra, late ninth century. Its outer walls enclose a prayer space larger than nine football fields.

monuments, and within a few decades the city extended along the Tigris for twenty-four miles. Baghdad continued to function as a commercial and intellectual center, but it was no longer of political importance.

The Assertion of Regional Autonomy

The move to Samarra only postponed the resolution of the crisis, which could hardly be solved by creating yet another imperial capital, especially as the economy was heading into a slow decline. The problem of the rebellious Turkish mamluks became only more serious. These military slaves, totally dependent on the caliph for their subsistence, could be loyal to the death to him when his support for them was unquestioned; on the other hand, they could pose a threat to him when doubts arose regarding their own security. In 861, the caliph al-Mutawakkil (847–861) punished a corrupt Turkish officer by seizing his property. In retaliation, a group of Turkish soldiers murdered him. The relationship between the soldiers and the court had become so poor that no caliph was able to repair it. The remainder of the decade was a period of anarchy during which three of the four caliphs who came to power were assassinated. The chaos in the capital ended strong central control over the provinces, and local leaders were quick to seize the opportunity to enhance their own power at the expense of Samarra. A Turkish general by the name of Ahmad ibn Tulun was appointed governor of Egypt in 868, but he took advantage of the confusion in the capital to establish an autonomous regime. He did not formally reject the authority of the caliph, but he stopped sending Egypt's critically needed revenue to Iraq. Under Ibn Tulun and his descendants, Egypt remained autonomous for almost four decades.

The insecurity of Abbasid society is reflected in both the religious and political developments of the period. The eleventh Imam of the Imamiya died in 874, and the Lesser Occultation began at that time. The same decade witnessed the transformation of Isma'ilism from a little-noticed underground activity into a major challenge to Abbasid power. In the eastern parts of the caliphate, dramatic political developments were taking place. Between 867 and 873, a coppersmith, al-Saffar, led a rebellion in Khorasan and Afghanistan and established the Saffarid dynasty there. Although the Saffarids did not sever relations with the caliph, they openly expressed their contempt for him, and they sent the revenue from their area to Samarra only at their pleasure, rather than on demand. By the beginning of the tenth century, the Saffarids were in turn ousted by the Samanid regime, which became truly independent of Baghdad. The new dynasty, based in Bukhara, continued to have the prayers in the mosques said in the name of the caliph, but it did not send revenue to his treasury at all. Moreover, the Samanids began a program of patronizing Persian literature as a way of declaring cultural independence from Arabic influence. During the ninth century, a revival of Persian literature had already been encouraged at the provincial courts of Iran, and the so-called "new Persian" had begun to adapt the Arabic alphabet and borrow certain Arabic words, as well as to borrow from motifs in Arabic poetry. Under the Samanids, the revived interest in the Persian heritage developed into a magnificent literature of epic poetry celebrating pre-Islamic heroes without becoming anti-Islamic in sentiment. We shall see examples of this later.

An unexpected challenge to the Abbasid government during this period was also in some ways the most threatening. The tens of thousands of African slaves who had been brought into southern Iraq in order to try to revive agricultural production were treated brutally, and in 869 they arose in revolt. They overwhelmed the local garrison, and for the next fourteen years the rebels, known as the Zanj, maintained a stronghold in southern Iraq, constantly threatening Baghdad with attack and depriving the caliphate of the revenue from its most productive province. The magnitude of this rebellion can be gauged by the fact that the rebels captured the military city of Wasit and the major city of Basra. Throughout the period, the rage that the ex-slaves felt about their treatment was expressed in the ferocity of their fighting. They massacred the inhabitants of the cities they captured and destroyed mosques and other public buildings. Because of the danger, commerce over the important Persian Gulf trade route was diverted to Iranian ports and to the Red Sea. When the revolt was finally quelled in 883, the consequences were severe: Basra had been destroyed, large-scale land reclamation projects were never resumed, and the major trade routes had shifted permanently.

In 892, in an attempt to revive the fortunes of the empire, the Abbasid government began the formidable project of moving the government apparatus back to Baghdad. Abandoned, Samarra's vast and magnificent mud-brick structures began to melt into the desert, becoming a metaphor for the fortunes of the dynasty as the economic crisis of the caliphate accelerated. The political disintegration of the empire played a major role in this regard. The Samanid seizure of power ended the prospects of revenue coming from Khorasan, and the drying up of the Persian Gulf trade route starved both the customs revenue and the local retail trade. The land revenues from southern Iraq, which had already been declining before the Zanj revolt, continued to plummet. By the early tenth century, the revenues from the once-wealthiest province were one-third what they had been during the time of Harun al-Rashid. Egypt became increasingly autonomous throughout the tenth century and was able to reduce the amount of revenue sent to Baghdad. The reduction of the flow of revenue from the Nile valley (and Palestine, which was controlled by the Egyptian regime) was a catastrophic blow to the Abbasid court, for it meant that insufficient revenue was available to pay the army. The result was a state of perpetual mutiny.

In a desperate effort to bring order to the capital, the caliph in 936 agreed to give a Turkish general responsibility for both civil and military administration. The caliphal office, which had been weak for several decades to that point, now became ineffectual for over two centuries. But even this fateful step did not bring stability. The devolution of power from the caliph to a general triggered a jealous struggle among the local military elite, leading to a decade of turmoil in Baghdad. The stage was set for a well-organized outside force to march in and take control. In 945, the Buyid clan did just that.

The Buyids were from Daylam, in the Elburz mountain range. Because it was a wild and remote area, it served as a refuge to people throughout history who wanted to keep imperial governments at arm's length. During the late eighth century, Alids began to seek refuge in the area, and over the next hundred years, this remote area became a stronghold of both Zaydi and Imami Shi'ism. In 932, a Daylami named 'Ali ibn Buya, along with two of his brothers and a few hundred infantrymen, ventured south into Fars. This province, the heartland of the old Sasanian empire, had remained prosperous throughout the previous century, even as Baghdad suffered blow after blow. One of the few revenue-producing provinces left to the Abbasids, Fars had only recently fallen victim to the depredations of some renegade soldiers from Baghdad and was ripe for the plucking. In a single battle, 'Ali won control of the area, and from his base in the provincial capital of Shiraz, he and his brothers sought to expand their area of control. In 945 one brother, Ahmad, negotiated a takeover of Baghdad, and the following year al-Hasan conquered the Iranian plateau from Rayy to Esfahan.

The Buyid brothers and their immediate descendants ruled their provinces as a confederation. Utterly pragmatic, they acknowledged the spiritual authority of the caliph and asserted that he had appointed them to their posts. Ahmad assumed the title of Commander of Commanders, while 'Ali and al-Hasan took the title of governor of their respective provinces. Despite the connotation of the titles, 'Ali remained the most influential of the three rulers, and he sealed the issue by adopting as his title Shahanshah, a Sasanian title meaning "King of Kings." The first generation of Buyid rulers seem to have been Zaydi Shi'ites, but later they provided generous support to Twelver Shi'ism. Although the Buyids did not try to force their subjects to adopt Shi'ism, the Sunni Abbasid caliph was humiliated to be under Shi'ite control. After eighty years of splendor in Baghdad and a century of decline, the Abbasid caliphs had been reduced to figurehead status.

The Fatimid Caliphate

In the preceding chapter, we saw that the Isma'ilis were the Shi'ites who regarded Isma'il's son Muhammad as the Imam when Ja'far al-Sadiq died in 765. After a century of underground activity, they reemerged as militant social and religious activists. One faction of Isma'ilis even set up a rival caliphate, challenging the Abbasid caliphate in Baghdad. This was a development of major importance for Muslim history. Shi'ites had verbally expressed their disdain of the Sunni caliphate, but never before had a competing caliphate actually been created. For over two and one-half centuries, the Fatimid caliphate would pose a threat to Sunni political and religious dominance.

Isma'ili Activism

The first two centuries of Muslim rule had brought about a dramatic urbanization of southwestern Asia, transforming the economic and social relationships of the area. By the middle of the ninth century, the Arab tribal aristocracy that had been dominant during Umayyad times was a secondary influence, having been shouldered aside by a ruling class composed of merchants, military leaders, administrators, religious leaders, and landowners. Many of the new elite were the offspring of marriages between Arabs and local women, and some had no Arab lineage at all. The striking wealth of the cities, and the relative impoverishment of the peasants and the bedouin, became a focal point of grievances that led to rural unrest. As we have seen, the Abbasid caliph had become more remote than before, causing some Muslims to mumble about their "Sasanian prince."

It was in this period of growing social cleavage, a widespread perception of injustice, near anarchy in some regions, and the erosion of the legitimacy of the Abbasid regime that, after more than a century of underground activity, Isma'ilism burst onto the scene. From the outset, the movement served as a vehicle of social protest and promised that the existing order would be overthrown in favor of a just and egalitarian society. Isma'ilis preached that Muhammad ibn Isma'il never died, but rather remained alive in seclusion. His return as the Mahdi was imminent, at which time he would eliminate the corruption, favoritism, and oppression inherent in the materialist society that had been built on the trade of luxury goods and the exploitation of the poor. He would inaugurate a new age of justice and abrogate the old law. In the meantime, his intermediaries provided spiritual leadership to his followers. Initially, the peasants and bedouin were the most responsive to the appeal, but over time a small group of the intelligentsia became involved in the movement, as well as substantial numbers of artisans and day laborers.

Much about the reemergence of Isma'ilism is obscure, and the evidence is partial when it is not contradictory. Some of the confusion is due to the obsession for secrecy characteristic of an opposition movement; some is the result of genuine confusion on the part of observers, who could not distinguish among the many Shi'ite groups competing for followers; and some is due to the fact that the Isma'ilis' enemies slandered them when they were not confused by them. It is clear that more than one group of Isma'ilis arose toward the end of the third quarter of the ninth century.

One of these groups came to be known as the Carmathians. They had their demographic support in Syria, Iraq, and the Persian Gulf coast. Because of their proximity to Baghdad, they were a serious threat to the Abbasid regime, which they vowed to destroy. They attacked several Abbasid installations during the 890s and developed a fearsome reputation. They captured Bahrain from the Abbasid governor in 900 and maintained a prosperous state there for almost two centuries. The Carmathians of Bahrain gained favorable publicity among the poor as a result of their policy of sharing material goods equally, whereas notorious rumors (such as the sharing of wives) gained it equal disrepute among its detractors. Bahrain became the base for numerous raids against the Abbasids, including the capture of the large city of Basra.

The Carmathians became infamous for their massacres of pilgrims en route to Mecca. Making the pilgrimage was arduous and dangerous under the best of circumstances, but for extended periods of time, particularly during the years 902–906 and 923–939, Carmathian raids caused pilgrims to realize that performing the hajj could be an act of martyrdom. An episode in 930 won everlasting opprobrium for the sect when a group of Carmathian raiders attacked Mecca and carried away the Black Stone from the Ka'ba. It was kept in Bahrain until 951, when it was returned for a large ransom. On the one hand, this act of theft and desecration caused most Muslims to loathe the Carmathians; on the other, it helped to show how irrelevant the Abbasid caliph had become. Combined with their regular attacks on pilgrims, the theft demonstrated that the Abbasid caliphate had no power outside the metropolis of Baghdad. Bahrain remained a regional power until the second half of the eleventh century, when it began to experience political and economic problems. In 1077, a bedouin army defeated and destroyed it.

Another Isma'ili group appeared in Iran and Iraq in the 860s that resulted in the Fatimid movement. Its leaders, based in the lower Tigris River valley, established networks of agents throughout southern Iraq. Soon the Isma'ili headquarters was transferred to Salamiya, north of Damascus. Because of its implicit—and often explicit—criticism of the existing social and political order, the organization came under increasing repression by the Abbasid government. Already having developed a complex underground system of secret cells that communicated with each other across vast distances, the Isma'ilis now accelerated their efforts to spread their message of an alternative to the Abbasids. By the end of the ninth century, Isma'ili missionaries were organizing cells in villages and cities from North Africa to India.

As noted in Chapter 3, the Isma'ili leader at Salamiya, 'Abd Allah, left Syria in 902 and made his way westward. The traditional account of the reason for this move attributes it to a schism within the Isma'ili leadership. There is evidence that in 899 'Abd Allah began suggesting to the leadership of the group that he would soon publicly announce that he was the Imam himself, rather than merely a spokesman for him. He also claimed that he was descended from Ja'far al-Sadiq's son 'Abd Allah rather than from Isma'il. These were stunning revisions of accepted doctrine and came as a great shock to many Isma'ilis. They had been accustomed to denigrating the followers of any claimant to the Imamate of Ja'far al-Sadiq other than Isma'il and his son Muhammad. For 'Abd Allah to claim that a rival of Isma'il's line was the true Imam required a greater shift in loyalties and identity than many Isma'ilis could muster. Many of them revolted, and in 902, 'Abd Allah was forced to flee.

After spending several years in hiding in Egypt, 'Abd Allah made his way to the Maghrib, where Isma'ili missionaries had gained a large following among the Kutama Berbers of Ifriqiya. Making his way in 905 to the Kharijite oasis settlement of Sijilmasa on the fringe of the Sahara, 'Abd Allah took up residence there in the guise of a merchant. He made contact with missionaries in Ifriqiya who were loyal to him. In 909, they overthrew the Aghlabids in 'Abd Allah's name. The following year, they escorted him from Sijilmasa to Qayrawan, where he took power in the royal suburbs of the city.

A Second Caliphate in the Umma

As the self-proclaimed Imam, 'Abd Allah also adopted the title of Mahdi and was known thereafter as 'Abd Allah al-Mahdi. Since he claimed descent from Ja'far's son 'Abd Allah, in a technical sense his mission was not Isma'ili at all: It traced its origins to Isma'il's brother, rather than to Isma'il himself. As we shall see in Chapter 6, one of his descendants reclaimed the Isma'ili mantle several decades later. The followers of al-Mahdi's organization eventually came to be known as the Fatimiya, or the Fatimids, which suggested descent from 'Ali and Fatima. This claim, of course, was not unique to his group, but it is the name that became permanently associated with it. The Fatimids themselves apparently did not use the word *Fatimid*. They simply called themselves *dawlat al-haqq*, which means "the legitimate governmental authority."

The ruling elite realized the importance of the Aghlabid navy that they inherited, and they enlarged it for military and commercial purposes. Their orientation toward the sea took graphic form when 'Abd Allah created a new capital on the coast and named it Mahdiya, "(The City) of the Mahdi." The Fatimid navy captured Sicily, raided the coasts of France and Italy, and plundered Genoa. The fleet dominated the central Mediterranean and threatened the trade of the Muslims of the Iberian Peninsula. The Fatimids also made great efforts to increase the existing trans-Sahara trade and were able to enhance Ifriqiya's importance as a commercial center for goods from both the Mediterranean basin and the sub-Saharan region.

The Fatimids did not try to convert the Sunnis of Ifriqiya by force, but they did gain a reputation for harshly suppressing some of the Sunni leaders. They may have been provoked: The Sunni leaders had quite often deliberately antagonized the Aghlabids, as well. The Fatimids did force all the mosques to institute the slightly different Shi'ite version of the call to prayer and to proclaim the Friday sermon in the name of the Fatimid caliph-Imam.

Ifriqiya turned out to be a fortuitous location for the Fatimid Empire to begin, because most of North Africa had fragmented into numerous ministates after the Berber Revolt of 740. No major power threatened the Fatimids in their early days, but these small states would be vulnerable when the Fatimids were ready to attack. Almost all of the neighboring states were led by Berbers, and many of them had adopted Kharijism. Kharijism was popular among Berbers because of its sanctioning of the overthrow of an unjust ruler, its egalitarianism, and its insistence that even a non-Arab could become caliph. Several of the Kharijite Berber states that were founded in the mid-eighth century became important in the trans-Saharan trade. Tlemcen and Sijilmasa (modern Rissani, Morocco) were among the first of these. Tahart (modern Tagdemt, Algeria) was founded by Rustam, a Kharijite of Iranian origin. It deserves special notice. It became the seat of the Rustamid dynasty, which had a remarkable history. Despite the Kharijites' preference for political decentralization and their antidynastic bias, the sanctity and dignity of the Rustamid dynasty enabled it not only to hold power from generation to generation, but also to hold the respect of other Kharijite oases all across the northern fringe of the Sahara. Its reputation as a center of learning attracted Kharijite scholars from as far as Iran.

Most of the Kharijite settlements from Tahart to Tripoli adhered to the Ibadi variant of Kharijism, and their inhabitants tolerated the sins of fellow Muslims much more generously than the original Kharijites did. The original Kharijites typically insisted that the commission of a sin automatically made a Muslim an apostate, thus deserving the penalty of death. By contrast, Tahart became famous for its religious toleration, and it welcomed Christians, Jews, non-Kharijite Muslims, and adherents of different subsects of Kharijism. Ibadism even at this early date was hardly distinguishable from Sunnism. Nevertheless, it was attractive to many Muslims—usually dwelling in small towns in remote areas—to whom it was important as a badge of dignity, piety, and spiritual egalitarianism.

Berbers were also the overwhelming majority west of Tlemcen and the Atlas Mountains, but Kharijism was not as prominent there. The most dynamic development in Morocco during the pre-Fatimid period was the arrival in the 780s of an Alid named Idris ibn 'Abdullah. He was from Mecca, but it is not clear whether he was a refugee from Abbasid persecution or a missionary. Apparently a Zaydi Shi'ite, he quickly won a following among some local Berbers, and in 790 he captured Tlemcen. Before his death the following year he subdued most of the interior of northern Morocco. His son Idris II was born a few months after his death and was recognized as Imam at the age of eleven. Idris II reigned for more than two decades, establishing his dominance in the region from the Sous River in southern Morocco to some one hundred miles east of Tlemcen. He welcomed into his new capital city of Fez an influx of Shi'ite Arabs from Iberia and from Qayrawan after unsuccessful rebellions in those Sunni-dominated regions. By the time of his death in 828, the area around the city was largely Arabized, and Fez had become the dominant city in the region. With the establishment of two large mosques at mid-century, the city began challenging Qayrawan as a center of Islamic learning in North Africa.

Politically, however, there was no chance that Fez would soon become the capital of a major power. The first two Idrisids seem never to have ruled over a defined territory, and upon the death of Idris II the towns acknowledging his authority were divided among several of his sons. Morocco remained splintered into many feuding principalities. It remained largely Berber for many centuries, although considerable numbers of Arab adventurers and entrepreneurs came into the area over the next two hundred years. Because of the Atlas mountain ranges, these immigrants tended to be funneled along the Mediterranean coastal plain to the Atlantic plain and then south, or into the oases on the eastern slope of the Atlas, and thence to the Sous River. Both of these areas had access to trade (maritime commerce for the former and the trans-Saharan trade in gold and slaves for the latter), whereas the interior of Morocco did not offer many economic opportunities. As a result of this pattern of settlement, the Arabization and Islamization of Morocco took place on the periphery of the country. By the tenth century, the Umayyad dynasty in the Iberian Peninsula was attempting to secure its influence among these commercial settlements.

The Fatimid task, then, was to subdue as many of the small principalities as possible before the Umayyads of Iberia gained a strong foothold in the Maghrib. The Fatimid targets were weak, but numerous, which entailed many battles and sieges. At the core of al-Mahdi's army was the cavalry of the Kutama Berbers of western Ifriqiya. They were rivals of the largely Zanata Berbers of the southern oases, and control of those commercial oases was critical for Fatimid prosperity. The political and economic rivalry of the Kutama and Zanata Berber groups was overlain by religious differences. The Fatimids and the Kharijites hated each other. The Kharijites placed a premium on piety and strict observance of ritual, and their egalitarian ideals included the conviction that truth was accessible to all. The Fatimids, by contrast, viewed ritual as the outer truth that was not as important as the inner, spiritual truth; their organizational hierarchy of religious officials was the absolute opposite of religious egalitarianism; and they taught that individuals have access to different levels of truth.

Al-Mahdi had spent four years (905–909) of his life as a fugitive in the Kharijite stronghold of Sijilmasa, but he did so inconspicuously. When his identity was discovered, he had been placed under house arrest. Once his supporters began their campaign to place him in power in Qayrawan, they turned on the Kharijites with a fury. One of the Fatimid army's earliest conquests in 909 was Tahart, where the Rustamids were massacred. Other Kharijite oases from Tripoli to Tlemcen fell and were also treated with brutality. By 917, al-Mahdi's army had captured Fez, and the Fatimids were well on their way to domination of the entire Maghrib.

Al-Mahdi's most important goal, however, was to conquer Egypt. The fertile Nile valley would be an ideal location from which to coordinate the plan to dominate the Muslim world. The Abbasid grip on Egypt had weakened since the late ninth century, when the Tulunid governors became increasingly autonomous. Al-Mahdi launched campaigns against Egypt as early as 913–915, and again in 919–921, but was thwarted when the Abbasid army intervened both times. Al-Mahdi died in 934, and his son launched a third campaign against Egypt, once again without success. The Fatimid regime planned a fourth campaign, but it was aborted when a rebellion broke out among the Berbers of the Maghrib in 943. The Fatimids lost the entire Maghrib temporarily, and the capital city of Mahdiya was even besieged. For the next two decades, the Fatimid government was forced to concentrate its efforts on consolidating its power in the Maghrib. It relied increasingly upon the Kutama Berbers and the empire's urban population, who feared the unruly mountain and desert tribes. Not until the last third of the century would the Muslim world know how powerful this new Fatimid state could be.

The Umayyad Caliphate of Cordoba

The Iberian Peninsula witnessed the rise of yet a third caliphate within the Umma during the first half of the tenth century. Its emergence was not inspired by a challenge to Baghdad, for the Abbasids never controlled the peninsula. The area's links even with the Umayyad central government in Damascus had been tenuous from the first, due to the great distance of the province from the capital and the preoccupation of Damascus with the northern and eastern frontiers of the empire. Commercial and cultural links with the Arab east remained close, but the Muslims of the Iberian Peninsula developed a distinctive identity that facilitated the declaration of a separate caliphate.

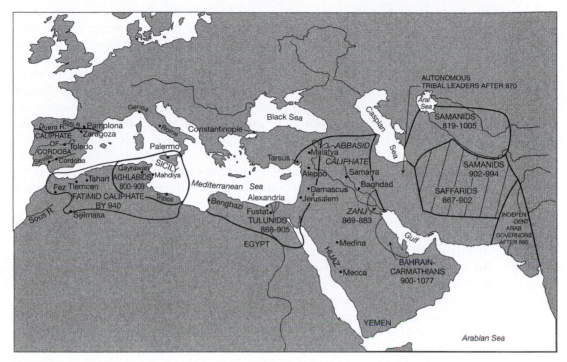

MAP 4.1 Political Fragmentation of the Umma, to 950

The Consolidation of Umayyad Power

Muslim raiders rapidly and easily subdued the Iberian Peninsula between 711 and 720, except for the north, where prolonged, vicious fighting took place. Historically, the mountain people of the north had always resisted domination by the government of the south, whether Roman or Visigothic, and that pattern continued under the Muslims. The peoples of the north were, themselves, separated from each other by high mountain ridges. Although they spoke mutually intelligible dialects, they formed distinct communities. The Muslims were primarily interested in the northern section simply to protect their own lines of communication, for they quickly realized that the area had little wealth to offer. Indeed, when the small principality of Asturias revolted about 720, the Muslims made little effort to quell the rebellion, preferring instead to begin a series of raids north of the Pyrenees into southern Aquitaine and Provence that lasted for several decades. The Muslims would eventually regret not having stamped out the revolt in Asturias. For the moment, however, Asturias was merely an arid and stony hill country, offering little for the effort that securing it would require. The wealth of the cities, monasteries, and churches in southern France, on the other hand, proved to be irresistible.

Despite the ease of the Muslim conquest of the Iberian Peninsula, the area was not politically stable under the Umayyads of Damascus. The primary threat to the dynasty was not that of the native population, but rather factional rivalry among Arab tribes. As a result, governors found that they were often opposed simply because of their tribal identity, and their authority was constantly challenged. The rivalry among the Arabs made the society vulnerable to the Great Berber Revolt of the 740s, which spread into the peninsula from North Africa. Several thousand Syrian troops, arriving from Damascus, suppressed the rebellion in Iberia. The uprising, however, had so shattered the administrative structure in North Africa that Damascus could not reestablish control over the Iberian peninsula, and it became autonomous. Moreover, in 750 a famine spawned by a sustained drought forced thousands of Berbers who had settled in the northwestern and north central parts of the peninsula to migrate to the south, allowing Asturias to annex much of the vacated territory. For the next three centuries, the valley of the Duero River formed a permeable and elastic frontier between Christian and Muslim regions. Increasingly, Arab writers referred to the Muslim-held territories—as opposed to the Christian-dominated areas of the peninsula—as *al-Andalus* (hereafter, Andalus). The original meaning of the term is an object of speculation.

The Abbasid revolution was an epochal event for most Muslims, but its impact on Andalus was unexpected. The Abbasids attempted to eradicate the Umayyad family, but one of the princes, 'Abd al-Rahman, escaped into Egypt and then into North Africa. There his heritage served him well, for he was able to find refuge among the Berber tribe from which his mother had come. From the Maghrib he made contact with Umayyad partisans who had sought refuge in Andalus, and he learned that his family had support among powerful units of the Syrian troops there. With their help, he resurrected the Umayyad dynasty, establishing a power base in Cordoba. The family would rule from there for almost three centuries, until 1031. 'Abd al-Rahman, not surprisingly, refused to recognize the Abbasid caliph, and he assumed the title of *amir*, which suggests "commander" or "leader." The Muslims of Andalus thereafter maintained close cultural contacts with the eastern regions of the Muslim world, but acknowledged no religious or political authority outside the peninsula.

The Umayyad name held no mystique for the bulk of the Arab and Berber tribes in the peninsula, however, and 'Abd al-Rahman had to lead military campaigns almost until his death in 788 in order to gain the submission of the Muslim warlords. One episode in 'Abd al-Rahman's campaigns made its way into the literature of the Franks. In 777, Arab and Berber chieftains in the foothills of the Pyrenees asked Charlemagne for help in resisting the encroachments of the Umayyad ruler. The Frankish king, who was in the early stages of his own conquests, recognized an unexpected opportunity to limit the power of a rival and simultaneously to secure territory on his southwestern frontier. When his army arrived at Zaragoza (Saragossa) in 778, however, the city's ruler changed his mind and closed its gates to him. After an unsuccessful siege, Charlemagne was forced to withdraw through the western Pyrenees. At Roncesvalles, his rear guard, commanded by Roland, was attacked and massacred, inspiring the Frankish epic *The Song of Roland*. The actual identity of the attackers, whether Basques or Muslim Arabs or Berbers, has not been conclusively determined, but Muslims received the blame in the poem. 'Abd al-Rahman captured Zaragoza and Pamplona the following year.

The Umayyads reigned over Andalus from their capital of Cordoba, but they never managed to rule the region as a centralized state. Even after 'Abd al-Rahman II (822–852) introduced Abbasid-style administrative offices and practices in an effort to centralize control, Berber and Arab tribes remained powerful down to the end of the dynasty in 1031. The central government was dominant, but the tribes tested its strength through frequent revolts. The native Hispano–Romans, both Christians and new converts to Islam, also engaged in periodic revolts against the government. The new converts seem to have been rankled by the same irritant that had bothered new converts in Umayyad Damascus: the privileges of the Arab elite.

Andalus was ethnically and religiously the most diverse polity in western Europe during the period from the ninth to the thirteenth centuries. It embraced the majority Hispano–Roman Christian population, a large Jewish minority, and the Muslims, among whom were the Arabs, Berbers, and a growing number of Hispano–Romans. The Arabs and Berbers, as conquering and garrisoned soldiers, served in the army all over the country, but a difference emerged in the pattern of settlement of the "civilians" of the two groups. The Berbers scattered all over Andalus, but in the mountains that form the perimeter of the central plateau (the Meseta), they greatly outnumbered the Arabs and became identified as a troublesome mountain people. The Arabs, on the other hand, tended to settle in the fertile lowlands, prominent among which were the Ebro and Guadalquivir valleys and the Valencian coast. The Jews, as in Christian Europe, were found primarily in urban areas.

The Muslims had conquered a land whose agriculture was typical of the Mediterranean region: sheep herding in the mountains and winter crops of wheat and barley, olives, and grapes in the valleys. Vegetables were grown on small irrigated fields in the Ebro valley and in Valencia. The Muslim settlement had a profound effect on the agriculture of Andalus and, subsequently, of Europe. The Arabs found that the old Roman irrigation systems, which were used to pump water from rivers into fields, had fallen into disuse. They repaired them and introduced into Andalus the noria, or water wheel, and irrigation from wells. The result was both an increase in the area of cultivable land and the ability to grow crops during the hot, dry summer.

The impact of the Muslim invasion on the variety of crops grown in Andalus was even greater. Due to the enormous extent of the conquests by the Arab armies in the seventh and eighth centuries, a remarkable diffusion took place in edible plants. Arabs in Andalus brought in plants from Syria, Berbers introduced crops from North Africa, and both groups experimented with new crops from as far away as Iran and the Indian Ocean basin. As a result, Andalus was soon home to the date palm, sugar cane, oranges (the Valencian orange and the tangerine—named after Tangier, across the Strait of Gibraltar—attest to the popularity of the oranges grown in the western Mediterranean), lemons, grapefruit, apricots, almonds, artichokes, rice, saffron, sugar, eggplant, parsnip, and lemons. Cotton, the mulberry tree, and the silkworm also made their first appearance in the Iberian Peninsula at this time. Elaborate gardens patterned after the Persian style became commonplace, and in the literature of the day Andalus—particularly the rich agricultural province of Valencia—became a model for paradise. Because of the new crops and the improved irrigation systems, as many as four harvests per year were now possible, greatly increasing the productivity of the land and the density of the population.

The newly productive agriculture stimulated the economy of Andalus. Little commerce took place with the underdeveloped Christian areas to the north of the Pyrenees, but a lively trade developed between Andalus and the eastern Mediterranean, with both Byzantines and Abbasids overlooking political differences in order to benefit economically. The most important goods exported from the west were silk cloth, timber, agricultural products, and gold from west Africa. Toledan steel had been famous since Roman times; in the form of cutlery and swords, it was in high demand, as were Andalusi copper utensils. The Andalusian breed of horses became one of the most prized in European history. Although its origin is disputed, most equine specialists think that it was the result of local mares having been bred with the North African Barb horse, which was brought in during the eighth-century invasion.

As had been the case in southwestern Asia, the international economy stimulated urbanization. The cities of Andalus blossomed, in startling contrast to the absolute dearth of urban life in western Europe before the eleventh century. Toledo, the old Visigothic capital, continued to flourish, but was supplanted in importance by cities to the south and east. The heart of Andalus was the Guadalquivir valley, and Cordoba was the center of Umayyad power. 'Abd al-Rahman I had revived the city when he made it his capital, and he is responsible for having begun construction of the Great Mosque, now famous throughout the world for its architectural splendor. 'Abd al-Rahman II enhanced the cultural life of the city with his patronage of music, poetry, and religious works, and he authorized a major expansion of the mosque. 'Abd al-Rahman III (912–961) founded a new complex of palace and official buildings at Madinat al-Zahra, some four miles outside the city walls. A veritable palace city, its size can be gauged by the 4100 marble columns that lined it. During the tenth century the grandeur of Cordoba, with its libraries and creature comforts, awed Europeans and Muslims alike. It may well have had a population approaching 100,000, at a time when Paris and London were muddy villages. Seville, the second city in size and influence, may have been home to over 80,000 inhabitants by the eleventh century.[2]

A Third Caliphate in the Umma

The Umayyad dynasty in Andalus experienced the pinnacle of its power in the tenth century. The late ninth century, ironically, provided little hope for that possibility, as the administrative reforms of which 'Abd al-Rahman II was so proud did little more than provoke uprisings against the attempts to centralize power. As a result, in 912, 'Abd al-Rahman III inherited an amirate whose authority had shrunk to little more than the environs of Cordoba. By then, regional power was in the hands of many different strongmen, some of the most powerful of whom were local converts to Islam, or *muwallads*. 'Abd al-Rahman III was determined to enhance his power, and throughout his long reign he fought almost constantly. During the first half of his career, he concentrated on subduing the rebels in Andalus and challenging the Fatimids in the Maghrib; then, during the second half, he concentrated on the struggle with the Christian kingdoms to the north. By the last decade of his reign, several of the Christian kingdoms were forced to pay him an annual tribute.

In the year 929, he announced that he was not merely an amir, but rather was the true caliph of the Islamic world. He may have claimed the caliphate as a result of Fatimid activity. As we saw before, the Fatimids had seized power in Ifriqiya twenty years earlier and had immediately laid claim to the caliphate. Furthermore, the Fatimids expanded what had been the Aghlabid navy and soon dominated the western Mediterranean. The implicit Fatimid threat to Andalus from the sea was compounded in 922 with the Fatimid capture of Fez. Whereas previous Umayyads might have been restrained from claiming the caliphate for fear of appearing presumptuous, now

'Abd al-Rahman III could claim it as the true champion of Sunnism, in opposition to the Shi'ite Fatimids and the remote and weak Abbasids.

The declaration of the Umayyad caliphate in Andalus raises the intriguing question of how many Muslims were in the peninsula by the mid-tenth century. What proportion of the society, after all, would be affected by the new claim? Some historians think that rapid conversion to Islam took place in the country during the first half of the tenth century and that, by midcentury, a Muslim majority existed. According to this view, conversion continued to the end of the eleventh century, by which time eighty percent of the population was Muslim. Other historians assume that Christians always remained the majority.[3] The evidence is inconclusive for either position, but 'Abd al-Rahman's claim of caliphal status does suggest that Andalus had at least a large Muslim minority, whose numbers, wealth, and power made their cultural hegemony incontestable. Arabic was the lingua franca, both formally and informally; the manners and tastes of the Umayyad court were the arbiters of the social graces; and the transformation of the economy gave the Muslims great legitimacy and prestige.

It is worth noting in this regard that the substantial number of Jews in Andalus became Arabized, as most Jews throughout the Muslim world did. Little is known of them before the tenth century, but from the early tenth to the mid-twelfth centuries, Andalusi Jews experienced a revival of literature, science, and philosophy, and they wrote in Arabic, using Hebrew script. Many of them served as important court figures, the most famous being Hasday ibn Shaprut, the physician to 'Abd al-Rahman III. His diplomatic services and patronage of the arts made him an important figure. Prior to the twelfth century, Jews throughout the world could hardly hope to live under more favorable circumstances than in Andalus. A pogrom did take place in Granada in the eleventh century, but it was the exception that proved the rule: It was a reaction by the common people against the great influence that Jews exerted at the court.

The extent of Arabization among Christians is unclear. It was once thought that Arabized Christians—Mozarabs—were the most dynamic element within the Christian community. However, no Christian literature in Arabic has survived, in contrast to a large corpus of Latin literature that still exists. The evidence suggests that most Christians could speak Arabic, and in cities such as Toledo, used it exclusively. Moreover, it is clear that many of the Christians who fled as refugees to the north in order to live in Christian societies had Arab names. On the other hand, the frequent, small-scale riots of Christians in the cities of central and southern Andalus, and the absence in the Christian literature of references to cultural developments outside the Christian community itself, suggest a religious community that sealed itself off from Islamic influences. The term, Mozarab, appears to have been an epithet hurled at Arabized Christians by other Christians who considered them to have betrayed their heritage. The Mozarabs did not leave a cultural legacy, unlike the Arabized Jews.

At midcentury, the caliphate of Andalus was in an enviable position. Its two caliphal competitors were on the defensive. The Abbasid caliph had become a puppet first to his own Turkish guard, and then to the Daylami Buyids, and the Fatimid caliph was fighting for his life against the Berber revolt in North Africa. 'Abd al-Rahman III even contributed to the discomfiture of the Fatimid ruler by supplying several Berber chiefs with supplies and arms. His family's honor had been reclaimed with the establishment of a second Umayyad caliphate at the very time that the Abbasid usurpers had apparently faded into insignificance. His society was becoming Arabized and Islamized to such a degree that he could reasonably expect it to become the dominant region of the Muslim world within a matter of decades.

Economic Networks

The political and religious fragmentation of the ninth and tenth centuries contrasted sharply with developments in the economy of the Muslim world that were tying the regions together more closely than ever before in history. The Arab conquests of the seventh and eighth centuries had consolidated into one empire many previously hostile states and regions. Under the central administration of the Umayyads of Damascus, these far-flung regions enjoyed rapid communication and participation in a single huge market. The new garrison cities required food, building materials, and other everyday necessities that often had to be brought in from a considerable distance away. These demands stimulated migration, manufacturing, and commerce. Craftsmen, merchants, scholars, soldiers, and adventurers traveled to distant regions of the empire and encountered new foods, tools, implements, and styles of architecture and fashion. They brought home with them new tastes and demands, further stimulating trade. The vast area from the Indus to Andalus became a single economic unit, stimulating agricultural diversification, industrial production, international trade, and urban population growth. Despite the loss of central political control that took place after the overthrow of the Umayyads of Damascus, the economic and communication channels remained remarkably open.

A Single Economy

Agriculture formed the base of the economy almost everywhere. In most parts of the Muslim world, agriculture was dependent upon irrigation. In the Iranian areas, the dominant irrigation system had long been based on *qanats*, underground canals that might extend from the foothills of mountain ranges into the surrounding plains for as many as thirty miles (although the typical length was one to three miles). Along the Indus, Tigris, Euphrates, and Nile rivers, elaborate networks of basins, canals, and dikes had been in place for thousands of years, employing water wheels, the Archimedes screw, and other lifting devices to move water to where it was needed. As these areas were incorporated into a single economic system, the techniques and the crops that were grown as a result of their use became available to other, distant regions. The most striking illustration of the process was the adoption of the noria, or Egyptian water wheel, in Andalus, and the subsequent cultivation in that peninsula of citrus fruits, sugar cane, and other vegetables and fruits from Egypt and Iraq.

The cities depended on the surplus produced by local farmers so that their inhabitants, in turn, could produce manufactured goods. Like most advanced societies of the period, the Muslim world's primary manufactured product was textiles. Fars in southwestern Iran was probably the most important center of textile production, but others became famous, as well: Egyptian cottons and linens were in high demand, and Mosul and Damascus became immortalized in the fabrics known as muslin and damask, respectively. Damascus and Toledo were famous for their carbon steel, and customers sought out Toledan steel and Damascened sword blades.

Despite the excellent quality of the textile and metal industries, however, the glass industry may have achieved the highest level of artistic and technical sophistication. Glass was first manufactured in southwestern Asia in ancient times, and Muslims continued the tradition of innovation. Glassmakers in Baghdad developed spectacular new styles of relief cutting and decorated their products with the forms of running animals and plant scrolls. Glass makers in Egypt invented luster painting and gilding, in which gold leaf was applied to an object that was then fired to fix the glass.

The most noteworthy feature of the economy of the Muslim world was international trade. Commerce, of course, had taken place among the various regions of Eurasia and Africa for centuries. Rome had traded with Han China and with East Africa, and even the hostile Byzantines and Sasanians had traded with each other. But the fact that Muslims now ruled the huge area from the Indus to the Atlantic resulted in profound changes. Whereas Sasanian–Byzantine commerce had been largely an exchange of luxury goods, the same trade routes by the early Abbasid period carried an astounding variety of goods destined for mass consumption, including textiles, foodstuffs, and utensils. As a result, new crops and new craft techniques spread rapidly across the vast trading network, transforming diets and material culture.

Muslim merchants between the Nile and Amu Darya had regular contacts with Andalus and the Maghrib. In fact, the extent of the travels undertaken by merchants in this period is quite remarkable. Documents describe merchants from Khorasan who accompanied their goods to Andalus and Andalusi merchants who personally sold their goods in the Iranian highlands. Except in winter, ships made regular voyages between the eastern Mediterranean and the Maghrib, both individually and in convoys. Caravans made the route from Egypt to the Maghrib year-round. As a result, the eastern Mediterranean was in contact not only with North Africa and Andalus, but also with West Africa.

Overland Trade

International trade was conducted overland and by sea. Most of the world's long-distance trade before the advent of the railroad in the nineteenth century went by sea if possible, due to the much lower costs and shorter times offered by sea travel. In the Muslim world, however, overland caravans played a more important role than in many other developed societies. One reason for that was its geographical setting. North Africa sought the goods of West and Central Africa, from which it was separated by the Sahara, and the great land mass of southwestern Asia made it impossible to ship goods by water from, say, Syria to Khorasan. This motive for long-distance overland trade was matched by the means to accomplish it: the domestication of the camel in the first millennium B.C.E. Camels offered a rugged, low-maintenance, "off-road" means of transportation with a quarter-ton cargo capability and an "all-terrain" ability that carts and wagons simply could not match.

Just as irrigation systems were designed to compensate for the arid climate in most parts of the Muslim world, so international trade was valued most for filling the region's chronic need for timber and most metals. The purchase of timber and basic metals in the central Islamic lands was made possible by the abundant supplies of gold and silver that became a feature of the first three centuries of Muslim history. The Iranian plateau had ample supplies of silver, but the new Muslim regimes made special efforts to obtain control of trade routes with access to sources of gold. The main gold mines that supplied the Muslim world were in West Africa and were linked to the Muslim world by caravan routes across the Sahara. The trade with West Africa was immensely profitable, for the Muslims were able to exchange cheap products such as beads and metal pans for gold.

The Sahara is so large (the size of the United States), hot, and dry that it is easy to assume that it is a trackless waste. In fact, however, several caravan routes wound their way for a thousand miles through the desert, following water holes and funneling a lucrative trade in gold and slaves from the south. North African states had long competed for control of these routes. The most westerly route linked the gold mines of Ghana with Sijilmasa, which quickly became the largest North African market for gold and slaves. Tahart, Qayrawan, and Tripoli were other major distribution points for the trans-Saharan trade. The commodities arriving at these points might be destined for ships or for other caravans that followed well-established routes along the North African coast. (Qayrawan gets its name, in fact, from *qayrawan*, the Arabic word from which we derive *caravan*.)

From these and other caravan cities, Muslim merchants embarked upon trading ventures that might take them away from home for months, or even years, at a time. Other merchants sent agents to be permanent representatives in sub-Saharan towns. These merchants were emissaries of a flourishing urban civilization and received favored treatment at the hands of West African rulers. Their literacy in the Arabic language—the diplomatic and commercial language of North Africa—made them doubly valuable to the rulers, and they and their families increasingly served the royal courts as secretaries and interpreters. Because many of them were Ibadis in the early centuries of Islam, it is probable that the earliest converts in West Africa were also adherents of Ibadi Islam. By the tenth century, Muslim merchants and officials occupied separate quarters of several West African towns along the upper Niger River and the Senegal River, and several rulers of the area had become Muslim. Rarely did West African rulers attempt to impose Islam upon their subjects. On the contrary, almost all of them were sufficiently astute politically to make a point of displaying the rituals of the traditional religion at court while patronizing Muslim scholars and merchants. As a result, Islam had little impact on the countryside until several centuries later.

Because the large cities of the Muslim world were confident of obtaining regular supplies of gold, the gold dinar (derived from *dinarius*, the standard unit of Byzantine currency) became the standard unit of Muslim coinage, usually worth ten silver *dirhams* (a term derived from the Greek *drachma*). The high-quality gold and silver coins minted by Muslims meant that the cities of the region could obtain the goods they needed from anywhere in the known world. A particularly dramatic demonstration of the utility of the coins is seen in the caches of thousands of silver dirhams (struck in Samanid Bukhara) that have been discovered in northern Europe, attesting to the large volume of trade between the far north and the Muslim world. Russians and Scandinavians were too primitive to be able to use the scientific instruments, fine fabrics, paper, and ceramics that Muslims had to offer. Thus, when Muslims purchased timber, amber, honey, wax, furs, and white slaves from northern Europeans, they paid in gold and silver.

A Commercial City in the Mediterranean

The expanding networks of trade facilitated the flow both of goods and people. Scholars, merchants, and missionaries traveled extensively. During the tenth and eleventh centuries, several Muslim geographers became immortalized by virtue of their trenchant descriptions and analyses of what they saw during their long journeys. Ibn Hawqal (ca. 920–ca. 980), a native of northern Iraq, explored from Khorasan to Andalus. His Surat al-Ard is a particularly good source for comparing the means of production in both agriculture and manufacturing across the Muslim world. In the excerpt that follows, he describes the market layout in Palermo, Sicily, which served as a conduit of goods between Europe and North Africa. He admired the landscape and architecture of Sicily, but he was quite critical of its inhabitants, whose character he believed to suffer from overconsumption of onions!

Among the countries in the hands of the Muslims, Sicily, by virtue of its fine situation, may be put in the same class as [Andalus]. It is an island in the form of an isosceles triangle, with its apex to the west. Its length is seven days' journey; its width, four... Sicily consists mainly of mountains, castles, and fortresses. Most of its soil is inhabited and cultivated. The only famous city is Palermo, the capital..., which is on the seashore. It consists of five quarters, adjoining and not separated by any distance but with their boundaries clearly marked.

... Palermo is surrounded by a huge stone wall, high and strong. It is inhabited by merchants. There is a great cathedral mosque, which was built as a Christian church shortly before the Conquest.... Facing Palermo there is a town called Khalisa, with a stone wall inferior to that of Palermo. Here live the Sultan and his entourage. There are two public baths but neither markets nor inns. There is a small cathedral mosque, the Sultan's garrison, a naval arsenal, and the administrative offices. It has four gates in the north, south, and west, but in the east there is the sea and a wall without a gate.... The quarter known as the Quarter of the Slavs is bigger and more populous than the two cities I have mentioned. In it is the seaport. There are springs which flow between this place and [Palermo], and the water serves as a boundary between them.

There is a quarter known by the name of the mosque of Ibn Saqlab. It is also big but has no streams, and its inhabitants drink from wells. By its edge flows the river called Wadi 'Abbas, a broad and swift stream on which they have many mills, but their gardens and orchards do not make use of it.

The New Quarter is large and adjoins the quarter of the mosque. There is no division or demarcation between them, and both are unwalled, as is also the Quarter of the Slavs. Most of the markets are between the mosque of Ibn Saqlab and the New Quarter. They are as follows: the olive oil sellers in their entirety; the millers, the money changers, the apothecaries, the smiths, the sword cutlers [polishers?], the flour markets, the brocade makers, the fishmongers, the spice merchants,... the greengrocers, the fruiterers, the sellers of aromatic plants, the jar merchants, the bakers, the rope makers, a group of perfumers, the butchers, the shoemakers, the tanners, the carpenters, and the potters. The wood merchants are outside the city. In Palermo proper there are groups of butchers, jar merchants, and shoemakers. The butchers have nearly 200 shops for the sale of meat, and there are a few of them inside the city at the beginning of the main road. Near them are the cotton merchants, the ginners, and the cobblers. There also is another useful market in the city.

SOURCE: *Islam from the Prophet Muhammad to the Capture of Constantinople. II: Religion and Society.* Edited and translated by Bernard Lewis. New York: Walker and Company, 1974, 87–89.

The upper two images are the obverse and reverse of a Sasanian-style coin that the Umayyads continued to strike for several decades. After the Arabization and Islamization policies of 'Abd al-Malik, coins of any Muslim state resembled the coin shown in the lower two images. It contains no human representation, and its Arabic inscriptions are from the Qur'an.

In the east, the famous Silk Road through Central Asia was an important link between Iran and China. Actually, there was no single Silk Road, but several roughly parallel routes that had been conduits of commerce and ideas since 500 B.C.E. or earlier. Under the Han dynasty (206 B.C.E.–220 C.E.), the links between Iran and China became a matter of Chinese state policy, and trade became regular and important. Transoxiana became the central link in a great network of roads that connected the Mediterranean with Ch'ang-an, the capital of several Chinese dynasties, including those of the Han and T'ang (618–907). Merchants from the Syrian coast followed a path through Rayy to Bukhara and Samarqand; merchants from the Aegean Sea would cross Anatolia and then arrive at the Transoxiana oases either by crossing the Caspian Sea by ship or by following a road to Rayy.

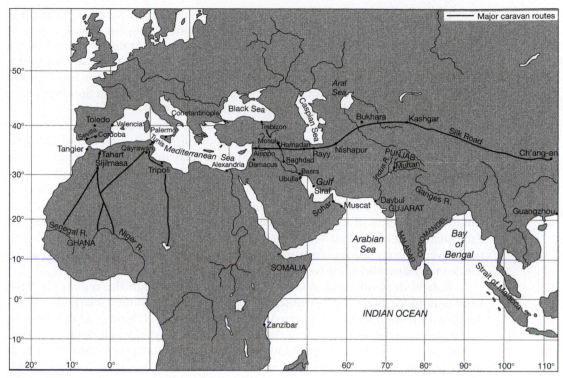

MAP 4.2 The Tenth-century Muslim Trading Zone

From Samarqand, the routes to China were all daunting. The road due east scaled formidable mountain ranges so high they caused altitude sickness; the more indirect route to the north was across steppe land, and thus less exhausting, but was often contested by competing tribes or states, making the journey risky at best. Thus, the Silk Roads encouraged a thriving trade in luxury goods and provided a route for the introduction of Chinese technologies and techniques into the Muslim world that craftsmen readily adopted.

Maritime Commerce

Overland trade, however, was a long and dangerous undertaking, even with camels. The bulk of the trade between the Muslim world on the one hand, and India and China on the other, took place by sea, utilizing the Indian Ocean. Until the beginning of the tenth century, the center of Muslim commerce in the Indian Ocean was the Persian Gulf. The metropolis of Baghdad served as an enormous siphon that attracted staples and luxuries of every kind. Even as it imported timber and metals overland from the north and west, it served as a magnet for luxuries coming by sea. Large ships bearing goods from China and South Asia tied up at the wharves of Ubulla, the port for Basra, where stevedores transferred their cargoes to river boats bound for Baghdad. There the boats unloaded their cargoes from all around the Indian Ocean basin: porcelain, silk, spices, precious stones, perfumes, incense and scented wood, and slaves.

Other ports in the Gulf—Siraf on the Iranian coast, and Sohar and Muscat in Oman—also became flourishing entrepots of world trade during this time. Goods from China were highly valued, and even in the pre-Islamic era Arabs had established a colony in Canton (Guangzhou) in order to have direct access to Chinese silks, porcelain, lacquerware, and other goods. The Muslim community in Canton was expelled in 879 by the T'ang dynasty, and many of the merchants resettled in Southeast Asia, where they reestablished trading connections with the Gulf.

Direct trade with China, however, was rare. The long distances and the need to synchronize one's schedule with the monsoons meant that a round trip to China required a year and a half. As a result, the Muslim carrying trade was focused on the western half of the Indian Ocean basin. Merchants who wished to trade with the residents of East Africa could send vessels on winter's northerly monsoon to reach most of the east coast of Africa, and the southeasterly monsoon brought them back in summer. As a result of this trade, Muslim communities began to appear along the Ethiopian coast of the Red Sea in the eighth and ninth centuries. By the tenth century, several communities containing Muslim Arab traders were established along the Somali coast, and a few could be found as far south as Zanzibar.

East of the Gulf, Sind was an important stop. Although the region had long been famous for its agricultural potential, pre-Islamic Arabs valued it largely as a conduit for trade from India. Conquered by the Muslims in 711, Sind gradually became autonomous in the second half of the ninth century. Daybul was a flourishing port of call for merchants crossing the Indian Ocean, and it was open to influences from many regions. Four hundred miles up the Indus River, Multan became the major Muslim city in the Punjab (the region that is defined by the five large tributaries of the Indus). Sind was predominantly Buddhist at the time of the Arab conquest, although Hindus were in the process of persecuting them and forcing them out of the region. Hinduism itself, only just beginning to be established, did not weather the invasion well, and Islam gradually replaced it along the length of the Indus. Multan became notorious in the Sunni imagination when it fell to Fatimid-supported Isma'ilis in 977. Despite the efforts of certain Sunni rulers to crush the Isma'ilis, they maintained a significant presence in Sind for over two centuries and expanded into Gujarat.

Muslims also established trading communities on India's Malabar Coast, south of Gujarat. Jews and Nestorian Christians, along with Arabs from Yemen, had established settlements there in pre-Islamic times, and the Arabs in the area rapidly Islamized after 650. Malabar had traditionally supplied spices and luxury goods to the Mediterranean region, and its merchant community served as middlemen for the commerce of the Indian Ocean. The coastal plain is separated from the rest of India by the Western Ghats, a steep escarpment that extends parallel to the Arabian Sea for over seven hundred miles, insulating the coast from political and cultural developments inland. As a result, Malabar's contacts with the rest of the world were by sea, and hence with Southeast Asia, Arabia, and East Africa even more than with the rest of India. This orientation allowed the Muslims of the region to develop a quite different identity from those who subsequently settled the interior.

In contrast to the thriving trade of the Indian Ocean basin, the maritime commerce of the Mediterranean was in a depressed state for several centuries until the end of the ninth century. Although merchants from Muslim territories (both Muslims and Jews) and from the Byzantine Empire continued to trade throughout the intermittent warfare that erupted between the two sides, most of their commerce was conducted overland with the Black Sea entrepot of Trebizon rather than through Mediterranean seaports. Maritime commerce in the eastern Mediterranean was jeopardized by the fact that the Byzantine navy conducted naval attacks on Muslim ports, and even great ports such as Alexandria and Antioch gradually lost population to interior cities located on caravan routes. In the western Mediterranean, the collapse of the Roman economy and administration in western Europe after the fourth century had resulted in an impoverished society that could not afford to import many goods. Trade thus declined in that area. Contacts even between Andalus and western Europe were few. The merchants of Andalus were much more interested in trade with the wealthier Byzantines and with Muslims to the east.

The late ninth century witnessed an important shift in the movement of Indian Ocean trade into southwestern Asia, with important consequences for Mediterranean trade. The mamluk revolt in Samarra, coupled with the Zanj revolt, contributed to political disruption and economic instability in the central lands of the Muslim world. As Baghdad declined, the Red Sea began to supplant the Gulf as the main trade route from India to the Mediterranean. In the tenth century, Egypt began to enjoy a prosperity that it had not experienced for hundreds of years, making it all the more attractive to the Fatimids of Ifriqiya. Merchants from several European cities, primarily Italian, began establishing regular contacts with Muslim ports in the eastern Mediterranean. The new European demand for Asian goods stimulated the economies of ports such as Alexandria and Antioch, setting the stage for a vibrant international trade in the eleventh and twelfth centuries.

Conclusion

The first half of the tenth century witnessed a development that must have distressed many Muslims. In 910, the Fatimids announced the establishment of a second caliphate in the Muslim world. They claimed that theirs was not merely a second caliphate, but the only legitimate one. Less than two decades later, however, in 929, the Umayyad dynasty in Andalus also claimed the caliphate. Sixteen years after that, the Buyids became the real power behind the Abbasid caliphate, raising the question of what function the caliph played in society. Prior to the tenth century, the caliphate had been a symbol of Muslim unity, but now it represented differences within the Umma. More important, the competing claims of three caliphs had to have raised religious anxieties for at least some believers. While more cynical or detached individuals could dismiss the fact of three caliphs as political posturing, at least some Muslims, who had been taught that the caliph represented God's authority on earth, had to wonder if they were recognizing God's actual representative. The situation was not unlike the schism that developed within the papacy in the fourteenth and fifteenth centuries, when two, and then three, popes challenged each other, causing great anxiety among the Christians of western Europe.

But the growing religious and regional identities within the Umma were transcended by a sophisticated and remarkably efficient economic network that tied all the regions together. Caravans and ships brought goods from locations half a world away. Not only were manufactured goods exchanged in this manner, but crops as well, resulting in a foreshadowing of the so-called Columbian exchange six hundred years later. Just as the voyages of Columbus opened up an era in which the flora and fauna of the western and eastern hemispheres would be exchanged, so was the ecology of the Mediterranean transformed by Muslim commerce.

In addition, as more and more Arab and Iranian merchants converted to Islam, the port cities and desert oases to which they moved or in which they established agencies became outposts of Islamic civilization. A Muslim diaspora began to extend around the Indian Ocean basin and in China. A similar development took place across the "sea" of the Sahara, as the "ships" of caravans brought Muslims into the oases of the desert and the cities of the sub-Saharan savannah, introducing the religion to those areas for the first time. These communities became centers of Islamic culture, and would eventually radiate monotheism and Islamic law into their hinterlands.

NOTES

1. Population estimates for Baghdad vary widely, with some estimates ranging up to one million. The most carefully reasoned seems to be Jacob Lassner's study, *The Topography of Baghdad in the Early Middle Ages*. Detroit: Wayne State University Press, 1970, p. 160. For the land area comparison with Constantinople, see the same source, p. 158.

2. Tenth-century Cordoba is frequently said to have had a population of half a million people, but Thomas Glick makes a good case for a considerably smaller population of 100,000. The city would still have dwarfed any urban center in contemporary western Europe, and its wealth and hygiene would have stood in even sharper contrast. See Thomas F. Glick, *Islamic and Christian Spain in the Early Middle Ages* (Princeton, New Jersey: Princeton University Press, 1979), p. 113. By contrast, Andrew M. Watson, a specialist in medieval agriculture, says that the city attained a population of one million. [See "A Medieval Green Revolution: New Crops and Farming Techniques in the Early Islamic World," in *The Islamic Middle East, 700–1900: Studies in Economic and Social History*, A. L. Udovitch, ed. (Princeton, New Jersey: The Darwin Press, Inc., 1981), p. 57, n. 45.]

3. See Glick, *Islamic and Christian Spain*, pp. 33–35, and Roger Collins, *The Arab Conquest of Spain, 710–797* (Oxford, U.K.: Basil Blackwell, 1989), p. 217, for contrasting evaluations.

FURTHER READING

General

Kennedy, Hugh. *The Prophet and the Age of the Caliphates*. London and New York: Longman, 1986.

The Abbasid Caliphate

al-Hibri, Tayeb. *Reinterpreting Islamic Historiography: Harun al-Rashid and the Narrative of the 'Abbasid Caliphate*. Cambridge, U.K.: Cambridge University Press, 1999.

Lassner, Jacob. *The Shaping of Abbasid Rule*. Princeton, New Jersey: Princeton University Press, 1980.

Lassner, Jacob. *The Topography of Baghdad in the Early Middle Ages*. Detroit: Wayne State University Press, 1970.

Sourdel, Dominique. "The Abbasid Caliphate." In P. M. Holt, Ann K. S. Lambton, and Bernard Lewis, eds., *Cambridge History of Islam*, vol. I. Cambridge, U.K.: Cambridge University Press, 1970.

The Fatimid Caliphate

Brett, Michael. *The Rise of the Fatimids: the World of the Mediterranean and the Middle East in the Fourth Century of the Hijrah, Tenth Century C.E.* Leiden, Boston: Brill, 2001.

Daftary, Farhad. *The Ismailis: Their History and Doctrines.* Cambridge, U.K.: Cambridge University Press, 1990.

Halm, Heinz. *Empire of the Mahdi: The Rise of the Fatimids.* Leiden: E. J. Brill, 1997.

Madelung, Wilferd and Paul Walker. *Advent of the Fatimids: A Contemporary Witness.* London and New York: I. B. Taurus, 2000.

The Umayyad Caliphate of Cordoba

Collins, Roger. *The Arab Conquest of Spain, 710–797.* Oxford: Basil Blackwell, 1989.

Glick, Thomas F. *Islamic and Christian Spain in the Early Middle Ages.* Princeton, New Jersey: Princeton University Press, 1979.

Jayyusi, Salma Khadra, ed. *The Legacy of Muslim Spain.* Leiden, New York, Koln: E. J. Brill, 1992.

Economic Networks

Ashtor, E. *A Social and Economic History of the Near East in the Middle Ages.* Berkeley, California: University of California Press, 1976.

Bulliet, Richard. *The Camel and the Wheel.* Cambridge, Massachussetts: Harvard U Press, 1975.

Goitein, S.D. *A Mediterranean Society,* 5 vols. Berkeley, California: University of California Press, 1967–88.

Hourani, George F. *Arab Seafaring in the Indian Ocean in Ancient and Early Medieval Times.* Revised and expanded by John Carswell. Princeton, New Jersey: Princeton University Press, 1995.

McNeill, William H. "The Eccentricity of Wheels, or Eurasian Transportation in Historical Perspective," in *American Historical Review,* 92, 5, December, 1987, 1111–1126.

Risso, Patricia. *Merchants & Faith: Muslim Commerce and Culture in the Indian Ocean.* Boulder, Colorado: Westview Press, 1995.

Watson, Andrew. *Agricultural Innovation in the Early Islamic World: The Diffusion of Crops and Farming Techniques, 700–1100.* Cambridge, U.K.: Cambridge University Press, 1983.

CHAPTER 5

Synthesis and Creativity

When the Arabs began their conquests in the 630s, their practice of Islam was rudimentary and simple. They possessed a body of scriptures, a few simple rituals, and the memory of specific teachings and acts of the Prophet that served as guides for behavior. In the seventh century, however, there had yet to emerge a class of Muslim religious specialists whose careers were devoted to the elaboration of the deeper meaning of the principles of the faith and to the production of devotional literature, guidelines for ethical living, and theology. The vast majority of Arab Muslims, in fact, were a handful of years—or even months—removed from polytheism.

The development of Islam as a major institutional religion began during the eighth century. After decades of expansion into new territories, it was becoming clear to some pious believers that guidelines for doctrine and correct behavior needed to be drawn up in order to stop the proliferation of quarreling sects and to obtain a consensus regarding doctrine, ritual, and ethics. Simultaneously, the Arabs now found themselves in the midst of millions of adherents of other major religions, whose institutions, doctrines, and rituals they found to be commendable or repugnant in varying degrees. They encountered bureaucratic organizations, civil and religious laws, social structures, cuisine, and types of entertainment that were entirely new to them. Which of these were compatible with the faith that the Prophet had brought to his people? What distinguished his community from those of Christians, Jews, and Zoroastrians, many of whose adherents were engaging in a polemical attack on the doctrines and rituals of Islam? Just as the internal dynamics of the community began the process of articulating the implications of the faith, so was there a need to mark off the boundaries between it and the other monotheistic religions. By the middle of the tenth century, the foundations had been laid for Islamic law and devotional life, and subsequent discussions would refer back to this period as the touchstone for debate.

During this period, it became commonplace to refer to those areas under the control of Muslims as the *dar al-islam*, or the House of Islam. Obviously, this region did not have a predominantly Muslim population in the early centuries, but it was one in which Islamic values were upheld and protected. The area of the world not under

Muslim control was referred to as the *dar al-harb* (the House of War) or the *dar al-kufr* (the House of Unbelief). It was the House of War precisely because the Qur'an enjoins believers to fight against *kufr*, or unbelief.

The Origins of Islamic Law

The history of Christianity is replete with doctrinal disputes, and as a result, theology became the chief intellectual discipline of that religious tradition. Islam, by contrast, is more similar to Judaism in that correct behavior takes precedence over doctrine, and law has been the major intellectual pursuit within these two religions. In the absence of the Prophet, Muslims sought guidance regarding how to live in accordance with God's will. Shi'ites looked to their Imams for that guidance. Sunnis found it in the Shari'a, or Islamic law.

Assimilation and Adaptation

During the earliest period of Islamic history, the Prophet served as the source of correct doctrine, the guide to the correct way to perform religious rituals, the judge for criminal acts, and the adjudicator of civil disputes. When he died, Muslims were forced to make radical adjustments in their lives. Not only did they lose their source of divine revelation, but they soon lost the intimate and compact community of which Medina and Mecca were the largest population centers. The caliph was now the ultimate authority on religious and civil matters within the community, but his capacity for remaining the central figure in this regard was limited. He was expected to make judgments within the framework established by the Qur'an, but it has only some eighty verses that deal with matters that can properly be called legal. In addition, the Ridda wars and the rapid conquests of Syria, Egypt, and Iraq greatly expanded the area under the caliph's jurisdiction. As a consequence, he became an increasingly remote figure to most Muslims, many of whom were moving to the newly conquered areas as soldiers, administrators, merchants, or other specialists. It was unavoidable that many important decisions regarding ritual behavior, property rights, commercial issues, criminal acts, and other pressing issues would be decided without recourse to the caliph.

An organized Muslim judiciary became established only after Mu'awiya seized the caliphate in 661. Under the Umayyads, each garrison city was staffed with an agent to implement the body of administrative and fiscal regulations and laws that the rapidly growing military empire needed in order to function. This agent or judge, called a *qadi*, had wide discretionary powers. Whenever possible, qadis would rule within the principles of the Qur'an, but often they had no choice but to utilize local legal traditions in order to make a ruling. In the absence of a comprehensive Islamic legal system, qadis relied on Sasanian, Byzantine, Jewish, and Orthodox canon law for many of their decisions. As a result, the legal administrative apparatus in different areas of the empire began revealing significant differences.

By the end of the seventh century, pious scholars began debating among themselves whether Umayyad legal practice adequately reflected the ethical values of the Qur'an. The motives of some may have included hostility towards the Umayyads, but in general these scholars were acting on the profound conviction that each human has a responsibility to obey the commands of God. Not only should a believer desist from evil acts and be sure to do the good acts himself, but he should also "command the right and forbid the wrong," an injunction that implied a universal responsibility for maintaining the public order. During the eighth century, several of the influential urban areas had clusters of scholars (sing. *'alim*, pl. *'ulama'*; hereafter *ulama*, the most common English transliteration) who sought to Islamize the law by using Qur'anic principles as the standard by which to evaluate the adequacy of Umayyad legal practices.

The unusual features of this movement of "legal review" were that it was conducted by pious scholars who held no positions of political authority and that it was not officially sanctioned by the Umayyad government. The ulama of Damascus, Kufa, Basra, Medina, and Mecca took the lead in this nascent jurisprudence. It soon became clear that, despite the intention of the scholars to use Qur'anic principles, differences began to develop among them. Syria, Iraq, and the Hijaz naturally had important differences in their social environments, and these were reflected in the legal thought that emerged from the cities within each region. For nearly a century, Muslims had adopted many local customs in each city, and even the pious naturally assumed that their local practice was identical with that of the first Muslim generation in Medina. The Qur'an, like any other revealed scripture, provides specific guidance on only a few of the issues that individuals in a complex society face. Unless a local custom conflicted with a Qur'anic directive or ethical principle, it was assumed to be legitimate. The religious scholars felt free to exercise their discretion when ruling on cases that presented original problems.

Groping Toward an Islamic Jurisprudence

With the advent of the Abbasids, the central government took an active role in encouraging the development of a legal system based explicitly upon Islamic values. The new regime hoped to gain legitimacy by supporting the demands for an Islamic law, and it saw that the empire's legal system would benefit from uniformity in the determination and application of law. The office of the qadi was encouraged to rely on the principles being articulated by the ulama. The new impetus for the development of an Islamic law led to the emergence of a generation of reformers who were critical of the approach of their elders. Whereas the first generation of jurists tended to accept current legal practice unless it violated some Qur'anic principle, the younger generation, working during the last third of the eighth century, insisted that the Qur'an and the example of the Prophet be the norms from which all jurisprudence be based. They viewed local consensus and the analogical reasoning of individual scholars, even if based on religious precedent, with suspicion. The earlier jurists had sought guidance from the *sunna* (meaning *way, custom,* or *practice*) of the first generation of Muslims, assuming that it ultimately derived from the example of the Prophet; now their successors explicitly sought only the Prophet's words and deeds. Those who sought guidance from the Sunna of the Prophet called themselves *ahl al-sunna wa al-jama'a,* or the People of the (Prophet's) Sunna and of the Community. They collected reports or traditions (sing. *hadith;* the singular form is usually used in transliterations as a collective noun) of the Prophet's declarations and his behavior in certain circumstances and urged that Hadith and the Qur'an be the sole standards for legal practice. They had a powerful argument on their side, for if the law were not in fact derived directly from the Prophet's words and example, what guarantee would the believer have that it was God's will?

The new emphasis on the Sunna of the Prophet resulted in great efforts being expended to discover it, and during the eighth and ninth centuries C.E., an enormous number of Hadith appeared. Several scholars organized the traditions into collections, the most famous and authoritative being those of al-Bukhari (d. 870) and Muslim (d. 875). The rapid appearance of thousands of Hadith raised suspicions that many were being fabricated, particularly when they attributed to the Prophet ideas or the use of technology that were anachronistic. Al-Bukhari, Muslim, and the other great collectors made efforts to assess the traditions by examining their internal evidence and by weighing the integrity of the scholars who were said to have passed them from one generation to another. According to legend, al-Bukhari examined 600,000 such traditions before deciding on the 2700 that he put into his collection. Although many Western scholars are skeptical that a majority of the traditions are authentic, most Muslims consider them to be as authoritative as the Qur'an.

The new initiative to codify God's will, however, only multiplied the differences among the various groups of ulama. According to tradition, literally hundreds of "schools" (sing. *madhhab*) of law emerged across the empire during the ninth century. These schools were not colleges, but rather circles of scholars who followed the methods determined by influential local ulama for ascertaining the principles of law. In most of the madhhabs that had a life span of several generations or more, the founding scholar's teachings were modified and elaborated considerably, perhaps even beyond recognition, but each one represented a cohesive social unit as well as an ideological perspective. The madhhabs differed from each other due to the wide variety of Hadith sources, differences in techniques of Qur'anic interpretation, variations in local customs and values, and differences over the scope that individual reasoning should be allowed in making legal judgments. The cleavage among the schools reached its height in the ninth century, when some Muslim scholars who were influenced by Greek philosophy asserted that the human mind is capable of determining which acts are good and which are bad, independent of revelation. The caliph al-Ma'mun (813–833) patronized this group, known as the Mu'tazilites, and he ordered all qadis and other government officials to adhere to their theories. Because the Mu'tazilite position seemed to threaten the primacy of the Qur'an, a scholar named Ahmad ibn Hanbal (d. 857) refused to submit to the ruling, even though he was persecuted as a result. His followers, the Hanbalis, insisted that acts were good or bad because God had decreed them so and that it was impious to reason why or whether they were so. Scholars should rely only upon the Qur'an and the Sunna of the Prophet.

The Development of the Shari'a

The numerous schools of religious law caused confusion and consternation among Muslims. How was one to know which most closely reflected God's will? By the middle of the tenth century, a consensus had developed on the broad outlines of a method for determining religious law. As a result, the number of schools rapidly declined and the Shari'a, or Islamic law, became the defining element of Muslim identity.

Hadith: Guides to Living

The thousands of Hadith provide guidance for a remarkably wide range of behavior. The following selections are excerpts from one of the two major collections of Hadith, the Sahih Muslim. *The isnad, or chain of transmitters, has been removed from each. Note how each Hadith cites a saying or act of the Prophet as a model for one's own life.*

'A'isha reported, The Messenger of Allah (may peace be upon him) said: Ten are the acts according to Fitra (the ritual acts that enable human nature to reach its potential): clipping the moustache, letting the beard grow, using the tooth-stick, snuffing up water in the nose, cutting the nails, washing the finger joints, plucking the hair under the armpits, shaving the pubes, and cleaning one's private parts with water. The narrator said: I have forgotten the tenth, but it may have been rinsing the mouth. (I, 192–193)

Salman reported that it was said to him, Your Apostle (may peace be upon him) teaches you about everything, even about excrement. He replied: Yes, he has forbidden us to face the Qibla at the time of excretion or urination, or cleansing with the right hand or with less than three pebbles, or with dung or bone. (I, 193)

Jabir said: Allah's Messenger (may peace be upon him) forbade that the graves should be plastered, or they be used as sitting places (for the people), or a building should be built over them. (II, 553)

Jabir b. 'Abdullah reported Allah's Messenger (may peace be upon him) as saying: Do not walk in one sandal and do not wrap the lower garment round your knees and do not eat with your left hand and do not wrap yourself completely leaving no room for the arms (to draw out) and do not place one of your feet upon the other while lying on your back. (III, 1388)

Buraida reported on the authority of his father that Allah's Apostle (may peace be upon him) said: He who played chess is like one who dyed his hand with the flesh and blood of swine. (IV, 1469)

Abu Huraira reported Allah's Messenger (may peace be upon him) as saying: Do you know who is poor? They (the Companions of the Holy Prophet) said: A poor man amongst us is one who had neither dirham with him nor wealth. He (the Holy Prophet) said: The poor of my Umma would be he who would come on the Day of Resurrection with prayers and fasts and Zakat but . . . since he hurled abuses upon others, brought calumny against others and unlawfully consumed the wealth of others and shed the blood of others and beat others, . . . his virtues would be credited to the account of one (who suffered at his hand). And if his good deeds fall short to clear the account, then his sins would be entered in (his account) and he would be thrown in the Hell-Fire. (IV, 1645)

SOURCE: Imam Muslim, *Sahih Muslim*, tr. 'Abdul Hamid Siddiqi. 4 vols. Rev. ed. New Delhi: Kitab Bhavan, 2000.

The Synthesis of al-Shafiʻi

Although the rationalists lost their official patronage by mid-century, they remained active in legal and philosophical circles for centuries. By the early tenth century, however, a compromise between the rationalist Muʻtazilite position and the Sunna-based Hanbali position began to gain acceptance in many of the law schools. The compromise was based on the work of a scholar, Muhammad ibn Idris al-Shafiʻi, who had died a century earlier, in 820. On the one hand, he had argued that the Qur'an and

Sunna of the Prophet were the sole material sources of the law, a position that sounded much like that of Ibn Hanbal. On the other hand, al-Shafi'i squarely confronted the reality that questions frequently arise in daily life that are not addressed in these sources, and hence require the use of reason. Unlike the rationalists, he did not allow the free exercise of reason or opinion (*ra'y*), but he did allow reasoning by analogy: If a case could be resolved on the basis of an analogy with the ethical principles expressed in the Qur'an, Hadith, or previous legal cases, the decision was valid. When a legal decision became accepted by the consensus of scholars across the Dar al-Islam, it could reasonably be considered to reflect God's will.

Thus, al-Shafi'i's theory actually recognized four sources of law: the two primary sources of the Qur'an and Hadith and the two derivative sources of analogy and consensus. This new model for jurisprudence was ignored for many decades after his death in 820, but rapidly gained acceptance in the early tenth century. Soon, any jurist seeking a solution to a legal problem was expected to consult the Qur'an and the Hadith first. If the issue was not addressed directly in those sources, he was to employ an analogy with cases that had been resolved. The result was a tentative conclusion that would be substantiated or rejected by the rulings of other jurists. In the event that it was corroborated by other rulings, it was said to have been confirmed by the consensus of the other ulama.

The growing uniformity within jurisprudence led to a general sense that God's will was being ascertained, and the rules that were developed for living the upright life were called the *shari'a*. The term *shari'a* had been used up to that time to denote the beaten path to a watering hole in the desert. If one did not know the path that the camels had taken repeatedly, death could result. Likewise, knowing and practicing God's will as revealed through the disciplined decisions of the ulama brought life to whoever submitted to it.

Consolidation of the Madhhabs

The Shari'a gradually became an essential element of Muslim life. Then as now, highly trained professionals were less likely to choose to live in rural areas than in cities, and it was thus much harder for peasants and pastoralists to gain access to educated qadis. Nevertheless, everyone was expected to choose which madhhab he would follow. Over the years, the growing uniformity of legal method had the effect of consolidating many madhhabs and reducing the number from which to choose. By the end of the thirteenth century, only a few schools were left. In some large cities, a choice still existed even as the number of schools declined, for one could find qadis from several madhhabs. For most people, however, the school they followed was in effect chosen for them because of the distinctly regional coloration that the madhhabs possessed.

Out of the numerous schools that emerged during the early period, four continued into the modern era to represent the majority of Muslims. The tradition from Kufa was named after one of Ja'far al-Sadiq's students, Abu Hanifa (d. 767), and was called the Hanafi school. It dominated in Iraq and Syria, and later spread to Anatolia, Central Asia, and India. The school in Medina was named after one of its greatest early scholars, Malik ibn Anas (d. 796), and is known as the Maliki school. It became paramount in North Africa and the Iberian Peninsula, and it spread into West Africa. The Shafi'i school, claiming descent from the original disciples of al-Shafiʻi, prevailed in Egypt, Yemen, East Africa, certain coastal regions of India, and in Southeast Asia. The Hanbali ma<u>dhh</u>ab derives its name from Ibn Hanbal, who was known for his theological disputes with the Muʻtazilites. Over the years after his death, however, his followers developed a ma<u>dhh</u>ab that argued for the primacy of the Qur'an and Hadith literally understood. (Ibn Hanbal is said never to have eaten watermelon, on the grounds that he found no precedent in the example of the Prophet.)

The Hanbalis were so hostile to the use of personal opinion that they placed sharp limits on the use of analogy. Regarded as the most conservative and traditional of the four schools, the Hanbalis nevertheless turned out to be the least bound by tradition. Because they did not feel constrained by the consensus of other scholars, in later centuries they were the most active in making new interpretations of the law to fit changing circumstances. The Hanbali ma<u>dhh</u>ab was influential in Baghdad and Syria until the fourteenth century. It was revived in the Arabian peninsula in the eighteenth century and remains dominant in Saudi Arabia today. It is also popular among reformist movements all across the Muslim world, whose members regard it to be the most congenial for allowing new interpretations.

The Shiʻites and Kharijites developed their own distinctive ma<u>dhh</u>abs, although they share much in common with the four discussed above. As we have seen, true sectarian identity took centuries to crystallize, with the result that the major developments in Islamic law took place in an atmosphere in which Muslims of all inclinations were in communication with each other. The Shiʻites maintained three major ma<u>dhh</u>abs, the most influential of which was attributed to Jaʻfar al-Sadiq, and is thus known as the Jaʻfari ma<u>dhh</u>ab. All Muslims agreed that the Qur'an and Hadith are the primary sources of the law, although the collections of Hadith used by the Ismaʻili and Twelver schools contain traditions that differ in part from the earlier collections due to an emphasis on the Alid tradition. Likewise, when Shiʻites began developing their own legal methods, they placed less emphasis on analogy and consensus than did the earlier ma<u>dhh</u>abs, since the decisions of the Imam had authoritative weight.

The Impact of the Shariʻa

By the ninth century, the Shariʻa was the authorized basis for qadis to make their judgments in court. The Shariʻa, however, was not a codification of laws to which a qadi could refer when confronting a case. It was largely a set of norms regarding how to live the godly life, and included a remarkably broad range of topics from the scholars who reflected on the duties that humans owed their Creator. In it one could find details on the proper way to consummate a marriage or to defecate, as well as regulations regarding contracts, theft, and inheritance. Despite the intent of its architects to provide guidelines for all of life, its primary utility was for issues relating to religious rituals, marriage, divorce, inheritance, debts, and partnerships.

Among the most notable legacies of the Shariʻa have been norms regarding the roles and status of women. Like other topics treated by the jurists, the decisions relating to women arose out of an interplay among Qur'anic injunctions, the Hadith, and deeply rooted customs of a given region regarding women's roles. The Qur'an itself insists on the essential equality of women and men (3:195, 33:35, 4:124), but it also suggests that God views men to be "more equal" in rights than women (4:34). Because the Qur'an became the chief source of the Shari'a, the jurists followed that lead. In addition, however, a Mediterranean tradition of honor and shame, a centuries-long Greek tradition of keeping women out of public life, the misogynistic teachings of some of the Christian theologians, and a Sasanian culture in which women were second-class subjects were powerful forces in the Fertile Crescent. At the Abbasid court—which was influenced by both Byzantine and Sasanian norms—the women were already being secluded even as the Shari'a began to be delineated. The jurists of Islam worked within societies influenced by one or more of these factors as they interpreted the Qur'an and the Hadith.

According to the Shari'a, a woman was to have a male guardian—father, husband, brother, or uncle—and the marriage contract was technically between the bridegroom and the woman's guardian, not the bride. A father could give his daughter in marriage without her consent if she had not yet reached age of puberty. Once a young woman had attained puberty, she technically could not be married against her will, but if she was a virgin, consent could be given "by silence," a condition which was often exploited. A woman could marry only one man at a time, whereas a man could have up to four wives and as many slave concubines as he could afford. (The Hanbali school recognized the legitimacy of the marriage contract to stipulate that the husband could take no concubines or additional wives, but the other schools did not allow that provision.) The woman was entitled to a dowry and to maintenance (food, clothing, and lodging).

All of the law schools agreed that the husband could divorce his wife unilaterally and for any cause, but the wife's rights to divorce were more limited. According to some legal schools, the husband could divorce his wife by simply stating that he had divorced her in the presence of witnesses, and she did not even have to be present or to be informed of the act. Women, by contrast, could obtain a divorce only by mutual consent or by petitioning a qadi. The Hanafi school allowed a woman to request a divorce on the grounds of impotence, whereas the Maliki school allowed a wife to cite impotence, cruelty, desertion, failure of maintenance, or the threat posed to her by her husband's disease. In the event of divorce, the woman would have custody of the children of the marriage and the duty of bringing them up until they reached a certain age (typically seven for boys and nine for girls) or until she remarried, in which case the children's age was irrelevant. At that point, the father or his family would assume custody of the children.

Women in urban areas from Transoxiana to Andalus did not play an active, visible role in public life either before or after the arrival of Muslims, unless they were from poor families that needed them to engage in trade, services, or the crafts. Most scholars agree that, if anything, the status of women in the area probably rose slightly in the formerly Byzantine and Sasanian territories due to the ethical principle of the equality of the sexes before God that runs as a leitmotif throughout the Qur'an. Legally, women were guaranteed a share of an inheritance, as well as the right to own and sell property. Many women from prosperous families did engage in business activities, but typically that meant renting out a shop, buying and selling property, and lending money—activities which did not necessarily thrust them into the public eye. On the other hand, the traditions of concubinage and seclusion that both the Byzantines and the Sasanians had practiced prior to the advent of the Muslims continued into the Islamic era and shaped Muslim mores in a profound manner. Women had clearly demarcated roles that left them subservient to those of men.

Qadi courts dealt with criminal cases as well as family issues, but the state increasingly appropriated the responsibility for criminal law because the Shari'a's rules of evidence precluded a qadi from investigating criminal cases. In principle, only oral testimony from reputable witnesses was acceptable. Written evidence was only occasionally acceptable, and circumstantial evidence was not recognized at all. Because of the constraints on the qadi in this regard, the state transferred the greater part of criminal justice cases to the police. Both commerce and taxation were also spheres in which governments increasingly found that they needed a more flexible framework than what the Shari'a provided.

Thus, although the Shari'a became a central feature of Muslim life, it never became a comprehensive law code for all of society's needs. Two parallel systems of law existed in the Islamic world: the Shari'a and one that served the needs of the state. As we have seen, the Shari'a itself arose not from the needs of the state, but rather from the sense of moral responsibility that pious Muslims felt toward God. The Shari'a was the guide to living a life acceptable to God. Rulers were willing to accommodate the Shari'a because it served as a guide for judges and its implementation gave religious legitimacy to the state that employed it. Nevertheless, governments frequently faced issues that the Shari'a did not address, and they utilized a variety of expedients for resolving their legal problems.

On the other hand, the Shari'a, because of its focus on the issues of marriage, divorce, and inheritance, was much better known to the public than the secular codes, and it was the system that provided a common identity from one end of the Islamic world to the other. The very fact that the Shari'a had not been created to resolve the issues of a given state endowed it with the capacity for universality, and when the political unity of the Abbasid empire began breaking up, it was the Shari'a that provided for a commonality among all Muslims regardless of their membership within a given state. Governments could come and go without affecting the stability of their respective societies.

The development of the Shari'a also seems to have been instrumental in crystallizing an identity for most of the Muslims who were not Alids. Oddly enough, we do not know when *Sunnis* began to call themselves by that term. However, the expression, *ahl al-sunna wa al-jama'a*, discussed earlier, evoked the confidence that this group had that God's will could be found when individuals cooperated in ascertaining the model of the Prophet's life. It set them in contrast to those who relied for such guidance on a supernaturally inspired individual such as the Shi'ite Imam. Those who came to be known as Sunnis argued that God's will could be ascertained in the legal sciences, which were based on guidance from the Qur'an, the Hadith, analogy with similar cases, and the consensus of learned and pious scholars. A Hadith from the Prophet was often cited that expressed this confidence: "My community will never agree on an error." Over the years, more and more of the Muslims who sought religious truth from the consensus of the community referred to themselves as Sunnis to distinguish themselves from the Shi'ites, whose sense of identity was already established.

Early Sufism

In the late seventh and early eighth centuries, as Shi'ism, the Hadith movement, and the Shari'a were developing, a devotional movement arose in Kufa and Basra that eventually became the most widespread and characteristic form of Islamic piety. Because some of its adherents wore the rough woolen garments that had been the characteristic clothing of ascetics in the area for centuries, the movement came to be called Sufism, and its members Sufis (sing. *sufi*, from *suf*, or wool). At the heart of Sufism was a burning passion to transcend the externals of religion and to experience the spiritual reality for which rituals and texts were the representation. Although Sufism would come to embrace a wide variety of devotional practices and ways of life, most of the early Sufis sought a personal relationship with God through a combination of asceticism, a concern for ethical ideals, and a mystical form of worship.

The Contemplative Life

For over a century, many of the most prominent Sufis were among those who were engaged in the gathering of the Hadith in order to have a guide for living according to the will of God. What set many of the early Sufis apart from the other Hadith collectors was their emphatic renunciation of this world. Some favored a mild form of asceticism, while others took self-denial to an extreme. Just as Shi'ism and the Hadith movement contained elements of pious opposition to the Umayyad dynasty, the private piety and asceticism of the Sufis were in many cases expressions of disapproval or even active opposition to the same governmental authority. Throughout the Umayyad period there were examples of individuals who shunned the trappings of wealth and who sought a highly disciplined life of the spirit that stood in sharp contrast to the increasingly flamboyant way of life of the Umayyad court.

Sufism cannot be reduced to a movement of political protest, however. A movement of pious self-discipline had arisen early within Islam. The Sufis point to the Prophet himself as their model, and he certainly led a simpler life than his political power and his access to the community's resources would have allowed him. Moreover, many passages in the Qur'an stress the necessity of focusing on eternal goals rather than on worldly, material ones. Still other verses suggest the nearness of God that complements his transcendence and that allows him to be approached in a personal relationship. One that had a central role in the development of an accessible God was, "Indeed we created man; and we know what his soul whispers within him, and we are nearer to him than his jugular vein" (50:16).

Those Muslims who felt the need to cultivate the life of the spirit had a wealth of traditions in their midst from which they could borrow. On the one hand, Sufism was an indigenous development within Islam. Mystics in all the world's great religions share in a quest for the purification of the heart, a disregard for—if not renunciation of—worldly concerns, and a search for a deeper knowledge of God. It is unnecessary, and even misguided, to try to identify the source of borrowing of these elements from other traditions, because the dynamic of the mystical quest leads inexorably to some form of these features. However, many references in Sufi literature make it clear that Muslim, Christian, and Jewish mystics exchanged information on the contemplative life. Christian monks were particularly influential: In eighth-century Iraq and Syria, Christians still outnumbered Muslims, and awareness of monasticism was unavoidable. Indeed, the literary sources make it clear that Muslim mystics deliberately sought out conversations with pious members of the People of the Book who seemed to exemplify genuine spirituality. Even the woolen clothing characteristic of early Sufis was almost certainly a direct borrowing from Christian monasticism.

Interest in this form of worship had grown by the beginning of the eighth century. In the urban environment of late Umayyad Iraq, a number of ascetics, itinerant preachers, and individuals referred to as *weepers* called the Muslim community to a more faithful adherence to God's will. The most famous of this group was Hasan al-Basri (d. 728). He had served as a soldier in the military campaigns of the late seventh century and was later appointed qadi, although he may never actually have served in that capacity. He became a critic of the regime and was often in trouble with the Iraqi governor for his remarks. He was noted for his bouts of weeping for his own sins and for those of Muslim society. He was a respected moral teacher, and people flocked to the mosque when he gave the sermon.

One of the important themes of the career of Hasan al-Basri was his emphasis on the purity of the intention of any religious act. He denigrated as worthless a religious act that was performed out of habit or even from a sense of duty alone. In the next generation, the celebrated female mystic Rabi'a (d. 801) extended the concept of purity of intent to the attitude of worship itself: "O God, if I worship you from fear of hell, burn me in hell; and if I worship you in hope of heaven, exclude me from heaven; but if I worship you for your own sake, do not withhold your eternal beauty." This theme became a central one in later Sufism, as the movement can be seen in large part as a quest for spiritual and ethical perfection. Herein lies the source of a long-running tension between Sufi adepts and many of the ulama who were concerned to establish the precise acts that God willed and those He forbade. Whereas the ulama would have agreed that intention must be inseparable from the act, Sufis often regarded the ulama's concern for particular behavior to be legalistic, formal, and bereft of true spirituality. Some Sufis, on the other hand, drifted into a disregard for religious law. The law, they believed, was useful for the masses, but was meant to be only symbolic for the spiritually adept.

One of the most compelling features of Sufism for Muslims everywhere was the new emphasis that it placed on the love of God. On the one hand, it is a mistake to overstate the contrast between the Sufi doctrine of the love of God and the theme of the wrath or justice of God, because every Muslim frequently made reference to the "merciful and compassionate" God to whom he was devoted. Moreover, the Qur'an has many references to the mercy, love, and kindness of God that lend themselves to a fully developed doctrine of the love of God. On the other hand, it is clear that the Sufis found love to be a major theme that had not been mined as diligently before. Sufi writers emphasized not only the love of God for his creatures, but also the love of the believer for God. Like Rabi'a, they taught that God should be loved for Himself alone, and that when the pure of heart approached God in this way, God in turn would draw near to man.

By the ninth century, the Sufi tradition had matured sufficiently that spiritual masters (sing. *shaykh* in the Arabic-speaking lands and *pir* in the Persian-speaking regions) were writing manuals that described the methods of discipline that had enabled their followers to develop their spiritual maturity. The manuals described a progression of the soul towards God that required the completion of sequential stages (*maqamat*) and psychological and gnostic "states" (*ahwal*). Sufi masters might identify as few as four stages or as many as one hundred, but even the most detailed "road maps" for the soul usually followed a basic progression beginning with repentance and moving through stages of asceticism, fear of God, longing for God, and love for God. Most initiates never attained the final stage(s); they remained in a state of arrested spiritual development at one stage or another. Only those who themselves would become shaykhs attained the highest stage. But the passage through even a limited number of stages was more than most humans had experienced, and the seeker who had made any progress felt gratitude to God. In each stage, God granted to the seeker a "state," or spiritual experience, that demonstrated to him the presence of God in a manner not accessible otherwise. The path required a long and arduous journey of many years, during which initiates learned the virtues of patience and gratitude, even for the hardships that came one's way. Gradually, their souls became open to the presence of God, and they developed a longing for intimacy for God. Finally, the way culminated in spiritual knowledge and the loving experience of God.

     The characteristic activity for a Sufi was meditation. While the practice of meditation has a multitude of variations, many Sufis began to utilize a devotional practice known as _dhikr_, or the ritual "recollection" or "remembering" of the name of God. Many worshipers simply chanted "Allah" repetitively; others chanted the formula "There is no god but God;" some would recite the ninety-nine names of God, perhaps aided by a rosary; still other would utilize a more complex invocation, accompanied by movements of the body, rhythmic breathing, or even music. Like the mantra of South Asia or the "Jesus prayer" of the Eastern church, the purpose of the _dhikr_ was to provide a focus for the soul to fix its gaze upon God and to free itself from the distractions of the world. In both the Muslim and Christian cases, the prayer reflected the idea that the name of God is sacred, and that the act of invoking it in some sense entails contact with the divine.

Testing the Limits of Transcendence

As the mystical tradition developed, some writers began describing in more detail the experience that awaited the elite mystics at the end of their quest. This spiritual state was described by the twin concepts of *fana'* ("passing away" or "annihilation") and *baqa'* ("survival"). After pursuing a difficult discipline of spiritual cleansing and renunciation of the world, mystics would achieve direct knowledge of God and enter a state of joy and rest. A defining characteristic of the mystical experience is that it is ineffable, for it is not accessible to reason or to empirical experience. Nevertheless, Sufis attempted to describe the experience as one in which their attributes or characteristics merged with those of God. Their worldly longings and physical nature would "pass away," whereas the direct knowledge of God survived. Some mystics described this experience as one of an intoxicating, rapturous union with God in which the self was extinguished and actually united with God.

     Appearing for the first time in the eighth century was the doctrine of "friendship" with God, which arose from the desire to seek a personal relationship with

God. An adept who had achieved a direct experience of God and had demonstrated superior spiritual insight was regarded as a "friend (*wali*) of God." Whereas the ordinary believer sought out God, God actually sought out his "friends." The term *wali* is often translated as "saint" in English, and if not confused with the term as found in Catholicism, it is a useful concept to express some connotations of the word. Sufis regarded their spiritual teachers as wise, and certainly revered them for their insights and piety; some followers revered their teachers to such a degree that they considered them to be in some sense a manifestation of the divine being. Some saints practiced alchemy, an avocation that reinforced their reputation as healers and workers of miracles, both during their lifetimes and afterward. Their tombs became places of pilgrimage to which those who had special needs would go to pray and present offerings. The "friends of God" thus became intercessors between ordinary human beings and God.

The quest to bridge the gap between God and mankind became at once one of the great strengths of Sufism and the source of many problems for it. The mystical path has often had difficulty fitting comfortably within the monotheistic religions of Judaism, Christianity, and Islam because of its attempts to overcome the gulf between God the Creator and His human creature. Monotheism places a heavy emphasis on the transcendence, or "otherness," of God, whereas mysticism seeks to bridge that transcendence and to overcome the gulf between the divine and the mortal. Many Muslims regarded the notion of fana' to be heretical, for it seemed to suggest the essential identity of God and humans. The belief that "friends of God" could become intercessors between humans and God also seemed to run counter to original Islamic doctrine and was the target of bitter attacks.

The tension reached its peak in the life and death of al-Hallaj (d. 922), originally from Fars in southwestern Iran. He joined a Sufi group in Iraq, but soon quarreled with Sufis there and in his home province, and he devised his own mystical path. He became a missionary to India and Central Asia, and then settled in Baghdad. His reputation for working miracles followed him to that city, and he developed a large popular following. He is widely considered to have uttered the cry "*ana al-haqq*" ("I am the Truth" or "I am the Real"), from which the authorities would have inferred his claim to be one with God. He was insistent that ritual acts in themselves were merely perfunctory, and that only their inner meaning had value. The court record of his subsequent trial reveals that his offence was his having asserted that the pilgrimage to Mecca could be performed in his own room. Whatever his actual assertions, he clearly suggested that in some manner he was a manifestation of God, and he seems to have sought out condemnation by the authorities, as though to demonstrate that he had not accommodated himself to the worldly order.

Al-Hallaj lived during the unstable time of the rise of the Isma'ilis, the Fatimid takeover of Ifriqiya, and the raids of the Carmathians. His extreme mysticism, coupled with indications that he had Shi'ite leanings, caused the ulama and the civil officials to regard him as a threat to their authority. If he and others were able to persuade the common people of the unimportance of ritual acts, or that Alids had a more legitimate claim to the caliphate than anyone else, then the entire religious and political order could be jeopardized. In 922, al-Hallaj was executed in a particularly brutal fashion. His enemies and his supporters alike agreed that, as his feet and hands were chopped off, he faced death with a remarkable equanimity and asked forgiveness for those who executed him.

The Accommodation of Sufism

As remarkable and revered as al-Hallaj was, his defiant disregard for ritual and prescriptive behavior did not represent the future of mainstream Sufism. Whether because of the threat of persecution or because it was increasingly clear to many Muslims that some of the doctrines associated with al-Hallaj could not be reconciled with basic Islamic doctrines, his teachings were permanently eclipsed by the path represented by al-Junayd (d. 910) of Baghdad. Al-Junayd, who had been al-Hallaj's teacher for a short time before they quarreled, was a gifted thinker who combined an ascetic mysticism with a quest for moral perfection. He is often referred to as the greatest figure in early Sufism, one who created a synthesis between the scrupulous observance of the Shari'a and a sophisticated theory of mysticism.

Al-Junayd managed to justify the doctrine of a direct experience with God and carefully used the terms *fana'* and *baqa'* without claiming the permanent "annihilation" of the human identity. According to him, the mystic's quest is possible only because of God's active enabling power: God guides and strengthens the seeker in his quest to "die to himself" (*fana'*) and "live in God" (*baqa'*). In some sense, the mystical experience recaptures the preexistent state of the human soul as a thought in the mind of God. As a result, the joyous experience of God's direct presence makes it impossible for the mystic to be satisfied with life in this world, and he is constantly yearning for God's presence. On the other hand, precisely because he is in this world, the point of "life in God" is to live everyday life transformed by God's love and guidance. The spiritual experience enables a Muslim to see the world through new eyes, and to become a model of piety for others to follow. Even though al-Junayd shared the common Sufi attitude that the law was secondary to the inward life, he stressed that both were essential.

Al-Junayd's synthesis was crucial, for it kept Sufism grounded in the ritual and prescribed behavior that provided the common identity for Muslims everywhere. By the tenth century, Sufism was still a minority movement, and in order for it to be accepted as a valid Islamic experience, it needed to demonstrate that it was compatible with the rituals and ethic of the evolving norms of the majority. Few could predict at the time that the Sufi approach would come to dominate the inner life of Islam from West Africa to Southeast Asia. That it did so is a testimony to the wisdom of leaders such as al-Junayd. Their great accomplishment was to combine the doctrine of a transcendent God with the experience of an immanent God who is closer to man than his jugular vein.

The Reception of Science and Philosophy

The Arab conquests of the seventh and eighth centuries obliterated the political barriers that had formerly separated the rich and varied cultures of the areas that lay between the Indus valley and the Atlantic. Not only did a massive migration of peoples occur in their aftermath, but they also provided an economic stimulus to both trade and agriculture. More than commodities and luxuries were traded, however. Architectural styles, potterymaking techniques, and concepts in philosophy, mathematics, medicine, and many other intellectual fields now made their way across this vast expanse faster than ever before. The result was that cultural traditions that had often developed in isolation from each other now began to interact on a regular basis. The scholars and creative artists in the Dar al-Islam were able to synthesize a wide variety of traditions and to make original contributions to them.

Science ("Natural Philosophy")

When the Arabs conquered Egypt and Syria in the 630s, they entered a cultural zone that had been exposed to Greek intellectual influences for a thousand years, ever since the career of Alexander the Great. Iraq, too, was conversant with the Greek heritage. Unlike Syria and Egypt, Iraq had largely lost the Hellenistic patina that it had acquired during the Seleucid era, but in the fifth and sixth centuries a considerable number of Nestorian and Jacobite (Syrian Monophysite) scholars entered Sasanian Iraq to escape Byzantine persecution. They brought with them their Syriac translations of Greek theological writings, medicine, astronomy, and philosophy. Iraqi Christians were welcomed into the Sasanian royal school at Jundishapur, located approximately one hundred miles east of the capital of Ctesiphon. Jundishapur was a particularly exciting intellectual milieu, for it combined Greek medicine and philosophy with a Persian literary tradition and Sanskritic medical and mathematical influences.

The Arabs themselves had a brilliant poetic tradition, they had an effective tradition of folk medicine, and they could navigate over land and sea by virtue of their knowledge of the heavens, but they were in awe of what they found in the newly conquered territories. They encountered Christians and Jews who could pose philosophical questions about Islam that Muslims could not answer simply because they had never thought in such terms before. Some Muslims quickly appropriated logic and methods of formal argument in order to debate scholars from other religions, and they found the tools useful for controversies within Islam, as well. We shall explore the use of philosophical reasoning in the religious sciences more fully in the next section, since it came within the context of a debate regarding the rightful place of philosophy in religious discussions.

Muslim scholars and rulers were also fascinated by the knowledge that their subject peoples had of numerous fields of study, but especially of astronomy and astrology (the two were not yet differentiated), alchemy, mathematics, and medicine. As early as the late seventh century, certain Umayyad princes commissioned the translation of texts in the field of alchemy and were performing their own experiments. The Abbasid caliph al-Mansur (754–775) commissioned the translation of some of the medical texts attributed to Galen and Hippocrates, and a few other texts were translated during the remainder of the eighth century.

Not until the ninth century, however, did the government organize a systematic approach to the acquisition and translation of foreign texts. Al-Ma'mun (813–833) institutionalized the translation process by establishing the Bayt al-Hikma, or House of Wisdom. This institution became the focus of a massive translation project and served as a library to hold the newly translated books. Scholars at Jundishapur were drawn to the Bayt al-Hikma to become the members of the first major translation project. Almost all the translators over the next two centuries were Iraqi Christians. The notable exception was the pagan Thabit ibn Qurra (d. 901), who was also the court astrologer and physician to the caliph al-Mu'tadid. Hunayn ibn Ishaq (809–873) determined the framework for the translation process. He acquired as many Greek manuscripts as he could of a given work, compared them to determine the most accurate version, translated the work into Syriac, and then consulted with Arabic specialists to prepare an Arabic translation.

At first, the works to be translated were those with an immediate practical application. Mathematics was an essential tool in the huge construction effort taking place across the empire; medicine and pharmacology were required to keep the caliph and others among the elite healthy; and astronomy–astrology made possible the determination of the propitious times for the caliph and others to implement important policies and to determine the timing of religious festivals. Alchemy held out numerous possibilities: Its practitioners explored the relationship of humans to the natural world, devised ways to purify the soul, and sought ways to transmute base metals into gold.

It was not long, however, before philosophical texts began to be translated. The educational curriculum of the Eastern Christians had for centuries required the study of logic prior to that of theology or medicine, and it quickly became a staple of Islamic education. The majority of the corpus of the surviving Greek philosophical tradition quickly became available in Arabic versions. Because "philosophy" and "science" had not yet been divorced into separate disciplines (likewise, as late as the era of Newton in the European tradition, "science" was usually referred to as "natural philosophy"), Muslim scholars who were interested in the new texts almost always combined an interest in both, and were philosopher–scientists, as their Greek forerunners had been.

One of the most notable scholars of this period was al-Khwarizmi (ca. 780–ca. 850). As his name indicates, he was originally from Khwarazm, but he spent his adult career in Baghdad. He is credited with introducing the Indian numerals into the Muslim world, replacing both the Roman numerals and the awkward Hellenic style of using alphabetic letters. Although the Arabs still call the Indian numerals "Hindi," the Europeans call them "Arabic" since they in turn borrowed them from the Arabs. The Indian numeric system was not the first to utilize the place value system or to have a concept of zero—both the Babylonians and the Chinese had a place value system and the Babylonians had a blank symbol—but its combination of a decimal system (the Babylonians used a base of 60) and a highly developed concept of zero to signify the "null number"—absolutely nothing—was a powerful innovation and an essential development for modern mathematics. Al-Khwarizmi's most famous mathematical treatise utilized the new system and compiled rules for the arithmetical solutions of linear and quadratic equations, for elementary geometry, and for the solution of inheritance problems faced in probate cases. No two scholars can agree on an English translation of the book's title, which contains the word *al-jabr*, meaning the restoration and amplification of something incomplete. The book later became so influential in Europe that "al-jabr" gave birth to the word *algebra*. Another of al-Khwarizmi's works was translated into Latin as *Algorismi de numero indorum* ("Al-Khwarizmi Concerning the Hindu Art of Computation"), immortalizing his name in our mathematical term *algorithm*.

Philosophy

In philosophy and medicine, too, Muslim scholars initially were attracted to the richness of other traditions, and then made profoundly original contributions to those traditions. Muslim philosophers, like medieval Europeans, tended either to be idealists, in which case they identified with Plato's tradition, or empiricists, in which case they considered themselves Aristotelians. Some small groups deliberately cultivated one or the other school, but for almost the entire period under question, philosophers thought that the two Greek philosophers were more alike in their thought than they actually were. For reasons that are not clear, by the time the translations were being made, the Greek tradition had attributed to Aristotle two works that were not Aristotelian at all. They have features in them that are so patently different from the thrust of Aristotle's own work that modern scholars are baffled that they could have been identified with him. Nevertheless, they became central to the subsequent Islamic and medieval Western Christian philosophical enterprise. One was the so-called *Theology of Aristotle*, which was actually a paraphrase of Books IV, V, and VI of the *Enneads* of Plotinus, the third-century philosopher whose writings form the basis for Neoplatonism. The other was the *Book of Causes* (known later in medieval Europe as *Liber de causis*), which was excerpted from the *Elements of Theology*, written by Proclus, a fifth-century Neoplatonist.

Neoplatonism was the substratum for the work that was done not only in philosophy, but in many features of Sufism and the theology of Shi'ism, as well. It was based on the work of Plotinus, who credited his teacher in Alexandria, Ammonius Saccas, with having provided him the basis for his thought. Plotinus postulates a universe at the head of which is a First Cause, or the One, which so transcends the world we know that Plotinus does not even wish to say that it "exists" or has "being" (which even makes it technically incorrect to say that the First Principle "is" at the head of the universe!).

The concept of the One and of an Unmoved Mover were familiar in the Platonic and Aristotelian systems, but Plotinus' contribution was to suggest that this wholly transcendent First Principle has no direct relation with the material world. He argued that it "emanates" an entity that he calls *nous* or the Intellect, which in turn emanates Soul, which in turn contains in itself all particular souls, including human souls. Soul in its turn emanates nature, or the phenomenal world in which we live. Later Neoplatonists made this scheme of emanations much more detailed, and linked it to the nine spheres of the Ptolemaic universe.[1] Each sphere, or heaven, had its own intellect and soul, emanated by the previous one. The whole universe is thus the result of a succession of emanations in which each principle produces the next lower principle. Each lower principle is, to the extent that its lower nature permits, the imitation of the higher.

The vision of Plotinus was essentially religious, and in fact his philosophy was one of the great "natural theologies" of history. Rather than depending on prophetic revelation, he found the divine in nature and accessible by human reason. Like Plato, he felt trapped in his corporeal body, and thought that the highest joy for man is union with the One, attained by purification and contemplation. In classic mystical fashion, he believed that if a person puts aside his identification with his corporeal self and attains to a state of pure thought, he can "return" in a sense to a union with the First Principle in a process that goes in the reverse direction from that of the emanations. The individual soul loses its identity and submerges itself in the One. As we shall see, this scheme helped to give shape to the Islamic mystical tradition.

The fact that Neoplatonism was a self-contained philosophical religious tradition made it in one sense a competitor to the monotheistic traditions of Judaism, Christianity, and Islam. It appropriated Aristotelian notions such as the eternity of the universe, the denial of the resurrection of the body, and the rejection of the notion that prophets have a special knowledge inaccessible to reason. Its doctrine that the human soul loses its individual personality upon the death of the body was also a problem for most Muslims and Christians. On the other hand, certain influential Christian theologians, such as Augustine (354–430), found in Neoplatonism a notion of the deity as a creative force, or energy, that was more sophisticated than that of a crudely anthropomorphic Creator. When combined with an allegorical interpretation of the scriptures, the emanationist theory made the traditions about a Creator God philosophically acceptable, and it avoided having to address the knotty problems of creation *ex nihilo* ("out of nothing").

Many Muslim intellectuals faced the same problems Augustine did. Some of them concluded that prophetic and philosophical knowledge are merely the allegorical and rational expressions of the same truth. Many of them believed that the apparent contradictions between scriptural and Neoplatonic views of creation, resurrection, and the personal soul could be reconciled when it was understood that the scriptural versions were allegorical expressions of more complicated philosophical truths. In the hands of Muslim philosophers and mystics, the Aristotelian–Neoplatonic synthesis became progressively more complex and sophisticated as they attempted to correct weaknesses and inconsistencies in earlier versions. Some of their problems stemmed from the basic incompatibility between Aristotle's actual system and the Neoplatonic overlay, whereas others lay in the inconsistencies between Neoplatonism and the doctrines derived from the Qur'an and Hadith.

Some of the translators in the Bayt al-Hikma made philosophical contributions of their own, but the first genuine philosopher to write in Arabic was al-Kindi (ca. 800–ca. 870), who gained the nickname "Philosopher of the Arabs." Al-Kindi, impressed by the *Theology of Aristotle*, asserted that the truths revealed through the prophets were metaphysical knowledge, and that there was no contradiction between philosophy and revelation. Despite his protestations, the emergence of philosophy within the Islamic world during the first half of the ninth century provoked a bitter debate about the role of reason within religion, just as it did within Christianity in various periods. As a result, philosophy almost from its inception among the Muslims came under suspicion. With few exceptions, the advances in philosophy would henceforth take place among informal circles of scholars who knew that they were viewed with mistrust, and their work never became part of the institutions of formal education. Those who supported the use of unfettered reason adduced several Hadith to show that learning had been praised and encouraged by the Prophet—"Seek learning, though it be in China," "The ink of scholars is worth more than the blood of martyrs," and "The search for knowledge is obligatory for every Muslim" were but a few of many such sayings—but to no avail. Their work in "natural philosophy" and mathematics was encouraged for its practical value, but because their philosophical speculations risked challenging the literal interpretation of the Qur'an, many Muslims regarded them as heretics, if not apostates.

Despite the handicaps under which the philosopher–scientists worked, the achievements of this group of scholars is nothing short of awe inspiring. As a result of their work, Arabic, which had been the language of revelation for the Muslims, now replaced Greek as the primary language of philosophical and scientific inquiry for the next several centuries. Numerous scholars made contributions that would be immortalized in the twelfth and thirteenth centuries when their works were translated into Latin. Here we will mention two of the most famous whose work dates from before the middle of the tenth century.

Abu Bakr al-Razi (ca. 865–ca. 932), known as Rhazes to medieval Europeans, was born in the Iranian city of Rayy and became a physician and head of a hospital there; he later took over the administration of a hospital in Baghdad. He was probably the greatest medical mind of medieval Muslim history, and became well known in Europe because of his compendium of medicine from the Greek, Syriac, and Indian traditions, and for his treatise on small pox and measles. His treatises were not mere encyclopedias, but rather were infused with a vividness and freshness that resulted from his work as a practicing physician and his keen attention to the details of symptoms and stages of illnesses. Despite the universal respect for his medical contributions, he was widely hated for his philosophical ideas, such as his denial of the eternity of the soul and his rejection of the concept of revelation. He argued that because God had imparted reason to mankind, reason rather than revelation would purify the soul and release it from the chains of the body.

Al-Farabi (ca. 878–ca. 950) was born in Transoxiana, probably of Turkic origin, but he grew up in Damascus. Al-Farabi studied in Baghdad under the great Nestorian and Jacobite logicians there, but soon surpassed them. Al-Farabi was not as extreme as al-Razi in his expression of the relationship of philosophy and revelation, but he made it clear that human reason, as utilized by philosophers, is superior to revelation. Ordinary people, however, cannot be expected to comprehend philosophical truth and so must be provided with the concrete and picturesque images by which religion expresses philosophical truths symbolically. Al-Farabi was the first major Muslim Neoplatonist, and subsequent Muslim philosophers used him as a touchstone to measure their own work.

A major part of al-Farabi's career, however, was devoted to the problem of the correct ordering of the state. As the authority of the Abbasid caliphate was collapsing in the tenth century, al-Farabi turned back to Plato's *Republic* for inspiration, and argued that the ruler must embody the highest intellectual as well as practical virtues. Reflecting Hellenic values, al-Farabi considered the required qualifications of the ruler to include intelligence, love of knowledge, moderation in appetites, and the love of justice, among others. By implication, he suggested that the political problems of his century were due to the absence of philosophers in the government.

The Development of an Islamic Theology

As is the case in Judaism and Christianity, Islam stresses man's obedient response to the sovereign Word of God. Within each tradition, sacred scriptures are the basis for doctrine, ritual, and pious behavior. As a result, great efforts have been made to preserve the integrity of the scriptures and to ascertain their full meaning. The adherents of all three religions have found, however, that the attempt to live a devout life based upon the guidance provided by the scriptures is beset with complications. Passages in the scriptures can be ambiguous, they can contradict each other (at least in their literal meaning), and they are not comprehensive (i.e., they fail to address every issue that a person will encounter in his or her life for which ethical, ritual, or doctrinal guidance is needed). In order to ascertain the will of God in such cases, pious scholars within each religion have utilized a variety of intellectual devices. They identify principal themes within the scriptures as a whole that clarify ambiguities or that harmonize apparent contradictions within specific passages, and they apply the principles found within the scriptures to specific situations confronted in everyday life.

Within Christianity these attempts led to the development of systematic theology. Islamic theology, like its Jewish counterpart, never developed into the comprehensive field of study that Christian theology did. In part, the reason for that lay in the fact that Christianity developed doctrines that required considerable exploration in order to be comprehensible: original sin, the Trinity, the nature and person of Jesus, the meaning of the crucifixion and resurrection, etc. Islam and Judaism are more preoccupied with simply ascertaining God's will through His law, and with following it. Muslims did develop a field of study, *kalam*, that is often translated *theology*. It has focused largely on analyzing the attributes of God and of His creation.

The Reception of Rationalism

The introduction of philosophical modes of thought into the Arabic cultural tradition had profound implications for the development of Islamic religious thought. In fact, although the developments in science and philosophy were the features of the intellectual achievement of the Muslims that caught the attention of medieval Europeans, Muslims first experienced the Greek impact in the field of theology well before the translation process in the Bayt al-Hikma made possible a philosophical tradition in Arabic. The pressures for the development of an Islamic theology came from disputes within the Umma and from forces impinging upon it from the outside world. Within decades of the Prophet's death, urgent questions were presenting themselves to the community that needed to be addressed.

The Muslims of Syria and Iraq found themselves among large communities of Jews and Christians who had been exploring questions such as free will for centuries. The discussion of these issues was shaped by the concepts and forms of argument developed by the Greek tradition, in both its Hellenic and Hellenistic phases. These communities raised questions that Muslims initially found difficult to answer because of the rhetorical methods employed. Many of the questions with which all of the monotheistic religions of revelation are now familiar were first put into stark relief for Muslims at this time: Are humans autonomous rather than agents of God's will? If we are not autonomous, how can God hold us responsible for our evil acts? Are we judged by our acts alone, or by our faith, or by a combination of them? If our acts matter, do they have to be motivated by good intention? Can we know the standards by which we are judged? If so, does that mean that God is compelled to act according to norms—such as justice—that limit His omnipotence, or can He act arbitrarily, unbound by standards which we might count upon? Can God be described by the attributes we use for human beings, such as just or loving? Is God all-powerful and all-knowing? If so, why does He permit evil?

The evidence suggests that groups of Muslim scholars were employing certain Greek concepts and patterns of argument by the early eighth century, both to defend their religion against the polemics of non-Muslims and to explore theological questions for themselves. By the time of the reign of the Abbasid caliph Harun al-Rashid (r. 786–809) a well-organized group emerged that was identified by its friends and its enemies alike as the "partisans of dialectic." These were the Mu'tazilites, whom we have already seen locked in a struggle with Ahmad ibn Hanbal. Based in Basra and Baghdad, they were not the only actors in the discipline of Islamic theology, but they were the dominant group for several generations. Mu'tazilism was the result of a desire to use Greek concepts and methods of argument in the defense of Islam. Most of its practitioners were not philosophers, although al-Kindi may be regarded as part of their circle. Characteristically, they relied upon analogy rather than upon the syllogism of the philosophers, and they were exclusively interested in exploring and defending religious topics. But the Mu'tazilites did set out to demonstrate to non-Muslims that Islamic beliefs were in accord with reason, and they tried to defend reason against those Muslims who insisted on the sole efficacy of faith. They were the first group of Muslim thinkers to give a systematic, rational treatment of religious beliefs.

The Mu'tazilites were famous for their five basic principles, two of which provoked the most discussion. One was that of "justice," which connoted for the Mu'tazilites their doctrine of free will and responsibility. The Mu'tazilites were convinced that they could vindicate the rationality of God's ways. They argued that good and evil are not arbitrary concepts whose validity is rooted in the dictates of God, but rather are rational categories that can be established by the use of reason alone. Hence, if God does not establish ethical categories but is Himself bound by them, His actions are predictable. If He is indeed just, He cannot condemn a man who does good, nor excuse a sinner. If God is just, then He can punish only if man is responsible for acting in an evil way, and man can receive a reward only if he is capable of doing the good on his own power.

The traditionalists, like Ibn Hanbal, instinctively felt that such a theology limited the power of God—either He is omnipotent or He is not. They could also point to verses in the Qur'an that supported the idea that God was ultimately responsible for evil as well as for good. Their position was that God determines what is right or wrong at any given time, so that His actions are both arbitrary and right. Hence, a man could live a righteous life and yet God could justifiably condemn him to hell. The traditionalists regarded the denial by the Mu'tazilites of God's right and power to do as He wills to be an affront to God's majesty.

The other Mu'tazilite principle was called God's "unity." It was aimed at both the Manichaeans (dualists who believed that God cannot be responsible for the evil in this world) and the Muslims who interpreted literally the anthropomorphic descriptions of God that are found in the Qur'an. With regard to the latter, the question became whether to accept revelation literally or to use reason to interpret revelatory images. The anthropomorphic position was articulated by the jurist Malik ibn Anas with regard to the issue of God's sitting upon the throne: The "sitting is known, whereas its mode is unknown. Belief in its truth is a duty, and its questioning a heresy." The Mu'tazilite approach to the problem betrays its philosophical underpinnings. To accept literally the attributes accorded to God in the Qur'an threatens God's unity and simplicity, for to posit attributes of God (such as His power, knowledge, life, hearing, sight, or speech) distinct from his essence suggests a plurality of eternal entities. The Mu'tazilites were uncomfortable asserting the eternality of any but God Himself. They declared that God is pure essence with no eternal names and qualities. His "attributes" are simply aspects of His essence.

The traditionalists, on the other hand, interpreted the Qur'an literally. They identified the Qur'an with the word—and words—of God. They argued that, since God is eternal and has speech, then His speech—an attribute—must be eternal. Since the Qur'an is His speech, it is eternal, as well. Thus, God's attributes, *contra* the Mu'tazilite position, are coeternal with Him, and the Qur'an is uncreated, not created. They viewed the Mu'tazilite position as an attack on the authority of the Qur'an and, indirectly, on the power of God.

These debates seem as hairsplitting to many of us as the Christian controversies over the nature of Christ which produced Monophysitism and Nestorianism. However, like their Christian predecessors, the principals in these controversies were determined to use the power of the state to enforce their opinion. The crisis came to a head during the caliphate of al-Ma'mun (813–833). Mu'tazilism appealed to him in part because he was a rationalist himself, and in part because the doctrine of the createdness of the Qur'an could more easily allow the caliph, like the Shi'ite Imam, to interpret and expand on the meaning of the Qur'an as he felt was necessary. A doctrine that insisted on the literal meaning of the Qur'an restricted the scope of such interpretation. Al-Ma'mun required that Mu'tazilite doctrines be followed by qadis and other officials whose decisions had an impact on policy. In the face of resistance to this decree, he instituted a tribunal in 833 to enforce the Mu'tazilite doctrine. The court used the threat of torture and death to force compliance. Only a few, including Ibn Hanbal, refused to recant the doctrine of the uncreatedness of the Qur'an. The obstinate ones were imprisoned, and some died from the harsh treatment they suffered. The persecution continued intermittently until 849, when the new caliph reversed the policy, and then it became the turn of the Mu'tazilites to be persecuted.

The Critique of Rationalism

The reaction against the Mu'tazilites was vehement. Despite the fact that even their Muslim critics had often commended them for their defense of Islam against attacks by competing religious systems, many Muslims inferred from their arguments that they regarded revelation to be secondary to human reason. It seemed to many of their opponents that, like the philosophers, they regarded reason to be the supreme organizing principle in the universe, and that God and His works were subject to its rules of logic. They appeared to regard revelation itself as valid only if it was consistent with the workings of reason. Ibn Hanbal spoke for many Muslims when he asserted that the Qur'an and the Sunna of the Prophet were the sole sources of Islamic doctrine and practice. It was the duty of Muslims to accept the literal meaning of the Qur'an at face value "without asking how" (*bi-la kayf*) ambiguous or puzzling doctrines could be reconciled with human reason. Ibn Hanbal's school of law arose as a reaction to the Mu'tazilite controversy. Its purpose was to ensure that the Qur'an— literally interpreted—and the Hadith were the sole basis for jurisprudence.

In the midst of the conflict between the rationalist approach of the Mu'tazilites and the literalist position of their opponents, other thinkers tried to find a middle ground. The most influential was al-Ash'ari (d. 935), whose work eventually became the basis upon which subsequent scholars fashioned the theology that became the intellectual rationale for Sunni doctrine. Al-Ash'ari was a former Mu'tazilite, but he was convinced that the Mu'tazilite emphasis on reason undermined faith. Claiming that he was following in the tradition of Ibn Hanbal, he set about to do battle with the "rationalists." The irony of the situation, which was not lost on the Hanbalis, was that al-Ash'ari was defending the faith with the very tools of the Mu'tazilites: philosophical terms and dialectical arguments. This came about by the necessity of the age, as al-Ash'ari realized that to defeat the Mu'tazilites he would have to meet them on their own terms.

Al-Ash'ari insisted without equivocation that the Qur'an was uncreated and that God possesses attributes that are in His essence. Realizing the trap that lay in store for him, he cautioned that God's attributes may not be said to be identical with His essence, nor can they be said not to be identical with it. Such attributes— such as speech, sight, and hearing—are not like those of His creatures, and must simply be accepted *bi-la kayf*. Al-Ash'ari also argued that humans are incapable of creating their own acts. Unlike the Mu'tazilites, who argued that humans have free will, and the Hanbalis, who claimed that God is the author of all acts despite the fact that man is responsible for his evil acts on the Day of Judgment, al-Ash'ari used the concept of "acquisition" (*kasb*) to try to account for the synergy of God and man in a given act. At the heart of the concept is the theory that the creation of the world is not a finished act, but an ongoing one, in which God is constantly making each moment possible. At each instant, God is the creator of all acts, and yet men in some sense "acquire" them.

Al-Ash'ari's attempt to reconcile God's omnipotence with man's responsibility for his own acts was rejected by the Mu'tazilites and Hanbalis alike. The Mu'tazilites saw that it precluded free will, and the Hanbalis were opposed to the use of rational arguments in support of doctrinal points. Moreover, the Mu'tazilites could not accept the literalist presuppositions of al-Ash'ari, and the Hanbalis refused to recognize that reason had any role in affairs of religion. Al-Ash'ari did have followers, however, and they continued to refine his approach in ways that became acceptable to most Muslims. By the middle of the eleventh century, "Ash'arism" represented a compromise between rationalists and those who placed a premium on faith, and became the major expression of Sunni theological thought. Hanbalis were a dwindling, if influential, minority, whereas Mu'tazilism practically disappeared among Sunni scholars and became associated with Shi'ism. It had become apparent to most scholars that the real conflict was not between rationalism and faith, but over the scope and the validity of reason in faith. The theologians, as opposed to the philosophers, could not accept reason as a source of new and certain knowledge, but they became increasingly sophisticated in their use of reason to demonstrate the truths of revelation.

Conclusion

Just as the middle of the tenth century represents a major watershed in the political history of the Dar al-Islam, it also marks a milestone in the development of Islam as a major religion. By that time, the principles for deriving the Shari'a had been established, and, as a result, Sunni Islam had its basic organizing principle. Shi'ism had become a sectarian movement, and the majority of its adherents were clustered into two groups. One of them had become known as the Isma'ili or Fatimid movement and had achieved political power in North Africa, allowing it to develop without fear of governmental persecution. The members of the Imami branch of Shi'ism, who heretofore had followed a "visible" and "present" Imam, became "Twelvers" after 874, awaiting the return of the Twelfth Imam, who was being groomed by God to return in triumph from his "occultation." The essential difference between Sunnis and Shi'ites seemed to be that the former sought God's will in a method of inquiry for determining the Shari'a, whereas the latter sought God's will in the first instance from a divinely guided descendant of Muhammad.

Sufism, too, had achieved an important milestone by the middle of the tenth century. The major issues of basic presuppositions and of the methods for achieving spiritual maturity had been established, but Sufism was still in its infancy in terms of organization and literature. Sufism offered new avenues for worshiping God, and its deep spirituality appealed to many. Conversely, it threatened others. Whereas some Sufis understood their quest to be the fulfillment of the Shari'a, others saw it as an alternative to the practice of the Shari'a, with the result that some of the ulama were deeply suspicious of it.

Muslims were also active in science, philosophy, and medicine in this period. The translations of the ninth century, in particular, made available the heritage of the Greco–Roman tradition and of India. Important work by Muslims in medicine, mathematics, and philosophy laid the foundations for subsequent generations of philosopher–scientists to make contributions that are still admired. Other Muslims were beginning to question whether the quest for knowledge independent of the scriptures was either worthwhile or pious.

It is noteworthy that the work of scholars in Iraq was central to the developments within Imami Shi'ism, the Shari'a, Sufism, philosophy, mathematics, and medicine during this period. The Muslims there—Arabs and converts, natives and immigrants—managed to create a tradition that was enriched by its sophisticated environment and yet remained a distinctly Islamic enterprise, inspired by the Qur'an and the example of the Prophet. After the mid-tenth century, the most important intellectual work would take place on the geographical periphery of the Dar al-Islam, rather than in its heartland. The glory days of the Abbasid caliphate were over.

NOTES

1. Ptolemy, the second-century Roman scientist, postulated a model of the universe that would shape the thought of scholars in the Christian, Jewish, and Islamic lands for over a millennium and a half. Like almost all other intellectuals, he assumed that the earth was at the center of the universe, and that surrounding it were spheres containing the various celestial bodies. The spheres contained the moon, the sun, each of the five planets, and the stars (which were equidistant from the earth, and hence all in the same sphere), as well as what many scholars referred to as the Primum Mobile, or the agency that drives the entire apparatus as a result of the First Cause, or the One.

FURTHER READING

The Origins of Islamic Law

Coulson, N.J. *A History of Islamic Law.* Edinburgh: Edinburgh University Press, 1964.

Hallaq, Wael B. *A History of Islamic Legal Theories: An Introduction to Sunni usul al-fiqh.* Cambridge, U.K.: Cambridge University Press, 1997.

Juynboll, Gualterus H. A. *Muslim Tradition: Studies in Chronology, Provenance and Authorship of Early Hadith,* Cambridge, U.K.: Cambridge University Press, 1983.

Schacht, Joseph. *An Introduction to Islamic Law,* Second Impression. Oxford: Clarendon Press, 1964.

Schacht, Joseph. *The Origins of Muhammadan Jurisprudence.* Fourth Impression. Oxford: Clarendon Press, 1967.

Early Sufism

Arberry, A. J. *Sufism: An Account of the Mystics of Islam.* New York and Evanston: Harper & Row, 1950.

Knysh, Alexander. *Islamic Mysticism: A Short History.* Leiden, Boston, Koln: Brill, 2000.

Peters, F. E. *Allah's Commonwealth: A History of Islam in the Near East 600–1100 A.D.* New York: Simon and Schuster, 1973.

Schimmel, Annemarie. *The Mystical Dimension of Islam.* Chapel Hill, North Carolina: The University of North Carolina Press, 1975.

The Reception of Science and Philosophy

Anawati, G. "Science." In *Cambridge History of Islam,* edited by P. M. Holt, A. K. Lambton, and B. Lewis, vol. II, pp. 741–79. Cambridge, U.K.: Cambridge University Press, 1970.

Fakhry, Majid. *A History of Islamic Philosophy,* 2d ed. New York: Columbia University Press, 1987.

al-Hasan, Ahmad, and Donald R. Hill. *Islamic Technology: An Illustrated History.* Cambridge, U.K.: Cambridge University Press, 1986.

Hill, Donald R. *Islamic Science and Engineering.* Edinburgh: Edinburgh University Press, 1994.

Lindberg, David C., ed. *Science in the Middle Ages.* Chicago and London: The University of Chicago Press, 1978.

Peters, F.E. *Aristotle and the Arabs: The Aristotelian Tradition in Islam.* New York: New York University Press, 1968.

Turner, Howard R. *Science in Medieval Islam: An Illustrated Introduction.* Austin, Texas: University of Texas Press, 1995.

Ullmann, Manfred. *Islamic Surveys II: Islamic Medicine.* Edinburgh: Edinburgh University Press, 1978.

Young, M.J.L., J.D. Latham, and R.J. Serjeant, eds. *Religion, Learning, and Science in the 'Abbasid Period.* Cambridge and New York: Cambridge University Press, 1990.

PART TWO

A Civilization Under Siege, 950–1260

By 950, Muslims were justified in feeling a sense of satisfaction in the accomplishments of the past. The agreement upon a methodology for jurisprudence had produced a comprehensive set of rules and laws that Sunnis accepted without question; after a bumpy start, the mystical life was becoming attractive to more and more Muslims; science and philosophy were being selectively incorporated into the Islamic theological framework; and a far-flung commercial network was increasing wealth and stimulating creative solutions to everyday problems. The result was the emergence of a civilization that could compare favorably with any that had existed in history.

Despite these achievements, many thoughtful Muslims shared a sense of foreboding about the future of the Dar al-Islam. In 950, three caliphs claimed exclusive legitimacy as leader of the Muslim world, and they were prepared to act upon those claims. The competing claims of authority were exacerbated by differences in religious creeds: The caliph in Cordoba was a Sunni; the one in Mahdiya was a Fatimid Shi'ite; and in Baghdad, the Sunni caliph was powerless, whereas the Buyid sultan—who exercised the real power in the Abbasid caliphate—supported Twelver Shi'ism. The sense of lost unity, both spiritual and political, has haunted Muslims ever since, and has been a major factor in the rise of reform movements for more than a millennium.

As it turned out, the next three centuries would confirm both the highest hopes and the worst fears of the mid-tenth century. The period from 950 to 1260 witnessed major cultural achievements—many historians judge its cultural productivity to have been one of the most spectacular in world history—but it is dominated by shocking violence and disorder. The first three centuries of Muslim history experienced violence, as we have seen, but it was episodic and most of it occurred between armies. In the second period, by contrast, we witness numerous examples of factional conflict among the inhabitants of the same city, persecution of subjects by their rulers, and "total war" tactics by invading armies, in which farmers and city dwellers alike suffered from ruined property or death, simply for being in the way.

The political history of the period 950–1260 can be divided in half to illustrate some important differences. The first half, 950–1100, provides a rough approximation for the period during which most of the violence was that of Muslims against other Muslims. This is the subject treated in Chapter 6. From eastern Iran to Andalus, new political dynasties came to power, and they did so in the only way they could, which was to overthrow the existing rulers. The second half of the three-century period, roughly 1100–1260, is the subject of Chapter 7. The degree of the violence intensified and tended to affect noncombatants more than previously. The origin of most of the violence was from outside the Dar al-Islam, and was initiated by non-Muslims. This is the period of the Reconquista in the Iberian Peninsula, the Crusades in Anatolia and Syria, and the Mongols in Iran and Iraq. Overlapping both of these periods is the in-migration of tens of thousands of Turkish warrior–herdsmen. Some of their leaders were devout Muslims and sophisticated leaders of great ability, but the vast majority of their followers were illiterate, only nominally Muslim, and were in search of plunder. Their initial impact was destructive, too, but the long-term effect of the irruption of the Turks into the Dar al-Islam would be not only constructive, but decisive, in shaping the character of Islamic civilization.

Chapter 8 returns to the topic of religious and intellectual developments that we last explored in Chapter 5. By the mid-tenth century, Muslim scholars were sufficiently familiar with the Greek and Indian cultural legacies to begin making major contributions of their own, and some of the most famous intellectuals in Muslim history produced their work during the next three centuries. Their achievements in science and philosophy were so impressive that western Europeans began a major translation process to transfer Arabic learning into Latin. On the other hand, a consensus developed among Muslims that the exercise of reason, unless guided by revelation, was a dangerous force in society. Increasingly, intellectuals who might have pursued a path in philosophy became mystics instead. Indeed, this was the period in which the most distinctive Sufi institutions—the lodge and the order—emerged.

Chapter 9 surveys the state of the Dar al-Islam as it was in the mid-thirteenth century, employing the concept of "commonwealth" that some scholars have adopted to characterize this vast and diverse portion of the planet which, for all its differences, constituted a single civilization. The scale of the violence of the period could have spelled the end of Islam. Islam's enemies, in fact, counted on that to happen. Precisely the opposite happened. Muslims proved to be highly resourceful, and developed new social institutions that enabled them to weather the storms that afflicted them both physically and emotionally. They had created a civilization that would not only survive, but would thrive, under the most severe conditions.

CHRONOLOGY

969	Fatimids conquer Egypt
998–1030	Reign of Mahmud of Ghazna
c.1000–1037	Career of Ibn Sina
1034-1060	Norman conquest of port cities in Ifriqiya

1058	Tughril Bey secures Baghdad for Saljuqs
1050s–1147	Almoravid Empire
1060–1091	Norman conquest of Muslim Sicily
1066	Norman conquest of England
1071	Battle of Manzikert
c.1085–1111	Career of al-Ghazali
1085	Toledo falls to Reconquista
1092	Civil war begins among Great Saljuqs
1094	Musta'li-Nizari schism among Fatimids; "Assassins" become notorious
1099	First Crusade conquers Jerusalem
1130	Hafizi-Tayyibi schism among Fatimids
1140s	First Gothic cathedral (Saint Denis)
1144	Edessa falls; first Crusader state to do so
1147–1269	Almohad Empire
c.1160–1198	Career of Ibn Rushd
c.1170	Emergence of Sufi lodges
1171	Saladin takes power in Cairo, ends Fatimid caliphate
1176	Battle of Myriokephalon
1187	Battle of Hattin
1189–1193	Third Crusade
1180–1225	Caliphate of al-Nasir, who attempts a renaissance of Abbasid power
c.1200	Emergence of Sufi tariqas
c.1200–1240	Career of Ibn al-'Arabi
1204	Fourth Crusade results in sack of Constantinople and creation of Latin Kingdom
1212	Battle of Las Navas de Tolosa
1215	Magna Carta issued in England
1219–1222	Chinggis Khan's campaigns in Muslim world
1236–1266	All of Andalus except Granada falls to Reconquista
c.1240–1273	Career of Rumi
1241	Batu defeats coalition army of Europeans at Liegnitz
1250	Mamluke era begins
1258	Hulagu destroys Baghdad
1260	Mamlukes defeat Mongols at 'Ayn Jalut
1261	Byzantines regain Constantinople from Latin Kingdom
1269	Marinids replace Almohads in Morocco

CHAPTER 6

Filling the Vacuum of Power, 950–1100

In 950, three cities claimed to be the seat of the legitimate caliphate. The next century and a half proved that each claim merely demonstrated that the Muslim world was hopelessly divided, both religiously and politically. The inherent weakness of each polity, and the emerging social strains in each region, rendered their claims ephemeral. Their petty concerns and evident weakness encouraged other ambitious leaders to make bids for power, with the result that the period witnessed frequent clashes for power.

The year 1100 is a convenient one with which to close the period. In the east, the Buyids fell in 1055 to a group of invaders called the Saljuq Turks. Their entry into the heartland of the Muslim world heralded the arrival of a dynamic ethnic group that would dominate large parts of the Dar al-Islam for centuries to come. A dynastic struggle for power within their ranks in the 1090s, however, left the Mediterranean coastline vulnerable to the invasion of the Frankish Crusaders at the close of the decade. In North Africa, the Fatimid empire became the greatest of the Muslim powers in the eleventh century, but it suffered a debilitating schism in 1094, also just before the Crusaders showed up to seize Palestine from it. In the west, the Reconquista claimed its first major triumph in 1085 by taking Toledo, but a new Berber dynasty known as the Almoravids immediately came across the Strait of Gibraltar from North Africa to prevent any more of Andalus from falling under Christian control. By 1100, the Almoravids had incorporated most of Andalus into their North African empire.

The Buyid Sultanate

In Baghdad, one of the first orders of business for the Buyids when they seized power in 945 was the regularization of pay for the military. They inherited from the Abbasid regime a practice that had begun as early as the ninth century of substituting

142

"tax farms" for the salaries due to officers. Because tax collection was so inefficient, the government was often short of cash to pay military officers and high civilian officials. The new technique entailed granting to officials the right to collect the taxes themselves from specific villages or districts. The system under the Abbasids had had only limited success due to its intermittent practice and to the fact that the officers in charge of the revenue of a district sometimes would not forward to the government the amount in excess due to the officer himself. The Buyids codified the practice, guaranteeing the officers that if their assignment was inadequate, another would be exchanged for it, and implementing audits that secured the amount due the government. The grant of a tax district is known as an *iqta'*, and it proved to have a long life in southwestern Asia. Its theoretical appeal to government officials is understandable, but in practice it proved detrimental to the economic productivity of the areas in which it operated. The officer in charge of local revenues was often tempted to extract more taxes than were due him whenever he saw any accumulated wealth, and as a result peasants and merchants soon learned that they had no incentive to improve their farms or businesses.

The early Buyids wore their Zaydi convictions lightly, but later generations made no secret of their Twelver Shi'ite sympathies. On the one hand, they did not force their sectarian identity upon their subjects and they never threatened the Sunni caliph. On the other hand, they did protect and encourage the practice of Shi'ism, which had been crystallizing in Iraq even before the Buyids assumed power there. Hasan al-'Askari, the eleventh Imam of Twelver Shi'ism, was in Samarra when he died in 874, and the scholars who began developing the idea of the Hidden Imam in the 940s were centered in Baghdad. During the 960s, the Buyid regime in Baghdad inaugurated two ceremonies that became central to the ritual life of subsequent Twelver Shi'ism. One was *'ashura'*, which memorializes the death of Husayn at Karbala. *'Ashura'* literally means "tenth," referring to the tenth day of the month of Muharram, when Husayn was killed. Over the next several centuries, the observance of the martyrdom eventually developed into an elaborate ten-day observance involving prayer, Qur'anic recitations, reenactments of the battle at Karbala, and, in some localities, self-flagellation by the pious as a way to share in Husayn's suffering.

The other festival that Shi'ites began to observe at this time was *ghadir khumm*, the celebration of Muhammad's designation of 'Ali to be his rightful successor. The basic assertion of pro-Alids all along had been that 'Ali and his family were the most qualified to rule. The early Shi'ites had claimed that the Prophet had designated 'Ali to be his successor at the pool (*ghadir*) of Khumm. Now, under a Shi'ite regime, that tradition could be publicly celebrated. When the celebrations were held, however, clashes between Sunnis and Shi'ites were common.

Throughout the period of Buyid rule, Baghdad lagged behind both Rayy and Shiraz economically and politically. Shiraz was the wealthiest city of the Buyid confederation, and Rayy became a thriving commercial center on the east–west caravan route. Baghdad did house the caliph, its physical size was still impressive, and scholarly life continued, but it was in the grip of perpetual economic and political crises. Daylami and Turkish soldiers frequently fought pitched battles in the streets, and the countryside was plagued with banditry.

In addition, the tenth and eleventh centuries witnessed a reassertion of nomads throughout the Fertile Crescent and western Iran. The Umayyads and early Abbasids had controlled the movements of nomads by means of a policy that combined the incentives of subsidies and the threat of force. The bedouin lost their subsidies by the ninth century and were displaced from the Abbasid army by the tenth century. They soon began raiding settlements in Syria and Iraq, and discovered that the decline of central authority and of economic stability enabled them to engage in attacks almost with impunity. Several local Arab and Kurdish families seized control of cities during this period, and created short-lived dynasties. By the end of the tenth century, competing Arab and Kurdish families ruled northern Iraq, northern Syria, the middle Euphrates valley, and eastern Anatolia. The most famous of the new ruling groups was the Shi'ite Hamdanid confederation, which controlled Mosul and Aleppo for most of the tenth century. The Hamdanids actually controlled a larger area than did the caliph or his Buyid "Commander of Commanders." They demonstrated their wealth and sophistication by patronizing famous artists and scholars. The Hamdanid ruler of Aleppo, for example, became the primary patron of the philosopher al-Farabi.

Compounding the disorder caused by the "bedouinization" of Syria and Iraq during this period was a century-long revival of Byzantine military power. The Byzantines began capturing Arab settlements in eastern Anatolia in the 930s, driving out the population. In the 960s, they retook Crete, captured Antioch and Tarsus, and sacked Aleppo. Aleppo was subjected to nine days of pillaging, and 10,000 Muslim children were said to have been dragged into captivity. Although the Hamdanids subsequently regained their position as rulers of Aleppo, they served thereafter at the sufferance of the Byzantines and had to pay tribute to them.

Under pressure from the street preachers and ulama, the Buyid regime in Baghdad attempted to mobilize against the Byzantine threat in the early 970s. Factions within the Turkish units of the Buyid army seized this chance to rebel against their masters, however, leading to a civil war that lasted from 972 to 975 and devastated Baghdad. Northern Syria remained vulnerable to Byzantine incursions, and over the next few decades vast expanses of Muslim settlement in the frontier zone along the Taurus Mountains were wiped out. Refugees flooded into Syria and northern Iraq, causing the Buyids and the caliphate to lose considerable prestige for their failure to stem the tide of the Christian enemy's incursions.

A resurgent Byzantine empire was ominous for the Buyids, but the security problem was intensified by the rise of yet another threat, this time from the east. After 1030, isolated groups of Turkish sheep herders and war bands began to filter into Azerbaijan and northern Iraq from Transoxiana. Themselves the victims of warfare in the east, they were desperately poor, seeking green grass for their sheep and plunder for themselves. Their arrival touched off chronic warfare between them and the local inhabitants. One group of these herdsmen temporarily captured Mosul in 1044. Challenged from the east and from the west, the authority of the Buyids by the middle of the eleventh century extended little farther than the environs of their three main cities. Even in the cities the sight was not pretty. Travelers reported that Baghdad had degenerated into a congeries of fortified hamlets, separated from each other by the desolate ruins of what once had been the greatest city in the world west of China.

The Advent of the Turks

By the middle of the eleventh century, the Buyids were suffering from a series of escalating challenges from the Byzantines, bedouin, and Turks. A clear-headed military analyst in Baghdad in the early eleventh century would have emphasized the need to concentrate Buyid military resources against the Byzantines and bedouin: They were, after all, formidable local threats. The Turks, fearsome as they might be, were based a thousand miles away in Transoxiana. Such a clear-headed analysis would have been wrong, as even rational calculation sometimes can be in the face of the unexpected. As it turned out, the Turks dispensed with the Buyids, Byzantines, and bedouin as though they were leaves before the wind. The coming of the Turks into southwestern Asia in the mid-eleventh century heralded a profound transformation in the relations of power in the Dar al-Islam.

The Turks were a new addition to the linguistic quilt of the Umma. Whereas Arabic is part of the Semitic language family and Persian is one of the Indo–European languages, Turkish is a member of the Ural–Altaic language group, which includes the languages of the Mongols and Koreans. Like the Arabs before them, the Turks quickly conquered a vast, sedentarized and urban-based society. Unlike the Arabs, whose language and religion transformed the civilization of the conquered areas, the Turks were quick to appropriate the languages and religion of the societies into which they moved. But even though they recognized that the culture of the new areas was superior to theirs, they had a sense that they were destined to be rulers over wide areas of the earth. Politically and militarily, they would prove to be the dominant ethnic group within the Umma for most of the next nine centuries.

Origins

Between the seventh and eleventh centuries, most Turks lived in the area north of the Syr Darya River and the Aral Sea and were divided into some two dozen competing confederations. A few Turkish groups—among them the Bulgars, Khazars, Cumans (the western Qipchaqs) and Pechenegs—made their way westward early in this period and played an important role in the early medieval history of eastern Europe. Others, notably the Qarluqs, Oghuz and eastern Qipchaqs, remained in the area north of Transoxiana.

From the early ninth century, Turks had interacted with Muslims in different ways. Individual Turks entered the Dar al-Islam as adventurers or as slaves, some served as mercenary soldiers of established states, and many others found the urban-based Islamic culture to be irresistibly attractive because of its dynamic culture. The Samanid state, with its capital in Bukhara, was the Muslim principality that had the most contact with the Turkish peoples. Even though it was a self-consciously Persian regime, its military force was composed largely of Turkish mamluks. Furthermore, although the economic base of the Samanid regime was the irrigated agriculture of Transoxiana, a large part of its wealth derived from the commerce of the slave trade, for the states of southwestern Asia had by the tenth century developed an insatiable appetite for slave soldiers.

In 961, one of the Samanid ruler's Turkish mamluks seized from his master the city of Ghazna (modern Ghazni) in what is now Afghanistan, where he proceeded to build a power base. In 994, his successor cooperated with the Samanid ruler of the time to repel an invading force of Turks from the Qarluq confederation, and as a reward he received control of Khorasan. Thus, by the end of the tenth century, the Ghaznavids had virtually independent control of the territories south of the Amu Darya. This empire was inherited by Mahmud of Ghazna (998–1030), who became famous for his wide-ranging military campaigns. He made at least seventeen major raids into India for treasure, striking as far south as Gujarat, plundering and destroying Hindu temples. The most successful, and infamous, of his conquests was the plundering of the immense temple complex of Somnath in 1025–1026, which resulted in the massacre of thousands of Hindus and the extraction of incalculable wealth. Mahmud boasted of how his troops smashed to pieces the golden idols there; he did not emphasize that the gold was then carried back to the treasury at Ghazna for him to enjoy.

The Ghaznavid state had long-lasting repercussions. As an aggressive Muslim regime based in what is modern Afghanistan, it was poised to be a base for the future expansion of Islam into South Asia, as we shall see in subsequent chapters. Culturally, it was equally influential. Mahmud's capital at Ghazna is obscure to most of us today, but prior to the thirteenth century it ranked among the three or four most culturally advanced cities in the entire Dar al-Islam. It attracted not only Turkish warriors, but also many learned authorities of Persian and Arabic culture—poets, historians, linguists, and mathematicians.

The Ghaznavids were Persianized Turks. Although the ruling elite were ethnic Turks, they continued the patronage of Persian art and literature that the Samanids had begun in Transoxiana decades earlier. The greatest literary work of the era was the *Shah-nameh,* or *Book of Kings.* This monumental epic of some 60,000 verses is an intriguing example of the Persian revival of the period. While it is not anti-Islamic, it is a celebration of pre-Islamic Iran, and can be read as an implicit criticism of the Arab conquest of Iran. Its author, Ferdowsi, is said to have worked on the poem for thirty years. For most of that period he lived under Samanid rule, but he presented the manuscript to Mahmud in 1010.

Mahmud also commissioned several outstanding architectural works which had a long-lasting influence. Iranian mosques were already beginning to incorporate into their design a Sasanian feature, the *eyvan,* or large vaulted hall closed on three sides and open to a court on the fourth. Several large mosques of this type were constructed in Ghazna. Over the course of the next century, the motif of a court surrounded by four eyvans came to dominate Saljuq mosque architecture and was used frequently in Iran and Central Asia for centuries to come.

Mahmud's large army, augmented by armor-plated war elephants, struck terror into the hearts of all his opponents. Although his raids may appear to the observer to have been largely in quest of loot, Mahmud insisted that he was championing the cause of Sunnism against both paganism and Shi'ism. He gained a reputation in the Muslim heartland as a champion of Sunni Islam, and although he was a brutal and exploitative ruler, he was praised by scholars for his patronage of the arts and sciences. Sunnis who chafed under Buyid rule looked to him as their deliverer, and to their delight he turned his armies westward late in his career. He captured Rayy from

The Birth of Rostam

Speakers of Persian still revere Ferdowsi's Shah-nameh, *and many of them know by heart large numbers of its verses. The figure from the poem who remains the most popular with Iranians is Rostam, a great hero who fought continually for the defense of Iran. The selection that follows relates details from the circumstances surrounding his birth and provides a flavor of the tone and style of the poem, even though the translation is in prose.*

The incident requires some background: The great ruler Sam had abandoned his infant son Zal at birth because the baby's hair was entirely white. The child was placed on the top of a remote mountain to die, but a great bird, the Simorgh, brought Zal to her nest and raised him as her own. Eventually, Sam learned that Zal had survived to become a towering figure himself and came for him. As Zal was leaving the mountain with his father, the Simorgh gave him one of her feathers and told him that, should he ever encounter trouble, he should burn the feather, and she would come to his aid. Zal soon met the beautiful princess Rudaba and, as the poem relates, their love grew, and wisdom fled: She was soon pregnant with their son, Rostam. The pregnancy, however, was difficult, and Zal was afraid that Rudaba would die. Remembering the feather, he burned it, and the Simorgh instantly appeared.

The Simorgh inquired, "What means this grief? Why these tears in the lion's eyes? From this silver-bosomed cypress, whose face is as the moon for loveliness, a child will issue for you who will be eager for fame. Lions will kiss the dust of his footsteps and above his head even the clouds will find no passage. Merely at the sound of his voice the hide of the fighting leopard will burst and it will seize its claws in its teeth for panic. For judgment and sagacity he will be another Sam in all his gravity, but when stirred to anger he will be an aggressive lion. He will have the slender grace of a cypress but the strength of an elephant; with one of his fingers he will be able to cast a brick two leagues.

"Yet, by command of the Lawgiver, Provider of all good, the child will not come into existence by the ordinary way of birth. Bring me a poniard of tempered steel and a man of percipient heart versed in incantation. Let the girl be given a drug to stupefy her and to dull any fear or anxiety in her mind; then keep guard while the clairvoyant recites his incantations and so watch until the lion–boy leaves the vessel which contains him. The wizard will pierce the frame of the young woman without her awareness of any pain and will draw the lion–child out of her, covering her flank with blood, and will sew together the part he has cut. Therefore banish all fear, care and anxiety from your heart. There is a herb which I will describe to you. Pound it together with milk and musk and place it in a dry shady place. Afterwards spread it over the wound and you will perceive at once how she has been delivered from peril. Over it all then pass one of my feathers and the shadow of my royal potency will have achieved a happy result."

Speaking thus she plucked a feather from her wing, cast it down and flew aloft.

(*Zal took the feather and obeyed his instructions. When his son was born, he named him Rostam.*)

Ten foster-mothers gave Rostam the milk, which provides men with strength and then, when after being weaned from milk he came to eating substantial food, they gave him an abundance of bread and flesh. Five men's portions were his provision and it was a wearisome task to prepare it for him. He grew to the height of eight men so that his stature was that of a noble cypress; so high did he grow that it was as though he might become a shining star at which all the world would gaze. As he stood you might have believed him to be the hero Sam for handsomeness and wisdom, for grace and judgment.

SOURCE: Ferdowsi. *The Epic of the Kings: Shah-Nama the national epic of Persia.* Translated by Reuben Levy. Chicago: The University of Chicago Press, 1967, pp. 47–48.

the Buyids in 1029 and harassed Buyid holdings in Kirman and Fars. At his death in 1030, he controlled an empire that extended from the border of Azerbaijan to the upper Ganges, and from the Amu Darya to the Indian Ocean.

While the Ghaznavids were securing their power in Afghanistan in the second half of the tenth century, clans from two of the Turkish confederations—the Qarluq and Oghuz—began crossing the Syr Darya into Transoxiana. The Qarluq group, led by the Qara-khanid dynasty, converted en masse to Islam about 960. In 992 the Qara-khanids seized Bukhara from the Samanids, and seven years later they took Samarqand. The Amu Darya now served as the boundary between the Qara-khanids and their rivals, the Ghaznavids.

Qara-khanid unity fractured within a decade, and rival Qara-khanid rulers assumed control of Bukhara and Samarqand. Like the Ghaznavids, the Qara-khanids ruled over a largely Iranian populace at first, but Transoxiana experienced a continual in-migration of Turks. The Qara-khanid rulers professed to accept the authority of the Abbasid caliph, at that time under the control of the Buyids, and they became a force for the propagation of Islam within Transoxiana and in surrounding territories. Again like the Ghaznavids, they patronized literature, but in this case, it was a new Turkish literature based on Arabic and Persian models, with the result that Turkish speakers had access to a wide range of Islamic literature. The dynasty further signaled its transition from a nomadic lifestyle to an urban environment with its financial support for hospitals, mosques, schools, and caravanserais in Transoxiana.

The Saljuq Invasion

The most famous of the Oghuz clans is that of the Saljuqs. They left the region north of the Aral Sea and entered Transoxiana in the 980s when the Samanids requested their assistance against other Turkish invaders. Still more migrated into the area in the early eleventh century when various branches of the Qara-khanids sought outside aid in their own civil war. Thus, the Saljuqs came into Transoxiana by invitation. It is not known if they had converted to Islam before they entered Transoxiana or after, but, like the Qarluqs, they converted collectively—the religion of the leader became the religion of the tribe.

In 1028, Mahmud of Ghazna imposed a major defeat on a band of Saljuqs who were raiding along the Amu Darya, and the survivors began migrating to the west as far as Azerbaijan, where their depredations harried both the Byzantine and Buyid governments. Seven years later, a group of Saljuqs, led by the brothers Chaghri and Tughril, arrived in Khorasan from Transoxiana, starving and begging for some grazing land. When Mahmud's son, Mas'ud, treated them harshly, they struck back and surprised themselves by defeating him. He granted them a small territory for grazing purposes, but they were no longer supplicants. They allowed their sheep to graze unrestricted in the oases of the northern Khorasan, with the result that crops were damaged. They also intercepted caravans and harassed the villages and towns of the region.

The inhabitants of the major cities of Merv and Nishapur had already been chafing under the heavy taxation of the Ghaznavids, and now their discontent increased, as it appeared that Mas'ud was not going to deliver them from the uncouth and dangerous nomads who did what they pleased with impunity. Despairing of any

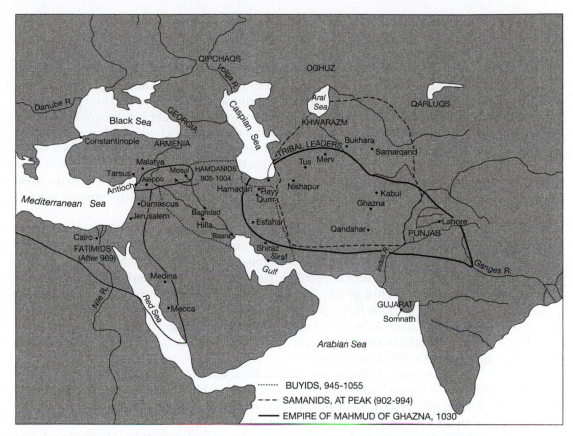

MAP 6.1 The Eastern Muslim World, 950–1030

help from the government in Ghazna, Merv surrendered to the Saljuqs in 1037, followed the next year by Nishapur. In 1040, Mas'ud finally attacked the Saljuqs, only to be soundly defeated. The Ghaznavid empire lost Khorasan forever, and henceforth was to be centered on Ghazna and Lahore.

As the new rulers of Khorasan, and with Mas'ud's successors barely able to keep them out of Afghanistan, the Saljuqs were in a position to carve out a large empire. They immediately conquered Khwarazm, on the lower Amu Darya, in 1042. The Saljuq leaders found much to admire in the Persian culture that permeated the new areas they ruled. Although they and their successors always remained proud of being Turks, they began to adopt certain features of the new culture for their own purposes. They saw the advantages of an efficient bureaucracy with a tax-gathering mechanism, and they admired the Persian literary tradition and architectural styles. They began recruiting Khorasani bureaucrats, the most talented of whom was Nizam al-Mulk, whose achievements we shall see later. They also began to incorporate into their army a unit of slave soldiers. Within two decades or so, mamluks would constitute the core of the Saljuq army, although the army would always contain larger numbers of Turkmen (nomadic Turks), accompanied by their families and herds.

Soon after the conquest of Khwarazm, Tughril and Chaghri agreed on a division of labor. Leaving Chaghri in charge of Khorasan, Tughril began a campaign of conquest westward across Iran. He defeated the Buyid ruler at Rayy in 1043, and over the next seven years he also captured Hamadan and Esfahan. He discovered that he had to rely increasingly on his mamluks and less on his Turkmen. Typically fractious and independent, the Turkmen's top priority was the acquisition of loot and of good grazing grounds for their herds. Tughril knew that he could not discipline them sufficiently to control their looting, but he did try to channel their looting into regions outside the provinces for which he had taken responsibility to protect. As a result, bands of Turkmen not directly under Tughril's control raided into Armenia, eastern Anatolia, and northern Iraq. As long as they were not causing havoc in the areas in which Tughril wanted his authority recognized, they served a useful purpose in weakening the administrative authority of his enemies.

From Esfahan, Tughril began negotiating for the surrender of Shiraz and Baghdad by their Buyid rulers. Baghdad, characteristically, was riven at the time by sectarian strife between Sunnis and Shi'ites, bedouin depredations, and schisms within its own army. Now it was further afflicted by Turkmen raids. The faction aligned with the caliph invited Tughril to take over the city from its Buyid overlords. In December 1055, he did so, with little effort. Soon, however, he faced two serious challenges. The first was a revolt by one of his brothers, who managed to secure a large following of Turkmen by charging Tughril with having begun to associate too closely with urban Arab and Iranian elites.

The second challenge was a threat from a Shi'ite conspiracy. By the 1050s, Fatimid missionaries had begun achieving considerable success in Iraq, as villagers and townspeople sought an alternative to their unbearable conditions. Fatimid agents pointed to the deteriorating conditions as evidence that the time was ripe for God to deliver the Iraqi people through the agency of his Imam. When Tughril took over the capital in 1055, many Iraqis were suspicious and even contemptuous of the Saljuq leader, whom they regarded as dangerous and uncivilized. Among the group that opposed Tughril was a Turkish mamluk military officer in the Buyid service called al-Basasiri. Al-Basasiri had become one of the most powerful members of the Buyid military establishment and was determined not to become subject to what he regarded as a bunch of sheep herders. He consulted with a Fatimid missionary as he planned to recapture Baghdad, only this time in the name of al-Mustansir, the Fatimid caliph-Imam.

Taking advantage of Tughril's absence when the Saljuq leader had to subdue the revolt by his brother, al-Basasiri inflicted a major defeat on the Saljuq army in 1057 and entered Baghdad in triumph the following year. He handed the Abbasid caliph over to Arab tribesmen for safe-keeping, instituted the Shi'ite form of the call to prayer, and said the sermon in the name of al-Mustansir. Thus, for almost a year, Baghdad formally acknowledged the authority of the Fatimid caliph. For purposes that are now obscure, the Fatimid wazir abruptly cut off aid to al-Basasiri, and Tughril, having crushed his brother's revolt, turned back to Baghdad. Upon defeating al-Basasiri, he carried out an intense persecution of the Iraqi Shi'ites, both Twelver and Isma'ili. The attempted Shi'ite coup d'ètat left the Saljuq regime permanently hostile to any form of Shi'ism.

Tughril's recapture of Baghdad was a momentous occasion. For many Sunnis who had become concerned about the political dominance of Shi'ism in Iraq, Egypt, and in scattered provincial dynasties, it was a ray of hope that the caliph's authority would be restored. In fact, although the Sunni Saljuqs respected the caliph as the Shi'ite Buyids could not, they had no intention of turning political or military control over to him. On the other hand, by destroying the Buyids, challenging the Fatimids, and in general persecuting Shi'ites, the Saljuq administration did play a major role in the consolidation of Sunni dominance over Shi'ism in most of southwestern Asia over the next century.

Tughril's consolidation of power was also a dramatic expansion of a process that had been underway since the beginning of the century: the growing importance of Turkish political and cultural power in the Muslim world. Tughril's contemporaries would have viewed his achievement as little more than the seizure of power by yet another regime. It was not a particularly impressive regime, supported as it was by unruly nomads. In fact, however, his arrival marked the advent in southwestern Asia of Turks as creators of empires rather than just as soldiers. As empire builders, they would create some of the most powerful states in the world over the next several hundred years, controlling territory from the middle Danube in Europe to the mouth of the Ganges in South Asia.

The Great Saljuqs and the Saljuqs of Rum

With the recapture of Baghdad in 1058, Tughril secured control of Iraq and western Iran. A year or two later, his brother Chaghri died in Khorasan and was succeeded by his son Alp-Arslan. When Tughril died in 1063, a council of elders chose Alp-Arslan to inherit the entire empire, from Iraq to Khorasan. Although Baghdad remained important as the seat of the Abbasid caliphate, and hence of the legitimacy of Saljuq rule, Esfahan became the seat of most of the Saljuq bureaucratic apparatus. Alp-Arslan left most matters of civil administration to Nizam al-Mulk, his Khorasani *vizier* (the transliteration for the Turkish pronunciation of *wazir*).

Alp-Arslan himself spent little time in Esfahan, for he was a tireless military campaigner. He secured regions that had been bypassed during the original campaign, disciplined renegade followers, and conducted campaigns in Armenia and Georgia designed to secure his borders against Byzantine threats. He also had to suppress a major revolt by one of Tughril's cousins, Qutlumish, who challenged Alp-Arslan's right to rule the entire empire. Alp-Arslan's rapid rise to power had created a crisis. He had not acted illegitimately, but the Saljuqs had no regularized process of succession to power. Like their fellow Turks, they followed a tradition that every member of the ruling dynasty had an inherent right to rule. Influential elders could agree upon a successor to the dead ruler, but any member of the family could legitimately challenge the selection. As a result, most Turkish domains were frequently embroiled in struggles for leadership, but the system also prevented the accumulation of power in a single lineage.

The Byzantine empire, for which the Saljuqs borrowed the Arabic name *Rum* (for Rome, pronounced "room"), now came under unrelenting Turkish pressure. The reason for this did not lie in policies of state: Alp-Arslan was not interested in

Lashkari Bazar, a wealthy Ghaznavid city of the eleventh and twelfth centuries.

conquering the Byzantine empire. In the wake of the Saljuq conquests, however, a constant stream of Turkmen flowed into western Iran, northern Iraq, and Azerbaijan. Bands of Turkmen, with their families and herds in tow, renewed the raiding of Azerbaijan and Byzantine Armenia and began extending their forays even into central Anatolia and northern Syria. Rarely were these raids authorized by Alp-Arslan. Many of the participants were even his enemies, including the sons of Qutlumish, who formed a cohesive group of raiders that grew steadily more powerful.

Nevertheless, the raids were rationalized as attacks on the infidel, in accordance with a long tradition of warfare on the frontiers of the Dar al-Islam. From the perspective of the Turkmen, Rum was a territory in which towns and villages could be raided, the dominance of Muslims could be asserted, and refuge could be sought from the hands of a central Saljuq authority that was becoming progressively alienated from its nomadic masses. From the perspective of Alp-Arslan himself, the more Turkmen who could be diverted into Rum, the fewer unruly nomads he had to worry about as he began laying the foundation for a powerful state. Thus began a tradition of Turkish *gazis*, or raiders, who harassed non-Muslim territories on the Muslim Turkish frontier.

The Byzantine authorities became increasingly concerned about the rising level of raids, particularly when one campaign took raiders to the heart of Anatolia at Iconium (Konya). Negotiations between the emperor and the sultan took place sporadically, but Alp-Arslan had nothing to gain from antagonizing thousands of Turkmen by limiting their raiding. The Byzantines suspected that he was secretly encouraging the raids, and when, in 1071, he embarked on a military campaign to capture Syria, the Byzantines decided to take advantage of his absence by attacking Azerbaijan. The sultan, who had advanced to Aleppo, had to turn back to protect his empire and met the Byzantine army at Manzikert (Malazgirt), near Lake Van.

The Byzantine emperor, Romanus IV Diogenes, had assembled almost the entire Byzantine army to confront the sultan, but the bulk of the army consisted now of foreign mercenaries, including the Norsemen of the Varangian Guard, Normans and Franks from western Europe, Slavs, and even Turks, including some from the Oghuz group itself. The various units were feuding among themselves, and key commanders even of the Greek units despised their emperor. The result was that up to one half of the army deserted on the eve of the battle, and the proud imperial military force was obliterated by the Saljuqs. The Battle of Manzikert, remembered thereafter by the Byzantines as "that terrible day," ranks as one of history's most decisive battles. The units of the vaunted Byzantine army either were destroyed in the battle or melted away into fragmentary and ineffective components.

Rum now lay open to invasion, utterly undefended. Conquest of the area was the last thing on the mind of Alp-Arslan himself—confronted with a threat by the Qara-khanids on his Amu Darya frontier, he launched a campaign to invade Transoxiana. Turkmen on the Anatolian frontier, however, now encountered no effective resistance to their encroachments into Rum and found no reason to leave the area after raiding. More and more Turkmen entered the area in search of grazing areas and raiding opportunities, and still others were invited in by Byzantine factions who were clashing with each other in the wake of the disgrace of Romanus Diogenes at Manzikert.

The Saljuq group led by the sons of Qutlumish were invited by the new Byzantine emperor all the way to Constantinople in 1078 in order to fight the emperor's enemies, and then were enlisted to fight a European rival. In return, they were given access to the city of Nicaea (modern Iznik), sixty miles from Constantinople. They turned it into the capital city of what came to be known as the Sultanate of Rum. Thus, in a remarkable irony, the Byzantines themselves encouraged Turkish immigration into central and western Anatolia, even providing the Saljuqs with cities to use as their bases. It would be several centuries before Turks constituted the majority of the population of Anatolia. But with their rapid dominance of its cities, it is little wonder that, in little over a century, the Franks of the Third Crusade would be calling the area Turkey.

Alp-Arslan met an untimely end during his campaign in Transoxiana. A prisoner was brought to his tent and, in a remarkable lapse of security, the man was able to stab the sultan, mortally wounding him. He was succeeded by his teenage son, Malik-Shah (1073–1092), for whom Nizam al-Mulk continued to serve as vizier. Like Alp-Arslan and Tughril, Malik-Shah was an able military leader. Early in his career he suppressed revolts by relatives who challenged his leadership, and he repulsed a Qara-khanid attack. Thereafter, however, he combined diplomacy and intrigue with his military skills and expanded Saljuq power into parts of Transoxiana, Syria, the Hijaz, Yemen, and the Persian Gulf. Only a few coastal towns of Palestine, including Ascalon, Acre (Akko), and Tyre, remained outside his control. The army that brought him victories and that made his diplomacy effective continued to evolve. Alp-Arslan had increased the number of slave soldiers in it, and at the height of Malik-Shah's career, the nucleus of his army was slave. Almost all the rest were mercenaries, rather than Turkmen.

The composition of the army was only one example of the assimilation of the Saljuq elite into the Perso–Islamic culture of the period. Malik-Shah's name is another. Whereas Tughril and Alp-Arslan are Turkish names, the name Malik-Shah derives from the new environment: *Malik* is the Arabic word for "king," and *shah* is Persian for "emperor." The young ruler was a patron of literature, science, and art, and he ordered the construction of beautiful mosques in his capital at Esfahan. Nizam al-Mulk, the native of Tus, worked hard to impose traditional Iranian administrative practices within the Saljuq court, and partially succeeded. He, too, was instrumental in providing patronage for great works of architecture and in establishing colleges of higher learning in Iraq and Syria that emulated similar institutions in his home of Khorasan.

Malik-Shah died in 1092, and with him died the unity of his empire. The Saljuq empire, with its ambiguous policy of succession, now faced a crisis. Contrary to Nizam al-Mulk's conviction that an autocratic regime was the highest expression of good government, the Saljuq state had continued to be administered in a decentralized fashion in deference to the traditional Turkish conception that the family as a whole should participate in the wielding of power. The provinces were granted a considerable amount of autonomy under the leadership of close relatives of the sultan. When Malik-Shah died, the family could not agree on his successor, and various princes fought each other with the armies at their disposal. For over a decade, civil war raged, centered on the struggle for the sultanate between two of Malik-Shah's sons. One of the sons died in 1105, worn out at the age of twenty-five, leaving Muhammad (1105–1118) the sole ruler, but he relied on a surviving brother, Sanjar, to govern Khorasan for him. Muhammad's dynasty came to be referred to as the Great Saljuqs, to be distinguished from the Saljuq Sultanate of Rum at Nicaea in Anatolia. Headquartered at Esfahan, Muhammad had hardly noticed that, during the civil war with his brother, Frankish warriors had taken control of his father's Mediterranean coastline.

The Fatimid Empire

The secretive and underground Isma'ili group surfaced in the ninth century and made a bid for political power as a group known to history as the Fatimids. In 910, the Fatimids seized power in Ifriqiya, and within a few decades they established their capital in Egypt. Fatimid Egypt quickly blossomed into one of the most advanced societies in the world, posing a serious threat to its Sunni rivals. Almost as quickly, however, it faded to second-rate status. By the end of the eleventh century, it occupied space, but was nearly irrelevant as a geopolitical factor.

The Conquest of Egypt and Palestine

When we last saw the Fatimids, their plans to attack Egypt were foiled yet again by the Berber revolt of 943. A revolt of this magnitude had not occurred in two centuries, since the Great Berber Revolt of 740 initiated the collapse of the Umayyad caliphate of Damascus. The Fatimid regime had to fight for its life at a time when it might have been able to take advantage of the Buyid seizure of power in Baghdad. The Sunni governors of Egypt, who also ruled Palestine (approximately the area occupied by modern Israel and Jordan), continued to acknowledge the legitimacy of the Abbasid caliph, but were on cool relations with the Buyid military leaders. Had the Fatimids been able to attack Egypt in the late 940s, the chance that they would not have confronted Buyid reinforcements was good.

It took almost twenty years for the Fatimids to restore their control over the Maghrib. By the 960s, they were once again prepared to turn east. Having failed three times to capture Egypt, the regime prepared carefully for the campaign of 969. One step that was taken was ideological: The official genealogy for the Fatimids was changed in order to attract the support of the far-flung Isma'ili community. The regime's founder, 'Abd Allah al-Mahdi, had claimed descent from Ja'far al-Sadiq's son 'Abd Allah. Without great fanfare, his grandson al-Mu'izz (953–976) consistently claimed descent from Isma'il instead, making the Fatimids "Isma'ilis" again.

Al-Mu'izz also was fortunate to have as his chief of armies one of the greatest generals of the age, Jawhar al-Rumi, a former Greek slave. Jawhar developed a formidable army. Its core was composed of the Kutama Berbers, but it was supplemented by growing numbers of Sudanese, Slavic, and Greek troops. This army put down the Berber revolt and recaptured Sijilmasa and Fez between 958 and 960. With North Africa pacified, al-Mu'izz set his sights on Egypt. This time the Fatimids won a surprisingly easy victory in 969.

Jawhar administered Egypt until the caliph-Imam al-Mu'izz arrived in 973. One of Jawhar's first official acts was to found a new capital city for his master. The existing capital, Fustat, had been created by the Arab conquerors of Egypt in 640 as a garrison city, and Jawhar's task was to create an imperial city that reflected the glory of the new dynasty. He laid out the boundaries of the new capital some three miles to the northeast of Fustat, calling it al-Qahira al-Mu'izziya, "Victorious (City) of al-Mu'izz," or Cairo. Surrounded by high walls, it was to be the center of government and of the Fatimid religion. For many years, it was almost exclusively composed of palaces, mosques, and barracks for the troops.

The new government initially sought to challenge Baghdad for the allegiance of the world's Muslims, but it ran into problems when its army began occupying territories in Palestine. The indigenous Carmathians of Syria called upon the aid of their compatriots in Bahrain, and the two groups joined together to thwart the eastward expansion of Fatimid rule. For eight years, they fiercely resisted their fellow Isma'ilis. They seriously impeded the Fatimid consolidation of power in Palestine, and they invaded Egypt twice before being decisively defeated. The Fatimids did manage to have the prayers in the holy cities of Mecca and Medina said in the name of the Fatimid caliph, but otherwise the expansionist aspirations of the Fatimids were largely disappointed. At its height at the beginning of the eleventh century, the Fatimid caliphate directly controlled Libya, Egypt, Palestine, and the upper Red Sea coast. Al-Mu'izz was content to rule Ifriqiya indirectly through the Zirid dynasty, a Berber family that had been rewarded for its loyalty with the governorship of the region when al-Mu'izz departed for Egypt.

Religious Policies

In light of the resources that the Fatimids had devoted to missionary activity and to the expansion of territory under their control, it would have been reasonable to expect that the new regime would attempt to turn Egypt into an Isma'ili society from which to convert the rest of the Muslim world. For over fifty years, the Fatimids had persecuted Ibadi Kharijism and Maliki jurists in Ifriqiya in a brutal campaign of terror and extortion. The campaign did scatter the Ibadis, but the martyrdom of Maliki ulama only increased the hostility of Sunnis toward the regime. By the 970s, the new leaders of the regime appear to have learned something from that experience. Although the Fatimid Imams did continue an active and wide-ranging missionary program all across the Muslim world and into Transoxiana and Sind, their religious policies in Egypt were benign. Isma'ili missionary activity, based on the model of a master and his initiates, was intended to bring about the conversion of spiritual adepts, not the masses. Prayers in the mosque were given for the Fatimid caliph, but otherwise Sunni prayers, doctrines, and ritual were hardly affected. During the first few decades of Fatimid rule, Fatimid law was dominant and held sway in the event of conflicts with Sunni schools, but by the middle of the eleventh century the Sunni schools were given equal status. The Fatimid authorities quickly adopted the observance of Ghadir al-Khumm and of Ashura from the Buyids. By the early twelfth century, they had introduced a festival of their own: Mawlid al-Nabi, the birthday of the Prophet. Although Ghadir al-Khumm, for obvious reasons, remains a distinctly Shi'ite festival, both Ashura and Mawlid al-Nabi are widely celebrated among both Sunni and Shi'ite communities today.

Sunni Muslims did experience occasional restrictions on their ability to worship, due to the fact that they were suspected of pro-Abbasid sympathies. Jews and Christians, on the other hand, who were tolerated in the rest of the Muslim world, found unique opportunities in Fatimid Egypt. Both of these non-Muslim religious groups were represented in large numbers in the government, particularly in the financial administration, which the Copts dominated. Twice—under al-'Aziz (976–996) and al-Hafiz (1131–1150)—Christians served as wazir. Jews served in high offices in such numbers that Abbasid partisans claimed that the Fatimids were actually a Jewish dynasty. During the Fatimid period, Copts were the majority in many of the rural areas and in towns that specialized in the manufacture of textiles. Whereas Sunni rulers (and insecure Fatimid wazirs) occasionally felt compelled to respond to the sensitivities or fears of the masses regarding religious minorities, the Imams, as divinely appointed agents, felt no such compulsion. Imams were even known to visit churches and monasteries and to observe Christian festivals such as Epiphany and the Coptic New Year. With the exception of al-Hakim, Imams did not persecute Christians or Jews. The street crowd, however, could become dangerous. At the death of al-'Aziz, who appointed a Christian wazir and otherwise showed toleration of Jews and Christians, a Sunni mob in Cairo plundered several churches and murdered several Christians.

The caliph-Imam who violated the policy of toleration was al-Hakim (996–1021). For this reason he is, unfortunately, the most famous of the Fatimid rulers. Eleven years old when he succeeded his exceedingly able father, he killed his regent four years later and ruled on his own authority. During the remainder of his reign, he ordered the execution of several thousand people, many of whom were important

The al-Hakim mosque (1013) and Cairo city walls (1087) from the Fatimid era.

officials in the government and who never knew why they were targeted. He issued edicts that required the markets to be open all night, and he forbade the consumption of watercress or of fish without scales. Once he ordered that representations of the Christian cross not be shown in public, only to issue an order shortly thereafter requiring Christians to wear the cross. He ordered the destruction of thousands of churches and synagogues, including the Church of the Holy Sepulcher in Jerusalem.

A little over halfway through his reign as Imam, al-Hakim became the center of a new religious movement. By that time, the Fatimids had been in power in Egypt for nearly half a century, and the apocalyptic expectations of many Isma'ilis that the regime would enact a radically new order had been disappointed by what appeared to be nothing more than yet another mundane regime. About the year 1010, certain religious leaders in Cairo began teaching to their initiates that al-Hakim was an incarnation or manifestation of the deity. The most visible spokesman for the cause was Muhammad al-Darazi, but soon devotees of the movement were to be found in considerable numbers all the way to Aleppo. They were being called *al-Duruz* (the Druze), a plural noun meaning "the followers of al-Darazi," apparently because of the active role of al-Darazi in the teaching of the new doctrines. Al-Darazi paid for his notoriety: He was assassinated in 1019, but it is not clear whether soldiers or jealous rivals within his own movement were responsible for his death.

In 1021, al-Hakim failed to return from one of his customary nighttime wanderings into the desert. Some suspected foul play, while those who worshiped him insisted that he had been placed in concealment by God. His successor as caliph persecuted the movement mercilessly, and soon the remaining members were to be found only in the mountains of Syria–Lebanon. The Druze, who call themselves al-Muwahhidun, or Unitarians, number about 300,000 today. They are not regarded as Muslims because of their unique doctrines and rituals.

In light of the apparent goal of the Fatimids while in Ifriqiya to dominate the known world, their subsequent actions in Egypt seem strangely unambitious. Aside from a persistent determination to maintain control of Palestine in the face of threats from various local and outside threats, the Fatimid government did not attempt any major conquests. In fact, after the reign of al-ʿAziz (976–996), peaceful relations were maintained with the Byzantines throughout most of Fatimid history. In 1038, one of the many treaties concluded between the two governments allowed the Byzantines to rebuild the Church of the Holy Sepulcher. As previously noted, the Fatimid government did not forcibly try to convert its own citizens, even though the mosque of al-Azhar, which was constructed in 970, became the setting for public lectures on the Ismaʿili school of law. Within the palace itself, the famous *dar al-hikma*, or House of Wisdom, trained missionaries for the purpose of spreading Ismaʿili doctrines throughout the Muslim world, but this nonviolent approach was the substitute for any campaigns such as the one that succeeded in taking Egypt. The Fatimid missionary activities reached their peak during the reign of al-Mustansir (1036–1094), with agents active in Iraq, Fars, Khorasan, and even Transoxiana. Al-Basasiri's short-lived coup in Baghdad in 1058 appeared to be a major triumph for these efforts at first, before the fatal breakdown in relations between al-Basasiri and the Fatimids.

The New Egyptian Economy

Despite the eccentricities and distractions of the reign of al-Hakim, the Fatimid state continued to thrive for several decades. From the late tenth century until the middle of the eleventh, it was the preeminent empire in the Mediterranean basin and in the Muslim world. Its wealth was based on the agricultural productivity of the rich Nile valley, but commercial contacts with areas as far apart as Morocco and India supplemented the economic base. The empire's own conquests in the Maghrib had established links there, and its missionary work had resulted in the presence of numerous Ismaʿili merchants in Sind and Gujarat, who worked to funnel as much as possible of the trade from those important commercial centers to Egypt.

The Fatimids had become established in Egypt at a fortuitous time in economic history. First, western Europe, which had been a poverty-stricken hinterland for the previous five centuries, was slowly developing a stable economy on the foundations of the medieval agricultural revolution. This in turn spawned the growth of towns where the agricultural surplus could be traded. The nobility and the new merchant class, their pockets brimming with newfound wealth, were developing a taste for luxury goods from the East. It turned out that both Christians and Muslims overcame their religious scruples when it came to trade—the emerging Italian maritime city–states and the Fatimids eagerly sought each other's trade.

Second, as we saw in Chapter 4, the Fatimids were the beneficiaries of changes in major trade routes. Much of the trans-Saharan trade shifted from Ifriqiya to Egypt when the Fatimids' traditional sub-Saharan suppliers saw that the new imperial market in Egypt was much more lucrative than the provincial markets of North Africa. The Fatimids also benefitted from the turmoil that began in Iraq during the late ninth century. South Asian merchants who had been accustomed to shipping goods through the Persian Gulf and across Iraq and Syria now looked for a trade route that could guarantee them safety and a demand for their goods. They found it in the Red Sea route, where the Fatimid navy controlled both the Red Sea and the eastern Mediterranean. A portage of one hundred miles from the Red Sea to Cairo linked the sea trade on both sides of the country. Spices, perfumes, and fine cloths from South Asia and Southeast Asia were in heavy demand all around the Mediterranean, and in return the Indian Ocean suppliers received the products of the Mediterranean hinterland: fine glassware, cloths, furs, and gold. Egypt itself was famous for producing remarkably high-quality fabrics, jewelry, pottery and crystal ware.

Ominous Developments

At the middle of the eleventh century the Fatimids began to experience a series of jolts that shook the very basis of their regime. The first was a factional conflict within the military. The Fatimid army had begun as a mixed force based on a Kutama Berber lance-bearing cavalry supplemented by Slavic and Greek infantry. The conflict with the Carmathians in Syria during the 970s, however, had demonstrated to the Fatimid commanders that the Berber lancers were vulnerable to mounted archers. As a result, the regime soon began importing both slave and free Turkish cavalry as mounted archers. Moreover, the change in the regime's base from Ifriqiya to Egypt meant that it was now more economical to employ Daylamis and black Sudanese in the infantry than the Slavs and Greeks, who were more difficult to obtain.

Within a few years two major rifts within the military were beginning to show themselves. One was that the privileged position of the Kutama had become threatened by the Turks, and the tensions were expressed by violent encounters between the two groups. The second was that the infantry, which achieved parity in numbers with the cavalry, began to demand more equitable treatment. Both conflicts had ethnic overtones. Within the ranks of the cavalry itself, Turks and Berbers were clashing as early as 1044 over scarce resources, and a civil war between units of Turkish cavalry and black infantry erupted in 1066. Cairo suffered extensive damage, and the violence in the countryside caused fields to be unattended, a factor contributing to a seven-year-long famine. The failure of al-Basasiri's revolt against Tughril Bey in Baghdad in 1058 was a blow to the morale of the regime, which had thought that its long-standing goal of capturing Baghdad was finally in its grasp. As if these miseries were not enough, a plague struck Egypt in 1063, and in 1069 the ruler of Mecca and Medina transferred his allegiance to the Saljuqs and had prayers said in the name of the Abbasid caliph.

The turmoil within the Fatimid military at mid-century led to such destruction and economic distress that in 1073 the caliph-Imam al-Mustansir was forced to seek the assistance of his governor in Palestine, Badr al-Jamali. Badr went to Cairo, where he combined the role of wazir with full military powers. Badr, a converted Armenian, was a forceful personality who realized that drastic steps had to be taken to save the regime. He brought with him thousands of his own Christian Armenian troops to be the core of his military force, and he began replacing the troublesome Turkish mamluks with Sudanese infantry, a trend that continued over the next century until the Sudanese units became the largest contingent in the army.

Badr al-Jamali's promotion achieved al-Mustansir's immediate goal, but it had two major drawbacks. First, the withdrawal of the Armenian troops from Palestine allowed Malik-Shah to seize most of Palestine with ease. Second, Badr never yielded the reins of power in Egypt until his death in 1094, leaving al-Mustansir as subservient to his military leadership as the Abbasid caliphs had been to military officers since the early tenth century. The position of the caliph-Imam in Egypt never regained its prominence.

The Nizaris ("Assassins")

The Saljuq court had been hostile to the Fatimids ever since the latter had supported al-Basasiri in his attempt to overthrow Tughril. Nizam al-Mulk, in particular, became increasingly concerned about the Fatimid threat because of a new militance among the Isma'ilis of Iran. In 1090, the former quietism of that group gave way to a policy of assassinating public officials. The architect of the new policy was Hasan-i

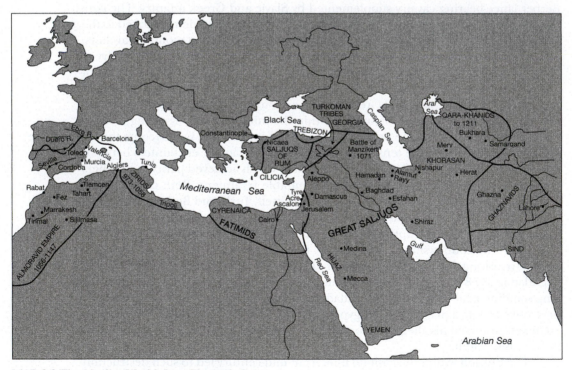

MAP 6.2 The Muslim World, Late Eleventh Century

Sabbah, an Iranian from the city of Qum. He had been trained in Cairo at the Dar al-Hikma and then returned to Iran, probably in the late 1070s. The Isma'ili message seems to have gained new strength in the aftermath of the Saljuq invasion, combining the traditional demand for social justice with a heightened sense of Iranian ethnicity formed in reaction to the Turkmen invaders. Isma'ilis were to be found all across Iran by the closing decades of the century, and Hasan found particularly strong support in the traditionally Shi'ite region of Daylam.

In 1090, Hasan acquired Alamut, a fortress in the Elburz range that proved to be impregnable for over a century and a half. Hasan began a campaign against the Saljuqs, who were doubly despised as defenders of Sunnism and as outsiders. Recognizing that winning pitched battles was not a realistic option, he began a policy of assassinating Saljuq officials. The legend arose that the agents who were sent out from Alamut for the purpose of murdering officials were administered hashish during a ritual. No evidence supports the idea that the drug was used in this way, but the agents nevertheless gained the nickname of *hashishin*, or hashish users. The English word *assassin* derives etymologically from this word, and Hasan's followers have been known as the Assassins for centuries. After killing several minor officials, the Assassins made a spectacular "hit" in 1092 by killing their old nemesis, Nizam al-Mulk, possibly in collusion with none other than Malik-Shah, who was clearly chafing after twenty years of the old Iranian's imperious tutelage.

Hasan's career took a turn in 1094, when a schism developed within the Fatimid movement. Al-Mustansir died a few months after Badr al-Jamali's death in 1094. Confusion over the succession process followed. The new wazir, Badr's son al-Afdal, favored the youngest son, al-Musta'li, but the eldest son, Nizar, claimed that his father had designated him to be his successor. In the subsequent conflict, Nizar fled Cairo, but was captured and murdered by being entombed within a wall. Al-Musta'li became the new Imam, but the supporters of the two sons formed factions that became bitter enemies.

The schism within the Fatimid ruling family in Cairo reverberated throughout the Isma'ili world. Al-Musta'li came to be recognized by most Isma'ilis in Egypt, many in Palestine, and by almost all Isma'ilis in Yemen. The Sulayhid regime in Yemen, ruled by the remarkable queen al-Sayyida al-Hurra al-Sulayhi (1084–1138), played a vital role in preserving the Musta'li line. She sponsored an extensive missionary activity in the Gujarat region of India on behalf of the cause, and the Musta'lis became permanently well-established there.

Hasan-i Sabbah, on the other hand, sided with Nizar's claim to be the Imam, and his considerable personal authority influenced many Isma'ilis in Syria and the vast majority of Isma'ilis in Iran to become "Nizaris." The upshot was that the "Musta'lis" had a visible caliph–Imam to follow, but one who was under the actual authority of al-Afdal, the Armenian wazir. The Fatimid state had become a hollow shell by this time and remained intact for another century only because of a peculiar set of international affairs that we shall examine in the next chapter. The Nizaris, on the other hand, claimed that a son of Nizar had been safely sequestered at Alamut. The masses of Nizaris never saw him, but Hasan served until his death in 1124 as the *hujja* or agent of the Imam who, he claimed, was in safekeeping. The Assassins were about to embark upon a period of history that would immortalize their name.

Hasan, therefore, by 1094 led a movement opposed to both the Saljuqs and the Fatimids. Because of Hasan's highly publicized activism, he attracted the support of Isma'ilis throughout Iran and Syria, and he soon came to rule over what was in effect a Nizari "state." It was not a territorial country with borders, but rather was composed of widely scattered fortresses, together with surrounding farms, villages, and, in a few cases, towns. These fortresses were located in eastern and southern Iran, the Elburz and Zagros mountain ranges, and northern Syria. Although occasionally a local Isma'ili leader might disagree with a policy adopted at Alamut, most of the time the various Nizari communities worked together with remarkable coordination. Hasan and his seven successors were commonly referred to as the Lords of Alamut. Alamut itself developed a reputation not only for terror, but also for being an intellectual center. As we shall see, Nizaris were remarkably active in the cultural life of the twelfth and thirteenth centuries. Alamut housed one of the world's greatest research libraries of the period and hosted many scholars–Twelver Shi'ites and Sunnis as well as Isma'ilis.

The Muslim West

The Muslim lands bordering the western Mediterranean enjoyed a halcyon period during the second half of the tenth century. The eleventh century, on the other hand, witnessed a profound change in the fortunes of the region. A combination of internal conflicts and foreign invaders threatened the very existence of the western wing of the Dar al-Islam and led to the permanent loss of Sicily and parts of Andalus.

Norman Invasions of Muslim Territory

A major theme in the history of the western Mediterranean basin in the eleventh century was the irruption into the area of a people known as the Normans. The Normans, more famous for William the Conqueror's exploits of 1066 at Hastings, had made a name for themselves years earlier in the warmer climes of the Mediterranean. It would have taken a keen eye at the time to discern in the bloody conquests of those brutal and avaricious knights the first inklings of a newly empowered Europe. In fact, however, they were the vanguard of an expansive Europe that was undergoing an economic revival and a "baby boom." Abundant food, commerce, cities, and education were finally coming to western Europe. The wealth and power of that society expressed itself in the military expeditions of the eleventh century by the knights of the Norman conquests, the Reconquista, and the Crusades. The earliest triumphs were by the Normans, and they inflicted territorial losses on the Muslims that have lasted to the present.

Beginning in the early eleventh century, small groups of Norman adventurers began entering southern Italy in search of their fortune. In that welter of small, feuding states they had been able to sell their services to local lords and then to take over from their erstwhile masters. Confounding their contemporaries, who assumed that, as cavalrymen, they were strictly land based, some of them took advantage of Zirid weakness as early as 1034 and began occupying port cities in Ifriqiya. Of much greater interest to them, however, was Sicily, which had the appeal both of proximity to the Italian peninsula and of prosperity.

Sicily had been under Muslim control for two centuries. The Aghlabids had slowly conquered the island from the Byzantines during the period 827–878. During that period, Sicily served as a base for Muslim raids into Italy, the most famous of which was the sack of the basilicas of St. Peter and St. Paul in 848. In 909–910, the Fatimids conquered the Aghlabids and thereby became the masters of Sicily. By mid-century, when the great Fatimid general Jawhar was preoccupied with reestablishing control over the Berbers of Ifriqiya and with planning the conquest of Egypt, the island had become in effect an autonomous province under a local Muslim dynasty.

Throughout its two centuries as a Muslim-controlled island, Sicily played an important political and cultural role. Like every other Mediterranean state of the period, its relations with its neighbors, Christian and Muslim alike, included piracy, wars, trade agreements, and cultural exchanges. The island's agriculture, like that of Andalus, achieved unprecedented prosperity as a result of new irrigation techniques, the breaking up of large land holdings, and the introduction of new crops such as citrus fruits, sugar cane, new vegetables, and date palms. Castles, palaces, mosques, and gardens patterned after Iranian models changed the landscape, and poetry, law, and Qur'anic studies flourished. Sicilian Christians and Jews assumed the typical status of <u>dh</u>immis, paying the poll tax, but allowed freedom of worship.

After about 1040, two developments led to the destruction of Muslim Sicily. First, the authority of the ruling Muslim dynasty was eroded, and Sicily fragmented politically. Then, in the 1060s, Robert Guiscard and his brother Roger began consolidating Norman power in southern Italy and eventually formed an alliance with the pope. They conquered Byzantine territories in the peninsula, and then in 1081 Robert began an anti-Byzantine campaign in the Balkans that was stopped by the Byzantine emperor only with Venetian help. Meanwhile, Roger, acting as his brother's vassal, began conquering Sicily in 1061. As in the case of the Muslim conquest of the island two centuries earlier, the task required several decades. It was finally completed in 1090. Roger's son, Roger II, brought about the unification of the Norman territories of Sicily and the Italian mainland in 1127, creating the new Kingdom of Sicily. The first Normans were intrigued by Islamic civilization, and under Norman patronage a flourishing synthesis of Islamic, Jewish, and Christian civilization occurred. In the twelfth century, however, the Reconquista and Crusades created a hostile climate for Muslims and Jews. Sicily was lost to the Dar al-Islam.

The "Hilali Invasion" of Ifriqiya

Muslims in Ifriqiya were concerned about a Norman conquest there, as well. Over a period of twenty-six years after 1034, the Normans methodically captured Tripoli, Jerba, Sfax, Sousse, Mahdiya, and Tunis. Whatever the Norman ambitions in Ifriqiya were, however, the invaders soon learned that a large-scale conquest was out of the question. The Norman army was not large enough to garrison all the cities and had to make alliances with local tribes. Moreover, the foreigners soon learned that the region was not as prosperous as it had been earlier. Ifriqiya still had the aura of its former glory under the Aghlabid (800–909) and Fatimid (910–973) regimes, which had stimulated a lucrative, long-distance caravan trade across the Sahara. Their lavish courts had placed a premium on luxury goods, and their possession of Sicily facilitated commerce with European ports. The creation of a network of merchants from Europe to Ghana had made merchants in many ports in Ifriqiya wealthy during the ninth and tenth centuries.

Sicily, however, became autonomous during the Fatimid wars to suppress the Berber revolts of the mid-tenth century, and its commercial links with Ifriqiya were loosened. Subsequently, the departure of the Fatimid court for Egypt in 973 diverted much of the Saharan trade from Ifriqiya to the much larger metropolitan area of Fustat–Cairo. Thus, by the eleventh century, Ifriqiya was already feeling the effects of a decline in the long-distance trade that had crossed the region. Information about the Norman presence in Ifriqiya is sketchy, but it is clear that the seizure of the port cities after 1034 was accompanied by raids into the hinterland and agreements with local tribes to secure cities for them. Agriculture may well have suffered from the raids and from the free hand given to the local nomads.

The diversion of the trade routes to Egypt, the Norman capture of the most important ports, and the crisis in Sicily after the Norman conquest began in 1061 might well have been sufficient to leave a permanent scar on the economic history of North Africa. All those developments, however, have been overshadowed in the annals and in epic poetry by yet another incident at midcentury. In 1051, the Zirid leader of Ifriqiya, whose regime had ruled an autonomous province under the Fatimids for decades, bowed to the pressure of his Maliki ulama and publicly humiliated the Fatimids by declaring his allegiance to the Abbasid caliph. In view of the Abbasid caliph's abject weakness in both religious and political affairs at the time (these were the last days of the Shi'ite Buyid regime in Baghdad), this declaration was particularly galling to the Fatimid court, and was viewed as a blatant insult. According to legend, the Fatimid wazir persuaded Imam al-Mustansir to punish the disloyal Zirid ruler and simultaneously rid his realm of a domestic problem: He encouraged a number of bedouin tribes that were posing a threat to villages in the Nile valley to migrate into Ifriqiya. The Banu Hilal and the Banu Sulaym were the most famous of the bedouin tribes that migrated westward.

The "Hilali invasion" has long been blamed for the economic catastrophe that undoubtedly occurred in Ifriqiya during the eleventh century. It has inspired Arab epic poetry and shaped our historical understanding of the period. Recent research on the economy of the era and the impact of the Norman raids has modified that picture considerably. There is no evidence that the Fatimids actually sent bedouin into Ifriqiya. The Banu Hilal and Banu Sulaym were Arab tribes grazing their herds to the west of the Nile, and they seem to have migrated west about the time that the Zirids made their declaration. The Banu Sulaym settled in Cyrenaica (eastern Libya), but the Banu Hilal continued to Ifriqiya. There they harassed the Zirids during the 1050s, forcing the ruling family to abandon Qayrawan and move to the better-fortified city of Mahdiya.

Other Arab tribes continued to move into the coastal plain of North Africa. Some stayed north along the Mediterranean coast, and others migrated along the eastern slopes of the High Atlas into southern Morocco. These incursions coincided with continued Norman raids along the coast of Ifriqiya. From Ifriqiya to Morocco, agriculture on the coastal plains was disrupted; the city of Qayrawan was largely abandoned and its economic and cultural influence plummeted; and Arab tribesmen feuded among themselves and with Berber tribes, making travel and commerce even riskier than before. The Normans soon drove the Zirids out of Mahdiya and captured the city. They also conquered Tunis, and contracted with a Berber chief to rule the city for them. They now controlled the important ports from Tripoli to Tunis.

The Arab nomads were no doubt destructive, just as they were in many other regions of the Dar al-Islam at one time or another. Their impact now seems to have been cumulative, however, rather than decisive. They were one factor, along with the slowing of long-distance trade and the Norman invasions, that led to the economic decline of North Africa. On the other hand, regardless of the precise economic role of this second Arab invasion, it did have a significant cultural legacy. It accomplished what the Umayyad conquest of North Africa had not: the gradual displacement of Berber by Arabic as the lingua franca of the North African coastal plain. The growing number of powerful Arab tribes caused their language and customs slowly to become dominant on the coastal plain, so that the region became in many ways a cultural extension of the Arab East. The majority use of Berber became confined to the mountains and the desert regions.

A Berber Empire

The Maghrib west of Ifriqiya was the largest area in the Dar al-Islam without a major state during the three centuries between the time of the Great Berber Revolt of 740 and the middle of the eleventh century. During that period the region witnessed the rise of numerous petty principalities such as Tahart, Sijilmasa, Tlemcen, and Fez. Most were Berber, while Fez was the notable Arab-led mini-state. By the middle of the eleventh century, however, a religious movement among a Berber tribe in southern Morocco gave rise to the Almoravid Empire, a state that would play a major role in the geopolitics of the era and help to lay the foundation for modern Morocco.

The seventh-century Arab conquest in North Africa had followed closely the contours of the areas of Roman settlement. In order to protect those areas from Berber incursions and from Byzantine naval attacks, Arab leaders established garrisons in forts along the lines of settlement and along the coast. Such forts in Andalus and in Ifriqiya came to be known as *ribats*. Often local citizens would supplement the regular soldiers in the forts as a civic and religious duty. During the ninth century, the long campaign by the Aghlabids to conquer Sicily had intensified this process, as garrisons kept a watch for signs of the Byzantine fleet, which occasionally attacked in retaliation. The men who lived in the forts—and especially the civilians who did so—were known as *murabitun* (sing. *murabit*). Thus, in the coastal areas of the western Mediterranean, as along many other frontiers of the Dar al-Islam (including the Andalusi–Christian frontier and the Turkish–Byzantine frontier), "warriors for the faith" had become a familiar feature of daily life.

As the military threat receded along the coasts, the ribats of Ifriqiya lost their military importance, and their combined military–religious function evolved into a religious one. They often developed into centers where men came to strengthen their devotional life through prayer and spiritual exercises. In Morocco, the process was almost the reverse: The term *ribat* had been used for centers of religious instruction since the ninth century, even in cases where there had not been a fort. Because they were usually situated in tribal markets or on former religious sites, they were nodes of interaction among mutually suspicious groups and the spiritual leaders tried to play a mediating role. Clashes did happen, however, and so the ribats of Morocco became fortified after having been set up for religious purposes. They were fortified religious schools.

From the late ninth century on, many of the murabitun felt compelled to move from the coasts of the Atlantic and Mediterranean into the Atlas Mountains and into the plains along the desert edge, where they could spread their faith among Berber villagers. There, because of their isolation from the trade routes, many of the Berbers had never encountered Islam or were only vaguely familiar with the rituals and doctrines of the faith. The murabitun taught the fundamentals of the faith, made charms and amulets for the sick and the lovelorn, and served as spiritual advisors. For many of the secluded villages, the murabitun were the first tangible contact with the world of Islam that they had ever experienced.

It was among the Sanhaja Berbers, who lived south of the High Atlas Mountains and north of the Senegal and Niger rivers, that a spiritual movement began that would transform the history of both the Maghrib and Andalus. The Sanhaja had been only lightly Islamized by the early eleventh century, but one of their chieftains returned from the pilgrimage to Mecca about the year 1035, accompanied by a young religious teacher. The teacher, 'Abdullah ibn Yasin, imposed a strict religious and moral discipline upon his followers and began to implement the Maliki law code in their affairs. Because of his emphasis upon the importance of the Shari'a, his movement—at least in the eyes of its critics—developed a tendency towards legalism. For a decade, the leaders of the new movement fought to spread their version of Islam among fellow Sanhaja groups. They closed taverns, destroyed musical instruments, and abolished illegal taxes. Because their religious fervor reminded others of the men of the ribat, they became known as *al-murabitun*, a term which has been anglicized as Almoravids.

During the 1050s, the movement began expanding into southern Morocco, and it gained a new leader in 1061 in the figure of Ibn Tashfin. He was a remarkable military and political leader, and under him the movement enjoyed tremendous expansion. In 1062 he established Marrakesh as his capital, and by 1069 he had control of Morocco. By 1082, his rule extended from the Sahara to the Mediterranean, and from the Atlantic to Algiers. For the first time in history this area was subject to a single political authority. Later in the decade, the power of this new state expanded into Andalus, as we shall see later in this chapter.

The Collapse of the Umayyad Caliphate of Andalus

The strong rule of 'Abd al-Rahman III (912–961) provided hope to some (and fear to others) that a powerful central government had at last been established in Andalus. Events were soon to demonstrate once again, however, that stability in the peninsula was dependent upon the personality of a charismatic ruler. By the last quarter of the century, the number of converts to Islam had swelled dramatically compared to a few decades earlier, and so had the number of Berbers and Slavs, both brought in by 'Abd al-Rahman III and his successor to bolster their armies. The society became splintered into factions. Arab tribes maintained feuds whose origins were often obscure, the social cleavage between Arab and non-Arab Muslims persisted, and Berbers who had been born in Andalus resented the arrival of recent Berber immigrants. Outbreaks of violence among the various ethnic groups became frequent, and the most commonly heard complaint was that of the arrogance of the Arabs. Many of the "Arabs" of Andalus in fact had mothers who were eastern European slave girls, but they continued to trace their origin patrilineally, and thus claimed high status by virtue of their Arab lineage.

When a weak ruler came to the throne in 1002, the stage was set for the various cleavages in society to widen irrevocably. The civil war that many had anticipated broke out in 1009 and did not end until 1031. By the conclusion of the conflict, the withered authority of the Umayyad dynasty had altogether disintegrated. The traditional political fragmentation of the peninsula reasserted itself, and the Umayyad caliphate's authority was replaced by over three dozen independent Muslim city–states. Arab historians have called the rulers of these tiny states *muluk al-tawa'if*, or "party-kings," suggesting that they were the instruments of one interest group or another. Some of these party-kings were Arabs; others were Berbers and Slavs. A branch of the Zirid family that ruled Ifriqiya went to Andalus to fight on behalf of the caliph during the civil war, but wound up taking control of Granada in 1012 and ruled it until 1090. The Zirids of Granada became famous for their alliance with the Jewish Nagrella family, which provided the chief administrators for the state.

Several of the small new states experienced unprecedented economic prosperity due to the fact that their surplus was no longer being siphoned off to Cordoba. The economic boom generated a cultural efflorescence that made the eleventh and twelfth centuries the golden age of Andalusi arts and letters, just as the tenth century had been the pinnacle of its political power. Cordoba's wealth, however, had depended upon the surplus extracted from other regions, and now that it was no longer able to obtain it, the city began to decline. Toledo, Zaragoza, and Seville benefitted the most from Cordoba's displacement. Of those three, Seville became the preeminent city of Andalus for the next two centuries.

The collapse of the Umayyad caliphate of Cordoba entailed a reversion to the status quo of most of the previous three centuries: political fragmentation in Andalus. Many, if not most, Muslims of the peninsula seem to have been more content with less power at the political center. As we have seen, the loss of political centralization even enhanced, rather than harmed, the economic and cultural life of eleventh-century Andalus. On the other hand, the feuding of the city-states seems only to have exacerbated the deeply rooted ethnic tensions of Andalus. In some Arab-dominated cities, Muslim Berbers were subjected to the sumptuary laws intended for Christians and Jews but rarely enforced on them. Berbers were even prohibited from riding horses or carrying arms. This humiliation was followed by an anti-Berber pogrom in Cordoba that spread to other cities, and in some clashes between Berbers and Arabs, acts of ritualistic cannibalism were committed on both sides. A revealing insight into the problems of Andalusi society is found in the plight of the last Zirid ruler of Granada, who, although totally Arabized, felt stigmatized by Arabs to the end of his life because of his Berber origins.

The disintegration of the caliphate played into the hands of the Christian kingdoms to the north, which were growing in strength. They had been prospering ever since the identification in 813 of a site in the extreme northwest of the peninsula as the tomb of St. James. It was soon christened Santiago de Compostela, and it became the third greatest object of Christian pilgrimage (after Jerusalem and Rome) during the Middle Ages. Because of the pilgrimage traffic, Asturias and Navarre increased in wealth. Utilizing its new wealth in its military forces, Asturias pushed to the south as far as the Duero River and then consolidated its power westward to the Atlantic. By the tenth century, it was increasingly known by the name of its southern region, Leon. Its dramatic rise to power was cut short in the middle of the tenth century, however, when its eastern province, Castile, broke away and became a rival kingdom. For the remainder of the century, Leon and Castile—as well as Navarre and Barcelona—were on the defensive against the caliphate, and suffered repeated invasions from 'Abd al-Rahman III and his immediate successors.

The eleventh century witnessed a reversal of the balance of power between the Christian north and Muslim south. The political fragmentation of the Muslims after their civil war (1009–1031) provided Christian states the opportunity to exact tribute from the weaker Muslim rulers just as the caliphate of Cordoba had exacted tribute from the Christians in the tenth century. Castile, in particular, became the beneficiary of Muslim weakness after the civil war. Many party-kings now paid tribute in the form of "protection money" to persuade Castile not to attack them. Muslim states not infrequently even allied with one or more of the Christian kingdoms against their Muslim rivals. The wealth of the Christian kingdoms expanded dramatically as the tribute money from Muslim states poured in and as agricultural lands were opened up in the Duero valley once the caliphate was no longer a threat to Christian settlement there.

By the third quarter of the eleventh century, Castile had come to expect the tribute as a right, and Muslim cities that refused to pay could expect a punitive campaign directed against them. The Muslims of Andalus had not been able to overcome their ethnic divisions and develop a cohesive identity within the framework of the Umma, even in the face of the growing menace to the north. They had gained temporary local freedom only at the expense of military weakness, which meant that in the long run they would fall victim to outside political control.

The Incorporation of Andalus into the Maghrib

While Ibn Tashfin was conquering the vast territory between the Atlantic and Ifriqiya under the Almoravid banner, Castile and Leon intensified their campaigns against the "party-kings" of Andalus, who belatedly realized the vulnerable position of their mutually hostile city–states. By 1082, the ulama of several cities in Andalus were appealing to Ibn Tashfin to aid them in thwarting the designs of King Alfonso VI of Castile. Ibn Tashfin, however, considered the urban Muslim elites of Andalus to be a decadent class, hardly more worthy of aid than were the Christians. He was not surprised when, in 1085, Alfonso took over Muslim Toledo, practically without a fight. This large city, which had represented the first line of defense against the Christian powers for the other Muslim city–states, had been under the "protection" of Alfonso for some years, and Alfonso had actually buttressed the authority of its inept and corrupt ruler against his fellow Muslim challengers. He had had to intervene several times to save the ruler from his own mistakes and crimes. Tired of expending energy in order to protect such incompetence, Alfonso decided to take over the city directly.

Despite Ibn Tashfin's dislike for Andalusi society, he viewed the Christian capture of Toledo as an assault on the Dar al-Islam that he could not ignore. He crossed the Strait of Gibraltar for the sake of Islam, but not to save the party-kings, for whom he did not bother to hide his contempt. In 1086, his Berber army defeated Alfonso's Castilian forces, and he laid siege to Toledo. While his army was investing Toledo, Ibn Tashfin applied to the Abbasid caliph—at that time under the leash of Malik-Shah and Nizam al-Mulk—for recognition as ruler of the Maghrib and for the right to use the title *amir al-muslimin*, or "commander of the Muslims." The title was remarkably close to the caliph's own title of *amir al-mu'minin*, or "commander of the faithful." The caliph, however, flattered to be recognized as possessing authority and desperate to exercise it, eagerly granted him both requests. Moreover, he could not be unaware of the fact that, thanks to the Almoravid movement, the Friday prayers in the Maghrib were being recited in the name of an Abbasid caliph for the first time in over three hundred years.

Despite having defeated Alfonso in the field, Ibn Tashfin could not retake Toledo by siege. Moreover, relations between him and the party-kings deteriorated quickly from suspicion to hostility. He and they belonged to two radically different cultures: He was pious and ascetic; they were worldly and self-indulgent. He was rustic and spoke Arabic with difficulty; they were cosmopolitan men who valued elegance, education, and refinement. He and his male followers wore veils whereas their women did not; this scandalized the menfolk of Andalus, whose women were veiled. When the party-kings failed to cooperate with Ibn Tashfin's military campaigns, his first impulse was to abandon them to their fate at the hands of the Christians, and he returned to Morocco. After several months of reflection in the quiet of his palace, however, his sense of responsibility for defending the Umma overcame his dislike for the Andalusi elites. He knew that it was his calling to keep the Christians out of Andalus and to reform the society along the lines laid out by Ibn Yasin. He returned to Andalus, and from 1090 until his death in 1106, Ibn Tashfin methodically captured all the city–states but Zaragoza, which did not fall to the Almoravids until 1110. Although he managed to capture and unite the Muslim city–states, he was not able to win back any significant territory that the Christians had captured prior to his arrival in Andalus.

Conclusion

By 1100, the Umayyad caliphate of Andalus was as dead as its namesake in Damascus. The Fatimid caliphate was under the control of its wazir–military general, just as the Abbasid caliphate was under the control of the Saljuq sultan. The institution of the caliphate had lost its aura for many Sunnis. The caliph was not a source of religious leadership. Doctrinal and ethical leadership was to be found among private scholars—the ulama—who discovered God's will by means of jurisprudence. A deeper, personal relationship with God was to be found by seeking out the guidance of a Sufi master (who, increasingly, might also be one of the ulama). The caliph was also not the model of the Just Ruler. The government itself was increasingly viewed as remote, oppressive, and interested in its subjects only for the taxes they owed. Shi'ites, on the other hand, were convinced that the problems of society were caused precisely because the majority of Muslims had not recognized that the only legitimate caliph was to be found in the lineage of Muhammad through 'Ali. That the Twelvers, Musta'lis, Nizaris, and Zaydis all disagreed over who the legitimate caliph-Imam should be was a stumbling block for the Sunnis, but it did not shake the confidence of the Shi'ites themselves.

The violence of the late tenth and eleventh centuries had been exhausting and destructive. The bedouin and Turkmen enjoyed the skirmishes, but all pious urban Muslims, at any rate, could agree that the struggle among ambitious warlords was an affront to God's desire for order and justice, and that invasions by nomads and by Christian Europeans were detrimental to the development of a cultured and stable life. What they could not know at the end of our period was that the violence of the previous 150 years was minor compared to what lay ahead.

FURTHER READING

The Buyid Sultanate

Kraemer, Joel L. *Humanism in the Renaissance of Islam: The Cultural Revival during the Buyid Age,* 2d ed. Leiden: Brill Academic Publishers, 1992.

Mottahedeh, Roy P. *Loyalty and Leadership in an Early Islamic Society.* Princeton, New Jersey: Princeton University Press, 1980.

The Fatimid Empire

Brett, Michael. *The Rise of the Fatimids: the World of the Mediterranean and the Middle East in the fourth century of the Hijrah, tenth century C.E.* Leiden, Boston: Brill, 2001.

Halm, Heinz. *The Fatimids and Their Traditions of Learning.* London: I.B. Taurus in association with The Institute of Ismaili Studies, 1997.

Lev, Yaacov. *State and Society in Fatimid Egypt.* Leiden: E. J. Brill, 1991.

The Advent of the Turks

Bosworth, C.E. *The Ghaznavids.* Edinburgh: Edinburgh University Press, 1963.

Bosworth, C.E. "The Political and Dynastic History of the Iranian World (A.D. 1000–1217)," in John A. Boyle, ed., *The Cambridge History of Iran,* vol. 5, *The Saljuq and Mongol Periods.* Cambridge, U.K.: Cambridge University Press, 1968.

Cahen, Claude. *Pre-Ottoman Turkey.* Tr. J. Jones–Williams. New York: Taplinger, 1968.

Cahen, Claude. *The Formation of Turkey.* Tr. and ed. by P. M. Holt. Harlow: Longman, 2001.

Sinor, Denis, ed. *The Cambridge History of Early Inner Asia.* Cambridge, U.K.: Cambridge University Press, 1990.

The Nizaris

Daftary, Farhad. *The Isma'ilis: Their History and Doctrines.* Cambridge, UK: Cambridge University Press, 1990.

The Muslim West

Abulafia, David. *Italy, Sicily and the Mediterranean, 1100–1400.* London: Variorum Reprints, 1987.

Abun-Nasr, Jamil M. *A History of the Maghrib in the Islamic Period,* 3d ed. Cambridge, UK: Cambridge University Press, 1987.

Safran, Janina M. *The Second Umayyad Caliphate: The Articulation of Caliphal Legitimacy in al-Andalus.* Cambridge, Massachusetts: Harvard University Press, 2000.

Wasserstein, David J. *The Caliphate in the West.* New York: Oxford University Press, 1993.

Wasserstein, David J. *The Rise and Fall of the Party-Kings: Politics and Society in Islamic Spain, 1002–1086.* Princeton, New Jersey: Princeton University Press, 1985.

CHAPTER 7

Barbarians at the Gates, 1100–1260

In the previous chapter, we saw that the Dar al-Islam suffered from major episodes of violence from the mid-tenth to the end of the eleventh centuries. But worse was yet to come. As the eleventh century waned, the Dar al-Islam began shrinking for the first time due to attacks from non-Muslims. Prior to that time, the Byzantine resurgence of the tenth century, the Norman conquest of port cities in Ifriqiya (1034–1060) and of Sicily (1061–1090), and the Castilian conquest of Toledo (1085) were rationalized as temporary defeats in the great ebb and flow of warfare to which everyone had become accustomed in frontier areas.

In 1099, however, the Crusaders seized Jerusalem after a three-year land campaign from western Europe. In itself this was not significant, for the Crusaders were eventually evicted from the eastern Mediterranean shores (unlike the Normans from Sicily and the Castilians from Toledo). What is significant, however, is that the Italian city–states that supplied them with provisions quickly dominated the entire Mediterranean sea. Muslim navies and commercial vessels would not be able to compete again until the Ottoman navy asserted its power in the sixteenth century. A little over a century after the fall of Jerusalem, the small Christian kingdoms in the Iberian Peninsula won a decisive victory in their so-called Reconquista, tolling the death knell for Andalus. Shortly thereafter, the pagan Mongols obliterated eastern Iran, cultural area, and at mid-century a second Mongol campaign conquered Iraq and threatened the very existence of the Muslim heartland. These events mark a major turning point in Muslim history.

The Period of the Crusades

For several centuries, Europeans launched numerous armed "crusades" against Muslims in a variety of locations. Usually, however, the phrase "the Crusades" denotes a series of military expeditions directed against targets in Syria and Egypt (and one against Christian Constantinople) during the century and a half after 1096. Only the first Crusade was an unambiguous success. The others were attempts to regain lands lost to Muslim counterattacks or, in the case of the Fourth Crusade, a looting operation against fellow Christians. By the thirteenth century, the presence of the Crusaders had been reduced to a few isolated castles; by 1291, they had all been evicted.

The First Crusade

Saljuq rule in southwestern Asia resulted in persecution for Shi'ite Muslims, but not for Christians and Jews. Some Christians—Armenians and members of other small churches—actually preferred Muslim rule to Byzantine Orthodox rule. The Christians of Anatolia, to be sure, suffered at the hands of Turkmen gazis before the battle of Manzikert, and in that battle's aftermath, they continued to suffer from lawless banditry. However, they were not singled out in the later period. Muslim peasants and townsmen who happened to be in the way of Turkmen bandits suffered as much as Christians. In those areas under the effective control of either the Saljuqs of Rum or the Great Saljuqs, Christians and Jews had little to complain about. It is true that Orthodox Christianity declined and ultimately disappeared in central Anatolia over the next several centuries, but that was due in large part to its isolation from the Orthodox urban centers on the coast, and not to a policy of persecution. The Saljuqs of Rum and the Byzantines viewed each other as rivals, rather than as implacable enemies. They engaged in trade and cultural exchanges and occasionally even aided each other militarily. Because of the turmoil caused by gazis in parts of Anatolia, it is not surprising that the Orthodox Church itself regarded the Turkmen as a disastrous agent, but the non-Orthodox Christians under the rule of both the Sultanate of Rum and the Great Saljuqs were effusive in their praise of their enlightened policies towards them.

The Christians under Saljuq rule, then, did not call upon western Europe for help. The Crusades were the result of a number of developments taking place within Constantinople and western Europe that coincided in the last decade of the eleventh century. In Constantinople, a new emperor, Alexius Comnenus (1081–1118), came to the throne ten years after Manzikert and began taking steps to bring stability to his empire. His first order of business was to arrange a truce with the Saljuqs of Rum, who had earlier aided various contenders for the Byzantine throne. In the course of the next decade, he secured his realm in the Balkans from Norman invaders and, with the help of Cuman (western Qipchaq) Turks, he became the first Byzantine emperor to inflict a decisive defeat on the Pechenegs, a Turkish group that had been marauding in the Danubian basin since the tenth century.

With his borders secure, Alexius could begin to build a solid foundation for a revival of Byzantine glory. One of his goals was to recruit mercenary soldiers from western Europe. Frankish and Norman heavy cavalry and armored infantry were among the most effective military forces of the age and had been important units in the Byzantine army until Manzikert. Having them in the army again would come in handy against future threats, whether from Normans or Turks. With that goal in mind, Alexius dispatched a delegation to Italy in 1095 to seek the pope's aid in recruiting soldiers.

The response was not at all what Byzantine emperor had in mind. When Pope Urban II conveyed the appeal at Clermont in November 1095, western Europe was in the midst of an unprecedented wave of religious enthusiasm as a result of the papal and monastic reforms of the previous decades. Moreover, the nobility of western Europe were experiencing economic hardship due to the "baby boom" that had begun in the eleventh century. As Urban's sermon spread by word of mouth throughout an overwhelmingly illiterate Europe in the winter of 1095–1096, many knights interpreted it to mean that Christians who helped deliver Jerusalem from the hand of infidels would have the opportunity simultaneously to gain whatever loot they could gather and to avoid time in purgatory.

Although Western Christians in general were moved by the appeal, local conditions determined the nature of the response. The Normans as a whole were already preoccupied. The descendants of William the Conqueror were still trying to consolidate power over the Anglo–Saxons thirty years after his victory at Hastings. Other Normans were busily conquering or consolidating their hold over territories in southern Italy, Sicily, North Africa, and the Balkans. The Germans were wracked with civil strife in the wake of the recent monumental conflict between their King Henry IV and Pope Gregory VII, and the Christians of the Iberian Peninsula were preoccupied with their conflict with the Muslims of Andalus.

Individuals from all those areas would go to the Holy Land, but it was the Franks, from the area we now know as France, who formed the bulk of the volunteers who went east on the first "armed pilgrimage." (The term *crusade* was not coined until much later.) Scattered throughout their various duchies, counties, and kingdoms, they had a variety of motivations. Many were prompted by deeply felt religious sentiments; others were interested primarily in the opportunity to gain glory and wealth; most embarked upon the venture for a combination of motives, and saw no contradiction in doing so.

Numerous groups headed off toward Constantinople, including the remarkable horde that followed Peter the Hermit. Others were little more than gangsters, who robbed and plundered their way across Europe until they themselves were robbed or killed. The primary force that is identified with the First Crusade, however, went to Constantinople in four groups, arriving between December 1096 and April 1097. Emperor Alexius was stunned by the arrival of the huge contingents, none of whom intended to give up their autonomy by submitting to his leadership. He warily aided the huge army in its siege of Nicaea, the capital of the Saljuqs of Rum. By a stroke of good luck, it was practically undefended, for the young Saljuq Sultan, Qilij Arslan, had recently left the city and led his army several hundred miles to the east in order to fight Turkish rivals who had challenged his power. He was unable to return in time to enter Nicaea, and his light cavalry lost a pitched battle with the Frankish heavy cavalry. The Byzantine emperor actually organized a clandestine rescue mission for the sultan's family and reunited them to him. He also managed to claim the city for himself when its population surrendered to him rather than to the Franks.

The Franks, who had come to fight "infidels," felt betrayed, and could not understand the nuances of the working relationship that the Byzantines and Saljuqs of Rum had established. They were convinced that their initial suspicions of the integrity of the eastern Christians were vindicated. They got their revenge a year later: When the city of Antioch finally fell after an eight-month siege in June 1098, the

Franks refused to turn the city over to Alexius despite their earlier commitment to do so. Even before the First Crusade had accomplished its mission, relations between the Byzantines and the Franks had become cold at best and were often hostile. The original intent of the expedition was long forgotten, and the Byzantines and Franks would never trust each other again.

Meanwhile, the Fatimids, who were recovering from the Musta'li-Nizari schism of 1094, were watching the campaign of the Franks with interest and curiosity. The wazir, al-Afdal, thought that it represented the beginning of a combined Byzantine–Frankish campaign to push back the Saljuqs, a prospect he found gratifying. He sent a note of congratulations to Alexius upon the fall of Nicaea and sent a delegation to the camp of the Franks during their siege of Antioch, offering a partition of Syria. He received no response to the offer, and he became increasingly uneasy. When, in the summer of 1098, he learned that Antioch had fallen, he seized several garrison cities in Palestine that the Fatimids had lost to Malik-Shah some two decades earlier. He left the area poorly defended, however, and the towns and garrisons of Palestine surrendered quickly in the spring of 1099 to the European invaders. Even Jerusalem, which the Fatimids thought was secure, fell to the Franks in July 1099 after a siege of only one month. In keeping with the pattern of previous sieges, the Crusaders massacred a large number of the population of the city, without regard for their religious affiliation. Al-Afdal sent an expeditionary force into Palestine to try to save the situation, but the Franks mauled it. He did not challenge them again.

The Franks had fought their way to Jerusalem, but they had yet to consolidate their gains. Over the next thirteen years, they secured the entire coast of the eastern Mediterranean, except for the two Fatimid-held cities of Tyre (finally captured in 1124) and Ascalon (captured in 1153). The conquered area was organized into four states. The County of Edessa was the least well defined territorially and the most vulnerable. It lay inland in northern Syria, straddling the Taurus Mountains as far east as the upper Euphrates valley. The storied city of Antioch became the focal point of the new Principality of Antioch, which lay on the upper Mediterranean coast from the Taurus Mountains to a point several miles north of the present Lebanese border. The County of Tripoli lay in the northern half of present-day Lebanon, and the Latin Kingdom of Jerusalem encompassed the territory included today within the borders of Israel and southern Lebanon.

The Europeans set up a society on the basis of what they knew, which was the Frankish feudal structure. It was not an exact replica, for the European landlords lived in towns in Syria, not in castles on their holdings, and the cash economy of southwestern Asia forced a revision in the pattern of service obligations to which the Franks had been accustomed in Europe. The local landowning class was completely replaced by Franks, and in each of the new states, the Franks ruled over a mixed population of Muslims and Christians. In several large areas, the indigenous Christians were the majority. The Catholic Franks characteristically regarded the local Orthodox and other Christians as suspect as the Muslims.

One indignity the Muslims had to endure was the payment of a poll tax, which had been the obligation of non-Muslims in the area for the previous four centuries. But in the towns, the indigenous merchants and craftsmen—Christians, Jews, and Muslims—retained some rights, just as their urban counterparts in Europe had obtained in the eleventh century (although Jews were not allowed to resettle Jerusalem for over a century). Some Christian Arabs even succeeded in becoming members of the knightly class, but such assimilation to Frankish mores was the only cultural interaction which interested the Franks. Whereas the Franks of Syria adopted certain features of local dress, medicine, and creature comforts, they had no interest in a cultural symbiosis. In this regard, they were quite different from their contemporaries, the Normans of Sicily and the Christians of the Reconquista in the Iberian Peninsula, who often took an avid interest in the scholarship and arts of the Muslims. Only a tiny number of the Franks even learned to speak Arabic.

The success of the expedition to Jerusalem had left the Franks confident of their superiority over their Muslim neighbors, but their new states were much more fragile than they realized. They feuded with each other, the leaders and soldiers were in a culture they did not understand, and they were surrounded by rival states. Perhaps most problematic for them was their dependence for leadership and protection on men who viewed their service in the region as temporary, with the result that Frankish manpower had to be constantly replenished just to keep the numbers stable. The Italian city–states of Venice, Pisa, and Genoa took advantage of this need to increase their seaborne trade in the eastern Mediterranean. Their fleets had assisted in the provisioning of the military expedition of 1098–1099 and even blockaded the besieged Muslim ports. Now their role was invaluable in bringing to the feudal states supplies, soldiers, and pilgrims who had money to spend.

Muslim rulers in the region were slow to respond to the Frankish challenge. They had been accustomed to defending their power against fellow Muslims rather than against foreigners. After the death of Malik-Shah in 1094, the Saljuq rulers of Damascus, Hama, Homs, Aleppo, Mosul, and other cities were rivals of each other as well as of their fellow Turks across the Taurus Mountains. Among the latter were the Sultan of Rum (who had relocated to Konya after his defeat at Nicaea) and his Turkish enemies in eastern Anatolia. Thus, the Crusaders had embarked on their enterprise with exquisite timing. Normally at each other's throats in Europe, they had united militarily just as the Saljuqs had splintered into a decentralized system that resembled feudal Europe in many respects. Had the Franks invaded Syria during Malik-Shah's reign, they might well have met with disaster. Instead, they were able to pick off the jealously independent city–states along the coast. All but the formidable Antioch proved to be relatively easy to subdue.

In addition to their rivalry with each other, petty Muslim rulers were also determined not to become subservient to the Great Saljuq sultan. Although theoretically still appointed to their positions by him, the local rulers of Syria were autonomous and had everything to lose by allowing troops from Esfahan to occupy their cities. The Great Saljuqs themselves were actually more interested in Iran than in Syria, but religious leaders, Sunni and Twelver Shi'ite alike, managed to inflame public opinion against the invaders. Demonstrations in Baghdad—still the seat of the Abbasid caliphate—forced the Saljuqs to respond. Sultan Muhammad, whom we last saw as the victor in the Saljuq war of succession after the death of Malik-Shah, organized several limited campaigns against the Franks beginning in 1110. These, however, were handicapped by lukewarm support from the local rulers in Syria. In 1115, a campaign sent by the sultan actually found the Muslim princes of Damascus and Aleppo allied with the Franks against him. After this betrayal, Muhammad vowed that he would not intervene against the Franks again.

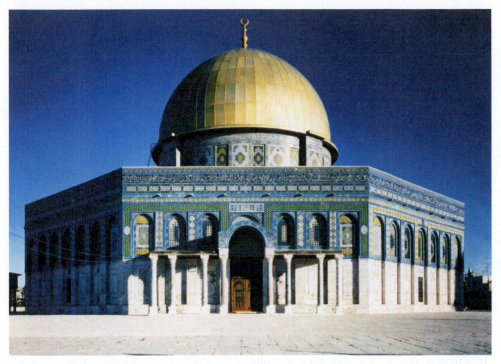

The Dome of the Rock mosque in Jerusalem, built by the caliph 'Abd al-Malik (685-705).
Its style was influenced by Byzantine architectural models.

The Ibn Tulun mosque in Cairo, completed in 877 by the Abbasid-appointed governor to
Egypt after whom it is named. It was influenced by Iraqi architectural models.

The mud wall around old Sana'a. In arid climates, both buildings and city walls could be kept in good repair even when made of mud.

A residential street in old Tunis, illustrating the emphasis on privacy to be found throughout most of the Dar al-Islam.

The walls of the citadel at Cairo. Saladin began their construction, using the labor of Crusader prisoners of war.

The ribat at Monastir. It was founded in the late eighth century, but the Aghlabids and Fatimids expanded it.

The interior of the Great Mosque at Cordoba, constructed between 784 and 987.

The Great Mosque at Qayrawan, constructed between 836 and 875.

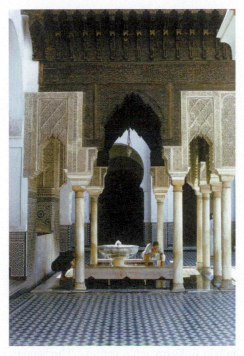

Men at ablution in the Qarawiyyin mosque in Fez. Originally built in the ninth century, it has been enlarged and modified several times.

The Congregational Mosque in Esfahan, built by the Saljuqs in the eleventh century.

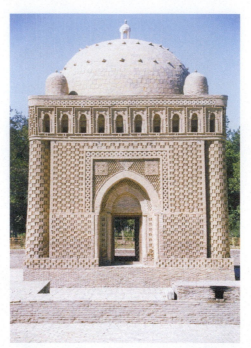

The Samanid dynastic tomb in Bukhara, tenth century. The Samanids were known for their fine decorative brickwork, and the tomb exhibits their skill on both the exterior and interior walls.

The gate to the Udaya Qasaba ("casbah," or citadel-palace complex), an Almohad monument in Rabat. It was built at the end of the twelfth century.

The stucco vault over the mihrab bay in the Great Mosque, Tlemcen, Algeria. It was built during the reign of the Almoravid ruler 'Ali ibn Yusuf, and was completed in 1136.

The tomb of the Il-khan ruler Uljaytu (1304-1317), in Sultaniya.

Cairo's Sultan Hasan madrasa-tomb-mosque complex (on the left), constructed 1356-1363. Elements of this Mamluke monument's style appear to be due to the influence of architects who fled Iran after the collapse of the Il-khan regime, some two decades earlier.

The Gur-i Amir, in Samarqand. Timur began its construction in 1398, and it became the tomb for him and several of his illustrious Timurid descendants.

Franks through Muslim Eyes

Few Muslims, even in Andalus, had had contact with Franks prior to the era of the Crusades. A widespread assumption among educated Muslims was that the Franks must be slow witted and boorish, for they lived in a cold climate and had contributed nothing noteworthy to the sciences. Syrian Muslims who were forced to live under Frankish rule after the First Crusade found little reason to change their opinion of them. In the passage that follows, a Syrian Muslim describes the Frankish custom of trial by combat. Under this legal process, the accused could challenge his accuser to a fight, and the community believed that God would favor the righteous person. A logical extension of this theory made it possible for either party to name someone else to take his place in the combat, for God would not give the advantage to the unjust, even if he were stronger. To a Muslim acquainted with the highly developed rules of evidence and procedure in the Shari'a, this system would seem bizarre.

I attended one day a duel in Nābulus between two Franks. The reason for this was that certain Moslem thieves took by surprise one of the villages of Nābulus. One of the peasants of that village was charged with having acted as guide for the thieves when they fell upon the village. So he fled away. The king [of Jerusalem] sent and arrested his children. The peasant thereupon came back to the king and said, "Let justice be done in my case. I challenge to a duel the man who claimed that I guided the thieves to the village." The king then said to the tenant who held the village in fief, "Bring forth someone to fight the duel with him." The tenant went to his village, where a blacksmith lived, took hold of him and ordered him to fight the duel. The tenant became thus sure of the safety of his own peasants, none of whom would be killed and his estate ruined.

I saw this blacksmith. He was a physically strong young man, but his heart failed him. He would walk a few steps and then sit down and ask for a drink. The one who had made the challenge was an old man, but he was strong in spirit and he would rub the nail of his thumb against that of the forefinger in defiance, as if he was not worrying over the duel. Then came the viscount . . . , i.e., the seignior of the town, and gave each one of the two contestants a cudgel and a shield and arranged the people in a circle around them.

The two met. The old man would press the blacksmith backward until he would get him as far as the circle, then he would come back to the middle of the arena. They went on exchanging blows until they looked like pillars smeared with blood. The contest was prolonged and the viscount began to urge them to hurry, saying, "Hurry on." The fact that the smith was given to the use of the hammer proved now of great advantage to him. The old man was worn out and the smith gave him a blow which made him fall. His cudgel fell under his back. The smith kneld down over him and tried to stick his fingers into the eyes of his adversary, but could not do it because of the great quantity of blood flowing out. Then he rose up and hit his head with the cudgel until he killed him. They then fastened a rope around the neck of the dead person, dragged him away and hanged him. The lord who brought the smith now came, gave the smith his own mantle, made him mount the horse behind him and rode off with him. This case illustrates the kind of jurisprudence and legal decisions the Franks have—may Allah's curse be upon them!

SOURCE: Ibn Munqidh, Usama. *An Arab–Syrian Gentleman and Warrior in the Period of the Crusades: Memoirs of Usāmah ibn-Munqidh (Kitab al-I'tibār)*. Translated by Philip K. Hitti. Princeton, New Jersey: Princeton University Press, 1987, pp. 167–168.

The politics of the area was immensely complicated. Several times during the first twenty-five years of the Frankish occupation, Muslim rulers allied with one or more Frankish rulers against fellow Muslims. In addition, local communities of Nizaris gained influence with the rulers of both Aleppo and Damascus and encouraged them to cooperate with the Franks, seeing the European newcomers as tools to be deployed against both the Fatimids and the Sunni rulers. The Fatimids themselves, although in possession of the wealth of Egypt, were remarkably weak after bouts with famine and plague and the schism of 1094. They never threatened the Latin Kingdom. From the time of Badr al-Jamali (the Armenian wazir from 1073 to 1094) until the end of the Fatimid state in 1171, the authority of the caliph-Imam was minimal. Most of the caliphs were minors when they came to the throne, and they were never allowed to assume full powers. Al-Afdal, Badr's son and successor as wazir (1094–1121), even abolished the distinctively Shi'ite festivals and closed the Dar al-Hikma. The Fatimid state was living on borrowed time.

The Franks on the Defensive

The Franks enjoyed a period of almost half a century before they were seriously challenged. A father-and-son team of Turkish warlords built up power in northern Iraq and Syria and then captured Egypt. A protege of this family, Saladin, continued the work of centralization and captured Jerusalem from the Franks. His successors in Cairo groomed Egypt to become the preeminent power in the Sunni Muslim world for the first time.

The Zengis

In 1127, 'Imad al-Din Zengi became the ruler of Mosul, in northern Iraq. The following year he took over Aleppo, unifying northern Iraq and northern Syria. In 1144, he attacked and captured the city of Edessa, the first of the Frankish-held cities to be retaken by Muslims. Before he could follow up on the victory, he was murdered by a Frankish slave in 1146 and his possessions were divided between his two sons. Zengi's exploits appeared to have died with him, as his miniempire was divided once again.

The fall of Edessa prompted the call for the Second Crusade. This expedition, however, was as disastrous as the first one had been successful. Edessa proved to be impregnable, so, in 1148, the Crusaders decided to conquer Damascus. Some of the Franks who had lived in the area for years objected to the decision, because the leaders of Damascus had been in a tacit alliance with the Kingdom of Jerusalem against the Zengi family for almost a decade. The Crusaders had their way, however, and laid siege to Damascus. Now, faced with a hostile takeover by Jerusalem, the Damascenes looked to Aleppo to help them. Imad al-Din's son, Nur al-Din Zengi, was the ruler there, and he was gratified for the opportunity to extend his influence where his father's had never reached. When he began marching south, the Crusaders abandoned their siege. When, in 1153, the Franks of Jerusalem finally captured Ascalon from the Fatimids, Damascus voluntarily submitted to Nur al-Din for protection from the Franks.

Christian Jerusalem and Nur al-Din's holdings in Aleppo and Damascus were now the two major powers in Syria. For either of them to dislodge the other would require the acquisition of further resources. Those resources seemed ripe for the taking in the Nile valley, where the Fatimids were growing ever weaker. Amalric, who became king of Jerusalem in 1163, made every effort to conquer Egypt, and Nur al-Din matched him step by step. Both led several expeditions into Egypt and even fought each other there. The Fatimid wazir, realizing how weak his country had become, played one power off against the other in an attempt to remain independent. He pretended to favor one side, and then the other; he promised tribute to both (and then would not pay); and he allowed envoys to view the Fatimid court ceremony, which even in the last, sad, days of the caliphate left observers awestruck.

Saladin

Despite the best efforts of the wazir, however, in January 1169 Nur al-Din's army, under the general Shirkuh, gained control of Cairo. Rather than dismantling the regime immediately, Nur al-Din authorized Shirkuh to become the new Egyptian wazir. When Shirkuh died a few weeks later, his nephew Salah al-Din, better known in Europe as Saladin, took his place. For over a year and a half, Saladin ruled Egypt without deposing the irrelevant Fatimid caliph-Imam. In September 1171, the caliph-Imam died, and Saladin took over as governor of Egypt. He formalized the change in the nature of the state by ordering that the Friday services in the mosques be said in the name of the Abbasid caliph. The Fatimid empire was at an end, after over two hundred fifty years of existence.

Nur al-Din, who had expanded his power to include Mosul in 1170, was now in possession of a large empire that extended from Mosul through eastern Syria and up the Nile valley. Despite the confidence that he and his father had invested in Saladin's family (both Shirkuh and Saladin's father Ayyub had served as governors for the regime), he became suspicious of Saladin's ambitions and had evidence that he was withholding tribute from Aleppo. As he was preparing a campaign to bring Saladin to heel, Nur al-Din died in Damascus in 1174, leaving Saladin the autonomous ruler of Egypt.

Shirkuh, Ayyub, and Saladin were members of the Kurdish ethnic group, which has long been concentrated in the mountainous areas of northeastern Iraq, northwestern Iran, and eastern Anatolia. Kurds are members of the Iranian peoples and speak dialects closely related to Persian. Saladin is the most famous Kurd in history due to his consolidation of political power, his severe crippling of crusader power, and his founding of a dynasty that ruled Egypt for several decades.

Saladin was faced with the task of reuniting the Muslims of Syria and Egypt, for upon the death of Nur al-Din his hard-won empire collapsed into feuding city–states again. Saladin now tried to reunite them under his own control. He gained Damascus easily in 1174, and it soon became his base of operations. (He never saw Egypt again after 1179.) The areas of northern Syria and northern Iraq resisted him ferociously, however, and it was not until 1186 that he was in effective control of both Aleppo and Mosul.

Meanwhile, he had a few minor clashes with Jerusalem, but remained on peaceful terms with that kingdom for most of the time. The notorious Reynald of Chatillon changed that relationship in the late 1180s. Reynald, master of the castle known as Karak on the Dead Sea, was a hothead who began attacking Muslim pilgrims and repeatedly violated agreements regarding the security of caravan routes that connected Egypt with the Hijaz and Syria. When Saladin demanded that Reynald pay restitution for his attacks, the latter contemptuously refused. Saladin declared war, and at the Battle of Hattin, fought in 1187 west of Lake Tiberias, Saladin destroyed the Frankish army. With most of the Frankish fighting force killed or captured, the Latin kingdom lay practically defenseless before Saladin. He took Jerusalem and several other cities, and by the end of the year, only Tyre was still in Crusader hands.

The Third Crusade (1189–1193) was the European response to Saladin's victory, but despite its initial all-star cast of European monarchs and the famous campaigns of Richard Lionheart, its gains were disappointing for the Crusaders. A few coastal towns were regained, including Acre, which became the new capital of the Latin kingdom, but Jerusalem remained in Muslim hands. Moreover, European chroniclers came to the shocking conclusion that Saladin conformed more closely to their ideals of chivalry than even their great hero, Richard. After months of campaigning that resulted in a stalemate, Richard and Saladin signed a truce in 1192 that provided a coastal strip for the Crusaders and gave Christian pilgrims free access to the holy places. Richard left for an eventful trip home, whereas Saladin died in 1193.

The Ayyubids

Saladin's dynasty—the Ayyubids—ruled Egypt, Syria, the Hijaz, and Yemen until 1250. The Ayyubids built a powerful state based on a military core of mamluks, most of whom were Qipchaq Turks from the region north of the Black Sea and Caspian Sea. The family distributed power widely: The sultan ruled all of Egypt directly, but he allowed relatives to rule as governors of the half-dozen major Syrian cities.

The Ayyubids oversaw a major rise in the status of Egypt in the Sunni world. Egypt had been blessed with remarkable agricultural resources for millennia, but under the Umayyads and Abbasids it had filled a distinctly secondary rank in status to Syria, Iraq, and Khorasan, which surpassed it in long-distance trade and cultural production. During the Fatimid period, when it was the center of an empire rather than the periphery of one, Egypt made significant gains. We have seen how it surpassed Baghdad as a channel for trade between the Mediterranean Sea and the Indian Ocean. Most historians believe that under Fatimid rule the majority of the Egyptian urban population had become Muslim, even though the Fatimids had not applied pressure to do so. Arabization of the country had also occurred, and the use of the Coptic language declined dramatically. The Ayyubid rulers now set out to establish Cairo as a major center of Sunni learning. They actively recruited scholars from Syria, Iraq, and Iran—all of which had heretofore produced far more scholars of note than Egypt—and their efforts were aided by the flight of scholars from Khorasan when the Mongols attacked in 1219. By midcentury, Cairo became the cultural capital of the Muslim world, a status sealed in 1258, when the Mongols destroyed what was left of long-suffering Baghdad. For almost three centuries, Cairo remained preeminent as the center of Islamic scholarship.

Saladin's campaigns had finally convinced Europeans that Egypt held the key to the control of Palestine. They launched two major crusades against the Ayyubids, but neither was successful. The first centered on the coastal city of Damietta during 1218–1221, the period of Chinggis Khan's invasion of Transoxiana and Khorasan. The other was during 1249–1250 and was led by the great Louis IX of France. It, too, began at Damietta, but the Crusader army was trapped and encircled as it made its way to Cairo. It was the last of the major Crusades.

The Crusade of Louis IX marked an important transition in Egypt's political history. In November 1249, the Ayyubid sultan al-Salih Ayyub (1240–1249) died just as Louis and his army were marching to Cairo from their base at Damietta. His widow was a Turkish woman, Shajar al-Durr ("string of pearls"), who had been his concubine, but whom he had married when she gave birth to his son. She and two of al-Salih's trusted advisors ruled as a triumvirate until al-Salih's eldest son, Turanshah, could assume the throne three months later. Only a few weeks after assuming power, however, Turanshah was murdered by a group of his father's mamluks. They then took the remarkable step of naming Shajar al-Durr to be their sultana, making her the first female to rule Egypt since Cleopatra more a millennium earlier.

At this point, the Syrian branch of the Ayyubid family, who had been chafing under the dominance of their relatives in Cairo, seized the opportunity to assert their power. Challenging the legitimacy of Shajar al-Durr's rule on the grounds of her gender and former slave status, they threatened to invade Egypt. The Egyptian mamluks, realizing they had created a political liability for themselves by naming a woman as their ruler, forced her to abdicate in July, and a power struggle began among various cliques within the mamluk organization. Over the next decade, many prominent individuals were murdered, including, in 1257, Shajar al-Durr herself.

In 1260, a mamluk named Baybars seized power and ruled for seventeen years. He showed that it was possible for the system of military slavery actually to rule the country. Because the Egyptian military slaves never relinquished power to a member of the Ayyubid family and subsequently created an empire, they are the only group of mamluks whose name is honored with uppercase letters: Mamlukes (Mamluks). We shall examine their history in more detail later, but here it is appropriate to close out the history of the Crusades by noting that Baybars and his successors waged war against the few remaining Crusader outposts in Syria until 1291, when they utterly destroyed the last ones.

Additional European military expeditions were directed against Muslim territories over the next two centuries, and most were conducted explicitly as Christian wars against Islam. They were all failures, and none of them reached "the Holy Land." Most historians regard them in a separate category from the activity that was focused on Palestine between 1096 and 1291 and is known as "the Crusades." The Crusades accomplished little that can be called positive. Western Europeans did become more familiar with geographical place names in the eastern Mediterranean, and they learned better techniques for building castles while residing in Syria.

Most of the consequences of the Crusades, however, were negative. The Franks made no effort to learn Arabic or to understand Islam, and thus made no contribution to cross-cultural understanding. The Muslims themselves were not unified in a countercrusade against the Franks. Individual Muslim rulers led campaigns against the Franks out of their own ambition, while Muslims not directly affected by the Crusaders had little interest in the conflict. Not surprisingly, Muslim attitudes towards local Christians hardened as a result of the Crusades. In some areas, particularly in northern Syria, some Christians cooperated with the Crusaders, leading the Mamlukes to regard their Christian subjects in general as potential fifth columnists. The great irony of the Crusades is that, whereas they began ostensibly as a relief effort by western Christianity to aid eastern Christianity, they created a permanent rift between the two communities. The Fourth Crusade, in 1204, attacked and sacked Constantinople. It created an undying hostility among Orthodox Christians toward Catholics, and the wanton destruction of the attack permanently damaged the ability of the city to defend itself.

The Loss of Andalus

As we saw in Chapter 6, the early eleventh-century civil war in Andalus resulted in the collapse of the caliphate and its replacement by some three dozen feuding city–states under the so-called "party-kings." The fragmentation of Muslim political and military power could not have come at a worse time for the Muslim community, because the Christian kingdoms to the north were beginning to share in the general economic expansion of eleventh-century Europe. The assertion of European power—and Christian identity—that took the form of the Crusades in the eastern Mediterranean had its counterpart in southwestern Europe in the so-called Reconquista. The military campaigns against the Muslims of Andalus were clearly not a "reconquest" in the strict meaning of the word, for these kingdoms were not heirs of the Visigothic kingdom that the Muslims had conquered in the early eighth century. However, it is important to realize that the Christians, by interpreting these campaigns as winning back territory for their people and for Christianity, had an ideological motivation—strained though it may have been—for their enterprise, whereas the Muslims did not. The Iberian Peninsula, in fact, because of its proximity to the rest of Europe, became the arena for more "crusades" than did the eastern Mediterranean.

Provisional Solutions: The Great Berber Empires

Had it not been for outside factors, Alfonso VI of Castile might well have brought the Reconquista to a successful conclusion at the end of the eleventh century. His stunningly easy victory at Toledo in 1085 was an ominous portent for the other, smaller Muslim principalities of Andalus. The remarkable political efflorescence of the Berbers, however, postponed the day of reckoning for most of them until the thirteenth century.

From at least the time of the Carthaginians, the Berbers had been subject to imperial powers who imposed themselves from afar. After the Carthaginians, the Romans, Byzantines, and Arabs had taken possession of North Africa's green and pleasant coastal plain. Some Berber groups, notably the Kharijite ministates of the eighth to tenth centuries, managed to create small, autonomous societies on the fringe of the vast desert to the south, but not until the eleventh century did a Berber empire appear. We saw in the previous chapter that the Almoravids created a huge empire in the Maghrib and then annexed Andalus. They were followed by yet another Berber empire, led by the Almohads. These two empires changed the course of history in the western Muslim world. They intensified the process of the Islamization of the Maghrib, they delayed the progress of the Reconquista by a century or more, and they set a precedent for large-scale political structures in the region.

The Almoravids

The key to understanding the new dynamism of the Berbers may lie in the role of the holy men, or murabitun, who extended the process of Islamization into central and southern Morocco. As we have seen, these were areas that were initially untouched by the Arabs, whose own settlements and influence extended along the Mediterranean and Atlantic plains, and along the foothills of the High Atlas. The Arabs regarded the interior of Morocco and the regions south of the Sous River as hostile, pagan territory.

When Ibn Yasin began his crusade to reform the Sanhaja along the lines of a strict adherence to the Maliki school of the Shari'a, this group of Berbers gained an ideological advantage comparable to that of the Arabs who swept out of the Arabian Peninsula in the 630s. Like the earlier movement, it combined the motivations of wealth and obedience to the perceived will of God. The result was a powerful complex of martial qualities: ambition, discipline, and fearlessness in the face of possible death in battle.

With this motivated force Ibn Tashfin conquered the western Sahara, the Maghrib, and Andalus. The consequences were immense. The presence of this large political unit stimulated trade all across the region. Of particular note was the intensification of commercial links with the gold- and salt-producing areas of West Africa. In later centuries, these links led to the Islamization of that region. Morocco, which had been largely neglected under the Arabs, for the first time became a commercial and urbanized society. Andalus, for the first time since the 740s, once again became an appendage of the Maghrib.

Unlike many rulers who used Islam as a cloak for their personal ambitions, Ibn Tashfin accorded respect and power to the ulama. He created a council for them, took them on his campaigns, and sought advice from them. The Almoravid regime was, above all else, a regime of the Shari'a as interpreted through the Maliki tradition. The jurists in the other three major madhhabs (the Hanbali, Hanafi, and Shafi'i) regarded the Maliki jurists as mavericks. The most influential Maliki practitioners still did not stress the importance of the prophetic Hadith to the degree of the other three major schools, preferring to rely more on their school's own body of legal precedent.

In the eleventh century, however, a reform movement was afoot in Andalus and in parts of the Maghrib. With the collapse of the Umayyad caliphate of Cordoba, legal scholars who wanted to reform Maliki practice by adopting the Shafi'i consensus of emphasizing the Hadith found it easier to engage in such labor, since they could migrate to whichever of the new city–states would allow it. Both the reforming scholars and their tolerant rulers tended to be either Andalusi Berbers or indigenous converts to Islam (muwallads), since the well-established Arab families tended to be conservative in this regard. The Almoravids sided with the conservatives.

Under Ibn Tashfin's son, 'Ali (1106–1143), discontent with the Almoravid regime began to mount. The expectation on the part of many Andalusis that Almoravid rule would increase the social mobility of non-Arabs to the higher political and religious positions was not fulfilled. On the contrary, the Almoravids reserved the highest military and political positions for themselves and allowed the Arab elites of Andalus to dominate the religious offices. The legal reformers were becoming increasingly frustrated with what they considered to be the narrow literalism of Maliki techniques of Qur'anic interpretation and the neglect of the Hadith in the interpretation of law. They could point to several weighty issues that they considered to be in urgent need of reform, but a relatively minor one was a powerful symbol of what they thought was deeply flawed about the current state of Maliki law as practiced by the Almoravids: The Sanhaja males who claimed to be upholding the Shari'a were veiled, whereas their women walked about in public with their faces uncovered. The Almoravids, in turn, regarded such criticism to be an attack on the legitimacy of their political power rather than a sincere attempt to join a universal consensus regarding the methodology of determining the Shari'a, and they began a policy of suppressing dissenters.

Many Andalusis were also critical of the rank-and-file Sanhaja troops. Not surprisingly, many of the troops had joined the Almoravid army to escape boring and poverty-stricken peasant lives and to live a life of high adventure. Many of them now became infamous for their indiscriminate looting. Both the Muwallads and the "old" Andalusi Berbers rapidly became disillusioned with the "new," rough Berbers who were ruling them. For Jews and Christians, the regime was even more problematic. They were frequently victims of persecution and extortion, with the result that thousands fled to the north, to Christian areas. 'Ali accused the Jews and Christians of Andalus of secretly aiding the Christian kingdoms, and he deported thousands to Morocco.

'Ali's policies have tarred the Almoravids with the charge of being hostile to Jews and Christians, but his policy toward Jews and Christians in Andalus stands in stark contrast to his policy in North Africa. In the latter region, western European Christian mercenaries (especially Catalans, from the area of modern Barcelona, ostensibly among his bitterest enemies) served in his cavalry, many of the empire's civil servants were Andalusi Jews and Christians, and many Christian artisans worked as free laborers in the construction of mosques in Morocco. His discriminatory policies in Andalus appear to have been provoked by fears of having fifth columnists in his ranks, since the threat from the north was so great.

The Almohads

'Ali's rule seemed secure, but during his reign a rival group of Berbers known to history as the Almohads began to challenge the Almoravid leadership. In part, this challenge was due to factional differences, for the challenge came from the Masmuda Berbers in southern Morocco. It was also, however, based on religious differences. When the Almohads replaced the Almoravids, they expanded the territory controlled by their predecessors, patronized the arts and scholarship, and left a lasting legacy to modern Morocco, Algeria, and Tunisia.

About the time 'Ali began to rule in 1106, a young man from southern Morocco made his way to Mecca to perform the hajj. This pilgrim, Ibn Tumart, stayed in the east for about a decade, studying with religious scholars in Saljuq-ruled Baghdad and Damascus. He returned to the Maghrib in 1118 with visions of Islamic reform (like most Muslims of the period, he does not appear to have been concerned about the recent invasion of the Franks into western Syria). The centerpiece of his program was the transcendence and oneness of God, and the rejection of pagan Berber customs that had been assimilated into Islamic practice. His emphasis on the oneness of God gained for his followers the nickname, the Almohads (*al-muwahhidun*, or "the unitarians").

Ibn Tumart derived two major corollaries from the theme of God's transcendence and oneness. The first was that the passages in the Qur'an that described God's characteristics should be interpreted figuratively rather than literally. He argued that the anthropomorphic interpretations characteristic of Almoravid Qur'anic studies infringed on doctrines of God's unity and oneness, for they made him manlike rather than transcendent. The second doctrine was that the legalism of the Almoravids was misguided. Ibn Tumart taught that only the Qur'an and Hadith should be accepted as guides for living a life pleasing to God, and he rejected all four schools of law.

Ibn Tumart's attacks on anthropomorphism and legalism, combined with his tirades against the Almoravid custom of allowing the women of the ruling family to be seen in public unveiled, put him on a collision course with the ruling regime. He found a responsive audience among his own people, the Masmuda Berbers of the western High Atlas Mountains. They were sedentary Berbers, and traditionally suspicious of the nomadic Sanhaja. Ibn Tumart established a ribat at Tinmal in the foothills of the High Atlas some seventy miles south of Marrakesh and began consolidating his power in the area by subduing rival tribes. He created a genealogy for himself that traced his descent from the Prophet, and he completed his ideological challenge to the Almoravids (and to all other existing political authorities) by claiming to be the expected Mahdi.

Ibn Tumart died in 1130 and was succeeded by 'Abd al-Mu'min, a Zanata Berber who had gained Ibn Tumart's confidence. The fact that 'Abd al-Mu'min was not a Masmuda Berber is significant. It demonstrated that the Almohads were serious about being less clannish and stratified than previous regimes. 'Abd al-Mu'min, who continued to insist that Ibn Tumart had been the Mahdi, assumed the title of Ibn Tumart's caliph. 'Abd al-Mu'min concentrated on taking over Almoravid territory during his thirty-three years as leader of the Almohads. From 1130 to 1147, he conquered Morocco, capturing Marrakesh in 1147 and making the Almoravid capital his own.

'Abd al-Mu'min's successes against the Almoravids encouraged the opponents of the Almoravids in Andalus. As early as 1140, some of the cities there were evicting their Almoravid garrisons and becoming independent. As a result, in 1143 the Christian kingdoms began taking advantage of the chaos to lay siege to many of the weak Muslim city–states. The most notable Christian victory of the period was the campaign led by the king of the nascent Portuguese state, who invited a combined force of English, Flemish, and Norman troops to join his Portuguese soldiers in a siege of Lisbon. The city fell to the Christian alliance in 1147. Upon the fall of Lisbon, 'Abd al-Mu'min invaded Andalus, and the Muslim city–states now faced the prospect of capture by the Christian kingdoms or by the Almohads. Several surrendered to 'Abd al-Mu'min, and several others put up only perfunctory resistance to him. As a result, during 1147–1148, 'Abd al-Mu'min came into possession of most of the southwestern quadrant of the peninsula. He then turned to the North African coast, where the Normans and their Berber allies were entrenched from Tunis east to Tripoli. He won Ifriqiya from them in 1160, and his son and grandson captured the Andalusi cities in Murcia and Valencia in the 1170s.

The Almohad regime was at the height of its power from about 1175 to about 1210. The empire was never totally at peace due to Berber rebellions in North Africa and wars against the Iberian Christians, but these disturbances were on the fringes of the empire. Most of the interior enjoyed peace and economic prosperity for extended periods of time. Marrakesh became the capital of a western Muslim empire that stretched from the central Iberian Peninsula to Tripolitania (western Libya). With the wealth derived from its control of the Saharan trade routes, the Almohad regime commissioned several spectacular architectural monuments that still remain, especially in Marrakesh, Rabat, and Seville. Almohad caliphs patronized scholars from Andalus, the Maghrib, Egypt, Syria, and the Hijaz. A literary and intellectual culture flourished in North Africa as never before. It was centered in Fez, but serious learning spread as far south as Sous—south of the Atlas Mountains—for the first time.

The Almohad Empire seemed secure against its divided Christian neighbors, particularly after its decisive victory over Castile and Leon at Alarcos in 1195. For several years after the battle, the Castilian king would not attack Almohad forces even when the latter marched through his territories around Toledo. The line that demarcated Muslim territory from Christian-controlled areas ran from just below Lisbon to just below Barcelona and seemed impregnable to Christian attack. Despite appearances, however, the Almohad empire had little support outside the Masmuda community. Its sudden collapse would toll the death knell of Andalus.

The Disintegration of the Almohads and of Andalus

The Almohad regime was not popular in Andalus, and it was the target of continuous revolts by Berbers and Arabs in its distant hinterlands in the Maghrib. Almohad doctrine was never successfully implemented. The teaching that Ibn Tumart had been the Mahdi seemed blasphemous to some, and the rejection of all the schools of Islamic law was not what the advocates of legal reform had in mind. They wanted to bring Maliki law into line with the methodological consensus of the other madhhabs, not to abolish it altogether. Moreover, to be without law proved to be impossible in the reality of everyday life. Even within Almohad ruling circles, the teachings of the founder came into question. In 1229, the Almohad caliph al-Ma'mun (1229–1230) proclaimed that there was no Mahdi other than Jesus. He also officially reintroduced Maliki law, naming members of the reform movement to positions as qadi.

In 1212–1213, the Almohads suffered almost simultaneous attacks from the north and the south. Throughout the whole period of their occupation of Andalus, they had benefitted from quarrels among the Iberian Christian kingdoms that made it impossible for the Reconquista to resume. With the accession to the papacy of Innocent III (1198–1216), that changed. Using both persuasion and the threat of excommunication, he organized a truce among the Christian kingdoms, emphasizing the peninsula's special status as a crusading zone. Moreover, a powerful new Christian kingdom had emerged during the first half of the twelfth century. Aragon, heretofore merely a province of Navarre, subsequently incorporated Catalonia and its great city of Barcelona. With Innocent's active financial support, in 1212 Alfonso VIII of Castile led the combined Christian forces at the battle of Las Navas de Tolosa, some seventy miles east of Cordoba. The battle shattered the army of the Almohads, although the victors fell to squabbling among themselves and did not take advantage of their opportunity to seize Andalus.

The following year the Almohad caliph died, leaving no adult son. In Marrakesh, disputes flared over the succession, and a Berber group known as the Banu

Marin, or Marinids, took advantage of the confusion to advance into the empire. The Marinids, pastoralists who lived in southeastern Morocco on the edge of the Sahara, had never submitted to Almohad control. Now they replicated the Almoravid and Almohad pattern of piecemeal conquests of the Maghrib and, in 1269, achieved the capture of Marrakesh. The Marinids moved their capital to Fez, and their leader took the title of caliph in the early fourteenth century. They remained the dominant power in Morocco until 1465.

In the wake of the devastation of the Almohad army at Las Navas de Tolosa, the Christian kingdoms were afforded the luxury of being able to quarrel for over a decade, secure in the knowledge that Almohad attention was focused on the Marinid threat. With the reunification of Leon and Castile in 1230, however, the foundation was laid for the definitive end of Muslim rule in the area. In the absence of the Almohad army and with the city–states fighting each other again, Castile conquered Cordoba in 1236 and Seville in 1248 (the latter with the aid of five hundred men sent by the king's vassal, the Muslim ruler of Granada!). The Muslim inhabitants of the two cities were then expelled and forced to find new homes in the area. When Aragon took the city of Valencia in 1238 after a two-year siege, the Muslims there, too, were expelled, leaving a practically empty city for Christians from Aragon to settle.

Over the next two decades the rest of the province of Valencia was systematically absorbed, and in 1266 Murcia fell. Meanwhile, between 1234 and 1249, all the lands south of Lisbon and west of the Guadiana River were brought under the authority of the Portuguese crown, and that country took on the shape that it would have to this day. Of the former territory of Andalus, only Granada remained as a Muslim province, and throughout its remaining history of two-and-a-half centuries it was rarely independent. Most of the time it was a vassal of Castile and was required to pay tribute; when it failed to do so, it suffered punitive raids.

Of all the regions won by the Umayyad conquests of the seventh and eighth centuries, Andalus was the only one to be lost permanently from the Dar al-Islam. The Frankish Crusaders had tried to take western Syria, but that goal had been unrealistic. The Franks' supply lines were overextended, and their neighbors were wealthy and populous Muslim regions whose retaliation for the almost unbounded aggression of the Frankish military culture could only be a matter of time. Very different conditions obtained in the Iberian Peninsula. The Muslims had established a vibrant economy and culture, but they could never transcend their ethnic and kinship rivalries, despite their shared religious values. By creating a myriad of belligerent city–states, they replicated the experience of the Greek city–states of the mid-fourth century B.C.E., which were absorbed by a less sophisticated, but more unified and motivated, Macedonia.

The Muslims who now found themselves to be subjects of Christian kings, however, were in a much more difficult position than were the Greeks under Philip II's Macedonia. How, they wondered, would they be able to be good Muslims in the Dar al-Kufr? Many devout Muslims believed that they had an obligation to emigrate (perform "hijra") from the lands of unbelief, while others convinced themselves that the situation might be only temporary, for God would not allow His work to be undone. Voluntary emigration is a hard choice to make, and under the circumstances of the time, it was not a popular one. The Muslim community may well have constituted the majority of the population in the Ebro and Guadalquivir valleys, as well as in the provinces of Valencia and Murcia, where the Muslims were almost certainly the majority. Very few individuals found the situation so unbearable that they felt compelled to leave for an unknown destination. Moreover, the kings of Castile and Aragon were intent on developing their new territories, and were not interested in deporting some of their most valuable subjects. Muslims had a reputation as skilled artisans and farmers, while the Jews were known as able administrators, physicians, and merchants.

The Muslims who remained under Christian hegemony eventually came to be known as Mudejars, a term derived from an Arabic word (*mudajjan*) which can mean "permitted to remain," but which also suggests "domesticated" or "put to use." The experience of the Mudejars differed from kingdom to kingdom and even among regions of the same kingdom, but in general during the thirteenth century their status was similar to that of the <u>dh</u>immis under Muslim rule. Just as the first generation of Muslim conquerors had turned some churches into mosques, now in many cities the major mosques were seized by Christians and turned into churches. Most mosques were left untouched, however, and Muslims were allowed to continue practicing their religion. The call of the muezzin still rang out, the faithful observed the daily prayers, the state recognized tax exemption for properties supporting religious purposes, religious schools stayed open, pilgrims were allowed to go to Mecca, and Islamic marriage and burial practices continued unchanged. Shari'a courts continued to function, and the qadis became even more important than before in their role as interpreters of the godly life. When Muslims testified in Christian courts, they were allowed to swear on the Qur'an.

On the other hand, the Mudejars had to contend with restrictions on their freedom which reminded them that they were second-class citizens. The most shocking was the experience of the Muslims in about six cities who were expelled from their homes and had to take residence outside the walls. Otherwise, their experience once again echoed that of the <u>dh</u>immis in the Dar al-Islam. In many places they had to wear distinctive clothing which set them apart from Christians; they were subject to certain annual dues and taxes paid to the crown and they had to pay tithes to the Church for property they bought from a Christian; in some cities they lived by compulsion in separate quarters of their own; city authorities often set aside separate days for the use of municipal bath houses by Christians, Jews, and Muslims; Christian families were not allowed to employ Muslim or Jewish girls as caretakers for their children; sexual relations between Christians and members of the other two groups were punished savagely; Mudejars were expected to abstain from work on Sunday; Muslim proselytizing was strictly forbidden, and in both Aragon and Castile Christian converts to Islam were executed; and a Mudejar who mocked the doctrine of Jesus as the Christ or who took the name of the Virgin in vain would be whipped for the first two offences and have his tongue cut out for a third.

Realignment in the East

While the condition of Muslims in the western Dar al-Islam was taking a turn for the worse, major developments were transforming the east. On the positive side, the Saljuqs of Rum achieved their pinnacle of culture in the first half of the thirteenth century, and the Nizaris achieved a peaceful modus vivendi with the Sunni world.

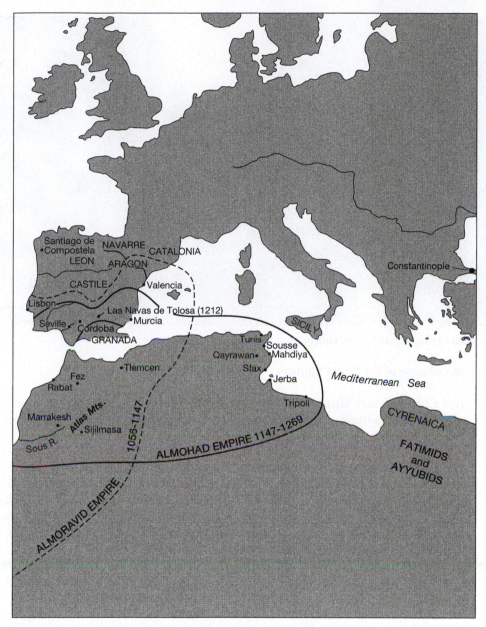

MAP 7.1 The Western Muslim World, 1100–1260

Among the negative developments in the region, the Great Saljuqs collapsed in the face of revolts from their own Oghuz people. A new Muslim power, the ruler of Khwarazm, took the place of the Great Saljuqs. Like many other high achievers who have won their success quickly, the new ruler of Khwarazm tended to be arrogant in his dealings with others. Unfortunately for him and millions of other Muslims, he offended a man named Chinggis Khan.

The Cifte Minareli madrasa in Erzerum, constructed by the Saljuqs of Rum.

The Collapse of the Great Saljuqs

While Christians and Muslims at both ends of the Mediterranean were involved in clashes that increasingly came to be seen as holy wars, the Saljuqs of Esfahan were preoccupied with their own affairs. As we have seen, the Great Saljuq, Muhammad, tried to organize resistance to the Crusaders from 1110 to 1115, but he became disgusted with his cousins who ruled Damascus and Aleppo when they stood with the Crusaders against him. From that time on, the Great Saljuqs had little to do with affairs in Syria. After Muhammad's death in 1118, in fact, the Saljuqs of Esfahan had little influence over affairs even in Iraq and western Iran. Family members ruling in those areas were embroiled in constant conflict with each other and deferred to Muhammad's brother Sanjar, who ruled Khorasan, as the Great Saljuq.

The turmoil in the western part of the empire resulted in a shattered economy. When cities were seized, they were stripped of their wealth, peasants routinely were subjected to confiscation of crops and livestock, and combatants often pursued a scorched-earth policy to deprive their opponent of provisions. By midcentury, the western capital was moved from Esfahan to Hamadan, but the Saljuqs were increasingly overshadowed by other provincial rulers and even by a revived Abbasid caliphate. Growing assertiveness by caliphs who took advantage of Saljuq divisiveness was capped by the career of the Abbasid caliph al-Nasir (1180–1225). He was able to brush off Saljuq control entirely, and he carved out a small province in Iraq over which he was supreme military and political ruler. In 1194, Tughril, the Saljuq prince of Hamadan, tried to reestablish his family's control over Baghdad, but al-Nasir sought assistance from the ruler of Khwarazm. In the ensuing battle at Rayy, Tughril was killed, bringing an end to the Great Saljuq presence in western Iran.

By contrast, the Sultanate of Rum recovered from its loss of Nicaea to the Crusaders and established its capital at Konya in 1116. Hemmed in by the Crusaders to the west and by Turkish rivals to the east, it was weak for several decades. By 1141, however, its chief Turkmen rivals had collapsed, and Konya's power began to increase. In 1176, the Byzantine Empire made the mistake of attacking the sultanate at Myriokephalon, resulting in a defeat almost as spectacular as that of Manzikert a century earlier. The victorious sultanate now had access to ports on the Aegean again, and within a few decades, Konya took over ports on the Black Sea and the Mediterranean, as well. Relations with the Byzantines soon improved. The Fourth Crusade in 1204 had Egypt as its announced goal, but its "armed pilgrims" sacked and captured Constantinople instead. As the Byzantine government relocated to Nicaea, it and the Sultanate of Rum once again became natural allies, united in their opposition to the Europeans and to the Armenians.

The sultanate continued to expand, and by the second quarter of the thirteenth century, it encompassed almost the whole of Anatolia. At its height, from 1205 to 1243, the sultanate impressed visitors by its economic vitality, its high level of urbanization, its impressive architecture, its generous patronage of the sciences, and its religious toleration. Of particular interest was this Turkish dynasty's conscious appropriation of Persian culture. The rulers of the period all had Persian names, and the chancellery used the Persian language in its documents.

Far to the east, in Khorasan, Sanjar ruled longer than any other Saljuq in history. His older brother had appointed him governor of Khorasan in 1097 when he was only about twelve years old. As the Great Saljuq after the death of his other brother Muhammad in 1118, he was an active military leader. Under his rule his capital city of Merv became a center of the arts and the intellect. In 1141, however, the Mongol tribe of the Qara-khitai defeated Sanjar's Qara-khanid vassals in Transoxiana, and Sanjar was unable to retake the province. In 1153, some of his own Oghuz troops revolted against him and held him captive for two years. The Oghuz engaged in an orgy of violence, during which many Khorasani cities were sacked and the great library at Merv was burned. Sanjar was released in 1155, but he was broken in health and died the next year. Oghuz chieftains and Saljuq amirs took advantage of his capture and his death to assert their own power, and Khorasan fragmented into a patchwork of competing principalities, much as Syria had done after the death of Malik-Shah over half a century earlier.

The resulting power vacuum allowed a former vassal of Sanjar, the governor of Khwarazm, to build up his power. Khwarazm's location on the lower Amu Darya allowed it to derive extensive wealth from irrigated agriculture, and it benefitted from a trade route that connected Khorasan with the valley of the Volga River. Khwarazm's rulers, known as the Khwarazm-Shahs, built up a remarkably strong power base in the late twelfth and early thirteenth centuries while in principle subject to the Qara-khitai. Tekish, the Khwarazm–Shah from 1172 to 1200, absorbed western Khorasan in the 1180s in a series of destructive campaigns, building up his reputation sufficiently for the caliph al-Nasir to call upon him in 1194 to help him defeat the last of the western Saljuqs. By 1212, his son Muhammad defeated the Qara-khitai Mongols and began annexing Transoxiana. Muhammad, however, had developed a reputation as a ruthless and rapacious tyrant, and many of the Muslim inhabitants of Transoxiana preferred the rule of the pagan Qara-khitai to the prospect of rule by him. They resisted his attempts to take them over, and Muhammad engaged in a particularly brutal campaign to subject the population. As a result, much of the great city of Samarqand was destroyed and had to be rebuilt. Muhammad continued his blitzkrieg over the next few years, and soon his empire incorporated territories from Afghanistan to Azerbaijan.

Sunni–Nizari Rapprochement

The disintegration of Great Saljuq power after the death of Muhammad in 1118 was the fulfillment of the dream of the Nizaris, but the consequences were not what they might have expected. The constant squabbling and warfare among the various branches of the Saljuq family, and between them and their subjects, caused the Assassins to lose their raison d'être. Their political murders no longer caught the public's attention amid the constant mayhem of the era, and yet they were not powerful enough to take advantage of the chaos by seizing power themselves. They became inactive for several decades.

The one major exception to the lower profile of the Assassins during this period was the career of the head of the Syrian community. Known to the Crusaders as the Old Man of the Mountain, he was Rashid al-Din al-Sinan, a native of Basra, whom the fourth Lord of Alamut had sent to lead the Syrian Nizaris in 1162. He remained the head of the community there until his death in 1192. Thus, he was a contemporary of the great Nur al-Din of Syria and northern Iraq, Amalric of Jerusalem, and Saladin. In typical Nizari fashion, he considered Nur al-Din and Saladin, who were Sunnis, potentially greater threats to his movement than the Crusaders were. Although he made enemies with the Hospitallers, in general he maintained peaceful relations with the Crusaders while making several attempts on the life of Saladin. Sinan was also often at odds with the leadership at Alamut. Despite the difficulties of communication among the widely flung Nizari "state," he was the only regional leader who occasionally pursued policies that ran counter to those of the central command.

The changed conditions of the region may well be responsible for two radical shifts in Nizari doctrine over the next half-century. In 1164, the Lord of Alamut, Hasan II, announced the arrival of the Last Day, the end of history. The exact meaning of Hasan's announcement is still debated. Most scholars agree that it entailed the long-awaited Last Judgment, when individuals would be assigned to paradise or to hell, and apparently at least some Nizaris understood it to mean the abrogation of the Shari'a. Many of Hasan's followers also inferred that he was claiming to be the Imam rather than merely his deputy. A year and a half later, one of his former followers stabbed him to death, but his son who succeeded him made explicit the claim that his father was a descendant of Nizar, and not merely a deputy or spokesman for him. From that point, the Nizaris recognized the Lord of Alamut as their Imam.

Thus, the Nizaris and the Muslim world at large were stunned in 1210 when their new Imam, Hasan III, repudiated Nizari doctrine and proclaimed the adherence of his community to Sunni Islam. The Abbasid caliph al-Nasir did not hesitate to welcome a potential ally in his effort to reassert caliphal authority against the Saljuqs, and many

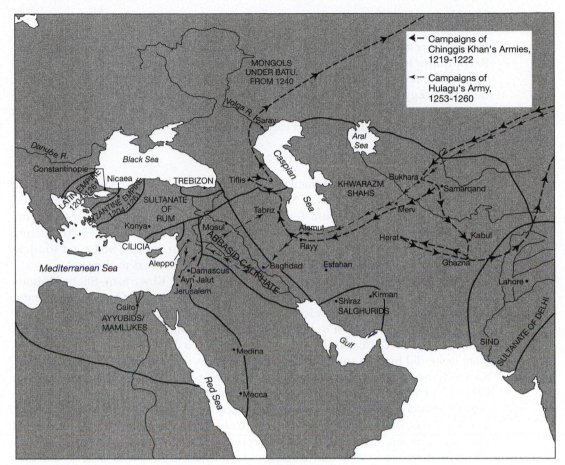

MAP 7.2 The Muslim East, 1200-1260

other Sunnis cautiously followed his lead in accepting the new "converts." Ulama from across southwestern Asia were invited to the regional Nizari centers to instruct the members of the community. Most Nizaris, however, assumed that the reason for the apparent conversion was a severe threat to the community and that this was really an instance of *taqiya,* or divinely sanctioned dissimulation. They were convinced that the stated adherence to Sunnism was merely a tactic for the survival of the Nizari community and that the Imam should continue to be recognized as such in private.

These conservatives were reassured in 1221, when Hasan III's successor, Muhammad III, reclaimed the position of Imam. Many Sunnis felt that their cynicism had been vindicated, but in fact relations between Nizaris and Sunnis from this point on were not as hostile as they had been. Assassinations of political and religious leaders were no longer automatically assumed to be the work of Nizaris, particularly since that tactic served no useful purpose in the revised doctrines of the community. Moreover, all Muslims, regardless of doctrinal affiliation, had a more important foe to fear: The Mongols had arrived.

The Mongol Campaigns

However presumptuous and brutish the Crusaders were and however shocking the Reconquista had proved to be by 1248, the Mongol campaigns of 1219–1222 and 1253–1260 were far more destructive. Between the Mediterranean and Central Asia, only Syria, Egypt, and the Arabian Peninsula remained free of Mongol destruction and subsequent occupation. The arrival of the Mongols marks a major turning point in the history of the Muslim world east of the Maghrib.

The Campaign of Chinggis Khan, 1219–1222

In the late twelfth century, a Mongol warlord by the name of Temuchin began asserting his dominance over the tribes of Mongolia near the Sea of Baikal. The process was largely completed by 1206, and Temuchin immediately began preparing for a campaign against the traditional target of Mongol nomads, China. By 1215, Temuchin, who gained the title of Chinggis (Genghis/Jengiz) Khan, had pushed as far south as the modern city of Beijing, and he began securing his borders to the west.

Chinggis established diplomatic contact with the Khwarazm–Shah, Muhammad. As we have seen, Muhammad had just defeated the Mongol Qara-khitai of Transoxiana and had rapidly expanded his territories. His achievements were genuinely spectacular, and he wanted to be recognized for them. Unfortunately, in the letter of diplomacy that Chinggis sent to him, Chinggis stated that he viewed the Khwarazm–Shah as he did his own sons. Muhammad, not knowing that he should be flattered, took offense at the remark. A few months later, when a delegation arrived from Chinggis protesting the massacre of several hundred merchants at the hands of one of Muhammad's governors, Muhammad ordered the execution of the Mongol envoys. This act was not only a brazen violation of a basic element of diplomatic protocol, but also one of history's greatest miscalculations of relative strength.

Chinggis began an offensive against Muhammad in 1219 with an army that may well have numbered 150,000–200,000 men. He took Transoxiana in the winter of 1219–1220, razing the great cities of Bukhara and Samarqand in the process. He rested during the summer heat, and then pursued a scorched-earth policy in Khorasan during the period from late autumn of 1220 into early winter of 1222. Nishapur, Merv, Herat, and other cities were destroyed stone by stone and their inhabitants massacred. The Mongol destruction of the eastern Iranian world is one of the great catastrophes of world history. Even when placed in the context of the region's violent history, it still elicits wonder and shock. The farmers and townspeople of Iran had been accustomed to destruction. During the two hundred years since the advent of the Saljuqs, they had experienced the wanton and irrational destruction of property by Turkmen, and the subsequent clashes of great armies among the regional powers had inflicted great loss on the area. Cities had been sacked, large numbers of civilians killed, and libraries burned. But nothing had prepared the inhabitants for what the Mongols would visit upon them.

When cities resisted Chinggis Khan's army, the walls and buildings were destroyed and the populations were massacred. Eyewitnesses from the era report seeing adjacent to such cities numerous pyramids of skulls that contained the heads of as many as 40,000 people each. It is true that we have to evaluate critically the reports of chroniclers, whose estimates of the size of armies and populations were not tempered with modern concern for demographic accuracy. In this case, however, the reports come from numerous sources and many locations and are supported by what we know of the subsequent economic and social history of the area.

The natural tendency of cities to resist an invader was met by the Mongols with utter destruction. Some artisans from the cities were spared and sent back to Mongolia or China so that their skills could be utilized, and thousands of peasants in the vicinity of the cities were sometimes herded ahead of the army to serve as arrow fodder at the next siege. Eventually, the residents of cities learned that, if they did not resist, a general massacre was not likely, but during the campaign of 1219–1222 that was not widely known, and the destruction to the cities and to the agricultural infrastructure was almost total. Thousands of ulama, secular scholars, and merchants fled in advance of the danger, seeking refuge farther west or even east. Many scientists and philosophers found refuge among the Nizari communities, while others fled all the way to Konya, Damascus, and Cairo in the west, and Lahore and Delhi in the east. The Mongol armies split into two major units. One pursued potential threats as far east as the Indus River, and the other circled the Caspian Sea, returning home through southern Russia.

Chinggis returned to Mongolia, where he died in 1227. His son Ogedai became the Great Khan, and his other three sons inherited the areas of Mongolia and the lands between China and the Caspian. In 1235, Ogedai authorized his nephew Batu to lead a campaign into the west, and western Russia was subdued over the next few years. By 1241, Batu commanded two armies in Europe. One delivered a devastating blow to the knights of eastern Europe at Liegnitz (modern Legnica, Poland), in April 1241. The other conquered Pest (the eastern half of modern Budapest). As western Europe trembled in the expectation of further devastating attacks, Batu abruptly reversed course and headed east. He had received word that Ogedai had died and that the Great Khan's son Guyuk, with whom Batu had earlier quarreled, was claiming the throne. Fearing an attack from Guyuk, Batu set up his command post on the lower Volga River. A settlement known as Saray grew up around it, and it became the commercial and administrative capital of an empire known to the Europeans as the Golden Horde.

Having established control over the Russian steppes, Batu now focused on securing control over the Caucasus. In doing so, his armies came into contact with the Sultanate of Rum, which had expanded by this time into eastern Anatolia. In 1243, one of Batu's generals informed the sultan of Rum that he needed additional grazing land for his army. The sultan, realizing that any concession would result in Mongol dominance, challenged Batu militarily. At Kose Dagh, the Mongols routed the Saljuqs, and for the next several decades, the sultanate was a vassal state of the Mongols. It soon became embroiled in a civil war, and disappeared by the end of the century.

The Campaign of Hulagu, 1253–1260

In 1253, the Great Khan sent Chinggis's grandson Hulagu to conquer southwestern Asia. Hulagu made it clear that the destruction of Alamut was a high priority. He laid siege to Alamut in 1256 and promised safe passage to those who surrendered. The Nizari Imam stalled for several weeks, hoping for the onset of winter weather. During this period, he tried to appease the Mongol leader by authorizing the destruction of scores of his castles. Eventually, however, the Imam had no choice

The Nizari castle of Samiran, in the western Elburz Mountains.

but to surrender, and he and his family were sent to the Great Khan. En route to the Mongol capital, he and his family were killed, and his followers who were in the custody of Hulagu were massacred in violation of the terms of surrender. Muslim scholars who accompanied Hulagu received permission to salvage some of the immense library at Alamut, but most of it was destroyed. Other Nizari fortresses fell in the next fifteen years, sometimes after sieges of a decade or more.

After destroying Alamut, Hulagu proceeded to Baghdad, where he demanded the surrender of the city. The city resisted for four weeks and then surrendered. When the inhabitants left the city as demanded, however, Hulagu ordered them to be massacred, and the city was pillaged. The last caliph of Baghdad was then executed, either by being smothered in a carpet or by being rolled up in a carpet and trampled by horses.

By early summer 1260, Hulagu's troops were in Gaza, preparing for an invasion of Egypt. He sent an insulting ultimatum to the slave–soldiers who were still engaged in their ten-year-old, often violent, factional quarrels regarding who should lead the others. Many Muslims, both inside and outside Egypt, were impatiently waiting for some dynasty to take control of the state and bring these unruly Turks to order. The mamluk who held effective power at the time, Qutuz, showed no interest in seeking the advice of a nonslave master to deal with the Mongols, however. He took the initiative of prudently arranging a temporary truce with the few remaining Crusaders in Syria in the face of a Mongol threat that concerned both sides. Then, rather than waiting for the Mongols to attack, he moved toward them, advancing into Palestine.

As the two armies were preparing to meet each other in a showdown that would determine the fate of the Muslim world, Hulagu received a message that the Great Khan had died. Almost twenty years earlier, a similar message had saved Europe from Batu; now Hulagu headed east at once with most of his army, perhaps intending to present himself as a candidate for the vacant throne. He left the remaining Mongol force under the command of his general, Kit-buqa. Halfway across Iran, Hulagu received word that the succession crisis had been resolved, and he turned back. Before he could reinforce Kit-buqa, however, Qutuz met the latter at a site near Lake Tiberias called 'Ayn Jalut. The result was a crushing defeat for the outnumbered Mongols and the death of their general. Qutuz himself had only a few days to relish his victory until Baybars murdered him and seized power in Egypt.

Meanwhile, Batu's brother, Berke, succeeded to the throne of the Golden Horde, and converted to Islam. He was now exerting great efforts to secure his hold on the Caucasus. Hulagu knew that if he were to control southwestern Asia he would have to possess Azerbaijan, and so he based himself there in order to block Berke's expansion. From there he sent a second army against Egypt. It, too, was defeated. Rather than challenge the Mamlukes again, he set about consolidating his power in Iran and Iraq from his capital at Tabriz. His empire would become known as the Il-khanate.

Conclusion

After three hundred years of almost continual violence, the political map of the Dar al-Islam quite rapidly achieved a relatively fixed form in the decade before and after the year 1260. The expansionist designs of Muslim states and of neighboring powers alike seem to have been replaced by a focus on the consolidation of power. In the West, the Reconquista had achieved more in the twelve years from 1236 to 1248 than it had in the previous three hundred. Granada was the single remaining Muslim principality in the Iberian Peninsula, but the Christian kingdoms would not make another serious effort to capture it for over two centuries. The Marinids were in secure control of Morocco, and they would also remain in power for two centuries.

Egypt, Syria, and the Holy Cities were under the rule of the slave–soldiers, who would rule there until 1517. The Mamlukes were the most powerful Muslim regime in the Dar al-Islam in the thirteenth century, and their prestige was higher than perhaps any Muslim government in history due to their defeat of the Mongols at 'Ayn Jalut. They moved quickly to certify their place in the Sunni world by installing a member of the Abbasid family as the new caliph in Cairo. (Like his grandfathers, he turned out to be merely an ornament for the military court.)

The Mongol states of the Muslim world—the Il-khans, the Golden Horde of Russia, and the Chaghatay khanate of Central Asia—were likewise relatively stable compared with the irresistible aggression their people had shown for half a century. They did send out raiding parties and the occasional expedition, but none of them ever again conquered significant territory. The conversion of Berke of the Golden Horde to Islam held out the hope that other Mongol rulers might yet convert.

As it happened, these Mongol newcomers were turning out to be not so unfamiliar, after all: Both the Golden Horde and the Il-khanid armies had assimilated numerous ethnic groups as they moved west in their campaigns, and the single largest ethnic group in them was Turkish. The "Mongol" armies of both the Il-khans and the Golden Horde were largely Turkish by the time they began to consolidate their power at their respective capital cities. It was not lost on the public who had anxiously watched the events unfold at 'Ayn Jalut that the armies of the Mamlukes and of Hulagu's Mongols were both largely Turkish, fighting for control of Muslim southwestern Asia.

FURTHER READING

General

Lewis, Archibald R. *Nomads and Crusaders, A.D. 1000–1368.* Bloomington and Indianapolis, Indiana: Indiana University Press, 1988.

The Crusades

Gabrieli, Francesco. *Arab Historians of the Crusades.* Translated from Italian by E. J. Costello. Berkeley and Los Angeles, California: University of California Press, 1984.

Hillenbrand, Carole. *The Crusades: Islamic Perspectives.* New York: Routledge, 2000.

Hitti, Phillip K. *An Arab–Syrian Gentleman and Warrior in the Period of the Crusades: Memoirs of Usamah Ibn-Munqidh.* Princeton, New Jersey: Princeton University Press, 1987.

Holt, P.M. *The Age of the Crusades: The Near East from the eleventh century to 1517.* London and New York: Longman, 1986.

Maalouf, Amin. *The Crusades Through Arab Eyes*, Jon Rothschild, tr. New York: Schocken Books, 1984.

Powell, James M., ed. *Muslims Under Latin Rule, 1100–1300.* Princeton, New Jersey: Princeton University Press, 1990.

The Loss of Andalus

Abun-Nasr, Jamil M. *A History of the Maghrib in the Islamic Period*, 3d ed. Cambridge: Cambridge University Press, 1987.

Brett, Michael. *Ibn Khaldun and the Medieval Maghrib.* Aldershott, Hampshire/Brookfield, Vermont: Ashgate/Variorum, 1999.

Brett, Michael and Elizabeth Fentress. *The Berbers.* Oxford and Cambridge, Massachusetts: Blackwell, 1996.

Burns, Robert J. *Islam Under the Crusaders.* Princeton, New Jersey: Princeton University Press, 1973.

Cornell, Vincent J. *Realm of the Saint: Power and Authority in Moroccan Sufism.* Austin, Texas: University of Texas Press, 1998.

Fletcher, Richard. *Moorish Spain.* New York: Henry Holt and Company, 1992.

MacKay, Angus. *Spain in the Middle Ages: From Frontier to Empire, 1000–1500.* New York: St. Martin's, 1977.

Scales, Peter C. *The Fall of the Caliphate of Córdoba: Berbers and Andalusis in Conflict.* Leiden: E.J. Brill, 1994.

Wasserstein, David. *The Rise and Fall of the Party-Kings: Politics and Society in Islamic Spain, 1002–1086.* Princeton, New Jersey: Princeton University Press, 1985.

Realignment in the East

Daftary, Farhad. *The Assassin Legends: Myths of the Isma'ilis.* London: I. B. Tauris, 1994.

Daftary, Farhad. *The Ismailis: Their History and Doctrines.* Cambridge, U.K.: Cambridge University Press, 1990.

Morgan, David. *The Mongols.* Oxford: Basil Blackwell, 1986.

Saunders, J.J. *The History of the Mongol Conquests.* Philadelphia: University of Pennsylvania Press, 2001.

CHAPTER 8

The Consolidation of Traditions

The turmoil of the period from 950 to 1260 inevitably had an impact on cultural life. The fracturing of political unity, the militarization of society, and the repeated invasions meant that it was unlikely that large-scale, state-sponsored intellectual projects such as al-Ma'mun's Bayt al-Hikma would be funded again. Moreover, as a result of the conflicts, libraries were often burned and looted, patron-rulers were killed, and scholars themselves were sometimes kidnaped or killed. On the other hand, the very proliferation of small states meant that petty rulers wanted to enhance their status by patronizing the arts and sciences. It may be that more scholars and artists were funded under the political decentralization that characterized this period than would have been possible under centralization.

Thus, despite the hardships of the era, the period from the tenth through the thirteenth centuries was an era of cultural efflorescence in the Muslim world. Scholars built on earlier developments in science and philosophy, theology, and Sufism, and achieved a level of sophistication that awed their contemporaries in other societies. New institutions were devised within the Dar al-Islam to conserve and perpetuate the knowledge and skills learned, and scholars and rulers of other states—most notably in western Europe—made great efforts to borrow from the achievements of the Muslims.

Science and Philosophy

The ninth century witnessed the monumental project of translating Greek and Syriac texts into Arabic. During the next several centuries, Muslim scholars worked out the scientific, philosophical, and religious implications of those texts. Many of the scholars became famous throughout the Dar al-Islam for their original work in science, mathematics, and philosophy, but gained an even wider fame in Europe during the twelfth and thirteenth centuries when their own work was translated into Latin. On the other hand, it became clear that elements of the philosophical legacy from Greece were incompatible with certain interpretations of Islamic doctrine. The Aristotelian tradition, in particular, posed problems for Muslim intellectuals just as it would in the thirteenth century for European Christian intellectuals.

Mathematics and the Natural Sciences

One of the great mathematicians and physicists of the period from the tenth through the thirteenth centuries was Ibn al-Haytham (known later to the Latins as Alhazen), who was born in the Iraqi city of Basra about 975. He was well educated in religious studies and obtained a position as an administrator. He became so disgusted, however, with the religious bickering of the period—this was the time when Iraqi Sunnis and Shi'ites were particularly intolerant of each other—that he resigned from his position and devoted himself to science. Apparently a Shi'ite himself, he won a reputation for his scientific achievements in Basra, and then went to Egypt during the reign of al-Hakim, the Fatimid caliph-Imam. Ibn al-Haytham is famous for advances he made in geometry, astronomy, the theory of light, and number theory, but he is best known for making the first significant contributions to optical theory since Ptolemy, whose work was done in the second century. He is the first to have used the camera obscura, and his name is best known in the context of "Alhazen's problem," which he stated as follows: "Given a light source and a spherical mirror, find the point on the mirror where the light will be reflected to the eye of an observer." He contradicted Ptolemy's and Euclid's theory of vision that the eye sends out visual rays to the object of the vision; according to Ibn al-Haytham, the rays originate in the object of vision and not in the eye. He published theories on refraction, reflection, binocular vision, the rainbow, parabolic and spherical mirrors, spherical aberration, atmospheric refraction, and the apparent increase in the size of the moon and sun near Earth's horizon. He died in 1039.

A contemporary of Ibn al-Haytham was al-Biruni (973–1048), a native of Khwarazm. In an age of multitalented scholars, al-Biruni impressed everyone he met. Many consider him to have been the most erudite scholar of the period under review. He obtained positions in several Iranian courts, where he measured latitudes and longitudes between cities and measured solar meridian transits. In 1017, he was back home when Mahmud of Ghazna conquered Khwarazm. Al-Biruni was one of the many captives taken to Ghazna, and he remained a virtual prisoner of Mahmud for the rest of that ruler's reign. He was forced to accompany Mahmud on several campaigns to India, but he made the most of the experiences and subsequently wrote a massive and perceptive description of Indian society and culture. He mastered Turkish, Persian, Sanskrit, and Arabic, and he published numerous works in physics, astronomy, mathematics, medicine, history, and what we might call anthropology. He introduced techniques to measure the earth and distances on it using triangulation. He estimated the radius of the earth to be 3930 miles, a value not obtained in western Europe until the sixteenth century. His wide range of abilities is demonstrated in his having translated Euclid's works into Sanskrit.

'Umar Khayyam (ca. 1048–1122) was born in Nishapur. He is most famous in the English-speaking world for Edward FitzGerald's 1859 translation of the *Rubaiyat*, a collection of quatrains, only some of which can be attributed to him with certainty. He was an even greater mathematician and astronomer than he was a poet, however. Like al-Biruni, Khayyam complained of the difficulties that the constant wars caused for the scholarly life, and yet, like him, his accomplishments would have been notable even for a scholar in the most serene of circumstances. His first appointment was in Samarqand, but his achievements in music theory and algebra were already so great by the age of 25 that the young Saljuq sultan Malik-Shah invited him to help set up an observatory (without telescopes, which would be used for the first time in the seventeenth century) in Esfahan. For eighteen years he was the leader of a team of observers that developed important astronomical tables. He also began work on calendar reform and calculated the solar year to be 365.24219858156 days. (Today it is said to be 365.242190 days.) When Sanjar became the supreme sultan of the Great Saljuqs in 1118, Khayyam moved to his capital at Merv, which Sanjar was turning into a great center of Islamic learning. Among Khayyam's achievements is a complete classification of cubic equations with geometric solutions found by means of intersecting conic sections. He also realized that a cubic equation can have more than one solution.

Philosophy

The most influential of all the Muslim philosopher–scientists was Ibn Sina (980–1037), known later in Europe as Avicenna. He was born in Bukhara into an Isma'ili family, although he does not appear to have been one himself. His father held a position in the Samanid regime, and Ibn Sina grew up having access to the royal library. He was a child prodigy, mastering Islamic law and then medicine, and he became a practicing physician at the age of sixteen. He then began a study of metaphysics, and he reports that he had to read al-Farabi's work on Aristotle forty times before he understood it. His study of philosophy was interrupted by Mahmud of Ghazna's defeat of the Samanids. He escaped the fate of al-Biruni (with whom he had exchanged much correspondence) and headed west rather than east in search of patrons to support his intellectual pursuits. He spent the rest of his life serving in the courts of provincial Shi'ite rulers, first in Khorasan, then at the Buyid court in Rayy, and then successive posts in Qazvin, Hamadan, and finally in Esfahan. He served as court physician and twice was wazir, but the political intrigues endemic in the courtly life led to his being imprisoned at least once and his life endangered several times.

Remarkably, this man of affairs was one of the most productive scholars in history, and left a permanent mark in both medicine and philosophy. *The Book of Healing* is a vast philosophical and scientific encyclopedia that treats logic, the natural sciences, the four disciplines that the Latins called the quadrivium (arithmetic, geometry, astronomy, and music), and metaphysics. His *Canon of Medicine* is the most famous book in the history of medicine in both East and West. Although some scholars regard it as advancing very little beyond the medical compendium of al-Razi, its great accomplishments were its clarity, its comprehensiveness, and its classificatory system. As a result, it was used in the medical colleges of western Europe into the seventeenth century.

As great as his influence was in medicine, Ibn Sina is also widely regarded as having been one of the world's greatest philosophers. Basing his own work on that of al-Farabi, which had been the most sophisticated Neoplatonic work before the eleventh century, he took advantage of the fact that Greek thought had been a part of the Arabic tradition for two centuries. His writing is more confident and more original and, as a result, has been more influential. He infused the existing Neoplatonic system with more Aristotelian content, including a subtle discussion of the difference between necessary and possible being. He also tried to prove that it was possible, despite the Neoplatonic tradition, that a personal soul would survive death (rather than losing its identity in the One). Although he tried to reconcile Islamic doctrines and philosophy, the brilliant system that he created posed serious challenges to the revealed message of Islam, precisely because it was so persuasive to intellectuals.

The defense of the traditional religious doctrines fell to al-Ghazali (1058–1111), whom Europeans would later call Algazel. Born in Tus, in Khorasan, he was educated in schools near the Caspian Sea and in the Nishapur area, and he moved to Baghdad about 1085. In 1091, Nizam al-Mulk appointed him to the new Nizamiya college there, where he became a popular lecturer in jurisprudence and theology. Although possessed of a keen philosophical mind, his theological commitments made him hostile to the legacies of Neoplatonism and Aristotelianism. He wrote a summary of the views of al-Farabi and Ibn Sina entitled *Intentions of the Philosophers*. Designed to help his students understand Neoplatonism so that they could begin to criticize its weaknesses, it was so lucid and objective that thirteenth-century Europeans concluded that the book reflected al-Ghazali's own views, and they believed that he had worked in the same tradition as al-Farabi and Ibn Sina. The sequel to this book was a criticism of Neoplatonism entitled *The Incoherence of the Philosophers*, which was not translated into Latin, but was highly influential in the Islamic world. In it, al-Ghazali challenged the philosophers' denial of the resurrection of the body, their postulate of the eternality of the world, and their notions of causality, which had diminished the concepts of God's sovereignty and omnipotence and had rendered him subject to necessity.

Al-Ghazali's attack on philosophy triggered a response by Ibn Rushd (1126–1198), known in Europe as Averroes. By the twelfth century, some of the greatest advances in philosophy in the world were taking place in Andalus. Ironically, this was the period of the Almoravids and Almohads, who have a reputation today for anti-intellectualism. Ibn Rushd was well versed in the work of the great Andalusi Neoplatonists Ibn Bajja (ca. 1095–1138), known in Europe as Avempace, and he was the student and protegee of Ibn Tufayl (ca. 1100–1185), known to the Latin world as Abubacer. Ibn Rushd came from a family of jurists, and he himself was trained in medicine, the religious sciences, and philosophy. He was a qadi as well as a physician in Cordoba and Seville under the Almohads. He then became court physician to the caliph in Marrakesh in 1182.

The official religious ideology of the Almohad state made the Qur'an and Hadith the only sources of truth, a position which would seem to create a hostile environment for philosophy. The two caliphs whom Ibn Rushd knew, however—Abu Ya'qub (r. 1163–1184) and his son Abu Yusuf (r. 1184–1199)—were genuinely interested in philosophical speculation. Except for one brief period after 1194, when

Abu Yusuf was compelled by popular agitation to send Ibn Rushd back to Andalus and to burn his books publicly, the patronage and respect of the Almohad rulers saved Ibn Rushd from the anger of many of the more traditionally pious.

A member of the ulama as well as a philosopher, Ibn Rushd was determined to construct a case for philosophy that would not violate the norms of true religion. Ibn Rushd's philosophical role was to champion true Aristotelianism and to extricate it from Neoplatonism. His profound, yet lucid, commentaries on the texts of Aristotle earned him in Europe the nickname "The Commentator." He swept away the concept of successive emanations from the One and argued for a restoration of the original Aristotelian concept of the First Cause or Unmoved Mover, by which it can be argued that a multiplicity of Intelligences can come directly from God, rather than in successive emanations. He upheld the Aristotelian concept of the eternity of the world, but pointed out that this does not mean that the world is eternal by itself, leaving room for a way to finesse the problem of creation. Ibn Rushd also argued for personal immortality, even though medieval Europeans misunderstood him on this point until the fourteenth century.

In addition to numerous commentaries and original works, Ibn Rushd wrote the *Incoherence of the Incoherence*, a response to al-Ghazali's attack on philosophy. Al-Ghazali had equated philosophy with the Neoplatonism of al-Farabi and Ibn Sina, but Ibn Rushd was not interested in defending Neoplatonism. Rather, he wanted to demonstrate that the conclusions of philosophy, if well understood, were in harmony with revelation and were an infallible source of truth. If there are apparent conflicts between revelation and philosophy and a review of the philosophical reasoning reveals no mistakes in assumptions and logic, then the scriptures are obviously meant to be interpreted allegorically.

Ibn Rushd said that there are three types of learners: those who can reason philosophically, those who are convinced by dialectical arguments (the theologians), and those who are convinced by preaching, inspiration, or coercion. The Qur'an was intended for all three, but the meaning of the Qur'an is not readily apparent to all persons. Those who are endowed with the ability of philosophical reasoning are under a divine obligation to pursue philosophy, and they are not obligated to change the demonstrable truths obtained by that means just because they contradict the opinions of theologians. Theologians rely upon dialectic and rhetoric and are in no position to argue with the superior conclusions of philosophy. Moreover, the theologians are wrong to make public the various interpretations of ambiguous verses, for it could confuse or raise doubts in the minds of the masses. Ibn Rushd thought that al-Ghazali, as a mere theologian, was out of place to be scolding philosophers. His discipline lacked the rigorous methods and concepts that characterized philosophy, and he should have ensured that theology yields to philosophy, rather than the reverse.

Ibn Rushd is often regarded as the last great philosopher in the Islamic world. Such a judgment has to be qualified. Brilliant Muslim minds would continue to work out highly sophisticated systems of thought for centuries to come, but after Ibn Rushd, such systems were developed only within a theological context and are best described as philosophical theology. Ibn Rushd's defense of an open-ended quest for truth by rational means had little resonance in the Dar al-Islam. East of the

Maghrib, al-Ghazali's attack on philosophy had persuaded scholars that reason need-ed to be disciplined by the doctrines taught by the religious establishment rather than given free rein. In the Maghrib and in Andalus, domestic and foreign affairs com-bined in the early thirteenth century to bring a halt to the exuberant philosophical tradition that had taken root there in the twelfth century. The Maghrib continued to be a hostile environment for philosophy, and Andalus collapsed under the im-pact of the Reconquista, leaving only Granada. The ablest minds and the wealthiest patrons left the peninsula for permanent exile. After the early thirteenth century, the Muslims of the peninsula never again produced literature that interested Muslims out-side that beleaguered community itself.

The Sunni Resolution to the Tension between Reason and Revelation

Although most Muslim intellectuals remained suspicious of metaphysics, philosophical modes of reasoning and arguing made a lasting impact on Sunni Islam. At the be-ginning of the twelfth century, the new Islamic theology, in the person of al-Ghazali, had gone head to head with philosophy's most articulate exponent, Ibn Sina, and to most observers, the fight ended in a draw. Al-Ghazali's arguments were often better than those of either Ibn Sina or the later Ibn Rushd, and many of his critics and supporters alike noted that he had attempted to demonstrate the inadequacy of philosophy on philosophical grounds. Moreover, he admitted that he found many of the methods and results of philosophers to be highly useful; he conceded that they had made valuable contributions in logic, mathematics, ethics, and politics. Ironically, although al-Ghazali attacked Neoplatonism, his own metaphysics were shaped by Neoplatonism. He did not deny emanationism, for example, and he assumed the existence of the Universal Intellect and the Universal Soul.

Al-Ghazali was followed by two theologians who, if anything, were even more influenced by philosophy than he was: al-Shahrastani (ca. 1080–1153), who spent most of his career in his homeland of southeastern Iran, and Fakhr al-Din al-Razi (1149–1209, not to be confused with Abu Bakr al-Razi the physician whom we saw in Chapter 5), originally from Rayy, but who spent most of his career in what is today Afghanistan. Both scholars used arguments that employed new philosophical con-ceptions and logical methods, and the organization of al-Razi's work reveals his philo-sophical bent. In the first part of his theological work, he lays the logical and epistemological framework for his work; then he discusses metaphysical issues such as being, necessity, and possibility; and only then does he discuss the doctrine of God and other religious topics.

By the thirteenth century, a student could not expect to embark upon a course of study in theology without becoming thoroughly familiar with philosophical concepts and forms of argument as well as the long history of doctrine itself. Even the great Hanbali teacher Ibn Taymiya (1263–1328), who was unsparing in his criticism of philosophers and theologians, used his own profound command of both philosophy and kalam to attack his targets. Nevertheless, most of the ulama regarded kalam in the same way that al-Ghazali had: Theology could not lead to certainty in spiritual truths, but it was a useful tool for polemics and apologetics.

Consolidating Institutions: Sufism

The period from the tenth through the thirteenth centuries was decisive in shaping the organizational and conceptual framework for Sufism. The tenth century was a pivotal time for the mystics of Islam. As we saw in Chapter 5, al-Hallaj's lack of caution not only cost him his life, but it also forced many other Sufis into a defensive position. In the aftermath of al-Hallaj's execution in 922, Sufi leaders began justifying their manner of worship. Over the next two centuries, they wrote books explicating Sufi tenets in an effort to allay the anxieties and suspicions of the ulama, and most Sufis gave careful thought to the balance that they should strike between everyday ritual and the mystical path. Most found the writings of al-Junayd to be helpful in this regard. Some Sufi intellectuals began viewing their enterprise as a religious science just as law was, and wrote manuals discussing methods and technical vocabulary. As a result, by the eleventh century, Sufism had become much more acceptable to the majority of the ulama, many of whom were now Sufis themselves. Hanbali traditionalists continued to hurl invectives at Sufism, but by the twelfth century the cultivation of the inward life had become an accepted part of the Sunni experience. The Sufi experience offered a wide range of options. A practitioner could use it to develop self-discipline, to cultivate gnostic insight, or to pursue ecstatic experiences.

A powerful endorsement of the Sufi path appeared at the beginning of the twelfth century in the person of al-Ghazali, whose name is as closely linked with the history of Sufism as it is with philosophy and kalam. On the one hand, it is useful to point out that he was not a philosopher, that his contribution to kalam was less than other thinkers, and that he added almost nothing to the content of Sufism itself. On the other hand, his passionate engagement in the debates of his day contributed to the future direction of all three fields of thought. In 1095, al-Ghazali resigned his teaching post in Baghdad, apparently with the intention of abandoning his career as a jurist, theologian, and professor in order to serve God more completely as a Sufi. He apparently suffered from a severe emotional crisis that almost incapacitated him. Whether his crisis derived from a conviction that the intellectual life that he had led did not produce certainties after all, or from a revulsion at the worldliness of his fellow ulama, or from some other cause, is unclear. Whatever the reason, he lived for short periods of time in several cities of Syria (on the eve of the arrival of the Crusaders in Palestine) and Iraq before returning home to Tus. There he lived the life of an ascetic and mystic and attracted a group of followers. The Saljuq vizier persuaded him to lecture in Nishapur for three years, but he returned again to Tus, in northeastern Iran, where he died in 1111.

During this post-Baghdad period, al-Ghazali wrote a major work entitled *The Revival of the Religious Sciences.* In it, he argued that it was not by theological learning that one attained heaven, but rather by a life of moral uprightness and closeness to God, which could be attained through Sufi methods. Whereas theology was a necessary safeguard for true belief in its role of defending the faith, the truly pious life was the fusion of religious obligations and the mystical experience. Prior to al-Ghazali, many Sufis and critics of Sufism alike considered that the Sufi way of life began where the Shari'a ended, but his contribution was a persuasive demonstration that, on the one hand, the truly Sufi life embraced the faithful observance of all these duties, and on the other, that the inner meaning of the Shari'a was fulfilled in the Sufi life.

Al-Ghazali's profound influence in this regard can be seen in the fact that the Almoravid regime implemented a policy of hunting down copies of his *The Revival of the Religious Sciences* and burning them publicly. Al-Ghazali had become a hero to the dissenters in the Almoravid empire because of his defense of the mystical life and his insistence on the importance of the Shafi'i consensus in law. As a corollary of his defense of Sufism, he asserted that all learned Muslims, not just the official ulama, had a right to be heard on the issues of ethics and law. His rationale was that the combination of piety and learning was what qualified people to make public judgments, not scholastic credentials. In the conservative, highly stratified Almoravid society, such ideas were considered seditious. As a result, his followers were persecuted and his works were banned.

The Emergence of Lodges and Tariqas

As Sufism became more widely practiced, it made an important transition from an individual exercise to an organized, collective effort. The first step in this direction was the widespread appearance of residential lodges. In the first few centuries of Sufism, a student in a city typically studied with several spiritual masters. He might visit them in their homes or travel widely in order to learn from as many as possible. On the frontiers and in the rural areas, however, it was the Sufi masters who tended to be itinerant. It was there that mosques, forts, and other structures became meeting places for Sufis, and many of the buildings (except for the mosques) became temporary residences for students who would stay with the master for as long as he remained in the area. As we have seen, many of the fortresses, or ribats, of North Africa assumed this role, and soon the term *ribat* had both military and Sufi connotations. By the second half of the eleventh century, such lodges were making their appearance in large cities such as Baghdad and shortly could be found throughout the cities of the Dar al-Islam. At first they were used for a variety of religious purposes, but by the end of the twelfth century they were used exclusively for Sufi purposes. Such a lodge was usually called a *ribat* in North Africa, a *khanaqa* in Iran, a *zawiya* in most of the eastern Arabic-speaking lands, and a *tekke* in Turkish areas, although the high level of travel by scholars, merchants, and the pious meant that the terms were interchangeable in practically every region.

The next important step in the development of Sufism was the emergence of the *tariqa*, a term that has been translated as "order." Literally meaning "path," the tariqa was a unique spiritual discipline and an accompanying set of rituals that constituted the identity of a group associated with a particular zawiya. The tariqa consisted of a structured set of spiritual exercises to be learned and mastered by the student. These exercises were designed to bring the Sufi into direct communion with God and therefore became the focal point of the student's concentration. The exercises included a dhikr as well as the ascetic or contemplative practices that a novitiate struggled to master on his ascent to a personal experience with God. Both the dhikr and the spiritual exercises distinguished one tariqa from another.

We know very little about the origins and spread of either the lodges or the orders, but it appears that the very presence of multiple lodges in a given city produced a momentum for each lodge to become associated with a particular master's spiritual discipline. Once the concept became fixed that a student belonged to a particular order, the practice of initiation into that order became the norm. Sufis were now allowed to practice the method of an order only in return for a pledge of spiritual loyalty to the master or the local representative of a given order.

Like the lodges themselves, tariqas appear to have developed first outside the major cities. They began developing in the twelfth century, but became prominent only during the first half of the thirteenth century. The Abbasid caliph al-Nasir (1180–1225), who was attempting to rebuild the authority of his office, appointed 'Umar al-Suhrawardi (1145–1234) *shaykh* ("leader" or "master") of a ribat, with the proviso that the membership associated with it be limited to those who accepted the teachings of Suhrawardi's great uncle, Abu al-Najib al-Suhrawardi. Abu al-Najib was revered as the formulator of a spiritual discipline, and it was believed that he had a spiritual genealogy that could be traced back to the Prophet—that is, he had been taught by men who had been taught by men who had been taught by the Prophet himself.

This spiritual genealogy, or *silsila*, became a distinguishing feature of Sufi orders, just as the isnad was of the authentic Hadith. It guaranteed the soundness of the method by showing that it had been transmitted from one Sufi to another ever since the Prophet's generation. The master himself had received it in its pure form, and his successors passed it on to future generations, its authenticity attested to by the collective membership. The orders themselves gained their names from the names of the master who supposedly founded them, although often, as in the case of the Suhrawardiya order, the organization was founded after the master's death. Another such posthumous order was the Qadiriya, named after 'Abd al-Qadir al-Gilani of Baghdad (d. 1165).

The development of the orders marked a new stage in the history of Sufism. To that point, the mystical tradition had encouraged an independence of spirit and creativity, but the crystallization of the orders meant the imposition of a rigorous discipline on those who sought spiritual enlightenment through them. No longer were the teacher and his students in a mere relationship of instructor and pupil; now they were in a relationship of spiritual guide (*shaykh* or *murshid* in the Arab world; *pir* in the Persian-speaking regions) and disciple (*murid*). Disciples were to submit themselves unquestioningly to their master. As one Sufi put it, the disciple was to be as a dead body in the hands of its washer.

Because of the new sense of discipline, generation after generation of members of a particular lodge followed the same tariqa (or believed themselves to be doing so), and thus developed a group identity. They were persuaded that the teachings associated with the order could be traced back through the generations of masters, the order's founder, and eventually to the Prophet himself. Mystical wandering mendicants, healers, and spiritual advisers continued to be found throughout the Dar al-Islam, but henceforward the characteristic Sufi approach would be that of a disciple who belonged to a community led by a spiritual master.

Merchants or scholars who visited a city might join an order for a few months or years, and then return home and begin a branch of the order there. By this process, some of the orders gained adherents over huge areas. By the seventeenth century, the Qadiriya tariqa could be found from North Africa to India. Sometimes the branches remained remarkably faithful to the original tariqa, but in many cases the local conditions and traditions led to slight modifications in the ritual, with the result that many suborders emerged within the Sufi movement. By adapting to local needs, the

A Handbook for Sufi Novices

Abu al-Najib al-Suhravardi (1090–1168), after whom the Suhravardi (in Arabic: Suhrawardi) order was named, wrote a guide addressed to novices and laymen who wished to learn the rules of conduct of a Sufi. The handbook contains less material on the stages and states of the Sufi mystical path than it does on such matters as companionship, hospitality, and specific rules dealing with particular situations. It is a revealing insight into the importance that most Sufi orders placed on adab, *a term that suggests good manners, refinement, and proper behavior. The section reproduced here deals with the adab of eating.*

121.   The ethics and manners of eating. (Qur'an 7:31 is quoted.) One should give the poor to eat from what one is eating. One should say at the beginning of the meal "In the name of God." If one forgets to say "In the name of God" at the beginning, he should say this when he remembers....

122.   One should not be concerned about the provisions of livelihood nor should one be occupied in seeking, gathering, and storing them. (Qur'an 29:60 quoted.) The Prophet did not store anything for the morrow. One should not talk much about food because this is gluttony. In eating one should intend to satisfy hunger and give one's soul its due but not its pleasure. The Prophet said, "You owe your soul its due." Food should be taken like medicine [as an unpleasant necessity]. Gluttony should be avoided. One should not find fault in any food nor should one praise it.

⋮

124.   Sufis eat only food whose source they know. They avoid eating the food of unjust and sinful people. A Hadith: "The Prophet forbade us to accept an invitation to dinner by sinful persons." The Sufis refuse to accept the gifts of women and to eat at their meals.

125.   The Sufis do not disapprove of conversation during the meal. More of their rules of conduct in eating: to sit on the left leg, to use the formula "In the name of God," to eat with three fingers, to take small bites and chew well, to lick the fingers and the bowl. One should not look at the morsel taken by a friend. When he finishes his eating, he should say, "Praise be to Allah who has made the provisions of our livelihood more plentiful than our needs." It is not polite to dip one's hand in the food because one can get soiled with it [one should dip only three fingers].

126.   [On eating in company.] A Sufi saying: "Eating with brethren should be with informality (insibat); with foreigners, with nice manners; and with the poor (fuqara'), with altruism." Junayd said, "Eating together is like being nursed together, so you should carefully consider the persons with whom you eat." The Sufis prefer to eat in company.... When one eats in company, he should not withdraw from eating as long as the others are eating, especially if he is the head of the group. When the Prophet was eating in company, he would be the last one to finish.

⋮

130.   Three obligations of the host and three of the guest. The host should present only licit food, keep the times of prayer, and should not withhold from the guest whatever food he is able to give. The guest should sit where he is told by the host, be pleased with what is given to him, and should not leave without asking permission of the host. The Prophet said, "It is a commendable custom (sunna) to accompany the guest to the door of the house."

Source: al-Suhrawardi, Abu al-Najib. *A Sufi Rule for Novices: Kitāb Ādāb al-Muṛīdīn.* An abridged translation and introduction by Menahem Milson. Cambridge, Massachusetts and London, England: Harvard University Press, 1975, pp. 57–59.

lodges enabled Sufism to became a mass movement. The orders encouraged those who could to live in the lodge and to engage in the fully dedicated life of an adept, but many of them encouraged those who had families and full-time jobs to participate as much as they could, if only to engage in the dhikr once or twice a week. Moreover, the masters freely gave of their spiritual guidance to anyone in need of reassurance and healing. As a result, the masses revered them during their lifetime and sought out their tombs after their death.

In the large cities, the members of the lodges were in close contact with the mosque system, and the shaykh might even be the imam of a major mosque. Thus, "middle-class" Sufism usually maintained practices and doctrines that did not run afoul of the developing cosmopolitan consensus regarding the acceptable doctrines and practices in Islam. Among the illiterate in the cities, and especially in rural and frontier areas, however, Sufi practices could include features quite unrelated to the written tradition of Islam. Some of these practices came into Sufism from local pre-Islamic traditions and were initially viewed by Sufi masters as harmless baggage that enabled new converts to make the transition to Islam. Howling, fire eating, sword swallowing, and juggling became associated with the rituals of some orders.

The result was a syncretism that made some Muslims uneasy. On the one hand, the persistence of pre-Islamic religious elements facilitated the conversion of vast numbers of people who otherwise might not have found the religion attractive. By combining these elements with piety and faith in God's love, Sufism made important contributions. On the other hand, some ulama were aghast at features that suggested ancestor worship or idolatry, as well as an ignorance of the Shari'a. The highly charged tension continued between those who assumed the role of guardians of the Qur'an and Hadith on the one hand, and those who were willing to make compromises in order to expand the Umma on the assumption that converts would gradually assimilate into correct practice.

Speculative Mysticism

Although the mystical experience itself cannot be subjected to rational analysis or description, many so-called "speculative" mystics have tried to understand how the mystical experience is possible at all and what it can reveal about the nature of God and of the human soul. As a result, many Sufis were attracted to the new sciences and philosophy that became available as a result of the translation movement of the ninth and tenth centuries. Alchemy was highly popular among Sufis. Its practitioners were sometimes engaged in the attempt to transform base metals into gold, and they were even more concerned to transform imperfect souls into perfect ones through the spiritual discipline that alchemy offered. Some Sufis became well known for both their spiritual exercises and their elixirs.

Philosophy, however, had an even more powerful impact on the mystical expression of Islam. Certain features of Neoplatonism and of gnosticism appealed to many mystics for the same reason that they had been popular among pagans, Jews, Christians, and Muslim rationalists. Neoplatonism not only furnished the cosmology that allowed mystics to explain their progress toward union with the One in the reverse order of the emanations, but it also had a complex theory of the divisions of

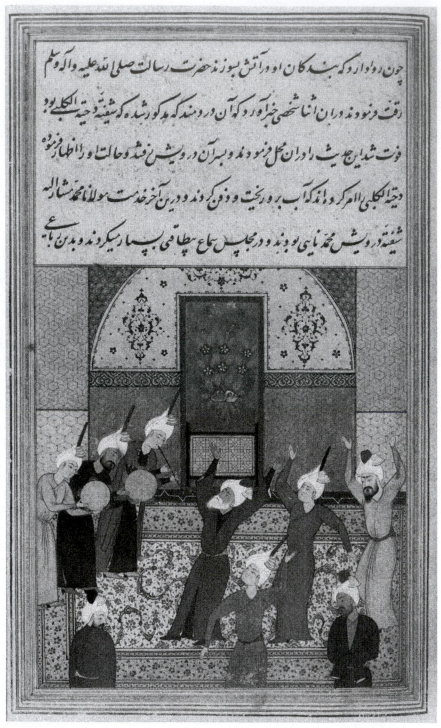

A sixteenth-century Persian painting of a Sufi pir dancing with his disciples.

the human soul that enabled them to explain their spiritual progress in mastering one aspect or another of their lower selves. Gnosticism taught that spiritual elites were in possession of a special knowledge that was different from knowledge gained by the masses or from empirical observation. Moreover, this knowledge was different from (and better than) even what passed as wisdom: It was obtained by direct contact with God's presence.

Neoplatonism and gnosticism provided the framework and the concepts for the development of ideas that played an important role in Sufism for hundreds of years. A major example is the understanding of the significance of the Prophet himself. The earliest Muslims viewed Muhammad to be a prophet and a warner, but his image inevitably acquired additional characteristics due to his role as the model of the pious life. With the aid of Neoplatonic concepts, the doctrine of the preexistence of Muhammad and the concept of Muhammad as the Perfect Man emerged, developments that run parallel to the Hellenistically influenced Christian ideas of Jesus of Nazareth as preexisting Logos and Perfect Man. The doctrine of the *mi'raj*, or the ascent of the Prophet to heaven (from Jerusalem), became fully developed during this time. Based on an ambiguous passage in the Qur'an (17:1), it soon was fleshed out in the Hadith and then was further elaborated among Neoplatonic Sufis. For the latter, it became a powerful paradigm for their own spiritual ascent into the presence of God.

Another legacy from Neoplatonism and gnosticism was the development of the concept of *al-Qutb*, "the Pole" or "the Axis," introduced by the Sufi theoretician al-Tirmidhi (d. 932). Al-Tirmidhi (who was nicknamed al-Hakim, the term used to refer to Greek philosophers), wrote that saints, or walis, govern the universe. They are ranked in a hierarchy, according to their spiritual insight, with al-Qutb at the pinnacle. Over the next few centuries, these ideas were developed in great detail, and walis were considered to be responsible for everything that happens in this world. Several Sufi masters claimed to be the Qutb of their generation, and some Sufis believed that a Muslim had to know the Qutb of his era or be regarded as an infidel. Al-Qutb was also known as the Seal of the Saints, a concept that disturbed some ulama because it could be construed to detract from the status of Muhammad as Seal of the Prophets.

In the twelfth and thirteenth centuries, several speculative mystics produced works that have been a source of inspiration for Sufis to the present day. Three are of particular importance for our purposes. Shihab al-Din Yahya al-Suhrawardi (1153–1191) was from the same town and had a similar name as the man who created the Suhrawardiya order, but he is nicknamed al-Maqtul (the murdered) to distinguish him from the other one. As a young man, he settled in Aleppo at the court of Saladin's son, Malik al-Zahir. Al-Suhrawardi attempted to create a philosophical base for an Islamic mysticism that combined elements of Neoplatonism, Zoroastrianism, and gnosticism. The central theme of his work is the metaphor of God as Light. With the help of this image, al-Suhrawardi could substitute illumination for the Neoplatonic concept of emanation; both the creation and the sustaining of the universe are the result of the constant production of light that characterizes God. The mystical experience itself is understood as a process of illumination, and the soul's fate after death depends on the degree of illumination that it obtained during life in the body.

Al-Suhrawardi was critical of Aristotelian categories, and dismissed all definitions and categories as mental constructs. For him, all reality was a single continuum, possessed with more or less of a degree of Being. God is pure Being, whereas nature has less Being. This interpretation of the universe is variously called pantheistic or monistic, for it suggests that nothing exists except God. By suggesting that the world is in some sense God, and that there is no distinction between God and His creation, al-Suhrawardi undercut a basic tenet of revealed monotheism. His ideas were too bold for the leading ulama of Aleppo, and they prevailed upon Malik al-Zahir to have him imprisoned and then killed. His ideas of Illuminationism, however, survived to influence mystics of the Persian-speaking world for centuries.

Meanwhile, in Andalus, a young man was reaching maturity who would have an even wider influence. Ibn al-'Arabi (sometimes rendered "Ibn 'Arabi") was born in Murcia in 1165. Sometime between 1198 and 1201, he set out on the hajj and never returned to Andalus. He remained in Mecca for several years, and then visited many other cities over the next quarter of a century before settling in Damascus in 1223. He died in 1240. Ibn al-'Arabi's ambition was to give philosophic expression to the important mystical doctrines that had been developed to that point. Like al-Suhrawardi, Ibn al-'Arabi employed ideas from gnosticism and Neoplatonism, and his erudition was formidable. His output, which included both poetry and prose, was prodigious. His writings have always been difficult to understand. Much of his work drew upon sources with which his readers were not familiar; he was fond of metaphors; and many of his ideas seem to contradict each other. As one can imagine, modern readers who grapple with his books in translation find his thought to be quite obscure. But precisely because his work combines a brilliant philosophical scheme with provocative imagery and ambiguous concepts, generations of Sufis have been able to find within his work many passages that reflect their own transcendental experience.

At the center of Ibn al-'Arabi's thought is a God who is inconceivable and unknowable, and whose only attribute is self-existence. And yet, God wishes to be known, and so He created the world. The universe exhibits His characteristics, serving in a sense as a mirror for His attributes. Longing to be known by individual souls, He makes His names known to us, that we may at least know Him in part. This partial self-revelation explains why each individual has a different conception of God, and why the various religions describe Him in different ways.

Just as Ibn al-'Arabi became *al-shaykh al-akbar* ("Great Master") for subsequent generations of speculative mystics, another thirteenth-century Sufi genius became known as Mawlana ("Our Master" in Persian; it is rendered Mevlana in Turkish) for the unsurpassed beauty of his poetry. Jalal al-Din al-Rumi (1207–1273) was born in Balkh, in modern Afghanistan. Leaving home just before the onslaught of Chinggis Khan, his father led his family on a circuitous route westward, eventually settling in Konya. Thus, Jalal al-Din grew up under the Saljuqs of Rum and, as a result, this poet who hailed from the eastern Islamic world has forever been known as Rumi. Rumi succeeded his father as a teacher of the religious sciences in Konya, and he also became a Sufi master, leading a circle of devoted disciples. In 1244, he met a wandering mystic named Shams al-Din, whom many found to be boorish, but in whom Rumi discovered the Divine Beloved. He became totally preoccupied with his relationship with Shams, and his family and disciples finally drove "the Beloved" from Konya. Rumi fell into a depression, and his family summoned Shams back to the city. Rumi's single-minded obsession resumed, however, and in desperation, his jealous disciples and children killed Shams.

The death of Shams was a life-changing event for Rumi. The experience of loss and of love turned him into a poet, and he developed a passionate interest in music and dance. He produced a collection of poetry dedicated to his beloved, and then, in 1249, he met a goldsmith whose deep spirituality reestablished for him a relationship similar to the one he had had with Shams. After the goldsmith's death, he formed a similar relationship with Husam al-Din Chelebi. Husam became the inspiration for Rumi's most famous work, the *Mathnawi* (*Masnavi*) which contains 26,000 couplets. The *Mathnawi* was inspired by the music of the world around Rumi—formal music, the music of nature, and of the everyday world of work, such as the ringing of the coppersmith's hammer. It contains fables, stories, proverbs, and the poetic evocation of the spiritual nature of the everyday world. For Sufis of the Persian-language world, it is second in importance only to the Qur'an as an inspirational text. At Rumi's death, Husam succeeded him as the leader of his spiritual circle and was in turn succeeded by Rumi's son Sultan Walad. Sultan Walad created the order that became known as the Mevlevi order, better known in the West as the Whirling Dervishes, whose musical, mesmerizing dance recapitulates the ecstasy and joy of Rumi's life and spiritual quest.

Ibn al-'Arabi, Rumi, the Egyptian Ibn al-Farid, and other Sufi poets of the thirteenth century produced one of the most powerful literary traditions in history. Rhythmic, sensuous, lucid, and yet deliberately obscure, it has provided pleasure and spiritual inspiration (as well as having provoked a powerful opposition to it by those who sense that it goes beyond the bounds of acceptable forms of worship). Since the mystical experience cannot be described, but can only be communicated through metaphor and analogy, poetry was found to be a far more appropriate medium for it than prose. In addition, the symbols and evocative imagery that are more easily expressed through poetry can also convey the mystical perspective that transcends the categories of rational thought. In their meditations upon the divine, Sufi poets borrowed subjects and themes from secular poetry to create allegories. A discussion of divine love could include a quatrain such as the following:

> Last night my idol placed his hand upon my breast,
>
> he seized me hard and put a slave-ring in my ear.
>
> I said, "My beloved, I am crying from your love!"
>
> He pressed his lips on mine and silenced me.[1]

In much the same way that Jews and Christians have found in the Biblical *Song of Songs* a metaphorical expression of the love between God and humans, so Sufis found in images of human love, of nature (the rose, the nightingale, the ocean), and even of forbidden pursuits (idols, wine, taverns, and temples) ways to express the ineffable truths of God's relationship to his creatures. The beloved represents God, and is usually portrayed in Persian poetry as a beautiful boy. Occasionally, in Arabic poetry, the beloved is a female, as in the works of Ibn al-Farid and in Ibn al-'Arabi's love lyrics in Mecca, composed under the spell of a young Persian-speaking lady. The idol, too, represents God; wine expresses the intoxication of God's love; the tavern can be the divine presence (where the lover drinks the wine of God's love); and the tavern keeper often represents the Sufi master. Puckishly, whereas the tavern and tavern keeper are positive symbols, the mosque and preacher usually represent hypocrisy or, at best, legalistic and empty religiosity. Not surprisingly, many of the non-Sufi ulama found such lyrics reprehensible, but many others found them profound, enjoyable, and inspirational. Particularly in their Persian form, they influenced the literature of Central Asia and South Asia in lasting ways.

Consolidating Institutions: Shi'ism

The tenth and eleventh centuries were heady days politically for the Shi'ites, for they controlled a large part of the Dar al-Islam. The Carmathians were a threat in the Persian Gulf from their base in Bahrain from the early tenth century until 1077; the Buyids ruled parts of Iraq and western Iran from 945 until 1055; the Fatimids controlled Ifriqiya and then Egypt and parts of Syria from 909 until 1171; the Isma'ili dynasty of the Sulayhids ruled Yemen from 1063 until 1138; the Hamdanids were a northern Syrian power in the second half of the tenth century; and the Assassins were a feared presence in Iran and Syria from 1090 until 1256. In addition, small Shi'te states were scattered throughout remote areas of the Dar al-Islam.

The period also witnessed important developments in Shi'ite theology and organization. As we have seen, this remarkably fragmented and inchoate movement coalesced into four major branches. The Zaydi community remained remarkably unchanged. Concentrated on the periphery of the major states in mountainous regions such as Daylam and Yemen, its members created small states but had little interaction with the major powers of the region. The Fatimid movement split in 1094 into the Nizari and Musta'li branches. The Imamiya, who fragmented upon the death of the eleventh Imam in 874, regrouped by the early tenth century around the doctrine of the Occultation of the Twelfth Imam. The dissolution of the Yemeni and Egyptian Isma'ili states in the twelfth century and the persecution of the Nizaris in the thirteenth century after the Mongol invasion left the Twelvers the largest single group of Shi'ites.

Twelver Shi'ites

From the 870s to the 940s, the leaders of what had been known as the Imamiya stated that the Hidden Imam was communicating with his community through certain spokesmen. Because the Hidden Imam was regarded as the twelfth and final leader of the Imamiya, the movement has become known as Twelver Shi'ism. After about seventy years of this so-called Lesser Concealment, the doctrine changed to that of the Greater Concealment, according to which the Imam no longer has an official spokesman. The transition from the period of the Lesser Concealment to that of the Greater Concealment occurred about 941, shortly before the Buyids seized power. Under their patronage, the Twelver Shi'ites flourished in Iraq and western Iran for a century.

During the Buyid period, Twelver scholars developed doctrines that answered some of the vexing questions that accompanied the end of the period of a present, or visible, Imam after 874. They taught that the twelfth Imam continues to provide guidance to his community despite his concealment. Although he has no single spokesman or agent, he does communicate through dreams and visions to highly-educated, spiritual ulama. When the Saljuqs conquered Baghdad from the Buyids in 1055, the leading Twelver intellectuals moved to Hilla, in southern Iraq, to escape persecution. There they developed the doctrine that the Imam had delegated his judicial authority to those who had studied jurisprudence. Thus, he continued to serve as a guide to his community, as well as to intercede with God for his followers. Because he is also the Mahdi, shortly before the Day of Judgment he will return to bring justice to this corrupt world. After a cataclysmic conflict with the forces of evil, he will rule the earth for several years. Then Jesus and the first eleven Imams will come, as well as prophets and saints who have previously brought the word of God and who have striven to establish righteousness on earth.

The doctrine of the Concealment of the twelfth Imam had important repercussions for the Twelver Shi'ites. One was that it provided a stability to the movement that it had never previously enjoyed. During the first two centuries or more of Shi'ite history, the Imamis had been less organized and less ideologically identifiable than the Isma'ilis, and had actually been in danger of fragmenting irretrievably in the late ninth century. However, during the tenth and eleventh centuries, they began to rally around the doctrine of the Hidden Imam and to develop doctrines and institutions that provided them with continuity and a stronger identity.

A second consequence of the new doctrine was that Sunni persecution of the sect became less pronounced. Until the doctrine of the Occultation was developed, the various Imams had been at least potentially political as well as religious figures. Although the Imams themselves had not led political uprisings since the time of Husayn, several pro-Alid agitators had proclaimed revolts in their name, and the Imams were suspect in the eyes of the political authorities because of these revolts and those of Zaydi activists. Any "present" or "visible" Imam would inevitably be perceived to be a political threat to the established order, and, as we have seen, several were persecuted and others died under mysterious circumstances. After 874, with the removal of the twelfth Imam from the political arena, Sunni authorities did not consider Twelver Shi'ism to be a threat and were able to coexist with it much more easily than they could Isma'ilism for several centuries. By the thirteenth century, Twelver Shi'ism was clearly the strongest and largest of the Shi'ite groups.

The Isma'ilis

The Isma'ilis enjoyed a period of great influence and power in the eleventh and twelfth centuries. In the first half of the eleventh century, the Fatimid empire was rivaled in the Muslim world only by the Ghaznavid empire under Mahmud. The factional conflicts and famines that began to afflict the empire during the 1060s greatly weakened it, but the schism of 1094 that resulted in the Musta'li-Nizari rift paradoxically left the perception that Isma'ilism was even more powerful than before. To many Sunnis and Twelver Shi'ites, it appeared that Hasan-i Sabbah's fortresses in Iran and Syria were simply an extension of the Fatimid state and that Isma'ilism was poised to dominate most of the Dar al-Islam. In reality, of course, the Fatimid

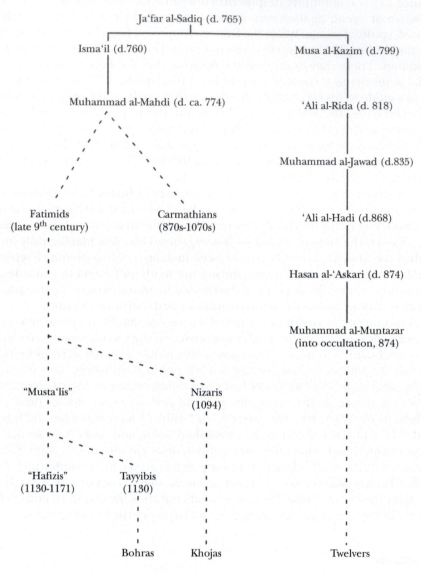

The Isma'ili (Sevener) and Imami (Twelver) Shi'a

movement had become greatly weakened, and it was saved from disintegration only by the fragmentation of the Saljuq empire at the very time of the Fatimid schism.

In 1130, the Fatimid movement suffered another blow. In that year the Fatimid caliph al-Amir was murdered, and yet another schism developed that would have a lasting impact. A cousin of the murdered caliph claimed the throne under the name al-Hafiz, and he was accepted by the Fatimid faithful in Egypt and Syria. In Yemen, however, where the policies of the Fatimid wazir al-Afdal were increasingly regarded as oppressive, many of the Musta'lis refused to accept al-Hafiz. Under the leadership of their queen, al-Sayyida al-Hurra al-Sulayhi (1084–1138), who had upheld the claims of al-Musta'li in 1094, the Yemenis asserted that an infant son had been born to al-Amir shortly before the caliph's murder, and that the infant, named al-Tayyib, was the legitimate ruler.

Because al-Tayyib never appeared in public in Yemen, his followers, the Tayyibis, claimed that he had gone into concealment. They asserted that the Imamate passed from him to his son, then from father to son thereafter. In the meantime, during the concealment, his guidance is administered through the *da'i mutlaq* (literally, "chief missionary"). The Tayyibi Isma'ilis, who seemed insignificant at the time compared to the center of the Fatimid movement in Cairo, outlasted the Fatimids. The latter group disappeared after Saladin seized control of Egypt in 1171, whereas the Tayyibis continued to thrive. The Tayyibi community in Yemen remained strong for several centuries, and over the years many of them migrated to Gujarat, where they became wealthy by virtue of their involvement in international trade.

The widely scattered Nizari Isma'ili state of the Assassins lasted from 1094 until 1273, when its last remnants were destroyed through the combined efforts of the Mongol conqueror Hulagu and the Mamluke leader Baybars. Although the Nizaris established their fortresses in remote, rustic areas, they cultivated a remarkably sophisticated intellectual life. Alamut, in particular, had become famous for its research library, and its leadership encouraged non-Isma'ili Muslim scholars to study there. The fall of Alamut to Hulagu and the subsequent murder of the Imam was a stunning blow to the Nizari community. Most of its members came to believe that the Imam's son had been hidden for safekeeping, and for the next two centuries Nizaris and their Imams lived secretively under the Mongols and successor dynasties. Discovering the Sufi relationship of master and pupil to be a useful cover for their own hierarchical structure, they pretended to be adherents of one Sufi brotherhood or the other. Because of continuing persecution, however, many Nizaris gradually migrated to South Asia. Thus, by the end of the thirteenth century, the two main surviving groups of Isma'ilis were the Nizaris and the Tayyibis, and both were gravitating toward the western coast of India.

The Impact of "The Foreign Sciences" and Jurisprudence

Shi'ism was profoundly influenced by the new intellectual currents of the ninth and tenth centuries. By the early tenth century, the Isma'ilis were incorporating Neoplatonism into their thought, enabling them to conceptualize the distinction between the exoteric (*zahir*) and esoteric (*batin*) features of the scriptures and of Isma'ili doctrines. This distinction allowed the leadership to justify their position as a spiritual elite who had a monopoly on the knowledge of the deep spiritual truths essential to salvation. The masses needed the Imam and the hierarchy of teachers that he installed in order to provide the allegorical interpretation of the scriptures and of Isma'ili literature which came to be the distinctive feature of Isma'ilism. The Fatimids backed away from this extreme position, however. By the time they had secured their position in Egypt, they insisted on the equal importance of the exoteric and the esoteric, and they were more careful than the Carmathians and their own descendants, the early Nizaris, to insist on the fulfillment of the requirements of the Shari'a.

Isma'ili and Twelver Shi'ite intellectual life took somewhat different directions from that of the Sunni community because of the centrality of the Imam in their doctrine. Philosophy and gnostic thought, under a cloud in the Sunni community, flourished among both of the main Shi'ite groups. Of the two communities, the Isma'ilis were the more attracted to complex cosmological doctrines adapted from Neoplatonism and even Indian philosophical systems. On the other hand, commentaries on the Qur'an are absent from Isma'ili literature of the period, for the Imam was the ever-present interpreter. The Fatimid Imam was often referred to as the "speaking Qur'an," whereas the book was known as the "silent Qur'an." Commentaries on the Qur'an were also rare within the Imami community until the doctrine of the Hidden Imam became firmly established. When the Imam was no longer present to interpret the scriptures, however, a demand arose for them.

The Imamis/Twelvers began as a Hadith-based movement, but they made a wrenching change to a rationalist one. Whereas the early Imamis agreed with Sunnis that the Hadith were a second source of law along with the Qur'an, they had quite different criteria for judging the authenticity of Hadith. Because of their hostility toward the first three caliphs and their supporters, as a rule they accepted only those Hadith that had been transmitted through a descendant of Husayn. The major center for Hadith collection and analysis in the ninth century was Qum. The scholars there refused to accept consensus and analogical reasoning as secondary sources of the law. They also espoused a view of God that was as anthropomorphic as that of the conservative Sunni Ibn Hanbal, and they were as convinced as he was that the fate of individual humans was determined in advance by God. Many also insisted that the Qur'an had been tampered with; otherwise, they said, it would be clear how central the career of 'Ali and his family was meant to have been.

Under the Buyids, Twelver scholars soon found a welcome home in Baghdad. In that cosmopolitan capital, a Twelver rationalist school of thought arose that challenged the traditionalism of Qum. It was in Baghdad that Mu'tazilism made its comeback. Although the Imamis and the Mu'tazilites had been associated together during the reign of the Abbasid caliph al-Ma'mun because of his patronage of both groups, their actual linkage was not firmly established until the early eleventh century. By that time, Mu'tazilism had become thoroughly discredited within Sunnism because of the ascendancy of Ash'arism, but Twelver scholars in Baghdad began to adopt it. Under Mu'tazilite influence, the anthropomorphic elements of the Qur'an began to be interpreted allegorically, humans were declared to be responsible for their own actions, and reason was accorded an important role in the development of theology. The Qur'an in its existing text was recognized as legitimate, albeit in need of esoteric interpretation.

Several eleventh-century Twelver scholars argued that the fundamental truths of religion are derived in the first instance from reason alone, and it is indefensible to rely exclusively upon the teaching of religious authorities for knowledge of them. They clearly took Twelver Shi'ism beyond the Sunni consensus that reason is to be used to defend and justify doctrine. They also made no attempt to disguise their contempt for the anthropomorphism and predestinarianism of the scholars of Qum, and they ridiculed their reliance on Hadith, claiming that the traditions were full of obvious forgeries. Later scholars recognized the importance of selected Hadith, but the victory of the rationalist school was so complete in the eleventh century that the Hadith scholars had to wait until the seventeenth century to challenge it successfully.

In practical terms, the doctrine of the Imamate and the greater Shi'ite regard for reason resulted in surprisingly few major differences between Shi'ite and Sunni versions of the Shari'a. A few differences in prescribed rituals developed. Until the twentieth century, the Friday midday service was not as important for most Twelver Sh'ites as for the Sunnis because of the absence of the Hidden Imam, the legitimate prayer leader. Twelver legal rulings sanctioned the growing practice of visiting the shrines of Imams, and for some pilgrims these trips were as important as the hajj. The most important shrines were those of 'Ali at Najaf and of Husayn at Karbala (both in Iraq) and of 'Ali al-Rida at Mashhad (in northeastern Iran). Most of the significant differences in legal practice, however, lay in provisions for marriage and inheritance. The most famous of these was the practice of temporary marriage among Twelvers: Couples can contract a marriage for a day or longer, explicitly stipulating that it is meant to be a temporary marriage. Historically, travelers have been the most likely to contract a temporary marriage, although couples initiate it for a variety of reasons.

The Transmission of Knowledge

The ferment of ideas in the Muslim world had major consequences for the Dar al-Islam and parts of the Dar al-Kufr alike. Within the Dar al-Islam, new institutions emerged in order to preserve and transmit to future generations the knowledge that was becoming the cultural legacy of a new civilization. In the twelfth and thirteenth centuries, Europeans engaged in a massive effort to transmit the achievements of Islamic civilization to the Latin Christian civilization.

Schools

As a community based on scriptures, Islamic society had always valued education. Study was regarded not merely as an intellectual endeavor, but also as an act of piety and worship. In the earliest period of the Umma in Medina, the Prophet's compound served as his home, the communal place for prayers, and a site for religious, moral, and legal instruction. In later years, as Muslims erected mosques in the new territories that they conquered, the mosque remained the primary locus for religious instruction. Teachers would occasionally offer instruction in their homes to eager pupils, but the mosque, as the community center, offered the advantage of a large space, a central location, and the appropriately spiritual atmosphere. Mosques were usually the location where one could find the local *kuttab* or *maktab* (a school for Qur'anic instruction) and, for advanced students, courses in Hadith and grammar.

As cities grew, a distinction arose between the small, neighborhood mosques and the large, official mosques to which much of the populace and the ruling elite would repair for the main Friday noon service. The term for a mosque in general is *masjid*, from the Arabic root, *s-j-d*, meaning to prostrate oneself (in prayer, in this case). Most mosques are referred to by that word, but an officially designated central mosque is called a *jami'*, which suggests a place where a large group gathers. It is sometimes referred to as a congregational mosque, to distinguish it from the masjid, which can be quite small. The imam of a congregational mosque delivered the weekly sermon and invoked the name of the ruler and caliph, acknowledging his legitimacy. A major city such as Baghdad or Damascus had a handful of congregational mosques (although Cairo had more) and hundreds of regular masjids.

Instruction could take place in masjids, but the congregational mosques naturally assumed the most prominent role in education beyond the level offered by the kuttab. In some cases, the government appointed teachers to posts in the congregational mosques. Many teachers, however, were beneficiaries of the largesse of wealthy patrons, while others relied upon the income from the tuition they charged their students. Students from out of town usually lived in a hostel, often called a *khan*, and might be the fortunate recipients of a stipend provided by a benefactor who had set up a religious endowment (*waqf*) for that purpose. Although the Shari‘a prescribed how a person's estate should be allocated to his or her heirs, it allowed people to designate part or all of their estate to be a waqf. By setting aside part of one's estate as a waqf that would result in the construction and maintenance of a public service such as a mosque or khan, a person was gaining favor with God and prestige for his family within the community.

By the tenth century, a new type of school emerged in Khorasan that offered advantages over the mosque-school model. Perhaps originally of Buddhist origin in Central Asia, in the Islamic world it came to be called the *madrasa*. In essence, it was a boarding school that combined teaching halls with a prayer hall and living quarters for the students, visiting scholars, and perhaps for the professor. The madrasa achieved widespread dissemination throughout the Islamic world in the second half of the eleventh century, when the Saljuq vizier Nizam al-Mulk established his Nizamiya madrasa in Baghdad and then provided the patronage for several others throughout the Saljuq realms. The institution eventually made its way across North Africa and into Andalus.

The madrasa never displaced the mosque as an educational institution. In fact, Muslims were never precise in distinguishing between the two, because education and worship took place in both. (Even the Sufi khanaqa, as a center of formal learning, was occasionally referred to as a *madrasa*.) Like the mosque, the madrasa was not a government-sponsored school. All madrasas were the result of personal patronage. Wealthy individuals would either provide a grant during their lifetime or leave a bequest stipulating that after their death the funds be applied toward the construction of a madrasa. A madrasa might enroll as few as ten students or as many as several hundred. The young scholars often received tuition scholarships. Sometimes they enjoyed stipends, as well, but more often than not they had to pay for room and board.

Students did not seek out madrasas or mosques on the basis of an institution's reputation. Instead, students sought out individual scholars under whose tutelage they wished to study. Madrasas and mosque schools were not characterized by a formal curriculum and did not offer an institutional degree. Most schools had a single lecturer, but several scholars were available on and off campus for private study. Students came to a school not to master a given curriculum, but to deepen their mastery of a certain field of study by working closely with a prominent scholar in the field. Some students might choose to focus on Arabic grammar and would therefore explore grammar, philology, and literature. Others might focus on Qur'anic exegesis, in which case they would also mine the most influential commentaries on the Qur'an, as well as become experts in Arabic grammar. Others might focus on

The Buyuk Karatay madrasa in Konya, constructed by the Saljuqs of Rum.

mastering the field of Hadith studies, in which case they would study the various collections of Hadith and the biographies of the transmitters of Hadith.

The "foreign sciences" (science and philosophy) were not usually found in madrasas or mosques, although many of their libraries provided interested students access to the Greek legacy, and a few professors actually taught them in courses that were listed under the rubric of Hadith or grammar. Usually, however, the scholars who were proficient in any of the sciences or philosophy held positions as advisors, astrologers, or physicians at the courts of the rulers in the Dar al-Islam. Students who wished to learn science or philosophy usually had to seek out a scholar in the privacy of his home. The disadvantage of this system was that science and philosophy had no institutional structures within which they could develop. The critique of one's ideas and the sharing of knowledge that a community of scholars can provide were limited by the need to travel to visit other, like-minded, scholars, or by sending manuscripts by courier to scholars at a distance. Philosophers, in particular, were vulnerable to politically influential critics and to the whims of patrons. By the late twelfth century (the period of Ibn Rushd), the practitioners of philosophy encountered greater difficulties in their work. Religious authorities and pious scholars were relentless in their insistence on the limitations, and the dangers, of knowledge that was not intended solely for the glorification of God.

Students who engaged in advanced studies in mosques and madrasas were all respected for their knowledge of the religious sciences, but it is probably fair to say that the "stars" of the religious colleges were those who were engaged in the study of the Shari'a. They typically learned the subjects noted earlier, since they were prerequisites for the study of the law. They also studied the sources and methodology of the law, the body of decisions arrived at in one's own school of law, differences of opinion within one's own school of law and between one's school and the other schools, and *jadal*, or dialectic, the mode of argument that in western Europe became the heart of Scholasticism.

The typical classroom activity in learning the law involved the raising of a question—real or hypothetical—by one person (often the professor) and the reasoned response to it by another, using precedent and logic. Then, another student would attempt to rebut the reply, resulting in a "disputation." The goal of this method was to produce legal scholars who were masters of massive amounts of facts and who could organize the material into a logical manner consistent with the spirit of the Qur'an and Hadith. This practical activity, however, often carried over into public. Since there was no Pulitzer Prize or National Book Award in those days to recognize intellectual achievement, many of the legal experts felt the need to put their hard-won skills on display. Like two swordsmen, it was not uncommon to see two scholars debating a point in an arranged public debate, each trying to bolster his reputation by defeating the other in argument.

Islamic education was based on the relationship between the student and the teacher. The students sought a license from an individual scholar, not the institution. A student might develop his skills by spending a few months with a teacher and then move on to another, or he might spend as long as twenty years with a particular scholar. When a teacher was convinced that his student had mastered the books he was studying, he granted him an *ijaza*, or imprimatur—a written statement certifying that he had placed his stamp of approval on the student. Thus, the former student had established his link in the chain of authorities stretching back to the Prophet that authenticated the texts at the core of Islam. He could go on to study with other scholars, or he could attract younger ones to himself on the basis of the seal of approval that he had gained. The silsila, or chain of authorities, was as important in the certification of scholars as it was in Sufism and the authentication of Hadith.

The students who attended mosques and madrasas were males, but education was not limited to males. Indeed, because education was perceived as a form of worship, the quest for knowledge was widely regarded as a duty of every Muslim, male or female. Some males opposed the education of female students, just as many European males opposed female education into the late nineteenth century, but such opposition was not a majority opinion. We know of no female professors or students in madrasas who taught or studied along with men; many women nevertheless received ijazas. Due to the injunctions regarding sexual propriety, it was more convenient for women to gain ijazas from relatives, who could instruct them informally rather than in a classroom setting. Nevertheless, many women studied with scholars who were not family members and received ijazas from them. Some of the scholars they studied with were men, but others were women. The daughters of the learned elite sometimes became famous Hadith transmitters and were visited by students from all over the Muslim world. They bestowed ijazas upon men and women alike.

The Legacy to Europe

Although the study of science and philosophy was increasingly constrained within the Dar al-Islam, the scientific and philosophical contributions of Muslims began to be noticed by a western Europe that was slowly recovering from the sustained economic crisis of the early medieval era. Medieval Europe had preserved very little from its Greco–Roman heritage. A few of Aristotle's treatises on logic and Plato's Timaeus survived in monasteries, but little else. Europeans knew Islamic culture through the two areas closest to them, Andalus and Sicily, and as early as the tenth century monks from France were crossing the Pyrenees to study "Arabic learning." In the tenth and eleventh centuries, some of these monks began to translate texts from Arabic to Latin. The most important of these efforts were the translations of Galen by Constantine the African in the third quarter of the eleventh century.

During the last quarter of the eleventh century, two developments in Christian Europe provided the stimulus for a wholesale appropriation of Arabic texts. The first was that Europe was beginning to experience an economic revival. The new urban centers were enjoying a building boom, universities were emerging, and a middle class was growing. The second development was the European military expansion that began annexing formerly Muslim territories. Normans established their kingdom in Sicily and southern Italy between 1060 and 1091. In Palermo, Roger established a cosmopolitan court where Greek, Arabic, and Latin were all in use, and he patronized several Muslim scholars. Southern Italy and Sicily had maintained their commercial contacts with Constantinople, and the international atmosphere in the new Norman kingdom stimulated the translation of numerous Greek and Arabic texts into Latin. When Toledo fell to the Reconquista in 1085, a more massive process of translation began that matched the accomplishments of the Bayt al-Hikma two centuries earlier.

Although not formally organized in the way that al-Ma'mun's institution had been, the production of Latin translations of Arabic texts in the Iberian Peninsula attracted scholars from all over Europe, and it soon became systematized. Translation centers were established in the Ebro valley, Pamplona, and Barcelona, among other places, but the most famous was at Toledo. The Toledan school developed after 1165 under the leadership of Gerard of Cremona, and was most notable for its translation of the works of Aristotle. The translation technique that became characteristic of these institutes was for native scholars who were fluent in Arabic (a few of whom were Muslims, but most of whom were Jews) would translate the texts into a Romance dialect (usually Castilian or Catalan), and a Latin specialist would then translate into Latin. Alternatively, since much of the corpus of Arabic texts had already been translated into Hebrew by the Jewish community of Andalus, the texts were rendered directly from Hebrew into Latin. The translators found that many of the Arabic terms used in the philosophical, mathematical, alchemical, agricultural, and other texts (some of which had themselves been borrowed from Greek or Persian) had no equivalents in Latin or in the spoken languages of Europe. As a result, they were introduced into the Latin texts almost unchanged, introducing numerous new words into Europe (for examples of English words which are derived from Arabic, see the list in the accompanying table).

ENGLISH WORDS DERIVED FROM ARABIC

A Select List

admiral	azure	jar	satin
adobe	camel	jasmine	sequins
albatross	candy	lemon	sherbet
alchemy	carafe	lilac	sine
alcohol	carat	lute	soda
alcove	caravan	magazine	sofa
alfalfa	cipher	marzipan	spinach
algebra	coffee	mascara	sugar
algorithm	cotton	mask	syrup
alkali	crimson	mattress	taffeta
almanac	damask	monsoon	talc
amalgam	divan	mummy	tambourine
amber	elixir	muslin	tariff
apricot	gazelle	myrrh	tarragon
arsenal	ghoul	nadir	zenith
artichoke	giraffe	orange	zero
assassin	guitar	racquet	
azimuth	hazard	saffron	

Hundreds of texts were translated. The first Latin Qur'an was produced in 1143, and two years later al-Khwarizmi's algebra appeared in Latin. The works of Aristotle, Ptolemy, Euclid, Galen, and other Greek scholars were finally available to medieval Europeans, and the Muslim scholars who elaborated upon their work, such as al-Razi, Ibn Sina, and Ibn Rushd, were acknowledged to be as authoritative as the Greeks themselves. By the thirteenth century the pace of translation from Arabic decreased in the Iberian Peninsula, while it increased in Italy and Sicily due to the patronage of Frederick II (1198-1250).

The results of the translations were explosive. As in the Dar al-Islam, the introduction of Aristotle's works into Christian Europe caused an uproar. The primary battleground was the University of Paris, where the faculty of liberal arts fought the faculty of theology over the issue. Aristotle, Ibn Sina (Avicenna), and Ibn Rushd (Averroes) were intellectual heroes to the former and villains to the latter. In 1210, a council of bishops met in Paris to denounce heretical doctrines deriving from Aristotelianism, such as the eternity of the universe. In 1215, the university prohibited the teaching of Ibn Sina's recently translated commentaries on Aristotle, upon pain of excommunication from the Church. Despite the dangers, groups such as the "Aristotelians" and "Latin Averroists" sprang up. The scholars Albertus Magnus and Roger Bacon championed the reception of Aristotle's works, but the most famous Aristotelian of the period was Thomas Aquinas. Although he tried to mediate between the Averroists and those who adhered to the Platonic–Augustinian tradition, the masters of Paris condemned twelve of his own Aristotelian theses in 1277, three years after his untimely death.

The rigorous demands of scientific rationalism had confronted Christians in Europe just as they had Muslims several centuries earlier. It would require several centuries for the dust to settle, but the course of events took a different turn in western Europe from that of the Muslim world. Eventually, a Western philosophical tradition emerged that was independent of theology, and the Scientific Revolution is widely regarded to be at least in part the ultimate result of the assimilation of an Aristotelian attitude that takes the material world more seriously than did the Platonic one. Those developments are far too complex to be accounted for here, but some scholars suggest that they were made possible in part because of the institutional structure of education in western Europe. In western Europe, universities began to emerge out of cathedral schools in the twelfth century. Their basic curriculum was that of the seven liberal arts: the trivium (grammar, rhetoric, and logic) and the quadrivium (geometry, arithmetic, music, and astronomy). Further study could be pursued in law, theology, and medicine.

Unlike the madrasa, then, the cathedral school and the university provided an institution within which scientists, philosophers, and theologians studied in adjacent facilities. As a result, intellectuals in all disciplines were forced to grapple with issues raised in the others. Just as important in the long run was the fact that both the cathedral schools and the universities were legal corporations whose rights were guaranteed by charters. As a result, the faculties were able to set their own curriculum regardless of who endowed the school. As a consequence of these two factors, science and philosophy were able to continue to develop with institutional support despite vehement objection from critics who felt that vital religious principles such as God's absolute sovereignty were at risk. As we shall see, science and philosophy by no means disappeared in the Dar al-Islam, but the lack of a nurturing institutional environment did gradually impose handicaps on their further development.

Conclusion

The period 950–1260 was crucial to the development of doctrines and institutions that we identify with Islam today. It is important to recognize that fact, and it is important not to distort it. Some historians have called this the Golden Age of Islam, as though the centuries after 1260 represent a decline. Others have assumed that Islam attained a fixed form during this period and has not changed significantly since then. Neither of these positions is tenable. The history of Islam shows strong parallels with the history of Christianity, in which the first three centuries were crucial for narrowing the possible routes of development of doctrine, and the next three centuries witnessed the development of its most characteristic institutions and doctrines. Both traditions have continued to evolve and adapt to changing circumstances.

The period from the tenth through the thirteenth centuries is remarkable in light of the great intellectual achievements that were made in the teeth of upheavals and destruction. At a time when Europe and China were enjoying centuries of immunity from invasion, the Dar al-Islam experienced repeated episodes of destruction. Despite these obstacles, the life of the mind flourished. The impact of al-Ghazali's work in the Almoravid empire is illustrative: Al-Ghazali had written his *The Revival of the Religious Sciences* in the first decade of the twelfth century in Tus, and, within a decade of his death in 1111, it was causing an upheaval in Morocco and Andalus, 3700 miles and many frontiers away. A similar rate of transmission and assimilation of a book across a comparable distance is inconceivable in any other part of the world at the time. A more well-known testament to the creativity of Muslim intellectuals during this period was the intense engagement with their thought that took place in European universities after the century-long process of translating their works into Latin.

The violence of the period may not have been without its cultural consequences, however. The rise of the khanaqa coincided with the decrease in the scope allowed for philosophical exploration among Sunnis. Some scholars have suggested that the flourishing of Sufi lodges and the proliferation of tariqas were responses to the grim security conditions of the twelfth and thirteenth centuries. Sufi brotherhoods, or orders, can be viewed as voluntary support groups that provided material and spiritual sustenance and were often linked to the *futuwwa*, the self-defense groups often found in city quarters in the eastern half of the Dar al-Islam. When the civil and military institutions failed to provide security, the brotherhoods provided spiritual comfort, collective defense, and communal aid.

Philosophical reasoning, on the other hand, was viewed by many people as a threat to the community rather than as an instrument of defense and security. That has been a common reaction in every society from the time of Socrates until now. It is a particularly characteristic response in societies whose religion is based on divine revelation, because of the difficulties in defining the proper scope of reason as opposed to that of revelation. The thirteenth-century uproar in western Europe that resulted when Aristotelianism was introduced from Andalus is a case in point. The contrast between the fate of philosophy in western Europe (where it subsequently thrived) and in the Dar al-Islam (where it subsequently struggled) is quite striking. No definitive explanation is possible at this time, but it is useful to keep in mind that Christians in western Europe no longer worried about the survival of their civilization. They were actually confident and aggressive. Muslims of the thirteenth century, on the other hand, had to wonder what God had in store for them next. From Andalus to eastern Iran, entire societies had been destroyed or were under siege. This was a time to conserve what was certain and not to speculate on the possible, particularly when such speculation could injure the faith. Twelver Shi'ite scholars could exercise reason more confidently in this regard than their Sunni counterparts, for they knew that the Hidden Imam would not allow them to mislead his community.

A striking characteristic of this period is that Iraq ceased to be the center of intellectual creativity. Important work continued to be produced there, but the intellectual "stars" tended to come from Andalus and Iran. Particularly noteworthy is the Persian renaissance of this period. This was a movement that began in the mid-ninth century, but gained momentum only under the Samanids in the late tenth century. Thereafter work in the Persian language became remarkably creative. For the first time, the religion and culture of Islam became available in a language other than Arabic. Remarkably, most of the powerful Turkish dynasties that ruled large areas of the Dar al-Islam for the next seven centuries adopted the Persian culture for their court, with the result that Persian styles became dominant from Anatolia to India. Arabic continued to be the primary language of the religious disciplines and of science and philosophy, but Persian became the language of belles lettres and was increasingly used as a language of scholarship, as well.

NOTES

1. From *The Shambhala Guide to Sufism*, by Carl W. Ernst, Ph.D., (c) 1997 by Carl W. Ernst. Reprinted by arrangement with Shambhala Publications, Inc., *www. shambhala.com*. The discussion on pp. 157–178 is particularly useful. For another excellent discussion of Sufi poetry, see Annemarie Schimmel, *Mystical Dimensions of Islam* (Chapel Hill, North Carolina: The University of North Carolina Press, 1975), pp. 287–343.

FURTHER READING

Science and Philosophy

Nasr, Seyyed Hossein. *Three Muslim Sages: Avicenna, Suhrawardi, Ibn 'Arabi.* Delray, New York: Caravan Books, 1976.

Peters, F.E. *Allah's Commonwealth: A History of Islam in the Near East 600–1100 A.D.* New York: Simon and Schuster, 1973.

Turner, Howard R. *Science in Medieval Islam: An Illustrated Introduction.* Austin, Texas: University of Texas Press, 1995.

Watt, William Montgomery. *Islamic Philosophy and Theology: An Extended Survey.* Reprint Edition. Edinburgh: Edinburgh University Press, 1996.

Watt, W. Montgomery. *The Formative Period of Islamic Thought.* Edinburgh: Edinburgh University Press, 1973.

http://www-history.mcs.st-andrews.ac.uk/Indexes/Arabs.html

Consolidating Institutions: Sufism

Cornell, Vincent J. *Realm of the Saint: Power and Authority in Moroccan Sufism.* Austin, Texas: University of Texas Press, 1998.

Ernst, Carl W. *The Shambhala Guide to Sufism.* Boston & London: Shambhala, 1997.

Knysh, Alexander. *Islamic Mysticism: A Short History.* Leiden, Boston, Koln: Brill, 2000.

Schimmel, Annemarie. *Mystical Dimensions of Islam.* Chapel Hill, North Carolina: The University of North Carolina Press, 1975.

Trimingham, J. Spencer. *The Sufi Orders in Islam.* Reprint, intro by Voll. New York: Oxford University Press, 1998.

Consolidating Institutions: Shiʻism

Daftary, Farhad. *The Ismailis: Their History and Doctrines.* Cambridge, U.K.: Cambridge University Press, 1990.

Madelung, Wilferd. *Religious Trends in Early Islamic Iran.* Albany, New York: Persian Heritage Foundation, 1988.

Momen, Moojan. *An Introduction to Shiʻi Islam.* New Haven, Connecticut: Yale University Press, 1985.

The Transmission of Knowledge

Berkey, Jonathan. *The Transmission of Knowledge in Medieval Cairo.* Princeton, New Jersey: Princeton University Press, 1992.

Chamberlain, Michael. *Knowledge and Social Practice in Medieval Damascus, 1190–1350.* New York: Cambridge University Press, 1994.

Colish, Marcia L. *Medieval Foundations of the Western Intellectual Tradition, 400–1400.* New Haven and London: Yale University Press, 1997.

Halm, Heinz. *The Fatimids and Their Traditions of Learning.* London: I.B. Taurus in association with The Institute of Ismaili Studies, 1997.

Huff, Toby E. *The Rise of Early Modern Science: Islam, China, and the West.* Cambridge, U.K.: Cambridge University Press, 1995.

Pedersen, Johannes. *The Arabic Book.* Trans. Geoffrey French. Princeton, New Jersey: Princeton University Press, 1984.

CHAPTER 9

The Muslim Commonwealth

The Arabs involved in the conquests of the first century of Islamic history had been driven by an esprit de corps that allowed them to dominate their huge empire for a century, despite serious internal feuding. By the Abbasid period, however, no single ethnic group could generate a similar dynamism. Moreover, the fact that the new empire attempted to base its legitimacy on a monotheistic religion practically guaranteed eventual fragmentation. Whereas polytheism offers a wide range of religious expression for a society's members and can defuse conflicts over religious issues, monotheism is typically plagued by clashes over the correct interpretation of the one true faith. Ethnic, religious, and purely personal factors had splintered the political unity of the Muslim Umma within a short time.

On the other hand, among many Muslims, the sense of belonging to a single community provided a powerful bond that transcended many of the linguistic and other cultural differences that could have proved ultimately divisive. A Muslim empire ruled by an Arab oligarchy was gradually replaced by what some scholars call a "Muslim commonwealth," in which individual Muslims found a common identity with others all across the Dar al-Islam. The fact that there were multiple caliphs did not create sharp divisions among Muslims. The Qur'an was the common text of all Muslims, regardless of sect, and one's devotion to it made him or her a self-conscious member of a well-defined community, clearly set apart from those who did not recognize it. It was written in the Arabic language, which also served as the medium of commentaries on the Qur'an, devotional materials, and legal thought. Despite the decline of the political importance of the Arabs themselves, their language permeated the entire Dar al-Islam as the primary language of learning, even in the face of the persistence—and even revival—of certain local languages. By mastering Arabic, an individual could converse with educated Muslims everywhere and could take advantage of a valued skill that could lead to high-status careers in law or education in general. Travel between independent Muslim states (and even between Muslim states and their non-Muslim neighbors) was practically unrestricted, enabling merchants and scholars to foster ties with Muslims in other areas.

The Muslim world developed a remarkable cultural unity despite the overthrow of the "Arab empire" of the Umayyads and the rapid disintegration of Abbasid power. From the tenth through the thirteenth centuries, Shi'ites, Sunnis, and shamanists held power in several different areas of the Muslim world; Iranians, Berbers, Turks, Kurds, and Mongols replaced Arabs as the ruling ethnic group in several polities; and utter devastation occurred in several areas. Nevertheless, the development of a distinctive Islamic culture continued without interruption. Just as the Shari'a had developed independently of state patronage, so the economic, social, and cultural life of the Muslims continued to develop without reliance upon any given political order.

Remarkably, the rise of numerous independent Muslim states did not result in a reassertion of the barriers that had hindered commerce and cultural exchanges between Byzantines and Sasanians. Although Muslim states feuded with each other, they did not erect obstacles to travel, trade, or the pilgrimage to Mecca. Scholars, missionaries, merchants, and pilgrims traveled widely throughout the Dar al-Islam and communicated developments in law, science, engineering, devotional material, etiquette, and numerous other facets of the various evolving Islamic societies over vast distances. The different regions of the Muslim world retained unique characteristics inherited from their pre-Islamic culture, but they were increasingly able to share a common Islamic culture, as well.

Frontiers and Identities

Today, after two centuries of experience with nationalism and the nation–state, we take for granted clearly demarcated boundaries, checkpoints, passports and visas, nationalist emotions, patriotism, and numerous other characteristics of the modern state. These paraphernalia of the modern nation–state are, in historical terms, recent phenomena. When studying the premodern history of any region of the world, it is important to understand that boundaries and personal identities functioned quite differently from the ways they do now.

Frontiers Defining the Dar al-Islam

When nation–states became defined in the modern period, physical features such as rivers, mountain ranges, and straits were convenient and easily recognized markers that could serve as fixed borders for the countries that shared them. In the premodern era, such phenomena were not viewed as dividing lines. The Strait of Gibraltar, for instance, which so "obviously" separates Africa and Europe to modern eyes, was not viewed as a border by the inhabitants of the peninsula or of North Africa until the twentieth century. The Umayyads of Andalus, the Almoravids, the Almohads, and later, Spain, considered the strait as a water highway.

Rather than relying on borders, rulers had a sense of where their effective power lay and where it diminished. Cities were the seat of power for Muslim rulers, and in their vicinity the troops wielded effective control (as long as they were not rioting themselves), but the further away from the city, the less control was exercised. This was particularly the case when the territory at a distance from the capital was mountainous or arid, for such areas were too unproductive to justify the expense of administration, and they provided havens for rebels. Much as the illuminated areas of individual street lamps at night fade imperceptibly into the penumbra that lies between them, so there existed "penumbras of power" between rival polities where legitimate authority was ambiguous and where warlords, bandits, or adventurers of various types operated with considerable impunity. The best that the central government could hope to do was to play one group in these penumbras against another. This would effect at least temporary cooperation by means of bribes or punitive expeditions.

The Seas

Muslims were aware of several types of frontiers. One was the sea. The Indian Ocean during this period was viewed almost exclusively as a highway of commerce, whereas the Mediterranean offered both commerce and the threat of war. In the Indian Ocean, Muslims sailed almost unmolested, except for the need to coordinate voyages with the monsoons. As a result, Muslim settlements spread along the east African coast. Between the tenth and thirteenth centuries, over two dozen Muslim coastal communities sprouted on the African coast as far south as Kilwa, on the southern coast of modern Tanzania. The Muslim presence on the East African coast fostered the development of Swahili culture. *Swahili* itself derives from the Arabic word *sahel*, or coast, and it came to denote the speakers of a Bantu lingua franca along the coast from Kenya to Mozambique. Heavily influenced by Arabic, the Swahili language and material culture came to characterize the Islamized population of the East African coast after 1100.

The much smaller Mediterranean Sea was ringed with numerous states. Their proximity to each other resulted in frequent contacts that could be either hostile or commercial. Frequently, they were engaged in war and commerce simultaneously. By the eleventh century, merchants from Venice, Amalfi, Genoa, and Pisa were becoming active at Alexandria and Antioch, even before the Crusades began. The Fatimids were pleased to trade with them and provided them with perfumes, cloth, gold, cotton, alum (a fixative used by cloth manufacturers), and, especially, pepper. By the era of the Crusades, Muslims were finding that the Europeans had goods they could use. The major commodities were timber, furs, and metals, especially copper, lead, iron, and tin. European silks became increasingly popular, and Italian-made arms were imported in large quantities, despite papal threats of excommunication to any Christian who sold arms to the enemy Muslims. Muslim fleets held the advantage in the Mediterranean until the era of the Crusades, but during the twelfth century the Italian city–states began to dominate both the eastern and western basins.

The Land

There were two types of land frontiers: the kind that separated the Dar al-Islam from the Dar al-Kufr, and the kind that separated the realm of one Muslim ruler from another. The former, of course, was usually the most dramatic, because the jurists agreed that Muslims were under an obligation to conduct jihad into lands unfortunate enough not to be under the guidance of the Shari'a. Raids were not only permitted, but encouraged, into the Dar al-Kufr, and only there could one enslave people. Thousands of miles of such frontiers existed in North Africa and in the east. Muslims along those frontiers did not face major competing powers due to the huge expanse of desert or formidable mountain ranges that were characteristic of those areas. Long-distance trade flourished even in these areas over well-defined routes, and occasional raids might take place from the depths of the Sahara. In the east, invasions were not a threat from what is now Pakistan and Afghanistan, but, as we have seen, the frontier beyond Transoxiana was highly active and proved to be a conduit for numerous nomadic Turkish and Mongol groups. For almost a thousand years, the Central Asian frontier would prove to be a lucrative route to China, a source of manpower renewal and ethnic diversity for the Umma, and the origin for an occasionally catastrophic blow to lives and property.

At both ends of the Mediterranean, a quite different frontier evolved from that in North Africa and on the eastern edges of the Iranian cultural zone. In Andalus and Anatolia, Muslim and Christian powers faced each other for centuries across frontiers that might vary from ten to one hundred miles wide. The frontier in either zone would shift from time to time and, due to almost constant raiding and skirmishing, some parts of it were depopulated. When an army from one side attacked the other, it departed from heavily populated areas defended by forts and passed through less densely populated areas. Eventually, the troups encountered only widely scattered, impoverished settlements, interspersed with gradually decreasing numbers of friendly fortified outposts. The army then began confronting enemy outposts, more and more enemy settlements, and then the enemy's populated regions.

For over two centuries, the Duero River valley in the Iberian Peninsula served as the center of the frontier between Muslim and Christian authority. This "no-man's-land" was subject to sudden raids by murabitun from the Muslim side and their counterparts from the Christian side. Little is known of the nature of the Christian irregulars along the frontier during the early centuries of the history of Andalus, but the advent of the Almohads spurred the Christian kingdoms to approve the creation of three monastic orders of knights (Santiago, Alcantara, and Calatrava), which were modeled after the murabitun.

Nevertheless, the dynamics of life along the frontier were not characterized by an unremitting hostility toward the other side. Despite the demands of distant popes to conquer all of the peninsula, Christian rulers operated within specific local restraints and opportunities, and the people who actually lived on the frontier often found that they had much in common with the "enemy" who lived in their vicinity. The Umayyads of Andalus were usually preoccupied with subduing recalcitrant petty Muslim rulers rather than trying to expand into Christian territory. As we have seen, Muslim rulers sometimes allied with Christian rulers against fellow Muslims, and Christians allied with Muslims against fellow Christians.

Even some of the greatest "heroes of the faith" on either side, inspected closely, reveal a striking ambiguity of cultural and even religious loyalty. The most famous of these was probably El Cid, or Rodrigo Diaz de Vivar, one of the most celebrated figures of the Reconquista. A Christian nobleman from Castile, he lost favor in Castile and moved to Zaragoza, where he served the Muslim ruler there for a decade, fighting both Christian and Muslim rivals of his master. During the mid-1080s he refused to become involved in the critical campaigns against the invading Almoravids when they posed a genuine threat to the existence of an independent Christian presence in the peninsula. When he had the chance, he seized the Muslim city of Valencia in

1094 and ruled it until his death in 1099, defying rival Muslim and Christian rulers. Diaz's ambivalent identity is apparent in the honorific by which he is known —"El Cid"—which derives from the term *al-sayyid*, an Arabic term of respect and honor. The legend that grew up around El Cid over subsequent centuries, portraying him as a champion of Christianity against Islam, was obviously the result of a highly selective approach to his career.

A similar situation existed along the Anatolian frontier. The Taurus Mountains, as well defined as they are, did not suggest to either the Muslims or the Byzantines a natural border between the Dar al-Islam and the Byzantine territories. Although the Arab conquests did not push westward of them by much, Arab settlements did slowly extend onto the Anatolian plateau. The Arabs also swept to the northeast of the Taurus into Azerbaijan. As early as the reign of the Abbasid caliph al-Mansur (754–775), volunteers from Khorasan moved to this Byzantine frontier in order to engage in commerce and engage in jihad. Most of the Arab settlers lived in towns. By the middle of the ninth century, the largest of the towns were Malatya and Tarsus.

Both Malatya and Tarsus served as bases for attacks on the Byzantines, but Tarsus presents a special case. For the first two centuries of the Abbasid era, the city's economy was dependent on the institutionalization of jihad, or *ghaza*, as it was sometimes rendered. The latter term was an Arabic word used to refer to the bedouin raids or attacks on each other or on settlements. A raider in such an attack was a *ghazi*. Although jihad—usually understood as a war of conquest for the propagation of Islam or a war in defense of Islam against an outside threat—technically has a different connotation from *ghaza*; the chroniclers who reported on the activities of the Arab–Byzantine frontier used the two words interchangeably. This may reflect the changed reality of the time, when conquests did not come as easily as they had during the first century of Muslim history.

By the tenth century, the concept of jihad had become central to Muslim identity and had endowed frontiers with cosmic significance. By this time, the Shari'a had divided the world into two realms, the realm of Islam (Dar al-Islam) and the non-Muslim world, or realm of war (Dar al-Harb). A dweller in the realm of war was an enemy to whom the law offered no protection. Muslims had an obligation to attack him in his own realm, and if he entered the realm of Islam and was killed, no one was held culpable. Conflict with the inhabitants of the Dar al-Harb was assumed to last until the end of time. A permanent peace with the infidels was, therefore, an impossibility. A ruler could arrange a temporary truce if it served the interests of the Umma, but it was not legally binding. Jihad was understood to be a collective obligation: A group of Muslims had to be fighting at all times, or the community was guilty of a sin against God. Jihad became an individual obligation only when the ruler had mobilized an army in response to an enemy invasion.

Jihad was a serious matter of shedding blood, and thus the jurists framed it with numerous qualifications. Jihad could not be declared without first calling upon the target population to accept Islam or pay the head tax as a mark of tributary status. It was permissible to kill infidel warriors, but not women, children, old men, the blind, or lunatics, unless they were unexpectedly engaged in warfare. A Muslim commander was given wide latitude in his choice of disposing of male prisoners. He could kill them, enslave them, or free them as tributary subjects, but he could not allow them to return to the realm of the infidel. Women and children could only be enslaved or freed as tributary subjects. The rationale for these options was that returning a non-Muslim to the Dar al-Harb would extend the length of time necessary to conquer it, and the Shari'a did not provide for the possibility of an infidel's permanent residence in the realm of Islam other than as a slave or tributary subject.

The obligation of engaging in jihad was a requirement that God had enjoined upon the Umma as a whole—not one that the ruler could command. Individual participation was voluntary, and as long as a few were active, the collective requirement was fulfilled. Some of the *mujahidun* ("those who engage in jihad," often transliterated as "mujahideen") or ghazis were young men who engaged in raids for a short time before entering their intended careers as craftsmen, merchants, or scholars. They understood their service to be an act of worship as well as the fulfillment of an obligation, and they placed their perceived duty to God before their educational or career plans. Others were Sufis who saw jihad to be the outward expression of their inward quest. Still others made an occupation of raiding (some of them became quite wealthy from the spoils of war). The largest cities of the empire—particularly those of the Iranian plateau—financed the construction of ribats in Tarsus where their young men could stay while engaging in jihad/ghaza. They also supplied them with food and spending money until they acquired spoils from their raids. Muslims clearly viewed Tarsus as a permanent base for raiding Byzantine lands, and the expansion of territory was not the objective. This phase of ghaza ended in 965, when the Byzantines embarked upon their reconquest of the area and depopulated Tarsus.

The Byzantine frontier again became the scene of institutionalized raiding under the Turks a century later. As we have seen, the first bands of Turkish herdsmen who entered the Buyid realms of the Dar al-Islam in the early eleventh century caused havoc in Iran, Iraq, and Azerbaijan. When the Saljuqs replaced the Buyids at midcentury, they tried to direct the Turkmen's attention to Anatolia and away from Muslim territory. After Manzikert, in 1071, most of the Anatolian plateau lay open to the Turkmen. Christian villagers remained the majority population on the Anatolian plateau for two or three more centuries, but the constant threat from raiders increasingly concentrated the Christian population along the edges of the peninsula. During the twelfth and thirteenth centuries, Armenian Christians were concentrated in eastern Anatolia and in south-central Anatolia around the bend of the Mediterranean (Cilicia), while Orthodox Christians were concentrated in the extreme western littoral and along the Black Sea coast. As the Sultanate of Rum grew in power at Konya from 1116 until its defeat at the hands of the Golden Horde in 1243, Turkish raiders operated in the zones between the Sultanate of Rum and the Christian societies.

The Turkish raiders of the no-man's-land between the Muslim and Christian polities were known as *gazis* (the transliteration of "ghazis" when applied to the Turks). The Turks of Central Asia, like the bedouin of the Arabian Peninsula, regarded raiding as part of their pattern of subsistence, to supplement the meager return from their herds of animals. When they arrived in Anatolia, they typically did not immediately settle down, but rather continued to herd and raid. They soon learned that raids on Muslim neighbors resulted in unpleasant punishment from the central authorities, but that those same authorities encouraged the raiding of nearby Christian territories.

The Turks, like the Arabs before them, rationalized their raids as a religious act, and other Muslims came to understand them as such. The frontier society of the gazis offered an adrenalin rush to adventurers, a sense of freedom to those who felt

Jihad in the Shari'a

This selection regarding the rules pertaining to jihad comes from a legal treatise by the Egyptian Shafi'i scholar Ahmad ibn al-Naqib (d. 1368). Jurists from the other schools of law differed over details (some would reject the permissibility of destroying property of the enemy, for example), but this text reflects a widespread conception of jihad: The Dar al-Islam is in a constant state of potential or actual war with the Dar al-Harb; actual conflict should be taking place somewhere at all times; the engagement in jihad by a few Muslims relieves the obligation on the Umma as a whole; jihad is viewed as both a defensive reaction against hostile non-Muslims and as an aggressive act that follows a rejected ultimatum from a Muslim ruler to non-Muslims in the Dar al-Harb to accept Islam or pay the poll tax.

Jihad is a communal obligation. When enough people perform it to successfully accomplish it, it is no longer obligatory upon others. Jihad is personally obligatory upon all those present in the battle lines. Jihad is also obligatory for everyone when the enemy has surrounded the Muslims. Those called upon are every able-bodied man who has reached puberty and is sane . . .

It is offensive to conduct a military expedition against hostile non-Muslims without the caliph's permission.

Muslims may not seek help from non-Muslim allies unless the Muslims are considerably outnumbered and the allies are of goodwill towards the Muslims.

The caliph makes war upon Jews, Christians, and Zoroastrians until they become Muslim or else pay the non-Muslim poll tax [and thereby become dhimmis]. The caliph fights all other peoples [idolaters] until they become Muslim.

It is not permissible to kill women or children unless they are fighting against the Muslims. Nor is it permissible to kill animals, unless they are being ridden into battle against the Muslims, or if killing them will help defeat the enemy. It is permissible to kill old men and monks [who fight Muslims]. It is unlawful to kill a non-Muslim to whom a Muslim has given his guarantee of protection provided the protecting Muslim has reached puberty, is sane, and does so voluntarily.

Whoever enters Islam before being captured may not be killed or his property confiscated, or his young children taken captive. When a child or a woman is taken captive, they become slaves by the fact of capture, and the woman's previous marriage is immediately annulled. When an adult male is taken captive, the caliph considers the interests [of the community] and decides between the prisoner's death, slavery, release without paying anything, or ransoming himself in exchange for money or for a Muslim captive held by the enemy. If the prisoner becomes a Muslim then he may not be killed, and one of the other three alternatives is chosen.

It is permissible in jihad to cut down the enemy's trees and destroy their dwellings.

A free male Muslim who has reached puberty and is sane is entitled to the spoils of battle when he has participated in a battle to the end of it. After personal booty, the collective spoils of the battle are divided into five parts. The first fifth is set aside, and the remaining four are distributed, one share to each infantryman and three shares to each cavalryman. From these latter four fifths also, a token payment is given at the leader's discretion to women, children, and non-Muslim participants on the Muslim side. A combatant only takes possession of his share of the spoils at the official division.

As for personal booty, anyone who, despite resistance, kills one of the enemy or effectively incapacitates him, risking his own life thereby, is entitled to whatever he can take from the enemy, meaning as much as he can take away with him in the battle, such as a mount, clothes, weaponry, money, or other . . . .

SOURCE: Ibn al-Naqib, Ahmad ibn Lu'lu'. *Reliance of the Traveller: A Classic Manual of Islamic Sacred Law.* Edited and translated by Nuh Ha Mim Keller. Revised edition. Beltsville, Maryland: Amana Publications, 1999, pp. 600–606

oppressed under a centralized government, the possibility of wealth to the needy, and a ripe field of untutored souls to the missionary. Like most frontier areas, it was egalitarian in the sense that if a man could contribute to the goals of the group, he was accepted into it. Despite the fact that gaza was increasingly rationalized as a specifically Islamic religious act, identities and loyalties were as fluid as on the Iberian frontier. Occasionally Christians who had been victimized by gazas sought to join a gazi band, in a classic example of the attitude expressed by the phrase, "if you can't beat them, join them." Gazis not only accepted non-Muslims (and non-Turkish Muslims) as compatriots, but also shared the spoils equally with them. A Christian ruler (ostensibly defending his realm against the Muslim threat) who was fighting a fellow Christian would occasionally invite gazis to join him in a campaign, and gazis would occasionally seek alliances with Christian rulers against "wayward" fellow Muslims.

Since gazis accepted non-Muslims into their raiding societies, it is not surprising to learn that they were more tolerant of religious differences than most urban Muslims were. On the one hand, they became much more active as missionaries than the ulama in any time or place have been; on the other hand, they commonly venerated the shrines of local Christian saints, just as Christians of the rural areas visited Muslim spiritual teachers and venerated the shrines of Muslim saints. Gazi society was characterized by folk religion rather than by the intellectualized and formal Islam of the cities. As such, its version of Islam was often scorned by the ulama. Illiteracy was high in rural peasant areas anywhere; the uncertainties and fluidity of the frontier could only exacerbate the situation. Inevitably, religion on the frontier was different from its urban cousin and it was syncretistic, whether among Christians or Muslims. The Turkish nomads and semi-nomads themselves were originally shamanists. As they passed through Iran and into Anatolia, they picked up their knowledge of Islam from popular preachers, Sufi adepts, and members of persecuted sects who sought the safety of remote regions out of fear of persecution. In the process, they combined elements of their original spiritual practices with Shi'ism, Sunnism, popular Christianity, and other local religious legacies.

Frontiers within the Dar al-Islam

If hostile empires failed to demarcate exact boundaries between each other, the separation of Muslim polities from each other was even more imprecise. Like the frontiers that surrounded the Dar al-Islam, internal frontiers were a function of the diminishing power that cities exerted over their hinterland. Deserts, mountains, and sheer distance ultimately reduced the power of a Muslim ruler until he had to cooperate with regional strongmen, who in turn had to negotiate with rulers on their other frontiers. Thus travel among the various Muslim polities required flexibility and adaptation to changing circumstances, but it was rarely complicated by legal obstacles.

In order to understand the achievements of the peoples of the Muslim world prior to the formation of nation–states, it is important to realize that they were able to travel remarkably freely, regardless of their religious affiliation. When traveling from one part of the Muslim world to another, they would be recognized as *different* from the indigenous inhabitants, but they were not regarded as *alien*. Christians and Jews were allowed to travel great distances without harassment, provided they could demonstrate that they had paid their taxes. Even Christians from Europe were allowed access to important commercial cities, although their movements were often restricted. Linguistic barriers were not a major concern, either, since traveling scholars and merchants of any of the three main religions knew at least some Arabic, which played the role of an international language throughout the Dar al-Islam just as Latin did in western Europe. Due to the patronage of Persian literature by the Samanids and Ghaznavids, the Persian language increasingly became the lingua franca from Iran to South Asia.

The major challenge that travelers faced was not presented by powerful Muslim rulers, but rather by the absence of such power in the frontier regions. It was there that scholars, merchants, pilgrims, and others who were traveling overland were most likely to be attacked by bandits. If they survived the hazards of the less secure areas, they would not know when they had passed definitively from one "country" to another until they approached towns and cities dominated by a different amir. Upon entering the gates to the town, they would encounter customs booths and other signs of official monitoring. Local authorities would check the travelers' papers. While passports would not be required, the officials would make sure that foreigners from the Dar al-Kufr paid for the protection that they would enjoy and that Christians and Jews from other regions in the Dar al-Islam were carrying documentation that they had paid their taxes in their home regions.

The contrast between the modern focus on state boundaries and the monitoring of "aliens," on the one hand, and the indifference toward such elements in Muslim societies of the tenth to thirteenth centuries, on the other, is best explained in terms of the different types of law obtaining within each. Modern states enforce a code of laws that is territorial and applies to all who are within the national boundaries, with the exception of those who hold diplomatic immunity. By contrast, even in the pre-Islamic era, the governments in the area that became the Dar al-Islam had considered their primary functions to be the provision of security and the collection of taxes, rather than the creation and enforcement of a code of laws that defined a territorial state. For Byzantines, Sasanians, and then Muslims, law was personal, rather than territorial. As we have seen, the Shari'a was not developed by the state, but by groups of scholars working independently of the state. "Foreigners," whether Muslim or not, continued to be subject to the laws of their own religious communities when they left their homes. The Muslim state did not have a set of laws to which it considered them subject.

Identities

Prior to the spread of the nationalist idea in the nineteenth century, the concept of "nationality" or "citizenship" was extremely rare, with the Roman Empire being one of the few exceptions. Otherwise, people conceived of their personal identity in terms of family lineage, residence in a particular village or city, participation in the rituals of a given religion, and the language they spoke. Within the Dar al-Islam, the most important identities were those defined and addressed by the Shari'a. Among these were religious affiliation, gender, and slavery. The issues of religious identity and the status of women are discussed in other sections of this book, but, at this point, a few observations on slavery are in order. In addition, the issue of ethnicity bears some exploration. Although it was not an issue of concern to jurists, it played an important role in the perceptions of others, in self-perception, and in the development of cultural expressions.

Slavery

Until the modern period, slavery was almost universally considered to be an unfortunate, but common, experience. The scriptures of Islam, like those of Judaism and Christianity, did not condemn the institution of slavery. On the contrary, the scriptures and their commentaries addressed slaves and slave owners alike, counseling them in how to relate to each other. Despite condoning slavery, the Shari'a discouraged, and eventually prohibited, the enslavement of both Muslims and dhimmis. Unlike the Christian world, the Umma also forbade the imposition of slavery as a punishment for debt or crime. Thus, to be a slave in the Muslim world one was born to slave parents, captured in campaigns of conquest, or purchased from abroad. Like the Roman and Greek worlds, but unlike the plantation slavery of the early modern period, slaves in the Muslim world were not used primarily for agriculture or mining, but rather for domestic purposes or in the military. Slaves were not unknown in large-scale agriculture and mining: The late ninth-century Zanj revolt in southern Iraq was the best-known case of the agricultural use of slavery, although they were also used on a few large estates in Andalus and North Africa. Large crews of slaves were also doomed to the brutal and hopeless conditions of salt mines in the Sahara and gold mines of Nubia. Nevertheless, nothing in the records available to us now suggests that agriculture and mining were reliant to a large degree on slave labor. Slaves were used primarily in homes, in shops, in the military, and as tutors and entertainers in the palace. Most of the earliest slaves owned by Muslims were captured in warfare, but by the Abbasid period, that source dried up considerably. The raids of Mahmud of Ghazna once again brought in a vast quantity of slaves, this time from India— contemporary accounts report a figure of over 50,000 Indian captives as part of the pillaging in the raid of 1018 alone—but conquest ceased being a primary source of slaves. Most slaves were purchased from abroad. Many came from Africa, both east and west, but even more came from Europe. The European slaves are usually referred to as Greeks or Slavs. Andalus became a thriving entrepot of the European slave traffic, and it was serviced primarily by Catalan and Italian merchants. Egypt, too, had a famous slave market, which offered for sale slaves from Africa and Europe alike. With the increasing demand for Turks in the many Muslim armies of the Dar al-Islam, Transoxiana became a major area in the long-distance slave trade. From the Samanid regime until the end of the fifteenth century, the trade in Turkish slaves became an important pillar of the economy of the region.

Muslims viewed slavery with ambivalence. On the one hand, the jurists ensured the legal existence of the institution by formulating a myriad of regulations that became enshrined in the Shari'a. Slaves were legally property and could not own or inherit property themselves. Courts of law usually did not accept their testimony. A slave owner had unlimited sexual access to his female slaves. According to Sunni legal schools, slaves were not to hold jurisdiction over freemen and were not to exercise religious functions.

On the other hand, the Shari'a admonished slave owners to treat their slaves humanely, and families commonly adopted their slaves. The Qur'an and Hadith made clear that the manumission of slaves was a commendable act, and the Shari'a provided various ways for manumission to happen. A master who stated in the presence of a witness, even in jest, that his slave was free would have to give him his freedom. Slaves whose masters were willing could pay for their freedom. A concubine who gave birth to the children of her master could not be sold thereafter; on his death, she and her children were free, and her children had a legal right to his property on the same basis as the children of his wife or wives. The concubines of caliphs were in a particularly ambiguous position. Technically slaves, their sons could become caliphs. The last two Umayyad caliphs were the sons of slave mothers, and all but the first Abbasid caliph were the sons of concubines.

Like concubines, eunuchs held an ambiguous social position. The Qur'an forbade the mutilation of slaves, and the Shari'a reinforced the stricture. As a result, it was illegal to castrate individuals within the Dar al-Islam, but a thriving trade developed for individuals who were emasculated on the frontiers. Most eunuchs were either Slavs or Africans, and although they are most famous for their role in the harems of powerful men, they also served as custodians of the Ka'ba and of the tombs of famous individuals. Moreover, within the Fatimid empire some eunuchs managed to gain a certain revenge for their mutilation as they became powerful military or political figures who wielded enormous authority over free Muslims. Jawhar not only served as commander of the Fatimid armies, but also exercised absolute power in the process of consolidating Fatimid power over Egypt in preparation for the arrival of al-Mu'izz. Several other eunuchs were Fatimid military leaders, governors of towns and provinces, chiefs of police, and muhtasibs.

The most distinctive feature of slavery in the Muslim world, however, was the widespread use of slave armies. Between the early ninth century, when al-Mu'tasim began building his slave units, to the thirteenth century, most armies between Egypt and Central Asia became organized around a nucleus of slaves. The Abbasids were seeking to escape dependence first upon the bedouin, who had provided the support for the Umayyad regime, and then upon the Khorasanis, who began to expect extra consideration for their role in the destruction of the Umayyads. The Buyids needed Turks to supplement their own Daylami infantry, and the Fatimids needed units of various types in order to be able to compete as a great power. Slave armies were, indeed, dependent on their patron and usually fanatically loyal. On the other hand, they perceived how vulnerable they were in the event of a cutoff of support, and they could turn on their master in a moment. For them to seize power themselves was hardly a possibility that al-Mu'tasim or any other of the early rulers could have entertained, but it was a logical step for the Ghaznavids and Mamlukes.

Ethnicity

The lack of a precise territorial concept among most peoples of the period in question, in any region of the world, accounts for the lack of specificity in their use of place-names. As we have seen, inhabitants of the eastern Mediterranean often referred to North Africa and Andalus alike as the Maghrib, or "West." Before the Crusades forced them to make some conceptual distinctions, they referred to the Byzantine Empire, the Italian Peninsula, and western Europe alike as *Rum. Khorasan* might mean the regions served by Merv and Nishapur and a large area to the south, or it might include Transoxiana. On the other hand, it was the Muslims themselves who first conceptualized "India" as a separate civilization. The Sasanians had used the term "Hind" for the area around the Indus River valley, but the Arabs applied the term to the collective civilization that was shaped by Sanskritic literature. This came to include not only the Indian subcontinent, but later included parts of Southeast Asia and Indonesia as well (hence our term *Indies*).

The strength of ethnic identities varied with period and place. During the Umayyad period, non-Arab Muslims discovered that their ethnic identity automatically classified them as inferior to the Arabs, and it is clear that during the Abbasid period, ethnic tensions within the armies were a major cause of strife. Because of their dependence on the ruler, slave soldiers were sensitive to any signal that another group was gaining an advantage over them, for such a development could be life threatening. Within the larger society ethnic identity remained important, if not as divisive as during the first century of Islam. In Andalus, Berbers felt that the Arabs never fully accepted them, right down to the end of the Reconquista. Like the Arabs, the Turks who invaded southwestern Asia in the eleventh century considered themselves superior to the peoples whom they conquered. The Saljuqs, in particular, made it clear that they were proud of their Turkish heritage, even while they were adapting to the mores and customs of their Iranian and Arab subjects.

Perhaps the most impressive instance of ethnic assertion, however, was the revival of certain aspects of Persian culture in the ninth and tenth centuries. The Arabic language had been the medium of religious scholarship for Muslims from the beginning, had become the language of administration in the late Umayyad and early Abbasid regimes, and had rapidly become a lingua franca for commerce and poetry throughout the Dar al-Islam by the ninth century. However, Persian remained the spoken language east of Iraq, and it soon became a major literary vehicle. The Tahirid regime, which served as governors for the Abbasid caliphate (821–873), began patronizing Persian literature, the Saffarid state (867–963) continued the tradition, and the Samanid state (892–1005) developed a special interest in the cultivation of Persian literature at their court in Bukhara. Dialects of Persian had long been the language of commerce for the overland trade in central Asia, and with the aid of court patronage, the Dari dialect of Persian now became a language of high culture.

In part, the revival of the Persian language was an expression of Iranian pride and resentment against Arab domination, causing a controversy as early as the eighth century that pitted proponents of Iranian culture against defenders of Arab preeminence. The poets and writers whose creativity resulted in the new Persian language, however, were not reluctant to borrow Arabic themes, styles, and vocabulary, as well as the Arabic alphabet itself. Except for the Qur'an itself, the texts of Islam now became available in a language other than Arabic for the first time. By the thirteenth century, some of the greatest Sufi literature would be written in Persian.

Because Arabic continued to be the dominant language of religious scholarship even in Iran, it was in the secular arts that the Persian themes particularly flourished. Numerous lyric poets attained a high degree of proficiency, but perhaps the most famous of the medieval Persian works of literature was Ferdowsi's *Shah-nameh*

(1010). Sasanian values and styles were also revived in political writings, inscriptions and coins, court ceremonies, architecture, and painting. The glittering culture impressed Turkish newcomers, who, although proud of their own identity, readily accepted the Perso–Islamic elite culture for their own purposes. Ferdowsi's dedication of his masterpiece to a Turkish ruler, consequently, was not merely in default of having a Persian-speaking regime to which to give it. Both the Ghaznavid and Saljuq regimes cultivated the Persian culture and adopted Persian as the language of administration (except for use in the Shari'a courts). Their patronage of Persian culture laid the foundation for it to become the dominant culture of South Asia for several centuries.

The City and the Countryside

Throughout history, cities have served as the centers of government, commerce, and culture for most societies. They had higher death rates than did the villages, because disease was more likely to be spread from person to person in the crowded cities. Many rural folks might also view the cities as dens of vice or as enclaves for the rapacious classes that sought to enrich themselves at the expense of the peasants. Nevertheless, cities held out the allure of wealth, power, and entertainment for rural inhabitants, and other than during periods of catastrophe, the migration pattern tended to be from the village to the city.

The City

As in all premodern civilizations, only a minority of the population of the Dar al-Islam lived in towns and cities. On the other hand, only China, among other regions of the world, could claim to have as many large towns and cities as the Muslim world did. The new patterns of trade and expansion that the Arab conquest helped to create had a powerful impact on the region's urban life. Not all cities shared the same experience. The truncation of the Byzantine empire and the long-term, intermittent, naval warfare in the eastern Mediterranean had a negative impact for three centuries on cities such as Alexandria and Antioch; a few interior cities, such as Hira, lost their raison d'etre altogether and disappeared; others, such as the caravan cities of Rayy and Hamadan, experienced an economic boom because of the stimulus for overland trade; whereas numerous others, such as Kufa, Basra, and Sijilmasa, were created for the first time.

Cities in the Muslim world had their own "personalities," just as cities as different as Boston and San Francisco do today. They were located in a wide variety of settings. Access to water inevitably shaped the city's contours: Some were on the coast, while others were on rivers, in oases, in the plains, or nestled in hills. Most were in arid to semiarid climates and could rely primarily upon mud-brick construction, but some were located in areas of moderate rainfall and needed to rely upon stone as the primary building material. Mud-brick construction tended to result in low skylines, but some stone towns and villages, particularly in Yemen and southern Morocco, contained buildings that rose ten or more floors. The legacies of Indian, Sasanian, Hellenistic, Byzantine, Roman, and Visigothic cultures, among others, influenced elements from architectural styles to the prevalence of bathhouses, churches, synagogues, gardens, and plazas. Some cities appeared from a distance as colorless as the earth that surrounded them, while others were highlighted with glittering tiles that covered the entirety of congregational mosques and other public buildings. As a result, travelers often remarked on the distinctive appearance of cities from one region of the Dar al-Islam to the other.

The center of public life in Muslim cities was the mosque. Cities had numerous neighborhood mosques in which the pious would perform their daily devotions, but the officially designated congregational mosques were the preferred venue for the Friday noon prayer and sermon. They were also the setting for primary schools and higher education, they served as a forum for deliberations and the expression of public opinion, and they were restful havens when the crush of urban life created the need for repose and quiet. Their minarets might be thin or thick, round or square, but they served as a beacon to prayer and a reassurance of the Islamic character of the society in which the traveler found himself.

The congregational mosque was necessarily surrounded by a large public space or square. Typically, the square connected the mosque with the central market. Muslim cities had one or more major markets, and most of the quarters of the city had smaller individual markets. The large market might be open air, or it might be covered with a roof. Some roofed markets in capital cities were huge, and over the centuries they might grow until they extended for a mile or more. The markets were usually organized according to the product being sold, so that the merchants of rugs and carpets would be consolidated in one area, while those who sold pots and pans of copper, brass, and other metals would be clustered together, and the sellers of glass objects would be found in yet another area. Often the shops in which the articles were sold also served as the workshop in which they had been produced. The butchers, tanners of leather, and blacksmiths, however, were almost always confined to the outskirts of the city for hygienic purposes or to reduce noise. Likewise, caravansaries tended to be located at the city's edge. In some important caravan cities, thousands of camels, donkeys, and other beasts of burden might be constantly coming into the city's environs, and the local inhabitants thought it best to keep both the animals and the foreign merchants at a distance.

European visitors to thirteenth-century Andalus and fourteenth-century Muslim India commented on the attention to cleanliness characteristic of the cities in those regions. All across the Dar al-Islam, cities boasted numerous bathhouses. The public bath, of course, was not unique to the Muslim world. It was a legacy of Roman and Hellenistic societies. Islamic insistence on ritual purity before prayer, however, ensured that the institution would flourish in the Muslim world. Muslim cities from Andalus to India enthusiastically adopted the bath, modifying its layout and function according to their needs. Because of its primary purpose, the larger baths were usually adjacent to the congregational mosques. Muslims soon had to admit that, quite apart from its function in providing the required ablution, the bath was admirably suited for the objectives for which the Romans most valued it: relaxation and social interaction. Muslims devoted much energy and attention to the construction and maintenance of baths, washing facilities, drains, and latrines, even as these amenities declined in use in western Europe after the collapse of the western Roman empire.

A bath in the Umayyad palace of Khirbat al-Mafjar. Note the mosaics in the floors.

Cemeteries were usually situated outside the walls of the town. Their layout reflected the Muslim preference to be buried facing Mecca. They tended to be active social areas. Groups of Sufis might live adjacent to the tomb of the master who began their method of achieving spiritual insight, and the tomb might well attract pilgrims, who often lent a festive air to the vicinity. Townspeople themselves often visited graves and used the cemetery as picnic grounds and strolling areas. Also located outside the city walls might be a *musalla*, or place to perform the salat, at festivals or other occasions when a huge number of worshipers might assemble together and even the congregational mosque was not large enough to hold them.

Residential neighborhoods in Muslim cities were nearly self-contained quarters. Pre-Islamic towns in the Arabian Peninsula had been organized by families and clans, so it was natural that garrison cities such as Kufa and Basra were organized along the same lines. Arab immigrants who settled in existing cities in Iraq, Syria, and Egypt followed a similar pattern. Even as more and more of the dhimmis converted to Islam in places as far apart as North Africa and Khorasan, most—but not all—cities in the Muslim world became organized into quarters that were based on kinship, ethnic group, religion, or occupation. They might contain a few hundred or a few thousand residents, and each would typically be served by a local mosque, market, public bath(s), and perhaps its own cemetery.

Cities in the Dar al-Islam did not develop municipal institutions that assumed responsibility for the governance of a legally defined urban area. Thus, the inhabitants of each quarter assumed the responsibility for the provision of essential services such as the adjudication of conflicts, security, sanitation, and the delivery of tax revenues to the authorities. Facilities such as hospitals, neighborhood mosques, fountains, madrasas, khans, and public baths were usually funded by private bequests and particularly by the dedication of waqfs, as we saw in the previous chapter.

Although some of the services that a quarter provided—most obviously the provision of water and sewerage facilities—required cooperation with other sections of the city, the quarters nevertheless became self-reliant and developed a sense of territoriality and identity. The head of the leading family in the quarter represented the neighborhood to the governor. In cooperation with the army or the police, he was responsible for maintaining order during normal times. Security was enhanced by a massive gate that marked the entry to a quarter, and it was closed at night. During periods when the central authority was weak, neighborhood security in cities from Anatolia through Iran was often assumed by groups of local youths. These were called *futuwwa* orders (sometimes also called *'ayyar* in the Arabic-speaking regions and *ahi* in the Turkish-speaking regions). *Futuwwa* in Arabic literally means "youth," and the motivation for the earliest futuwwa orders was a moral one. Most of them had a code of behavior stressing altruism, generosity, patience, gravity, and justice. Many of their members were models of the best civic and moral behavior. As a result, Sufi orders often became linked with them, and Sufis as far away as Morocco would later adopt their regimen as part of their own code of behavior.

Some of the futuwwa orders promoted sports activities, others were related to specific crafts, and others were mutual aid societies. The perceived obligation to help others contributed to the evolution of some futuwwa orders into militias when the power of the amir or sultan was weak and troops or police might not be reliable. Unfortunately, the young men could sometimes act more like youth gangs than disciplined militias, and they could be more of a threat to the local residents than they were a source of security. As a result, the term *'ayyar* is often used by the chroniclers to mean "brigands" or "troublemakers."

The futuwwa thus had an ambiguous status in society and an ambivalent relationship with the social and political authorities. They could be a force for cohesion or for disruption. On the whole, they tended to express the energies and causes of the disadvantaged and could applaud what they saw as "Robin Hood" behavior. The Abbasid caliph al-Nasir (1180–1225), who gained his autonomy from the Saljuqs, tried to institutionalize the futuwwa movement to further his own cause of social and political reform, but the destruction of the Abbasid caliphate soon thereafter ended whatever progress he may have made in that direction.

Security for the neighborhood quarters was enhanced by the fact that they were not easily accessible by the wider public. The wide streets in the vicinity of the main mosque, which had to accommodate hundreds, if not thousands, of persons, branched off into smaller arteries that in turn branched off into still narrower lanes that twisted and turned and finally came to an end as culs-de-sac in front of the doors of a handful of residences in the residential quarter. The streets in most cities anywhere in the world at the time would seem labyrinthine to modern observers, but the layout of cities in the predominantly Muslim world had a special character. When thirteenth-century

The corridor-like streets of a residential neighborhood in Fez.

Aragonese (whose cities would seem claustrophobic and mazelike to us) began consolidating their hold on Valencia, they expressed their astonishment at the narrow, twisting streets and labyrinthine layout of the Muslim cities there.

In part, this pattern can be explained by the fact that wide streets were not required in a society almost utterly devoid of wheeled vehicles. In addition, streets usually followed the contours of the elevation, in order to facilitate drainage after rains. In many cases, too, individuals tended to follow family members, members of the same craft or occupation, or fellow members of a religious sect or ethnic group into a particular neighborhood and to set it off deliberately from other neighborhoods. Modes of transportation, terrain, and affinity groups explain only part of the unique layout of Muslim cities, however. In the Iberian Peninsula, where one could expect continuity in the shape of cities over time, the Reconquista brought about a striking change: When the Portuguese, Castilians, and Aragonese built over preexisting Muslim cities, the new cities included twenty-five percent more public space than the Muslims had provided.

Clearly other forces were at work, whether in the Iberian Peninsula or in India. Some are attributable to Islam and others are not. One is a concern with privacy and gender segregation, which has both pre-Islamic and Islamic roots. Pre-Islamic housing in North Africa, for example, was characterized by an absence of ground-floor windows and few windows on the upper floors. In part, this was a function of the heavy walls needed to insulate rooms and the need to reduce the amount of light entering the house. Courtyards allowed the occupants access to fresh air and sunshine without having to be in the public eye. This concern for privacy extends even to the tents of nomads, where it seems likely that male and female spaces were demarcated even before the advent of Islam.

Instances of this pre-Islamic concern for privacy could no doubt be multiplied across the vast world of Islam. On the other hand, certain features of the Qur'an, Hadith, and Shari'a also encouraged a consciousness of privacy that was given expression in the design of buildings and streets. In order to ensure family privacy and modesty, qadis frequently ruled on the height of buildings, the placement of windows, and the comportment of individuals. Not all Muslims lived in courtyard houses, but the Islamic concern for privacy and gender segregation reinforced any preexisting parallels, affecting the whole range of housing from one-room structures to vast palatial complexes. In addition, qadis tended to favor the individual's property rights over concerns for the collective good except in the case of an overriding moral principle such as privacy. As a result, property owners had relatively free rein in their wish to build. Thus, buildings were allowed to infringe on public space, transforming streets into narrow, twisting defiles. The maze of streets created in effect an informal zoning system, which kept public activities and strangers away from most residential homes. A person traversing a city remained in public areas; a stranger who wandered into a residential area would be immediately noticed and monitored, if not accosted.

By the thirteenth century, cities all across the Muslim world were slowly assuming a variation of the same pattern. There was no "blueprint" for such a Muslim city—as we have seen, Baghdad began as a meticulously planned, circular city. Esfahan, Herat, and Shiraz also began as circular cities, but their original plans were submerged under the pattern that became the dominant model throughout the Dar al-Islam by the thirteenth century. Hamadan's original, square design was likewise lost to the characteristic model. Cities otherwise as culturally distinct as Herat in Afghanistan (founded by Alexander the Great), Baghdad in Iraq (carefully planned as the imperial capital of a Muslim empire), and Fez in Morocco (established by refugees from Arabia) all slowly adapted in their own way to the model.

The Countryside

The vast majority of people in the Dar al-Islam lived in rural areas. Most lived in villages, and their livelihoods were tied to agriculture. In some areas, such as Yemen, Lebanon, and Morocco, villages could be built in remote mountainous areas and the peasants tilled fields that had been carved out of the sides of the mountains as terraces. Perched on precipices and constructed out of local stone or even lava, the villages were virtual fortresses and discouraged attacks from their neighbors. Aside from running feuds with neighboring villages, the lives of their inhabitants were relatively unmolested. Most peasants, however, lived in the fertile river valleys or plains, and were subject to outside intervention. The food and fiber that they produced were essential to the survival of the local town and city, and therefore the local governor exerted considerable efforts to ensure that they were under his control.

Villages throughout the Dar al-Islam had traditionally been autonomous in the sense that they were self-governing. Christian and Jewish villages were allowed to practice their own preferred system of law. The lives of villagers in Iraq and Iran were the first to feel the effects of the iqta' in the tenth century, and, like peasants thereafter, their lot seems to have declined. As we have seen, the Buyids introduced the iqta' into Iraq. Later, the Saljuqs, Ayyubids, and Mamluks adopted the practice. An iqta' was originally a specified tract of land (usually agricultural land and the villages that supplied the manpower for it) temporarily assigned to a military officer in return for equipping, paying, and supplying a number of soldiers to the service of the sultan. The holders of the early iqta's knew that their possession of the land was temporary, and their sole interest was to exploit it. Maintenance of the irrigation systems would typically be neglected, and exorbitant taxes would be charged to the unlucky peasants. The consequences for agriculture were catastrophic in some areas. Because of the debts that cultivators amassed under such conditions, they could be as fixed on the land as securely as the serfs in western Europe. When the Saljuqs made iqta's inheritable, peasants reaped the benefits, as managers began to take an interest in long-term investments.

In addition to the exploitation that they usually experienced at the hands of local elites, many of the peasants from North Africa to Transoxiana were subject to the depredations of nomads. Most of the time, peasants and nomads lived in a symbiotic relationship with each other. The pure nomads required the grains, fruits, and tools that peasants could provide, while the peasants purchased draft animals, wool, and hides from the nomads. Many of the bedouin were not pure nomads, but semi-nomads who cultivated fields for part of the year and spent the rest of the year in pastures. Because of their wanderings, they often encroached on the fields of peasants. In the ensuing quarrels, the nomads had the upper hand in mobility and martial training, and the peasants usually lost. The temptation for bedouin to raid the storage sheds of the cultivators was always great, and because of the nomads' ability to subsist in harsh environments, it was difficult if not impossible for central authorities to punish them.

With the widespread breakdown in central authority during the tenth and eleventh centuries, the bedouin increased their depredations in the area from Iraq to Morocco, with the result that large tracts of cultivated land were abandoned. The twelfth century witnessed the violence caused by several Crusades, the Almoravids and the Almohads, and the endemic warfare of the late Saljuq period, and was followed by the two invasions of the Mongols. The suffering that the voiceless people of the countryside endured is limited only by our imagination.

Nomads and peasants had little access to education or formal religious instruction. The bedouin, in particular, were scorned by urban populations for their irreligion. Groups such as the Almoravids and the Almohads, who conquered under the banner of Islam, were regarded with jaundiced eye by many merchants and artisans, who regarded their version of Islam with suspicion and condescension. These Berber peoples at least had been instructed in the faith; most nomads were quite ignorant of the basics of Islam. Muslim peasants almost always had access to a village mosque, but their imam was unlikely to be well educated. Many of the parents in the village would be satisfied if he could teach their children the Arabic alphabet and drill them until they had memorized the Qur'an. Because villagers and nomads had an uncertain grasp of the doctrines of Islam, they were even more likely than their low-income cousins in the city to have recourse to practices that were residues of pre-Islamic religions and that were condemned by the ulama. They, however, turned to whatever could help them find meaning in an otherwise crushing existence.

Conversion to Islam

A major development in world history was the achievement of a Muslim majority in the region from North Africa to Iran by 1300. This outcome is not surprising, but it was also not inevitable. Muslim military conquests outside the Arabian Peninsula were never followed by widespread conversion. The mere imposition of Muslim political rule was sufficient to change the status of a country from the Dar al-Kufr to the Dar al-Islam. The Shari'a recognized the existence of non-Muslim populations within the Muslim state, and granted them a wide degree of autonomy in the application of their law and customs, as long as they paid their taxes (the payment of which was a major reason they were often not encouraged to convert).

A Muslim Minority

Conversion rates were slow during the Umayyad caliphate of Damascus and for some time afterward in most parts of the Umma. The Umayyads themselves were in part responsible for this. They assumed that Islam was for Arabs and that it was better for non-Muslims to pay taxes rather than to convert and not pay taxes. Other factors were at work, as well. Until the last decade of the seventh century, Muslim authorities continued to employ Greek and Persian as the languages of administration. Even after Arabic became the official language, for centuries to come, many Christians and Jews continued to hold important government offices in various parts of the Islamic world. As long as lucrative and prestigious employment was possible and conversion was optional, it was natural to continue with one's traditional religion. Christians dominated the financial bureaucracy of the Egyptian bureaucracy until the late nineteenth century, and more than one Christian served as wazir in the Fatimid state. Jews, especially, served as personal physicians to Muslim rulers. Personal physicians to rulers had unusually open access to the center of power, and their broad education often made them the most qualified officials in the palace. Some of them were granted awesome state power (and a corresponding vulnerability when things went wrong).

One's place in the social structure also played a role in rates of conversion. Peasants in most areas of the empire had little contact with the culture of the conquerors except with the hated and feared tax collector. As a result, they were even slower to convert than urban dwellers. Terrain also played a factor. The formidable mountains of the Taurus, Zagros, Elburz, Lebanon and anti-Lebanon ranges in the east, and the Atlas and other ranges in North Africa, were home to many peoples who were there precisely because they wished to avoid central authority. Shielded by the rugged terrain, they were more trouble to subdue than they were worth to any imperial government until the late twentieth century. As a result, they remained unconverted for centuries. If and when these groups did convert, it was often to a minority version of Islam, such as Shi'ism or Kharijism, and the mountainous areas in southwestern Asia and North Africa have remained refuges of minority groups to the present day.

The presence of dhimmis rarely presented a major problem for Muslims, although they were a reminder that not everyone had recognized Muhammad as the Prophet, even when presented with the opportunity. Occasional discrimination against Christians and Jews did occur, most notably under the Fatimid Imam al-Hakim, during the Zirid regime in Granada, and under the late thirteenth-century Mamlukes. It is significant, however, that the Muslim community did not develop an attitude to either Christians or Jews even remotely resembling the anti-Semitism that medieval European Christians directed towards the Jews in their midst.

Dhimmis were, to be sure, distinct from the Muslim population. In many cities, they tended to be concentrated in certain quarters of the city (although rarely were they the exclusive residents of a given quarter). They paid the poll tax, and the Shari'a developed sumptuary laws to regulate their behavior. These were irregularly enforced: The Umayyad caliph of Damascus 'Umar II and the Fatimid caliph al-Hakim were exceptional precisely because they enforced such laws. Nevertheless, they were on the books and were a constant reminder to Jews and Christians that they were subject, if protected, peoples. Examples of such regulations were the requirement to wear distinctive dress and to avoid wearing colors—particularly green—associated with the Prophet; a prohibition against carrying arms and riding horses; and a prohibition against building new places of worship and repairing old ones without permission.

Although some of the later Shi'ites believed that eating with, or perhaps even touching, dhimmis would obligate a Shi'ite to perform full ablutions before he could pray, most Muslims enjoyed unrestricted interaction with Christians and Jews and often celebrated their holidays with them. The Sunni schools of law agreed that the meats prepared by Jews according to kosher practices satisfied the ritual prescriptions of the Shari'a. On the other hand, apostasy from Islam to Judaism or Christianity was punished severely and often resulted in death. Muslim men could marry non-Muslim women (many marriages in the ruling class were of this type), but a Muslim woman could not marry a non-Muslim man. Implicit in this custom, of course, was the assumption that the male was the head of the family and that his religion would influence the rest of the family's members.

The Pace of Conversion Quickens

Forces were at work that did encourage conversion, however. Some were what may be termed negative factors. Some sought to escape paying the dhimmi tax, to gain legal equality with Muslims, or to improve their social status. The weakening of central authority seems to have played a role in mass conversion. In Iraq, for example, the Nestorian community had maintained excellent relations with both the Umayyad and Abbasid administrations and had avoided subjection to the more onerous features of the sumptuary laws. That changed with the caliphate of al-Mutawakkil (847–861), who was confronted with his fractious army, the expensive new capital at Samarra, and the explosive debate between the Mu'tazilites and Hanbalis over the relative merits of reason and revelation. The caliph, desperately seeking allies in his struggles, yielded to the demands of the antirationalist Hanbalis and enforced the harsher regulations. After the middle of the ninth century, the quality of life for Nestorians deteriorated markedly, and conversion rates rose.

The "bedouinization" of large parts of Iraq and eastern Syria during the tenth and eleventh centuries also accelerated the conversion process. The reassertion of bedouin autonomy in Syria and Iraq occurred simultaneously with the Hilali invasion of North Africa and bedouin predations in Egypt. The result was the raiding of villages and towns and the disruption of agriculture. The poor, as always, suffered, but in the long run it was the ruin of the landowning and merchant elite and of the monasteries that broke down the institutional structures of the Christian and Jewish communities in these areas, and led to their replacement by Islamic institutions.

On the other hand, it is highly unlikely that most converts to Islam left their original religious affiliation for "negative" reasons. Some did so primarily because they had been impressed by the piety and spirituality of individual Muslims, or because they found the simple, yet profound monotheism of Islam a more convincing model of the meaning of the universe than any other religion with which they were familiar. Many converts, no doubt, changed their religious affiliation for reasons they would have had difficulty articulating, because the change simply seemed like the natural thing to do. A variety of factors, positive and negative, would accumulate in their experience, and the impulse to convert was less explicit and conscious than tacit.

Today, many of us find it difficult to understand how individuals could change religions without coercion. Religious identity in premodern societies, however, was typically not a matter of an individual commitment to a set of doctrines. Rather, it was the product of one's community and involved ritual and the body of laws that guided one's life. When one's social situation changed, it was appropriate to change one's religion. In some cases, individuals made the switch, but we see many incidents in which whole families or communities converted en masse.

The military garrison cities played a major role in this process of gradual conversion. Founded in order to isolate the Arabs from the surrounding population, they quickly became centers for the dissemination of the Arabic–Islamic culture instead. Whether in Egypt, Iraq, or Khorasan, the large cantonments served as magnets for local craftsmen, traders, household servants, entertainers, and scholars. The policy of cultural insulation collapsed as economic symbiosis became a fact of life. Some non-Muslims became acculturated to the norms of the dominant cultural group by having learned the Arabic language and having adopted new habits of dress and manners. The adoption of the Arabs' religion was a next, natural step. For others, the process was reversed: Adoption of Islam led to cultural assimilation.

The process of assimilation was never a one-way process, however, as we saw when the Arabs adapted many Byzantine and Sasanian governmental practices to their own purposes. On the individual level, as well, one adapted to one's environment. In Khorasan, where tens of thousands of Arab warriors settled during the last third of the seventh century, Arabs assimilated to the local culture more dramatically than elsewhere. Not only were Arab soldiers placed in the garrison city of Merv, but they also settled in numerous small Iranian communities. Ordinary villagers and townsmen mixed frequently with Arabs, and the two cultures assimilated. The two groups engaged in a high degree of intermarriage, Arabs adopted Iranian dialects, and many Khorasanis converted to Islam during the early eighth century. Arab and Khorasani Muslims were already making common cause when Abbasid propaganda began to appeal to them, and ethnic distinctions became less and less apparent.

Later, the rise and increasing independence of the Tahirid, Saffarid, and Samanid dynasties from about 820 on seems to have accelerated the conversion process not only within Khorasan, but also throughout the Persian cultural area. These Iranian dynasties were explicitly Muslim, and yet they encouraged the development of a new Persian literature. It used the Arabic alphabet and borrowed motifs from Arabic poetry, but it glorified themes from pre-Islamic Iranian history and myth. By reasserting an Iranian cultural identity within an explicitly Islamic context, this new literary and cultural movement seems to have been particularly effective in making the transition from Zoroastrianism to Islam seem less of a betrayal of one's tradition and identity.

The actual rate at which conversion took place is not known. The process of conversion was not noted by the chroniclers of the day. Richard Bulliet's statistical analysis[1] of the history of the adoption of Muslim names in Iran concludes that, by the mid-ninth century, half the population of Iran had converted to Islam and that, by 882, half the population of Iraq was Muslim. He concludes that, by the beginning of the eleventh century, perhaps eighty percent of the population of Iran was Muslim. This method of calculating the rate of conversion is suggestive, but while the evidence for certain cities has to be taken seriously, generalizations can mask local variations. The cities in the regions of Fars, Jibal, and Kirman in Iran, for example, remained strongholds of Sasanian and Zoroastrian loyalties until at least the middle of the eleventh century. The populations of the major mountain ranges do not appear to have become Muslim before the twelfth century.

No agreement exists on when the population of other areas of the Dar al-Islam became a Muslim majority. Many scholars would agree that Syria and Egypt became majority Muslim societies sometime between the twelfth and fourteenth centuries, but cannot be any more specific than that. Regions as distant as Andalus, as we have seen, present special problems. The proclamation of the caliphate suggests a self-confident and dominant Muslim community, and yet scholars cannot agree on whether Islam was ever the majority religion there. Christianity seems to have disappeared from North Africa by the end of the eleventh century—the century of great disorder in Ifriqiya—but Judaism continued to maintain a viable presence there.

As the proportion of the Muslims in the population increased and the influence of the ulama over the people and the rulers was consequently enhanced, the position of <u>dh</u>immis deteriorated. The ulama tended to insist that rulers enforce sumptuary laws as a matter of obedience to the will of God. Mobs could put pressure on the political authorities to remove non-Muslim officials, and the safety of other members of the non-Muslim communities would be threatened by association. During periods of distress, large numbers converted to escape the humiliating conditions and the physical dangers they entailed.

The Issue of Authority in the Muslim World

The process of conversion to Islam seems to have contributed not only to social tension, but also to the breakdown of political unity in the Dar al-Islam. As long as the Muslims were a minority ruling elite, they had a vested interest in maintaining ties of affinity with each other across great distances. Whenever the percentage of Muslims in a given society approached half the population, the Muslims found themselves pulled by a variety of identities—familial, social, and ethnic—that often competed with their sense of being a part of the Umma. Just as social clashes among the Muslims within each polity increased, so did the likelihood of breaking from a caliph's political authority.

The office of the caliphate was a unifying factor in the early history of Islam, for it was the locus of political and religious authority for most Muslims. It proved to be a remarkable combination of fragility and durability over the first six centuries of Islam. It emerged as an ad hoc measure to carry on the work of the Umma in the absence of the Prophet. It was not a constitutional office—it was explicitly provided for neither by the Qur'an nor by the Prophet's instructions—and two issues remained controversial: the responsibilities and powers of the office, and the provision for succession to the office in the event of a vacancy.

A significant minority within the Umma rejected the Umayyad and Abbasid caliphs as illegitimate on the grounds that they were not lineally associated with 'Ali, whom they believed to have been the Prophet's choice to have been his successor. The numerous factions that adhered to this conviction at one time or another were collectively known as Shi'ites, and they followed their own candidates as the true Imam/caliph. Increasingly, as it became clear that their Imams (with the exception of the Fatimids) would have little or no chance to wield political power, the figure of the Imam became one of a heightened spirituality, a figure to whom God had granted spiritual insight available to no other mortal.

By contrast, the Sunni caliphal dynasties increasingly accentuated their worldly power by means of constructing finer palace complexes, devising ornate ceremonies, and taking on the trappings of a monarchy in general. Some of the early Abbasid caliphs did make at least implicit claims for more than mere temporal power: al-Mahdi (775–785); al-Hadi, "the Guide" (785–86); and al-Ma'mun (813–833)—who introduced the title of Imam for all subsequent Abbasid caliphs—were obviously attempting to compete with the Shi'ite doctrine of the Imamate. But they never took the task seriously enough to initiate a doctrinal change.

The true status of the Sunni caliphate became clear as early as 756, when the new Umayyad regime in Andalus refused to recognize the Abbasid caliph. Rather than being considered apostates for having rejected God's deputy, the Umayyads of Andalus were considered political rebels. Moreover, the Umayyad princes of Andalus did not feel compelled at the time to claim the caliphate for themselves, but claimed only the title of amir, leaving the relationship between the Muslims of Andalus and the caliph in suspension. The Abbasid caliph had no political or economic claim on the Muslims of Andalus and had no way of imposing religious doctrines or rituals on them. Andalusis in effect had no caliph, and yet were not the less Muslim for that. Thus, with the beginning of the partition of the first Umayyad empire, the

Abbasid caliphate revealed itself to be a dynastic monarchy, despite its appeal to Islamic legitimacy. The seizure of Egypt in 868 by Ibn Tulun and of large parts of Iran by the Saffarids in the 870s only confirmed the fact that challenges to the economic and political authority of the caliph had consequences no different from that of challenges to any other ruler.

In the early tenth century, two new caliphates, one in North Africa and the other in Andalus, arose to contest the monopoly of an increasingly beleaguered Abbasid caliphate. By the middle of that century, the Abbasid caliph was a mere figurehead for a military regime that administered affairs in Iraq and western Iran. After three centuries, Muslim society was further away than ever from achieving a synthesis between Islamic political ideals and Islamic political practice. The Umma had fragmented into such conflicting groups that a consensus regarding the structure and functioning of governance appeared impossible. Kharijites argued that a caliph was not even necessary if God's law was being followed; the various Shi'ite groups agreed that the Abbasids and Umayyads should not be caliphs but disagreed over who should replace them as the Imam/caliph; the Fatimids, the one Shi'ite faction that did install its chosen Imam, soon settled into Egypt, but did surprisingly little to transform their society; and Sunnis were dispersed throughout the three competing caliphates as well as in several autonomous provinces whose rulers paid only lip service to the Abbasid caliph.

Shi'ite scholars were greatly preoccupied with defining the meaning and importance of the Imam, who was central to their whole belief system. Sunnis, however, devoted surprisingly little scholarship to the topic of the caliph. Most references to the office appear in the work of legal scholars who were trying to connect the implementation of the Shari'a to his office. The first major systematic work that analyzed the nature of the Abbasid caliphate appeared only in the eleventh century, from the pen of al-Mawardi (d. 1058). His *The Rules of Governance* was written during the caliphate of al-Qa'im (1031–1075), who began asserting some independence of action against his Buyid amir. Al-Mawardi's book boldly declared that the caliph was still the chief executive of the Umma and was entrusted by God for a wide range of responsibilities: the protection of the traditional interpretation of Islam from the designs of innovators; the enforcement of the provisions of the Shari'a; the defense of the borders of the Dar al-Islam; combating unbelievers until they accept Muslim rule; the levying of taxes; the regulation of public expenditure; the appointment of qualified people to public office; and the regulation of public expenditure. Most of these functions, of course, were performed by the Buyid amir, but al-Mawardi blithely argued that this was due to the fact that the caliph had the prerogative of delegating his powers; if these responsibilities were usurped or otherwise corrupted, the caliph had the right of summoning aid to restore his rightful powers.

Al-Qa'im welcomed the advent of Tughril Bey, but any anticipated liberation from the restricted role that the Shi'ite Buyids had imposed upon him turned out to be chimerical. The Sunni Saljuqs were no more willing than the Shi'ite Buyids to allow al-Qa'im or any other caliph to reassert the power of his Abbasid predecessors. The cleavage between al-Mawardi's vision and political reality continued under the Saljuqs. Their leaders adopted the title of *sultan*, which derives from the Arabic word *sultah,* meaning "power." The Sultan claimed to wield power at the pleasure of the caliph, just as the Buyid amirs had. Resigning themselves to the fact that it was unlikely that the caliph would be actively involved in their governance, Sunni jurists accepted al-Mawardi's idea of the delegation of powers by the caliph to justify the system that was in place. Scholars such as al-Ghazali (d. 1111), who was born the year that al-Mawardi died, insisted upon obedience to governmental authority in the absence of a regularly constituted caliphate. His widely quoted argument was that the anarchy that would result from a rebellion against an unjust ruler would be more detrimental to the purposes of God than the ruler himself was.

We do not have a clear understanding of how Andalusi Muslims viewed the religious authority of their Umayyad caliph. At any rate, their caliphate disintegrated early in the eleventh century, and during its span of less than a century, it had almost no effect on the lives of Muslims outside the Iberian Peninsula. The Fatimid caliphate, although in theory invested with a high degree of religious and political authority, shrank to insignificance within a century of its conquest of Egypt. Although the Abbasid caliphate under al-Nasir did manage to regain control over a small state in Iraq for a short time during the twelfth and thirteenth centuries, it played no active role in most Muslims' lives after the ninth century. This is quite an important point, because many general history books portray the Abbasid caliphate as though it led a powerful empire until 1258 and discuss Hulagu's destruction of the caliphate as though it had dire repercussions throughout the Muslim world. These are highly misleading concepts, as should be clear by now.

The Abbasid caliphate did, in fact, play an important symbolic role in the lives of large numbers of Sunnis in the Muslim East (and to a lesser extent in North Africa). Despite the caliph's actual weakness from the early tenth century on, Sunni religious teachers taught that he was the supreme head of all the Muslims. He represented to the faithful an unbroken line of succession of authority and served as a symbol of Muslim unity from the time of the Prophet himself. He continued to serve as a source of legitimacy for many provincial rulers, as many Muslim rulers from the Maghrib to India sought an official document from the caliph, certifying that they had been "appointed" or "delegated" to rule on behalf of the caliph. These same rulers usually minted coins bearing the name of the caliph as well as themselves, and at the Friday sermon they ordered that the name of the caliph be recited. The weaker the caliph was militarily, the more convenient they found it to acknowledge his theoretical suzerainty. The fall of the Abbasid caliphate in Baghdad was no doubt troubling for many Muslims in the East. Its resurrection in Cairo shortly thereafter under the patronage of the Mamlukes seems to have assuaged most of the anxieties, however.

Conclusion

The enormous ambitions of the Arab empire of the early eighth century had been radically scaled down by Abbasid times. There was no single "Islamic" empire even at the start of the Abbasid period, due to the loss of much of North Africa and of Andalus, and by the end of the ninth century, most of the remainder of the old Umayyad empire had slipped from Baghdad's control, as well. The chances that the physical dimensions of the original Arab-dominated empire could have remained intact, of course, were practically non-existent. The breathtaking size of that empire challenged any attempts to provide security, and the plethora of cultures that the conquests had brought together complicated the task of identifying a common interest. And yet, a culture grew up across the breadth of the Muslim world that facilitated travel, commerce, scholarship, and technological innovation.

Perhaps the most interesting and ultimately determining feature of the Muslim commonwealth was that, in the absence of a single leader who combined both religious and temporal authority, the importance of the legal schools and their scholars became magnified. In an unusual development, the "law" that most people felt compelled to obey was not developed by their government, but by independent scholars: the jurists. A few of them served as qadis for the various rulers, but most remained private citizens, engaging in frequent discussion with others like themselves in order to attempt to reach agreement on the finer points of living the godly life. Some of them traveled widely, sharing thoughts with other jurists in distant parts of the Dar al-Islam. As a rule, they were much more respected than government officials themselves. As we have seen, the rulers developed their own set of commercial and criminal laws to supplement the Shari'a, but these had little impact on the majority of Muslims. Muslims expected their governments to enforce the Shari'a, but they knew that governments had not created it—it came ultimately from God, mediated through the jurists. A tension existed between the governments and the interpreters of the law that would shape Muslim history for centuries to come.

NOTES

1. Richard Bulliet, *Conversion to Islam in the Medieval Period: An Essay in Quantitative History.* Cambridge, Massachusetts: Harvard University Press, 1979.

FURTHER READING

For a good discussion of the concept of a Muslim commonwealth see Garth Fowden, *Empire to Commonwealth: Consequences of Monotheism in Late Antiquity.* Princeton, New Jersey: Princeton University Press, 1993, passim, and Hugh Kennedy, *The Prophet and the Age of the Caliphates: The Islamic Near East from the Sixth to the Eleventh Century.* London and New York: Longman, 1986, pp. 200–211.

Frontiers and Identities

Bonner, Michael. *Aristocratic Violence and Holy War: Studies in the Jihad and the Arab–Byzantine Frontier.* New Haven, Connecticut: American Oriental Society, 1996.

Brauer, Ralph W. *Boundaries and Frontiers in Medieval Muslim Geography.* Transactions of the American Philosophical Society. Vol. 85, Pt. 6. Philadelphia: The American Philosophical Society, 1995.

Chabbi, J. "Ribāt," in *The Encyclopedia of Islam, New Edition.* Vol. VIII. Leiden: E.J. Brill, 1995.

Goitein, S.D. *A Mediterranean Society.* Vol. I. Berkeley, California: University of California Press, 1967.

Hambly, Gavin R.G., ed. *Women in the Medieval Islamic World: Power, Patronage, and Piety* . New York: St. Martin's Press, 1998.

Imber, Colin. *Ebu's-su'ud: The Islamic Legal Tradition.* Stanford, California: Stanford University Press, 1997.

Lewis, Bernard. *Race and Slavery in the Middle East: An Historical Inquiry.* New York: Oxford University Press, 1990, p. 14.

Mélikoff, I. "Ghāzī." in *The Encyclopedia of Islam, New Edition.* Vol. II. Leiden: E.J. Brill, 1983.

Peters, Rudolph. *Jihad in Classical and Modern Islam: A Reader.* Princeton, New Jersey: Markus Wiener, 1996.

Wink, Andre. *Al-Hind: The Making of the Indo–Islamic World.* Vol. I: *Early Medieval India and the Expansion of Islam, 7–11e.* Leiden: E.J. Brill, 1990.

The City and the Countryside

Abu-Lughod, Janet L. "The Islamic City—Historic Myth, Islamic Essence, and Contemporary Relevance." *International Journal of Middle East Studies,* 19 (1987), pp. 155–176.

Ahsan, Muhammad Manazir. *Social Life Under the Abbasids.* London and New York: Longman, 1979.

Brown, L. Carl, ed. *From Madina to Metropolis: Heritage and Change in the Near Eastern City.* Princeton, New Jersey: The Darwin Press, 1973.

Burns, Robert J. *Islam Under the Crusaders.* Princeton, New Jersey: Princeton University Press, 1973.

Hourani, Albert, and S.M. Stern, eds. *The Islamic City: A Colloquium.* Oxford: Bruno Cassirer, 1970.

Insoll, Timothy. *The Archaeology of Islam.* Oxford: Blackwell Publishers, 1999.

Lambton, Ann K.S. *Continuity and Change in Medieval Persia: Aspects of Administrative, Economic, and Social History, 11th–14th Century.* Albany, New York: State University of New York Press, 1988.

Wheatley, Paul. *The Places Where Men Pray Together: Cities in Islamic Lands, Seventh Through the Tenth Centuries.* Chicago and London: University of Chicago Press, 2001.

Conversion

Bulliet, Richard. *Conversion to Islam in the Medieval Period: An Essay in Quantitative History.* Cambridge, Massachusetts: Harvard University Press, 1979.

Gervers, M. and R.J. Bikhazi, eds. *Conversion and Continuity: Indigenous Christian Communities in Islamic Lands, Eighth to Eighteenth Centuries.* Toronto: Pontifical Institute of Mediaeval Studies, 1990.

Levtzion, Nehemiah. *Conversion to Islam.* New York: Holmes & Meier, 1979.

Lorenzen, David N., ed. *Religious Change and Cultural Domination.* El Colegio de Mexico, 1981.

The Issue of Authority in the Muslim World

Fowden, Garth. *Empire to Commonwealth: Consequences of Monotheism in Late Antiquity.* Princeton, New Jersey: Princeton University Press, 1993.

Kennedy, Hugh. *The Prophet and the Age of the Caliphates: The Islamic Near East from the Sixth to the Eleventh Century.* London and New York: Longman, 1986.

Mikhail, Hanna. *Politics and Revelation: Mawardi and After.* Edinburgh: Edinburgh University Press, 1995.

Safran, Janina M. *The Second Umayyad Caliphate: The Articulation of Caliphal Legitimacy in Al-Andalus.* Cambridge, Massachusetts: Harvard University Press, 2000.

PART THREE

Mongol Hegemony, 1260–1405

The Mongol conquests dwarfed those of the Arabs, which had occurred some six centuries earlier. Between 1206 and 1260, the Mongols subjugated northern China, Central Asia, Iran and Iraq, eastern Anatolia, the Caucasus, and the vast steppe region from Mongolia to the area now occupied by eastern Poland. By 1279, they completed the conquest of southern China, as well. On the one hand, then, the achievement is greater than the Arabs on sheer scale. On the other hand, the Mongols did not create a civilization, and most of their conquests were lost within three generations.

The Mongols are not easy to dismiss as a destructive, one-time wonder, however. Despite the fact that they soon lost control of their possessions, their legacy was remembered, revered, and emulated for centuries thereafter throughout much of the vast region they had conquered. In western and central Europe, too, the legacy lingered, but in a peculiar fashion: Rumors that a great force to the east had brutalized part of the Muslim world during 1219–1222 sparked hope in Europe that a potential ally, perhaps even a Christian king, existed in the east that would help to destroy Islam. This was the origin of the legend of Prester John, a great Christian king in the East with whom the Europeans should join forces against Islam. The hope was so strong that when, in 1238, the Nizari Imam at Alamut and the Abbasid caliph in Baghdad jointly dispatched an embassy to Europe, appealing for help against the Mongols, they were rebuffed. Europe, particularly in the person of the Pope, was pursuing a diametrically opposed policy of attempting to form a great Christian alliance with the Mongol Great Khan—whom some thought to be Prester John—against the world of Islam. Even the crushing Mongol defeat of European knights three years later at Liegnitz did not dissipate the fantasy of Prester John, who continued to fascinate and lure Europeans for hundreds of years to come.

But the Mongols were not only the stuff of memory and legend. They transformed the world. These horsemen from the steppes who destroyed so many cities quickly began to rebuild urban economies once they assumed power. Few of their leaders appear to have appreciated the importance of agriculture, and that sector usually languished as a result. Long-distance trade, on the other hand, flourished as never before. From the Pacific to the Black Sea, bandits were held in check, caravanserais were constructed, and diplomatic contacts were established. The famous career of the Venetian Marco Polo in the last third of the thirteenth century would be unthinkable without the Mongols. He and his father and uncle traveled from Constantinople to Beijing and back with less fear for their lives or property than they would have felt had they journeyed anywhere in the Mediterranean basin. Taking advantage of the *pax Mongolica*, Venice quickly established a vast trade network that extended from the Pacific to Scandinavia.

The Mongol Empire affected the histories of all its neighbors as well as of peoples beyond their immediate reach. The history of a large part of the Muslim world was irrevocably altered. The Mongols and their desperately ambitious scion Timur Lang dominated western Asia for only a century and a half, but Mongol hegemony had such a profound influence on the course of Muslim history that it merits a separate section in this book. Chapter 10 establishes the historical framework for the period. It examines the history of the three Mongol states whose rulers eventually converted to Islam, traces the rise of three other powerful Muslim states during this period, and explores the destructive effects of the plague and Timur Lang on western Asia. Chapter 11 examines the cumulative effects of these and other events on Muslim intellectual and religious life. The evidence undermines the widely held view that the Mongol era caused Islamic civilization to decline. Despite frequent outbreaks of political chaos and the long-lasting economic depression of some regions, Islamic culture continued to thrive and break new ground in a wide variety of fields. More striking still, the period marks a transition from an era of several centuries during which the frontiers of the Muslim world had remained largely static to an age of remarkable expansion. In many respects, the period of Mongol hegemony marks the beginning of a golden age of Muslim history.

CHRONOLOGY

1210–1236	Reign of Iltutmish, founder of Delhi sultanate
1219–1222	Campaigns of Chinggis into Muslim world
1240s	Batu founds Saray, begins to administer his Qipchaq khanate
1250	Mamlukes seize power in Egypt and Syria
1253–1260	Hulagu's campaign
c.1250–c.1290	Career of Hajji Bektash
1260	Mamlukes defeat Hulagu's army at 'Ayn Jalut
1260–1265	Hulagu is first ruler of Il–khanate, establishes Maragha observatory
1261	Byzantines regain Constantinople from Latin Kingdom
1269	Marinids replace Almohads in Morocco
1271–1295	Marco Polo's adventures in the Mongol Empire
c.1280–1326	Career of Osman, founder of Ottoman dynasty
c.1280–1334	Career of Shaykh Safi al–Din

1291	Mamlukes capture the last Crusader castle in Syria
c.1290–1327	Career of Ibn Taymiya in Mamluke Empire
1310–1341	Third, and most successful, reign of Mamluke ruler, al–Nasir Muhammad
1313–1341	Reign of Uzbeg, and the Islamization of Qipchaq khanate
1325–1351	Reign of Muhammad ibn Tughluq of Delhi
1325–1349	Ibn Battuta's journey east; serves Ibn Tughluq seven years
1326–1362	Reign of Orhan of Ottoman sultanate
1334	Schism in Chaghatay khanate, Transoxiana is lost
1335	Collapse of Il–khanate
c.1335–1375	Career of Ibn al–Shatir
1347	First wave of plague
c.1350–1390	Career of Hafez
c.1350–1398	Career of Baha al–Din Naqshband
c.1350	Consensus has been achieved in most *madhhab*s that, theoretically, *ijtihad* is no longer permitted
1359–1377	Civil war in Qipchaq khanate; Toqtamish secures control by 1383
c.1360–1406	Career of Ibn Khaldun
1368	Ming dynasty overthrows Yuan dynasty of the Mongols in China
1370	Timur's career begins in Transoxiana
1381–1402	Timur's campaigns from Ankara to New Saray to Delhi
1405	Death of Timur

CHAPTER 10

The Great Transformation

By 1248, the Christian kingdoms of the Iberian Peninsula had seized all Muslim territory north of the Strait of Gibraltar except for the small principality of Granada. Over the next century and a half, they secured their control over this area, confirming that the Reconquista had succeeded in destroying one of the most populous and culturally creative zones of the Muslim world. Simultaneously, a similar process of conquest and consolidation of power was taking place in the eastern Muslim world. During the 1250s, the second major Mongol invasion of southwestern Asia took place. Millions of Muslims were now under the rule either of Christian Europeans or of pagan Mongols. For the first time since the Islamic calendar began, half or more of the world's Muslims were subject to governments dominated by non-Muslims.

In spite of the similarities, the situation in the eastern Muslim world differed from that of the Iberian Peninsula. The challenges facing Muslims in Iberia were insidious and chronic, but those in the east were violent and episodic and transformed the eastern Muslim world in profound ways. Whereas the Iberian Muslim community slowly suffocated under increasing restrictions, Muslims in three of the four Mongol empires rejoiced at the conversion of their rulers to Islam by the early fourteenth century. Their joy was short lived, for all three dynasties suddenly lost their grip on power in the middle third of the fourteenth century. Anarchy and widespread destruction became the order of the day. As the dynasties were collapsing, the worldwide epidemic of plague began its deadly work, leaving large areas of the Muslim world underpopulated. The first wave of the plague had hardly subsided when a half-Turk, half-Mongol warlord named Timur Lang began his career. His inexplicably vicious campaigns ranged from Delhi to Damascus and caused the horrors of Chinggis and Hulagu to pale by comparison. From 1380 to 1405, the very mention of his name sent panic into the hearts of multitudes, and his conquests laid waste to vast regions. The region from the Aegean Sea to the Ganges River had been violently shaken, with consequences that would reverberate for centuries.

The Mongol Khanates

Shortly before his death in 1227, Chinggis Khan gave each of his four sons a portion of his great empire. He did so in accordance with the ancient Mongol custom of establishing a home for the eldest son at the furthest distance and assigning the youngest to tend the family hearth. Accordingly, Jochi, the eldest, received the steppe land that lay north of the Aral sea and extended westward "as far as the hooves of Mongol horses have reached," whereas Tolui, the youngest, received the ancient Mongol homeland that is now eastern Mongolia. The second son, Chaghatay, and the third son, Ogedai, divided the lands that lay between those extremes. Ogedai succeeded his father as Great Khan, and his son Guyuk replaced him in the 1240s. In 1251, Tolui's eldest son Mongke became the Great Khan.

From his capital at Qaraqorum in modern Mongolia, Mongke (1251–1259) planned a new campaign of expansion. Leaders of Christian Europe hoped that he was Prester John, and they appealed to him to join them in a crusade against Islam, but he was unwilling to do so unless the Christian rulers and the Pope submitted themselves to him. Confident that the Lord of the Sky had entrusted the world to the Mongols, he embarked upon an ambitious campaign of conquest on his own terms. He sent one brother, Qubilai, to conquer the Sung dynasty in southern China and another brother, Hulagu, to subjugate southwestern Asia. When Mongke died, he was succeeded by Qubilai (1260–1294), who completed the conquest of China and is regarded as the first ruler of the Yuan dynasty (1279–1368) in China. He symbolized his new status by moving his capital from Qaraqorum to Beijing.

During the rule of Mongke and Qubilai, the Mongol domains became more or less institutionalized: The Great Khan ruled over Mongolia and China; Jochi's son Batu and his successors ruled over the Golden Horde in the vast steppe that extended from north of the Aral Sea almost to the Baltic Sea; the Chaghatay khanate ruled over the area that now comprises the Chinese province of Xinjiang and eastern Afghanistan, as well as the territory north of the Amu Darya River; and Hulagu's Il-khanid regime comprised Iraq, eastern Anatolia, the southern Caucasus, and Iran to just east of Herat.

The Qipchaq Khanate

Europeans from the sixteenth century on referred to the domain of Batu's successors as the Golden Horde. The origin of the name is lost in obscurity. The English word *Horde* derives from the Mongol word *ordu*, meaning "camp" or "domain," but the meaning of the term *Golden* has spawned considerable debate, with no consensus having emerged. The name Golden Horde is commonly used in English to refer to the entire period of the dominance of the Mongols on the Eurasian steppes. Europeans have also frequently referred to the people of the Golden Horde as *Tatars*, a word that has been very loosely used throughout history. Understood in its linguistic sense, however, it has some value, because the various Tatar dialects belong to the Qipchaq division of the Turkic languages. In fact, the Golden Horde's neighbors in the east knew it as the Qipchaq khanate, which is a more appropriate name for it. For ease of reference, this discussion will refer to the khanate as the Horde.

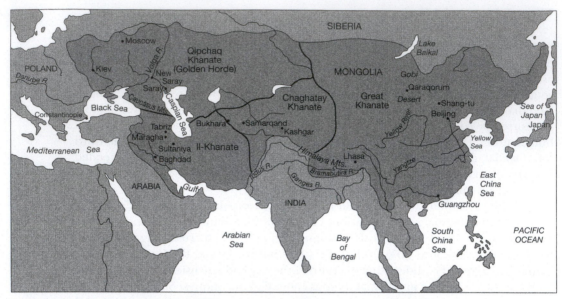

MAP 10.1 The Mongol Empire, ca. 1300

At its height, the Horde dominated the area from eastern Poland to the Siberian forests. The core was the vast, grassy plain known as the Qipchaq steppe that extended from northwest of the Black Sea to northeast of the Caspian Sea. This sea of grass was broken by three of the great rivers of Russia: the Dnieper, the Don, and the Volga. Batu had no doubt immediately recognized that the level, endless plains were ideal for his horse culture. The rivers complicated travel on an east–west axis, but facilitated travel and trade on a north–south axis.

This core region of the khanate was populated by numerous ethnic groups, but was dominated by the Qipchaq Turks. Batu's followers quickly became assimilated into the majority Turkish culture when their Mongol leaders intermarried with local Qipchaq elites and adopted the local language. The "Mongol" elite of the khanate always boasted of their lineal ties with Chinggis Khan and retained certain aspects of their Mongol culture, but they were soon indistinguishable from their Qipchaq subjects.

Our knowledge of the first century and a half of the history of the khanate is frustratingly scanty, due to Timur Lang's destruction of its cities in the 1390s. What we know about it is derived largely from the observations of outsiders and from archaeological evidence. It began with Batu, whose invasion in the late 1230s was as catastrophic for Russia as Chinggis Khan's invasion was for Khorasan. Catapults and battering rams pummeled cities into ruins, and thousands of people were slaughtered. The scale of the destruction is detected by art historians, who note that Russian artisanal skills declined permanently in the area.

The Horde exercised direct control over the Qipchaq steppe, but exacted tribute in a system of indirect control over the forested north and west. The latter region covered a vast area that included Russian, Ukrainian, Polish, Lithuanian, and Latvian cities. The most important among these were Kiev, Novgorod, and Moscow.

The ruling elite preferred to remain nomadic, whereas a majority of the population was settled. Unlike the Mongols in China and Iran, who assimilated to the local culture, the Qipchaqs did not live among the Russians or in any way become integrated into Russian society. On the whole, the rulers resisted the urge to raid and loot their territory, but retribution for failing to pay the quite heavy tribute was typically severe, and the armies would often engage in slave raiding even in areas that had not been targets of punishment.

The economy of this new empire was quintessentially Mongol, based on pastoralism and long-distance trade; the leaders of the Horde were interested in agriculture only insofar as it generated the revenue among the Russians that enabled them to pay tribute. Pastoralism was the means of subsistence that most Mongols wanted to retain, but they recognized the benefits that long-distance trade could bring. The security that the various Mongol regimes quite successfully enforced across the huge region from the Pacific Ocean to the Black Sea enabled merchants of all nationalities to benefit from the new commercial possibilities. Batu, like other Mongol rulers, was interested in trade, which would augment the revenues derived from taxes on peasants and townsmen. In pursuit of this objective, he established his capital of Saray near the Volga delta, situated at the crossroads of trade routes that connected China with eastern Europe in one direction and Scandinavia with Iraq and Iran, in the other. It rapidly became a commercial center with a distinctly international air. From the forested zones to the north came amber, furs, timber, Russian slaves, and honey, to be exchanged for textiles, tools, and scientific instruments from the Muslim heartland and for spices from the east.

Merchants from all nations were encouraged to live in the capital, and a wide variety of religious missionaries—Muslim, Russian Orthodox, Greek Orthodox, and Nestorian—were tolerated. The Russian Orthodox Church supported Mongol rule precisely because of the Horde's religious tolerance, and especially because of the tax exemption the regime allowed the Church. The Horde established correct relations with the Byzantines once the latter had recaptured Constantinople from the Italians in 1261, but they also welcomed Italian traders to Saray. Trade was encouraged with both the Latin Catholics and the Greek Orthodox, despite their hostility toward each other. The Mamluke regime took particular pains to foster good relations with the government at Saray because of the abundance of Qipchaq boys available to be shipped to Egypt as mamluks. Many Egyptian and Syrian craftsmen made their way to Saray to create objects of art in the Mamluke style. By contrast, the Horde's relations with its fellow Mongol regime, the Il-khanids, were hostile throughout the thirteenth century due to competing claims over the Caucasus. Several expensive wars drained the resources of both Mongol powers.

Too much can be made of the fact that Batu's brother Berke (1257–1267) was the first Mongol khan to convert to Islam. He did not pressure the remainder of the Mongol elite to convert, and he tolerated the Jesuit and Orthodox Christian missionaries who proselytized in his realm. Until the early fourteenth century, only one other khan converted to Islam, and shamanism remained the focus of the religious life of the masses. Nevertheless, Islam slowly became the dominant religion in the khanate. It had been the religion of the leaders of the Bulghar Turks along the middle Volga from the tenth century, but the religion had not expanded westward. During the era of the Horde, however, the caravans that plied the long-established routes between Syria and the lower Volga provided a means for Muslim merchants, scholars, and craftsmen, as well as wandering preachers, to make their presence felt in the realm. Mosques, the call to prayer, Ramadan observance, and numerous other signs of a growing Muslim presence provided strong witness to a vibrant Islam.

The definitive turning point in the religious history of the Horde was the conversion in 1313 of the khan Uzbeg (1313–1341). Like Berke, he did not force other members of the elite to convert, and Christianity maintained a strong and tolerated presence, but Uzbeg did expel shamanistic priests. During his reign Islam became well established as the dominant religion, at least in the urban centers. Muslims coming in from Syria or Egypt would have felt comfortable in the larger cities, particularly the capital, which Uzbeg moved upriver to New Saray on a site near the present city of Volgograd. By the end of Uzbeg's reign, the new city had large mosques and madrasas, and qadis were dispensing justice in Shari'a courts.

Uzbeg's rule represented the height of the Horde's wealth and prestige. Under him the Horde had become an international power feared and respected by other nations. Even during Uzbeg's lifetime, however, his eastern European vassals were beginning to become restless. During the reign of his two sons, Lithuania gained its independence and other regions began challenging Mongol power. With the death of Uzbeg's son Berdi-beg in 1359, the last of Batu's descendants was gone. The rival leaders within the Horde began fighting each other, and in the midst of the chaos, Moscow refused to pay tribute. A distant cousin of Berdi-beg, Toqtamish of the White Horde, seized New Saray in 1377. He crushed Novgorod and Moscow, and by 1383 he had restored Mongol control over Russia. The Horde seemed as strong as it had ever been, but Toqtamish's ambitions exceeded his good judgment. He unwisely challenged Timur Lang, who was building his power in Transoxiana. As we shall see, Timur would administer a defeat to the Horde that would shatter its mystique in the eyes of its subjects, and it would never again be so formidable.

The Il-khanate

In the aftermath of Chinggis Khan's conquest of eastern Iran during 1219–1222, a formal Mongol authority was set up only in the area of the former Khwarazmian Empire. In Khorasan and Transoxiana, anarchy reigned, interspersed with occasional Mongol raids. Hulagu's campaign through northern Iran, Iraq, and Syria in 1253–1260 inflicted further destruction in the predominantly Muslim world. Hulagu, however, proved to be a gifted administrator in the areas he had just devastated. He established his headquarters in northwestern Iran immediately after the destruction of Baghdad, and his state came to be known as the Il-khanid Empire. The name comes from *il-khan*, meaning "subject khan," in the sense of being subject to the Great Khan in China.

Like Qubilai and the leaders of the Horde, Hulagu valued the wealth that trade generated. He realized that he needed thriving cities in order to benefit from trade and that he would need a strong agricultural sector to feed the population of those cities. The southern half of Iran had not been harmed by the Mongol invasions of 1219–1222 and 1253–1260, but the northern half was in ruins. The irrigation system of qanats in Khorasan had not been rebuilt since the destruction of Chinggis Khan, and the riverine system of irrigation in Iraq had been destroyed during Hulagu's own campaign. He ordered the rebuilding of cities and the restoration of the irrigation works, but he was able to accomplish little in the five years remaining in his life. In his short reign, he did lavish patronage on art and architecture, inaugurating a policy that would eventually make his royal city of Tabriz widely admired for its beauty. He also built an astronomical observatory at Maragha, some sixty miles south of Tabriz, which became the most highly regarded scientific institute in the Muslim world.

Hulagu's efforts to rebuild Iran were handicapped by the fact that he was surrounded by enemies. The Mamlukes, the Horde, and the Chaghatay khanate were all hostile to him, forcing him to disperse his troops to confront them. The greatest threat was the Mamluke Empire, and Hulagu initiated contacts for an alliance with Louis IX of France against it, beginning a diplomatic correspondence between France and the Il-khans that lasted well into the next century. Hulagu's death in 1265 interrupted his plans to revive the economy that he and his predecessors had shattered so thoroughly in their conquests.

The next several rulers of the Il-khanid realm were remarkable for their lack of ability. For thirty years, the khanate was subject to constant infighting among the ruling elite and was the victim of neglect of the economic infrastructure. The population had suffered a catastrophic decline due to a combination of mass murder, famine, and flight, and it remained low. The peasants suffered particular hardship, for the Il-khanid rulers actually increased the taxes on villages compared to pre-conquest levels, even though both population and production had fallen precipitously. Mongol nomads stole peasants' livestock and grazed their horses on what had been prime cultivated fields. Most towns on both sides of the Euphrates were deserted, and Marco Polo described Baghdad as having been a "trading town" when he passed through it in 1272. Other major cities such as Nishapur lay in ruins until the early fourteenth century.

The early Il-khans were hostile to Islam. They had come out of a shamanistic background, but several of the leaders found Buddhism attractive. Many Buddhist monks came with Hulagu's expedition, and others arrived soon after he set up his capital. Buddhism remained strong among the male Mongol ruling elite, but many of the rulers, from Hulagu on, had Nestorian wives or concubines. For the first several decades of Il-khanid rule, the rulers clearly were more sympathetic to Buddhism and Christianity than to Islam. During this period, the Nestorian and Jacobite churches thrived across Iran as never before.

From the accession of Ghazan in 1295, those policies were reversed, and Christianity and Buddhism went into irreversible decline in the Il-khanid realm. Ghazan (1295–1304) was the greatest of the Il-khans after Hulagu. A Buddhist, he proclaimed his conversion to Islam in the first year of his rule and ordered the destruction of churches, synagogues, and Buddhist temples throughout the realm. He initiated many reforms in order to build up his regime's wealth and prestige. He began the restoration of irrigation systems, reduced taxes and exchange rates, and reformed the system of weights and measures. The agricultural economy began a slow recovery, and for over two decades, tax revenues showed a steady increase.

In contrast to the agricultural decline throughout the thirteenth century, the Il-khanid regime boasted a sparkling urban life in certain areas. Hostile relations with the Mamlukes had interrupted the historic long-distance trade with Syria and Egypt, but trade with China intensified. The Il-khans were also as eager to please

An illuminated manuscript from the Il-khanid period, revealing Chinese influences.

Italian and other European merchants as were their cousins in the Horde. Tabriz thrived on the new commercial life. Its location placed it on excellent trade routes. Iranian and Iraqi scholars and artists who had not fled to other lands in the face of the Mongol conquests made their way to Tabriz to enhance their careers. Hulagu's astronomical observatory at Maragha became famous for thousands of miles. Nasir al-Din al-Tusi, who had joined Hulagu's retinue at the siege of Alamut, was its first director, and it attracted astronomers and mathematicians from as far away as Andalus and China. It surpassed anything that Europe would offer until the career of Tycho Brahe in the late sixteenth century.

Under Uljaytu (1304–1316), Il-khanid literature, history, architecture, and painting blossomed. He constructed a new capital at Sultaniya, for which he commissioned magnificent tombs, mosques, bazaars, and schools. Because of close trading relations with the Great Khan in China, Chinese styles and techniques began to influence the plastic arts of the Il-khanate. The Chinese influence is particularly striking in the manufacture of porcelains and in the emergence of Persian miniature painting.

Just as it appeared that the Il-khans had established a regime that would enable them to create a stable administration and a thriving economy, family feuds broke out into the open. Uljaytu's son Abu Sa'id (1316–1335) was a devout Muslim, fluent in Arabic and Persian, musically talented, and determined to continue the rehabilitation of his empire's economy. In 1335, however, he was poisoned, and anarchy broke out as ambitious chieftains struggled for supremacy. By midcentury, Iran and Iraq had been carved up by numerous successor states headed by Mongol, Turkic, Iranian, or Arab families. The populace once again sank into poverty and despair, and then, as we shall see, the northern arc of Iran was devastated by Timur Lang. Not for two centuries did the area begin to recover economically.

The Chaghatay Khanate

The Chaghatay khanate was separated from the Il-khanid realm by the Amu Darya River and by a line of fortresses east of Herat. In the west, only the grazing areas of some Mongol and Turkic pastoralists separated it from the territory of the Horde. In the east, its territory extended into modern Xinjiang province in China, which encompasses the remarkable Tarim Basin.

The Tarim Basin consists largely of an absolutely barren desert the size of the state of Texas. The desert is surrounded by a series of oases that served not only as fertile crop-producing areas, but also as rest areas for the southern Silk Road. The oases exploit the fertile alluvial soil that has been washed down over the ages from the mountains ringing the basin on three sides. These are some of the most formidable mountain ranges in the world. To the west are the Pamir Mountains; to the north are the Tien Shan Mountains; and to the south are the Kunlun Mountains. All three ranges are covered perpetually in snow and are laced with numerous glaciers. Their average altitude is over 20,000 feet, and all have peaks that exceed 24,000 feet. The Pamirs have subranges that run east and west and others that run north and south; merchants on the southern Silk Road often experienced dizziness and nausea while crossing it. The Tien Shan are formidable barriers to transit between the Tarim and Mongolia, but predatory bands found ways to get through. The Kunlun, on the other hand, constitute an impenetrable barrier to Tibet in the south.

The Chaghatay khanate thus extended over vast steppe land, some of the world's most inaccessible mountains, and the sophisticated urban oases of Transoxiana. The khans themselves retained the original features of the Mongol traditions more than did their cousins in the Horde, Il-khanate, or Yuan dynasty. Whereas the Yuan and Il-khan dynasties became urbanized quickly and the Horde fostered the development of mercantile interests in their capital of New Saray, the Chaghatays remained nomadic in lifestyle and outlook. The ruling family did not settle down into one of the great cities. The closest to a capital that it had was an encampment between Lake Balkhash and the Tien Shan. The ruling family never lost its contempt for urban life, and they treated cities as fields to be harvested. The khans plundered and looted their own cities more than once. The fate of Bukhara is representative. Within twenty years of its destruction in 1220 by Chinggis Khan, it had largely recovered its prosperity. By the early 1270s, Marco Polo, passing through Khorasan, heard that it and Samarqand were the most splendid cities in Iran. However, in 1273, and again in 1316, the Chaghatay rulers sacked, burned, and depopulated Bukhara.

Kebek (1318–1326) was the first Chaghatay to prefer urban life to a nomadic existence, and under him Samarqand and Bukhara enjoyed a revival. Despite his efforts at rebuilding those cities, however, as early as 1334 the great Moroccan traveler Ibn Battuta found many of the mosques, colleges, and bazaars of Bukhara in ruins again. Because of the antipathy of most of the Chaghatays to urban life, we have little evidence to indicate that any of the rulers other than Kebek patronized literature and the arts. On the other hand, it is clear that long-distance trade continued to be conducted through Transoxiana throughout the thirteenth and fourteenth century. The repeated rebuilding of the cities of Transoxiana, and the pronounced Chinese influence on Il-khanid arts, speak eloquently of a well-established commercial life linking China and southwestern Asia which refused to die even in a hostile cultural environment.

The ruling elite of the Chaghatay khanate was a loose coalition of Mongols, Turks, and Uighurs (a Turkic-speaking people who inhabited the oases of the Tarim), in addition to a few Muslim Iranians who were appointed governors of Transoxiana. As in the Horde, Turkish culture soon became predominant. Shamanist religious practices remained strong among the nomadic population, although Buddhism made inroads, particularly among the nomads of the Tarim. The Uighurs, on the other hand, gradually Islamized, as did the Turkic nomads who settled down in Transoxiana.

In 1326, a new khan, Tarmashirin (1326–1334) came to the throne. He had been a Buddhist ("Tarma" in his name derives from "dharma"), but he became the first Chaghatay ruler to convert to Islam. When he converted, he required all the important leaders in the khanate to follow suit. The order antagonized his chieftains in the east, and they became restive. When Tarmashirin was unsuccessful in his attack on Delhi in 1327, these chieftains seized the opportunity to revolt. After seven years of civil war, the khanate split in 1334. The Tarim basin and the area north of the Tien Shan Mountains were paired in an unlikely entity that became known as Moghulistan. It remained a regional political actor for two more centuries, and members of the House of Chagatay exercised at least nominal authority in the area into the twentieth century. Ironically, the more wealthy Transoxiana was bereft of a central government. A handful of tribes dominated the area, and the towns and cities became prey to the raids of nomads and seminomads. The merchants and ulama of Samarqand and Bukhara could only hope for a leader to arise who would restore to their cities the vitality and glory of their fabled past. By the last quarter of the century, they would find him in Timur Lang.

Thus, all four of the Mongol empires collapsed quite suddenly within a period of just over thirty years. The Chaghatay khanate splintered in 1334, leaving only a minor principality behind; the Il-khans disappeared in 1335; the Horde collapsed in 1359; and in Beijing the Chinese overthrew the Yuan dynasty of the Great Khan in 1368. The only descendant of Chinggis Khan who still exercised authority was in isolated Mogulistan, and the only other Mongol with a powerful state was Toqtamish, who seized power in Saray in 1377. Despite the short period of formal Mongol rule, the Mongol legacy would continue to exercise a powerful effect on the imagination of the peoples of Central Asia.

New Centers of Islamic Culture

For six hundred years, the most influential forces shaping the legacy of the Qur'an and the Hadith into an Islamic civilization had been the creative communities of Iraq and Iran. Their decline had begun even before the Mongol threat, but the invasions of Chinggis Khan and Hulagu, followed by decades of Mongol misrule, were devastating in their effect. Now, as Iran and Iraq suffered, Muslim military power and cultural vibrancy shifted to the geographical fringes of the historic heartland. The Mamluke Empire, the Delhi Sultanate, and the Ottoman Sultanate assumed the dominant roles for the Islamic world in the thirteenth and fourteenth centuries. All three of them left permanent legacies for Islamic history.

The Mamluke Empire

The irruption of the Mongols into western Asia profoundly altered the geopolitics of the eastern Mediterranean. Egypt under the Mamlukes now rose to a position of influence that it had not enjoyed since Hellenistic times. By virtue of their triumph over Hulagu's army at 'Ayn Jalut in 1260, the Mamlukes of Egypt gained the respect and gratitude of Muslims everywhere. The regime continued to enhance its reputation for military prowess by repelling an Il-khan invasion of Syria in 1281, eradicating the last of the Crusader strongholds from the Syrian mainland by 1291, and by preventing further Il-khan attempts to annex Syria during the period 1299–1303. As a result, they expanded the control over Syria that rulers in Cairo had aimed for since early Fatimid times, and they occupied the Holy Cities of the Hijaz.

The Mamlukes constituted one of the most formidable military forces in the world from the thirteenth through the fifteenth centuries. Although that fact alone would merit their place in history, they attract attention primarily because of their unusual recruitment policy. Muslim governments had relied upon slave soldiers since the early ninth century, but the Mamluke regime is distinguished by the fact that the rulers themselves were of slave origin. The staffing of the highest positions in the state relied upon a well-organized system of slave importation and training. Slave merchants combed foreign markets—primarily in the Qipchaq steppe—for young boys ten to twelve years of age. They sold the boys to the sultan and to the several dozen amirs who were the most powerful men in the empire other than the sultan himself. These included the vizier, other chief court officials, provincial governors, and military officers. Each official then provided several years of training for the boys.

The "curriculum" included instruction in the basic rituals of Islam and rigorous drilling in the cavalry arts of the bow and the lance. The sultan, of course, was able to provide the most elaborate program. His slaves lived together in barracks, were drilled in the arts of cavalry warfare, and were taught basic literacy. They learned that their survival depended on loyalty to their master and to their fellow recruits. Upon completion of the training, their master granted them their freedom and gave them their military equipment and an estate to supply the revenue to maintain the expenses of their horses, arms, and armor.

The graduates of the sultan's school became members of the "royal mamluks," who numbered 5000–6000 during the late thirteenth and early fourteenth centuries. Enjoying the highest status of all the troops, they demanded to be stationed in or around Cairo rather than at posts remote from the center of power. The mamluks of the amirs were stationed in the provinces and at the homes of their masters. The Mamluke army, then, was characterized by an organization not unlike a feudal army of contemporary western Europe. At its core were the sultan's troops, who were loyal to him; supplementing them were the dozens of regiments that were loyal to their respective amirs, who in turn were loyal to the sultan. When the corps of the mamluks were supplemented by cavalry of the auxiliary units (freeborn troops who included local Egyptians, Syrians, and foreign soldiers of fortune), the regime could mobilize 40,000–50,000 cavalrymen, in addition to infantry.

Regardless of who their master was, the mamluks were intensely loyal to him and to their brothers in arms. This loyalty, by virtue of which the master was viewed as the mamluks' father and they called each other brothers, also meant that it was almost impossible for a mamluk who was transferred from one amir to another to be accepted by the new group. The sense of exclusivity also meant that the mamluks always felt a social distance between them and the society they ruled. They passed laws prohibiting civilians (Muslim as well as non-Muslim) from riding horses. They also adhered to a policy of marrying slave women (usually from the areas where they themselves came), and even their concubines were not of local origin. Some exceptions occurred, but local marriages were rare. Because the mamluks' sons by such wives and concubines were not slaves, they did not receive the training of the slave boys and found themselves overlooked in the competition for the best positions. They could serve in the lower status auxiliary units, but with the exception of several of the sultans' sons and brothers, they did not advance to the highest ranks. Thus, the perpetuation of the regime required the continual purchase of new slaves.

The Mamluke system was remarkable for its combination of power and latent anarchy. On the one hand, it fostered an esprit de corps among its soldiers that, combined with the high level of training, resulted in a formidable military force. On the other hand, the system of purchasing and manumitting slave troops created a system of cliques and factions that was a constant threat to peace and security. The system was most vulnerable during the process of succession to the leadership of the state. Each sultan wished to pass his office to his son, but the amirs demanded the right to ratify the choice of the next sultan. The amirs were not being presumptuous: They were adhering to the traditions of their common Turkish background, and they were well aware that the new sultan's "family" of troops would expect to displace the existing bureaucratic and military officials. Those who were threatened with the loss of their positions sought out allies among the other amirs, and those already in office did the same. Such a transition of power almost always led to fighting and scores of deaths.

The dynamics of this process were in evidence from the early years of the empire. Baybars, a talented and ruthless sultan, ruled for seventeen years (1260–1277). He named his son to succeed him, but his son was overthrown by Baybars' own troops. In 1293, another sultan was overthrown by a conspiracy of amirs, and his ten-year-old brother, al-Nasir Muhammad, was installed on the throne by yet another faction. He was deposed a year later, then reinstalled in 1299, only to be deposed again in 1309. By this time in his mid-twenties, the young ex-sultan seized the throne himself in 1310 and enjoyed the longest and most successful rule in Mamluke history (1310–1341). The nature of the Mamluke system guaranteed political instability, and its entire history was punctuated by frequent violence among the mamluks themselves. Fortunately, although the Egyptian and Syrian citizens whom the mamluks ruled were occasionally harassed and often exploited by them, they were not frequent victims of the political violence, which was largely restricted to the ruling elite themselves.

The mamluks who seized control of Egypt and Syria in 1250 from their "masters" in the Ayyubid dynasty were Qipchaq Turks. Their homeland was the Qipchaq steppe, which, as we have seen, had become the domain of the Horde a few years before the coup d'état in Cairo. The Mamluke regime needed a constant supply of slave soldiers, but the traditional supply route for them by 1260 lay through hostile Il-khanid territory. Baybars began a two-pronged diplomatic effort to develop a new supply route. In a fortuitous development for him, the Byzantines now reappeared in diplomatic affairs for the first time in several decades. The Byzantine royal family had been living in exile in Nicaea ever since the Venetians conquered Constantinople in the so-called Fourth Crusade of 1204. After decades of Byzantine frustration, the emperor Michael VIII Palaeologus (1259–1282) recaptured Constantinople from the Venetians in 1261. Threatened by the Venetians to the west and Turkish raiders to the east, the emperor needed to be on good terms with both Berke of the Horde and Baybars of the Mamlukes. He agreed to facilitate the mamluk trade between the Horde and Egypt, and he refurbished an Umayyad-era mosque in Constantinople as a gesture of good will to Baybars. He even made a promise to give Egypt military aid if needed.

Baybars also cultivated diplomatic relations with the Horde. The alliance became progressively easier to maintain because both regimes were Muslim, the Horde was continually assimilating to the Qipchaq culture into which the mamluks were born, and the two empires had no reason to quarrel over territory. On the other hand, both empires had hostile relations with the Il-khans, with the result that the natural trade routes through Iran and Iraq were never accessible. The two Muslim allies therefore maintained good relations with the Christian Byzantines in order to keep the shipping route open between Egypt and the Black Sea. The trade route opened up opportunities for merchants to purchase boys who were of Greek, Georgian, and Slavic origin as well, some of whom became mamluks. Beginning in the late thirteenth century, however, the largest number of non-Turkish mamluks were Circassians, members of an ethnic group whose origin was the area of the Caucasus on the northeastern shore of the Black Sea.

Baybars was as careful to develop economic ties as he was to cultivate diplomatic contacts. Mediterranean trade in the thirteenth century was dominated by

Europeans. The fleets of Italian city–states by that time had obtained a near monopoly of naval power. By virtue of Baybars' campaigns against the Crusader ports of Syria and Palestine (he captured all the remaining Crusader forts except Acre), the once-flourishing Italian trade with Syria was destroyed. Baybars realized that he could redirect that trade to Egypt, and he negotiated treaties with several Italian maritime powers in an effort to secure a share in the profits of the Mediterranean trade. Egypt's maritime commerce grew steadily in volume over the next century, and Alexandria experienced an economic boom as a result. The Mamlukes regained the dominant position in the trade between the Mediterranean and the Indian Ocean that Egypt had lost during the era of the Crusades. They maintained good relations with Venice and Genoa, whose ships transported most of the slaves from the Black Sea and whose merchants purchased the spices that came to Egypt from India and the East Indies.

Realizing the need for a vibrant economy to support their military machine and their high standard of living, the Mamlukes supported the crafts and manufacturing as well as trade. During the early fourteenth century, they invested in huge paper-making factories and sugar refineries. They encouraged the export of sugar to Italy, southern France, Catalonia, Flanders, England, and the Baltic Sea. The most important Egyptian industry continued to be the manufacture of cotton and linen textiles, both of which were in great demand during this period in both the Muslim world and in Europe.

With their wealth, the Mamlukes patronized learning and the arts. During the Mongol devastation of Iran and Iraq in the first half of the thirteenth century, both Damascus and Cairo had welcomed scholars and merchants fleeing the destruction of their homelands. Due to the influx of Iranian and Iraqi scholars, and the destruction of Baghdad in 1258, the two cities became the greatest centers of Islamic learning during the late Ayyubid period. As the capital city of the Mamluke empire, Cairo surpassed Damascus in importance and imperial stature, and it remained the cultural capital of the Muslim world at least until the late fifteenth century. Through patronage of culture, Mamluke sultans attempted to legitimize their rule by winning favor with the ulama and the masses alike. One time-honored way for rulers to impress upon the public the grandeur of their reign is through the construction of impressive buildings, and the Mamlukes were no exception in this regard. They vied with their predecessors in endowing magnificent madrasas, mosques, Sufi lodges, and hospitals, in addition to constructing enormous tombs for themselves. Some of the most impressive buildings to be found in Syria and Egypt to this day are the result of Mamluke patronage of monumental architecture.

Baybars installed a member of the Abbasid family as caliph in Cairo after he consolidated his power. It is impossible to assess the actual impact of this symbolic act. The caliph was not recognized outside the empire, and he wielded no influence in the government. On the other hand, his presence was politically useful for the government and psychologically important for many Egyptians and Syrians. More tangible were changes that the regime made in the patronage of the religious institutions. Previous Muslim regimes had favored one or another school of law, but the Mamlukes were the first to endow all four schools and to appoint qadis for each one.

The period 1260–1341 was the high point of Mamluke history, and the third reign of al-Nasir Muhammad (1310–1341) was its apogee. During al-Nasir's reign, there were neither famines nor plagues in the empire, a stark contrast with the late

Fatimid and early Ayyubid periods. The population grew, and prosperity soared. The death of al-Nasir Muhammad in 1341 marked the end of the golden age for the Mamlukes, even though they would continue to rule for almost two hundred more years, until 1517. Beginning in the last decade of the thirteenth century, ethnic rivalry between the Qipchaqs and the Circassians escalated, and fierce clashes broke out when al-Nasir Muhammad died. Struggles between the two groups caused chronic violence for the next forty years. Members of al-Nasir's family held the office of the sultanate during that time, but they were puppets of the factions who placed them on the throne. Thus, political instability in the Mamluke Empire occurred simultaneously with the collapse of the Mongol khanates.

To complicate matters, the plague, or Black Death, struck the Mamluke realm with at least the level of ferocity in 1348 that it did Europe, killing one-fourth to one-third of the population. For the next century and a half, the epidemics recurred at a rate of more than once per decade, causing the population to continue to decline. As agriculture and commerce plummeted, a Circassian group of Mamlukes seized power in 1382, and the Qipchaq era was over. The Circassians dominated the empire until their defeat at the hands of the Ottomans in 1517.

The Delhi Sultanate

The Arab invasions of 711–713 established an Islamic presence in the middle and lower Indus valley, but in terms of both geography and influence, the settlements there remained on the periphery of the Islamic world for several centuries. The Abbasids lost control of the area in the ninth century, and several of the towns in the valley soon came under the control of Isma'ilis who looked to Fatimid Cairo for guidance. In the eleventh century, however, Mahmud of Ghazna expanded his aggressive and predatory Muslim state into the Indus basin. The Ghaznavids inaugurated an era of seven centuries that would witness a series of powerful, autonomous Muslim states in South Asia (the area south of the Hindu Kush and Himalaya mountain ranges). Usually ruled by Turks or Afghans, each dynasty attempted to maintain an identifiably Muslim court in an overwhelmingly Hindu society. The model they found most congenial was the Islamic–Persian style that developed in northeastern Iran with the Samanid court of the tenth century. Until the advent of the Mughals, the greatest of these Muslim states was the Delhi Sultanate.

Mahmud of Ghazna laid the foundations for a powerful Muslim presence in South Asia. He raided the Punjab area as early as 1002, and captured Lahore in 1030. When the Saljuqs chased Mahmud's successor out of Khorasan ten years later, Lahore increasingly became the most important city in the remaining areas of the Ghaznavid Empire, and it developed into a thriving center of Islamic culture.

In 1173, an Afghan family from the region of Ghur seized power in Ghazna and began a systematic conquest of Ghaznavid holdings in the Punjab, which they accomplished by 1192. Not content with the Punjab, these Ghurids conquered Delhi in 1193 and occupied areas as far east as Bihar on the lower Ganges. Their military power can be gauged by the fact that, while they were conquering the Punjab and the Ganges, they were also winning Khorasan from the shahs of Khwarazm, often regarded as the greatest Muslim military power of the day until their defeat by

Chinggis Khan. The Ghurid realm grew until it extended from Bihar through Khorasan. But just as the Ghurids were poised to create a major state in South Asia, their ruler was assassinated in 1206, leaving no son to inherit the throne. The general who conquered Delhi for the Ghurids took over the reins of power in both Delhi and Lahore. But he in turn died in a polo accident in 1210. His former military slave, Iltutmish, then seized power. Iltutmish (1210–1236) is regarded to be the founder of the Delhi Sultanate, although it was over a decade before he made Delhi preeminent over Lahore.

Although the Delhi Sultanate was composed of several different dynasties, it is regarded as a single period in Muslim–Indian history because of the continuity of the ruling elite. Historians disagree on the issue of its duration. Some point out that it was the dominant state in South Asia from 1210 to 1398 and limit their treatment of the sultanate to the three dynasties of that period. Other historians include two later dynasties, in which case the sultanate's history is considered to last until the arrival of the Mughals in 1526. Regardless of how one defines the duration of the sultanate, each dynasty began of either Turkish or Afghan lineage. Like almost all other Muslim regimes (the major exception was that of the Mamlukes), the rulers might choose wives or concubines of strikingly different ethnic origin, but the patrilineal system of tracing one's ancestors made it natural for each generation to see itself as the heir to the founder of the dynasty and to identify with his ethnic origin.

The early Delhi Sultanate experienced the same degree of political turbulence that the Mamluke regime did. The entire period from 1210 to 1320 was one of political tumult among the ruling elite itself. Powerful amirs attempted to check the power of others, and violence often resulted. Between 1236 and 1296, ten sultans reigned, eight of whom averaged a reign of less than three years. Only one of the ten is known to have died a natural death. Despite having to confront almost constant challenges within the elite and violent changes of dynasties in 1290 and 1320, the sultanate successfully withstood threats from the Mongols. A Mongol expedition actually sacked Lahore in 1241, but between 1290 and 1327, the Chaghatay khanate's attacks were repulsed at least nine times.

In the periods between internal clashes and Mongol attacks, the sultanate expanded its area of control. By 1230, Iltutmish dominated a wide arc based on the Indus and Ganges river valleys. In that year, he sought and won recognition from the Abbasid caliph in Baghdad as the legitimate Muslim ruler of the area. By the early fourteenth century, the sultanate had extended its authority to Gujarat and the Deccan plateau, in addition to controlling most of the Ganges valley and the Punjab. Until the 1320s, the regime exercised authority in the conquered areas by a variety of means. The sultanate ruled directly in some areas, and in other areas it exacted tribute from Hindu or Muslim princes who were allowed to rule with little oversight.

The most influential of the Delhi dynasties was that of the Tughluq family, whose effective rule was from 1320 to 1388, although members of the family remained on the throne until 1413. Muhammad ibn Tughluq (1325–1351) was the most famous of the family. He was a fascinating figure of undoubted intellectual and creative talents, but his administration was a disappointment. On the one hand, he continued his father's military campaigns and managed to extend the authority of the sultanate over almost all of South Asia. His domain extended from the Himalayas almost to the southern tip of the peninsula, and from the Punjab to Bengal. He also defeated the Chaghatay ruler Tarmashirin at the very gate of Delhi in 1327, the event that indirectly resulted in the division of the Chaghatay khanate into Transoxiana and Mogulistan. He was an accomplished scholar, proficient in both Arabic and Persian, and he recruited numerous new qadis from abroad in a major effort to facilitate the implementation of Islamic law. Toward his Hindu and Jain subjects, he practiced a conciliatory policy of offering them high positions in the government, allowing them to build new temples and inviting them to court to debate philosophical and theological issues.

Although these policies seem like the strategies of an accomplished politician, Muhammad actually found it difficult to devise realistic policies for some important issues. His fastidious need for symmetry made it impossible for him to tolerate the variety of relations that existed between the central government and the multitude of provinces that were at least nominally subject to it. He instituted a uniform policy of direct rule for all regions, provoking widespread resentment in the areas that had been allowed a degree of autonomy by previous Delhi sultans. The biggest problem was in the Deccan plateau. The area was hundreds of miles south of Delhi, and the Hindu rulers there had no intention of yielding on the issue of indirect rule. Muhammad thought that he could resolve the problem of distance by moving the capital from Delhi to the more centrally located site of Dawlatabad in the Deccan, but the change was implemented in a heavy-handed fashion that provoked resentment among his own followers.

These, and other unpopular measures, were followed by a catastrophic drought and famine in the Punjab and the Ganges valley during the years 1335–1342. The suffering brought on by the drought became the pretext for widespread rebellions throughout the northern tier of the sultanate, forcing Muhammad to lead his army on repeated campaigns to the northern as well as southern provinces of his realm. He responded to the uprisings, and even to the whisperings of criticism of his policies, with brutal punishment that caused him to develop a reputation for cruelty. By the end of his rule, he had lost control of his southern possessions, including Bengal, and the support of most of his remaining subjects.

The reign of Muhammad's cousin Firuz (1351–1388) stood in sharp contrast to that of his own. Firuz practiced clemency where Muhammad had been brutal, although he responded to Muslim criticisms of his cousin's religious toleration by destroying newly built Hindu temples and promoting proselytizing efforts among the Hindu majority. He made a concerted effort to assist the agricultural sector of the economy by constructing irrigation projects, and he promoted employment by building a new capital city near Delhi. In the end, however, he had not made a convincing case for the continuing authority of Delhi. When Firuz died in 1388, a power struggle broke out among his sons and grandsons. Many of the Hindu and Muslim rulers of the provinces took advantage of the confusion to renounce their allegiance to the dynasty, plunging the sultanate into a civil war that lasted a decade.

Delhi was not on a major trade route and probably would never have become the center of the sultanate had it not been for the Mongol threat. Chinggis Khan's return route to Mongolia in 1222 passed through the Punjab, persuading Iltutmish to establish his headquarters at Delhi rather than at the Ghurid capital of Lahore. On the other hand, the valley of the Indus, the Punjab, and the Gangetic plain were all rich agricultural regions that supplied Delhi with wealth, and the acquisition of

Gujarat granted the city access to the wider world of commerce. Gujarat was famous for its fine cotton cloths as well as for its role as an entrepot. Commodities shipped there from Southeast Asia or East Africa would be transshipped to yet another port, such as Hormuz in the Persian Gulf.

As the capital of a rich and powerful regime, Delhi attracted soldiers, merchants, craftsmen, scribes, and scholars. Like Cairo and Damascus, it was a haven for refugees fleeing the depredations of Chinggis Khan and Hulagu. The Delhi sultans welcomed and offered patronage to foreign scholars and artisans, whose work enhanced the glory of the regime. Outstanding ulama were appointed to serve as qadis and administrators in the government, particularly during the reign of Muhammad ibn Tughluq, who seems to have been willing to trust foreign officeholders more than local ones. Most of the intellectuals who emigrated to Delhi came from Khorasan and Transoxiana, reinforcing the Persianate cast of the elite culture that had been bequeathed by the Ghaznavids to the Punjab. Poetry, music, and historical works composed in Persian flourished under the regime. Architecture, likewise, reflected the styles that had been developing in Iran and Central Asia. Magnificent mosques, Sufi lodges, madrasas, tombs, and palaces incorporated the vaulted halls, pointed domes, blue faience tiles, and gold plating of the Persian-speaking region. No contemporary Muslim city exceeded the architectural splendor of Delhi.

The sultanate shared many common characteristics with those of Muslim regimes to the west, but it was distinctive in one major feature: Not in several centuries had the Muslim rulers of any other major state represented such a small minority of the population. The population of the sultanate at its height (ca. 1310–1340) was remarkably complex linguistically. Over one thousand languages and dialects were spoken in South Asia. From the perspective of a Muslim government, however, the issue of religion was more vexing than that of language. During the thirteenth and fourteenth centuries, the Muslims of the sultanate were a tiny minority of the total population. For many Muslims the ultimate responsibility for any Muslim ruler was the protection and advancement of the faith. Although opinions varied regarding what this duty actually entailed, for most it seems to have included the enforcement of the Shari'a, the toleration of Jews and Christians within certain prescribed guidelines, and the eradication of polytheism.

In the Delhi Sultanate, the tension between the religious duty of the ruler on the one hand and the social reality on the other reached a level inconceivable in the rest of the Islamic world. The sultans depended on millions of Hindu laborers, troops, bureaucrats, carpenters, masons, metallurgists, bankers, and merchants. The Ghaznavids, the Ghurids, and the early sultans at Delhi exploited the religious issue when they raided Hindu towns and temples, but as the later sultans began to consolidate their holdings, they followed a more pragmatic policy. The fourteenth-century rulers Muhammad ibn Tughluq and his successor Firuz exemplify the range of possibilities available to the Muslim rulers of South Asia in their treatment of non-Muslims. The former's generosity to Hindus and Jains was criticized by devout Muslims, and the latter's punitive measures against non-Muslims contributed to the outbreak of the civil war that followed his death in 1388. As we shall see, the disorder of that period exposed northern India to perhaps the greatest catastrophe that it has ever experienced: the invasion of Timur Lang.

The thirteenth-century Qutb mosque in Delhi.

The Ottoman Sultanate

The third of the great Muslim states to emerge on the periphery of the Islamic heartland in the thirteenth century was that of the Ottomans. During the second half of the fifteenth century it achieved the status of an empire, and it went on to become one of the greatest and most durable states in world history. It collapsed only after World War I. During the period prior to the fifteenth century, when its territory was relatively compact and its reputation was only regional, its status may best described as that of a "sultanate."

Until the Saljuq defeat of the Byzantines at Manzikert in 1071, Anatolia was hostile territory to the Muslims and represented a seemingly impenetrable barrier to Muslim expansion. After the battle, the entire peninsula lay open to unlimited Turkish migration for a quarter of a century. In 1098, the knights of the First Crusade discovered that Nicaea (Iznik), just a few miles east of Constantinople, was the capital of the Saljuq Sultanate of Rum. They forced the sultanate back onto the Anatolian plateau, where the Saljuqs established their capital at Konya.

For the next two centuries, the pattern of settlement in Anatolia did not change much. The Turks controlled the central plateau and the east. The majority of the population under their control remained Christian peasants, although conversions and emigration ensured that the Christian population was slowly declining throughout this period. Three independent Christian states lay on the periphery of the peninsula. On the southern shore was the Armenian kingdom of Cilicia (sometimes known as Lesser Armenia). In the extreme west was the Byzantine state, which moved its capital to Nicaea when the soldiers of the Fourth Crusade captured and sacked Constantinople in 1204. The Byzantines returned the capital to Constantinople when they retook the city in 1261, but their former subjects in Trebizon, on the Black Sea coast, refused to recognize the new emperor and insisted on their independence. The zones between the three Christian states and the Turkish-controlled area were the domain of the frontier warriors known as gazis.

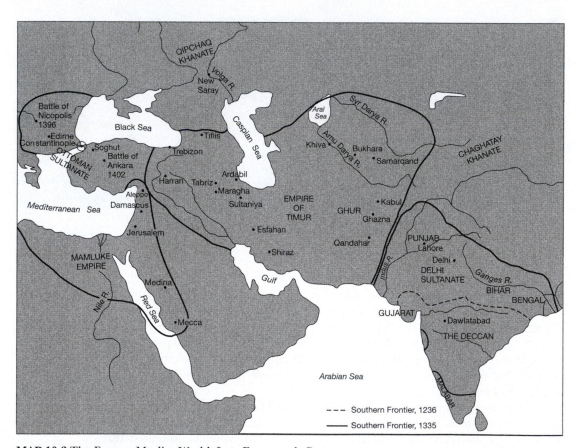

MAP 10.2 The Eastern Muslim World, Late Fourteenth Century

The Sultanate of Rum was the dominant Turkish power in the peninsula. It frequently cooperated with its neighboring Christian states, and as an urban society, it sometimes had tense relations with the gazis, or raiders, on the frontiers. Occasionally it restrained the gazis when their activities caused problems for their diplomatic relations with the Christian states. Despite the often peaceful relations with its neighboring Christian kingdoms, however, the history of the sultanate was punctuated by violence. For several decades, it had to contend for primacy with several other Turkish dynasties in the area, and after having established its supremacy, it had to subdue challengers. In addition, the dynasty followed the Saljuq tradition according to which the sons of the ruler fought each other for control of the sultanate upon their father's death.

Despite the frequent violence, however, the sultanate managed to establish an urban culture that was more vibrant than had been seen in Anatolia in several centuries. It synthesized several cultural traditions. Saljuq monumental architecture incorporated Byzantine styles, an emerging Turkish Sufi musical repertoire adapted Orthodox Christian musical themes for its own purposes, and Turkish immigrants were influenced by local customs and mores in countless ways.

Persian models of government, art, and literature also influenced the culture of the Rum sultanate. The early sultans admired the Persian cultural tradition, but the Persian influence became even stronger when Konya became a haven for Iranian refugees fleeing the destruction caused by Chinggis Khan in the 1220s. The products of the newly-arrived scholars, architects, and craftsmen transformed Konya into a lively cultural center. It became famous for its beautiful mosques, madrasas, caravanserais, and other monuments, as well as for the mesmerizing lyrics of the great Sufi poet Rumi, whose career unfolded there. Although non-Muslims probably constituted ninety percent of the population in the early thirteenth century, Konya's prestige aided in the Islamization of the sultanate. The visibility of mosques, the ubiquity of the call to prayer, and the fact that Islam was the religion of the ruling elite played important roles in the growing Islamic identity of the Anatolian plateau.

Mongol armies shattered the sultanate as decisively as they had destroyed other regimes and societies from China to central Europe. Batu of the Golden Horde challenged the sultanate at Kose Dagh in 1243 and won a decisive victory. The Saljuq army disintegrated, and Konya never again wielded effective influence outside its own environs. The sultanate withered away during several decades of tortured civil war, until it disappeared in the early fourteenth century. In 1260 Hulagu asserted his authority in the eastern half of the peninsula, and that region became part of the Il-khanate.

Although the Il-khanid regime continued to nourish the Persian strain in the high culture of eastern Anatolia, it also sparked a new wave of Turkish immigration into the peninsula. The second half of the thirteenth century witnessed the migration of tens of thousands of Turks into the area. Hulagu's conquests had left many of them displaced and in desperate straits; others had served as troops and were now in quest of further military adventures; and still others were simply taking advantage of new opportunities that had arisen in the wake of Hulagu's victories. As they entered Anatolia, the process of the Turkification of the peninsula accelerated. In the central region of the peninsula, neither the Il-khans nor the sultanate of Rum wielded effective authority, and it became a no-man's-land of anarchy. Many of the new immigrants resorted to sheer banditry to survive. Others continued to the fringes of the peninsula, where they augmented the existing groups of gazi fighters.

The Turkish migration began just as the Byzantines gained their revenge on their Latin enemies. When Michael Palaeologus unexpectedly recaptured Constantinople from the Venetians in 1261, the Byzantines eagerly anticipated a revival of imperial power. Unfortunately for them, they now faced a conjunction of challenges. To the west, rival Christian states—both Orthodox and Catholic—were planning to seize the wealthy Byzantine capital; and to the east, the new Turkish migrants were swelling the ranks of the gazis. The gazis were discovering that, when the Byzantines had relocated their capital to Constantinople, they had neglected their defense structure in Anatolia. After mid-century, the ambitious gazi chieftains who until then had been held in check by both Nicaea and Konya now began to carve out independent principalities in the western third of the peninsula. Many of the Turkish newcomers joined the ranks of the successful raiders, enabling some of the chieftains to establish thriving bases of power even along the Aegean coast. By the end of the century, some were hiring renegade Byzantine sailors to help them raid Aegean islands. Although the Byzantine emperor's diplomacy had protected his realm from the Sultanate of Rum, the Horde, the Mamlukes, and the Il-khans, it was futile against the gazi tradition, which had gained a new life with the arrival of large numbers of Turkish immigrants.

One of the gazi regimes was led by a chieftain named Osman, who was born in about 1260. He developed a power base at Soghut, only a few miles east of Bursa. From there, Osman had opportunities to tax merchants who were using the trade route that connected the Aegean with Central Asia, and he could raid Byzantine territory. By virtue of his successful raids, he attracted a growing number of gazis and adventurers. Many of the latter included Christians. Thus, the early Ottomans reflected the typical gazi band, which was not a group related by kinship ties, but rather a mixture of many different peoples, Turkic and Turkicized, who chose to participate in a dynamic organization.

At some point (possibly long after Osman's death), Osman's group became known as Ottomans, or "followers of Osman." Taking advantage of the Byzantines' deadly rivalries with the Bulgars, Serbs, Venetians, Genoans, and other Christian powers, they laid an extended siege to Bursa and took it in 1326, just after Osman died. His son Orhan (1326–1362) made Bursa his capital city, and from there he captured Nicaea (1329; later renamed Iznik) and Nicomedia (1337; later renamed Izmit), the last major Byzantine cities in Anatolia.

Osman and Orhan, like all contemporary successful leaders of volunteer military forces, had to provide outlets for the energies, appetites, and religious fervor of their followers. Success necessitated further success, for victories generated new recruits who expected glory and treasure, and the veterans of previous campaigns soon felt the need for new exploits. There is little doubt that Orhan would have eventually crossed the Dardanelles on his own, due to the fact that beyond it lay a vast territory that was Christian, wealthy, and increasingly riven by conflicts among weak states. As it turned out, however, in 1345, he was invited to cross by a Byzantine faction vying for power in the capital city, just as earlier Byzantines had invited the Saljuqs into western Anatolia at the end of the eleventh century. After enabling his Byzantine ally to gain the throne, Orhan remained interested in the Balkans. By 1361, he had captured territory from the Dardanelles to the old Roman capital of Adrianople (modern Edirne), which he made into his own capital.

The Ottomans arrived in the Balkans at an opportune time for their ambitions. The Byzantine Empire had shrunk to a mere shadow of its former self and comprised little more than the suburbs of Constantinople; the Serbian Empire of the great Stephen Dushan had lost most of its vitality at his death in 1355; and the peoples of the Balkans were suffering from the constant warfare of numerous petty states. Few of the inhabitants of the area, powerful or weak, felt a loyalty to a Balkan state at the time. Many of them sensed that the prospect of Ottoman overlordship could be no worse than what they were already experiencing. Due to the chaotic conditions, the Ottomans were able to recruit Christian knights to serve in their army, and in some battles, other Christians defected to the Ottoman side. Many Orthodox noblemen and soldiers of fortune made successful careers out of service to the Ottoman state. Many Christian peasants and townsmen benefitted from the stability offered by the Ottomans of this era, in contrast to the anarchy and exploitation characteristic of the Balkan Christian states of the fourteenth century.

Orhan's son Murat I (1362–1389) took advantage of the vacuum of power in the region. He consolidated his hold on Thrace, conquered Macedonia and southern Bulgaria, and forced the Byzantines to pay tribute to, and provide troops for, Ottoman campaigns. In 1389, his army, composed of Turks and Christian vassals, defeated a far larger force of Serbs and their allies at Kosovo. Murat was killed in the battle, and his son Bayezit (1389–1402) became sultan.

Murat and Bayezit laid the foundations for a future Ottoman Empire. Murat began the process of building a more reliable army than that of either the gazis or Turkish tribesmen in general, both of whom he regarded as unpredictable and independent minded. He created a unit of soldiers who were prisoners of war, and he instituted a centralized bureaucracy in order to collect the taxes required to support his growing empire. Bayezit expanded upon these initiatives. He implemented a levy of male children on Christian villages in the Balkans, who were then educated as Muslims and trained for either the military or the civilian administration. This recruitment mechanism was known as the *devshirme* system. The slaves in the military served in what came to be known as the Janissary corps (from "Yeni Çeri," or "New Force"). The Janissaries rapidly became the Ottoman army's primary infantry unit and were stationed around the sultan on the battlefield. Originally armed with pikes and bows and arrows, they later became famous for their effective use of gunpowder weapons.

As a result of his policies and leadership ability, Bayezit became a remarkably successful conqueror. Relying on the loyalty of his Christian vassals and Janissaries, he quickly conquered the western half of Anatolia from Turkish rivals, acquired large areas north of the Danube, and, in 1395, laid siege to Constantinople itself. By this time, all of the major European leaders had become aware of the potential threat of the Ottomans to their security, and they responded to the appeal of the Byzantine emperor for aid. The king of Hungary organized a huge army that attracted knights from France, Burgundy, England, Germany, and the Netherlands. This military force moved down the Danube in 1396, destroying Ottoman forts along the way. At the fortress of Nicopolis, however, Bayezit confronted the coalition's army and utterly destroyed it, sending a wave of terror throughout Europe.

While the siege of Constantinople continued, Bayezit turned to Anatolia again in 1397, and began conquering its eastern regions. By this time, the defunct

Il-khanate's domain in eastern Anatolia had been replaced by several Muslim Turkish overlords. Bayezit won battle after battle, until he had conquered the bulk of the peninsula. His territory, extending from the Caucasus to the Danube, was poised to become an empire. His brutal Anatolian conquests, however—accomplished with the aid of large numbers of Balkan Christians—had alienated many Turkish families in Anatolia, whose own hopes for leadership had been destroyed. They looked to Timur Lang to get their revenge.

Scourges

The fourteenth century was a difficult one for much of the world's population. The travails of the inhabitants of Europe are justly famous: famine, wars, the schism within the papacy, and the plague, which reduced the population by thirty to fifty percent. China also suffered from epidemics during this century, as well. For much of the predominantly Muslim world, however, the second half of the century was probably more wretched than for any comparably sized area on the planet.

Plague

The plague had already felled millions of people in China and India when it swept into southwestern Asia and Europe in 1347. Its sudden appearance and high mortality rate were shocking enough, but the symptoms of the disease made it even more terrible. Victims developed fever and shivering, and blackened swellings appeared in the neck, armpits, and groin, filled with dark and foul-smelling pus. Sometimes the swellings burst, causing the victim intense agony, and the stench of the escaping pus was so strong that many family members could not approach the victim. (The discolored swellings gave the disease its popular name, Black Death.) Many also experienced purple or red skin discolorations, internal bleeding, bloody urine, diarrhea, or vomiting. Many died from what appeared to be pneumonia, for their lungs filled with fluid, and they died of asphyxiation.

From Transoxiana to Egypt and Andalus, the Dar al-Islam suffered a serious blow from the pestilence. The Mamluke Empire's experience with the plague is the best-documented case in the Muslim world, and it suggests a population loss by the end of the century of at least one-third, a rate comparable to that of Europe. Rural and urban areas alike suffered depopulation, and the disease killed the livestock upon which agriculture and transport depended. Because of the depopulation of rural areas, orchards and crops were neglected, and food production dropped. Disease spread even more rapidly in the cities; the chronicles report a continuous procession of the dead being carried out the city gates to the cemeteries. Many of Cairo's neighborhoods were abandoned and had fallen into ruin by the end of the century. Hardest hit of all, it seems, were the royal mamluks. Refusing to leave the capital city and living in the close quarters of their barracks, the mamluks suffered huge losses. The struggle between the Qipchaqs and the Circassians had become intense by the time of the first appearance of the plague; what role it played in shifting the balance of power to the Circassians (who seized power in 1382) is a matter of speculation.

The Mamluke Empire entered a period of sustained decline in population, wealth, and military power. For reasons not understood, the pneumonic variety of the plague recurred repeatedly in the Mamluke Empire, and as a result, the mortality rates of several of the later epidemics were as high as the first one. At least fifty epidemics struck the empire over the next 170 years. The population of Syria and Egypt did not regain their preplague levels for several centuries. The regime's military power itself declined markedly due to the high rate of death among the royal mamluks.

Mamluke agriculture remained in a centuries-long state of depression, and the thriving industries of the fourteenth century went into steep decline. The one bright spot amid the gloom of the plague was that the Mamluke Empire did witness a boom in construction. New buildings, particularly madrasas, mosques, fountains, and tombs, went up in large numbers. Many of these may have been endowed by individuals hoping to escape the plague by their good works and by others grateful for having been spared from the plague. At any rate, as a result of the increased opportunities for constructing and decorating such buildings, urban artisans who survived the epidemics were well paid. In addition, Egypt continued to benefit from its role as an entrepot in the international spice trade. Its spice merchants joined the artisans as the only groups who prospered during the period from the mid-fourteenth to late fifteenth century.

Apart from the urban areas of the Mamluke Empire, our knowledge of the impact of the plague on the Muslim world is surprisingly limited. It is clear that the plague caused numerous villages in Palestine (within the Mamluke Empire) to be abandoned, and much agricultural land there reverted to the control of nomads. The ports of North Africa and of Granada were also hit hard by the epidemic. The disease struck the Iberian Peninsula during a war between Granada and Castile. It hit Granada's army before that of Castile, causing some Muslims to consider converting to Christianity as a prophylactic. Fortunately for their faith, the disease was soon raging among troops of Castile, as well. Alfonso XI, the king of Castile, was the only ruling monarch of Europe to die of the Black Death. The Ottomans were involved in the Byzantine struggle for the throne in the same year that the plague struck Constantinople (1347), but we do not know how the disease affected their campaigns.

Timur Lang

Shortly after the first incidence of the plague, another destructive scourge struck southwestern Asia. This was the army of the warrior Timur Lang, known to Europe as Tamerlane ("Temur Leng" is more accurate as a Turkic rendering of his name, but less widely used.) The ferocity and wanton destructiveness of his campaigns still provoke amazement and horror, and the victories of his undefeated army changed the course of history for numerous regimes. He came of age as the Mongol states were collapsing, and he found the heirs to those states to be easy prey. More impressive was the ease with which he defeated the Mamlukes, the Delhi Sultanate, and the Ottomans.

Timur (1336–1405) was born in the immediate aftermath of the schism within the Chaghatay khanate that erupted during the reign of Tarmasharin. He grew up near Samarqand, where the settled population was dominated by nomadic and semi-nomadic Turko–Mongol tribes. Timur himself could claim descent from the Mongols through his mother and from Turks through his father. During the 1360s, he developed a series of alliances with local chieftains and became a powerful actor in the affairs of Transoxiana.

In about 1370, Timur seized control of Samarqand and declared his intention of restoring the glory of the Mongol empire. He spent the next decade securing control of the frontiers of Transoxiana. True to the classic model, victories begat victories, for the vanquished armies became the reservoir for new recruits into his own army, and his forces grew exponentially. Unlike the armies of light cavalry characteristic of the Chinggisid conquests, however, Timur's armies gradually became a composite force. One element that made him such a formidable opponent was that he realized the advantages of combining the mobility of light cavalry with the shock force of heavy calvary. He also utilized infantry when it served his purposes, and he gradually adopted the new technologies of rockets and siege artillery.

In 1381, Timur began the conquests that made his place in history. His own explanations for the campaigns are not recorded, and historians have had to speculate on his motivations. To some observers, the needless bloodshed and physical destruction of the campaigns suggest that they were simple plundering operations, carried out to keep his volatile troops satisfied with booty. Other historians have speculated that the campaigns were begun in order to create a great commercial network that would allow Samarqand to recapture its glory, and that the accompanying violence was a technique to intimidate the local populations to submit to his authority.

Whatever Timur's motives may have been, by 1385 he had captured Herat, Khorasan, and all of eastern Iran, and during the course of the next year he conquered Esfahan and Hamadan, thus destroying the petty dynasties that had emerged in the aftermath of the collapse of the Il-khanid regime. Over the next nine years, he conquered Iraq and the Caucasus. During the 1390s, he led two punitive expeditions against Toqtamish of the Horde. Toqtamish, self-confident after having seized power over the Horde in 1377, dared to encroach upon Timur's territory in Transoxiana. Timur retaliated and punished him in battle, but Toqtamish foolishly challenged Timur again in Azerbaijan. This time, Timur systematically destroyed all the commercial cities in the Horde from the Black Sea to the Aral Sea. Although Timur was not able to capture Toqtamish, the latter's reputation was destroyed, and the destruction of the cities of the steppes caused irreparable harm to the economy of the Tatars.

During Timur's campaign against Toqtamish, revolts broke out all over Iran against his occupation. He brutally suppressed the revolts. Whole cities were destroyed, their inhabitants massacred, and towers were built of their skulls. After reestablishing control of Iran, Timur invaded the Delhi Sultanate in 1398. The Indian army, exhausted by the decade of civil war that followed the death of Firuz, was crushed. The killing and wanton destruction that characterized the Delhi campaign may be unsurpassed in history. The chroniclers report that Timur ordered the execution of tens of thousands of Hindu captives before and after the battle for Delhi. Thousands of them are said to have been skinned alive. The sack of Delhi went on for several days before the city was set afire and left in smoldering ruins. Members of the Tughluq dynasty continued to claim sovereignty in Delhi until 1413, but the city remained devastated. Over the course of the next century, Delhi slowly established itself as a regional power, but it would take over a century for it to eclipse its rival Hindu and Muslim states again.

Timur returned to Samarqand in 1399 with a vast amount of wealth with which to enhance the only city that he appears ever to have appreciated. He also brought back a herd of Indian war elephants, a novel weapon that he wanted to add to his arsenal. As usual, he spent only a few days inside the walls before retiring to his rural pavilion. Before the end of the year, he set out on a campaign to the west, and he again secured control over Azerbaijan. While there, he received emissaries from Turkish chieftains in Anatolia who were under his protection and learned that Bayezit had invaded their territories. Bayezit's action was an affront to Timur's honor and resulted in a tense confrontation between two of the most powerful men in the world. Neither one had a clear picture of the other's power, and both were reluctant to force the issue without more intelligence. Timur send a diplomatically worded dispatch to Bayezit, warning him to keep his distance from areas under Timur's authority. Bayezit replied not only arrogantly, but insultingly. Timur then attacked and destroyed the Ottoman outpost of Sivas, which had been under the command of one of Bayezit's sons.

Assuming that he had taught Bayezit his lesson, Timur then turned to the Mamlukes and attacked the city of Aleppo in 1400. The Circassian Mamlukes, reeling from the effects of recurring bouts with the plague, of famines caused by inadequate floods of the Nile, and of a worsening balance of trade with Europe, were in no position to contest the mighty Timur. Aleppo was sacked, and in 1401, Timur moved on to Damascus. There, the young Mamluke sultan had assembled his army, but when he heard of a rebellion in Cairo, he returned to his capital in haste. The abandoned army, confused and leaderless, straggled back to Cairo in disarray. The inhabitants of Damascus, now defenseless, agreed to pay Timur a heavy ransom not to be attacked. Once inside the walls, however, Timur increased the ransom demand tenfold. When the citizens protested, he ordered the city to be sacked, and the inhabitants were massacred. He spared the city's artisans, whom he sent to Samarqand.

By the fall of 1401, Timur was no longer concerned by a potential threat from the Mamlukes, and he headed toward the Caucasus for the winter. Learning of a rebellion in Baghdad, he ordered the city destroyed. Leveled for the second time in little more than a century, it would require more than four centuries for the city to become even a regional town again. Once in the Caucasus, Timur received news of Bayezit's continuing challenge to his claims in eastern Anatolia, and he resolved to decide the issue the following season. In July 1402, the two armies met at modern Ankara. Timur used his Indian war elephants to launch the attack. Once the battle had been joined, Bayezit's Turkish allies abandoned him, leaving him to fight Timur with his Balkan Christian vassals. He was defeated and captured, and died in captivity eight months later. Timur's army pursued the remnants of the Ottoman army all the way to the Dardanelles, where the Ottoman survivors were ferried across (for a price) by Genoese and Venetians.

Bayezit's sons began fighting each other for control of the Ottoman holdings, and they almost caused the destruction of everything that their ancestors had achieved. For the next nine years, their civil war allowed most of the local leaders in Anatolia and in the Balkans to regain their political independence, and both areas lapsed into near anarchy. To contemporaries, it appeared that the Ottomans were finished.

In the Presence of Timur

Anyone trapped within a city besieged by Timur would be consumed by anxiety of the worst kind. Such a fate befell one of the era's greatest scholars, Ibn Khaldun, when Timur besieged Damascus. The scholar's experience with Timur soon became "up close and personal" when the conqueror announced that he desired to see him. Timur received Ibn Khaldun graciously, and then informed him that he wanted him to write a detailed description of the Maghrib. Ibn Khaldun spent the next five weeks in Timur's camp writing his report, and he left a record of his experiences during that time. Foregoing an opportunity to portray Timur as a monster, he reveals a human side to Timur as well as his own obsequiousness in the presence of absolute power.

[After asking for the report on the Maghrib] he gave a signal to his servants to bring from his tent some of the kind of food which they call "rishta" and which they were most expert in preparing. Some dishes of it were brought in, and he made a sign that they should be set before me. I arose, took them, and drank, and liked it, and this impressed him favorably. [Then] I composed in my mind some words to say to him which, by exalting him and his government, would flatter him....

The news was brought to him that the gate of the city had been opened and that the judges had gone out to fulfill their [promise of] surrender, for which, so they thought, he had generously granted them amnesty. Then he was carried away from before us, because of the trouble with his knee, and was placed upon his horse; grasping the reins, he sat upright in his saddle while the bands played around him until the air shook with them; he rode toward Damascus....

When the time for Timur's journey approached and he decided to leave Damascus, I entered to him one day. After we had completed the customary greetings, he turned to me and said, "You have a mule here?"

I answered, "Yes."

He said, "Is it a good one?"

I answered, "Yes."

He said, "Will you sell it? I would buy it from you."

I replied, "May Allah aid you—one like me does not sell to one like you; but I would offer it to you in homage, and also others like it if I had them."

He said, "I meant only that I would requite you for it with generosity."

I replied, "Is there any generosity left beyond that which you have already shown me? You have heaped favors upon me, accorded me a place in your council among your intimate followers, and shown me kindness and generosity—which I hope Allah will repay to you in like measure."

He was silent; so was I. The mule was brought to him while I was with him at his council, and I did not see it again....

Then on another day I entered to him and he asked me: "Are you going to travel to Cairo?"

I answered, "May Allah aid you—indeed, my desire is only [to serve] you, for you have granted me refuge and protection. If the journey to Cairo would be in your service, surely; otherwise I have no desire for it."

He said, "No, but you will return to your family and to your people."

Source: *Anthology of Islamic Literature From the Rise of Islam to Modern Times*, with an introduction and commentaries by James Kritzeck. New York: Holt, Rinehart and Winston Inc., 1964, pp. 281–284.

Timur now began to prepare for the climax of his career: a campaign against the Ming dynasty in China. He set out from Samarqand in December 1404, but fell seriously ill as he approached the Syr Darya River. He died in February 1405. Contrary to Muslim practice, his body was embalmed and sent to Samarqand, where it was buried in the impressive tomb that he had constructed for that purpose, the Gur-e Amir. At his death, his sons and grandsons fought over the succession and lost all the territories that Timur had conquered, except for Transoxiana and western Afghanistan.

Timur's legacy would boast of impressive cultural achievements in Samarqand and Herat over the next century. Timur himself adorned Samarqand with beautiful architecture, gardens, and the equivalent of a national library, where books were copied, illustrated, bound, and stored. Elsewhere, however, the result of Timur's career was sheer destruction. The area from Delhi to Damascus had been laid waste, and combined with the effects of the plague in Syria and Iraq, the populations of a huge area experienced suffering and despair beyond comprehension.

Some historians have pointed out that Chinggis Khan and his Mongol successors usually employed cruelty as a means to gain submission. Timur, like Alexander the Great, seems to have simply enjoyed watching rivers of blood flow. What makes Timur's cruelty more difficult to explain is that all of his opponents were Muslim regimes. If he had been a pagan like his Mongol ancestors, his barbarity might be dismissed as a symptom of his hostility to an alien culture. Timur, however, like many of his fellow Turks and Mongols in Central Asia, easily combined residual shamanism with a commitment to Islam. In the name of Islam, he systematically destroyed the Jacobite church in northern Syria and western Anatolia, as well as the Nestorian church in Central Asia. He also claimed to be serving the cause of Islam in invading the Delhi Sultanate, which of course was ruled by Muslims. But his motives for the utter destruction of large numbers of Muslims across a wide swath of territory remain obscure.

Conclusion

The fifteenth century dawned on an eastern Muslim landscape utterly transformed from its contours of the early thirteenth century. From Syria and the Russian steppes in the west to India in the east, the whole order had been reworked several times in a century and a half. Muslim regimes, Mongol regimes, civil war, the plague, and Timur Lang had transformed the political and social order the way a tornado scrambles anything in its path. The Mongol conquests of the thirteenth century inflicted catastrophic damage upon Iraq and Khorasan. They had also inadvertently boosted the fortunes of the nascent Mamluke, Ottoman, and Delhi regimes by causing tens of thousands of intellectuals, craftsmen, and artists to flee to those havens. In the fourteenth century, the plague and Timur's campaigns laid waste once again to Iran and Iraq, but also threatened the very existence of the Mamluke, Ottoman, and Delhi states and societies. By the time of Timur's death in 1405, Delhi had been reduced to the status of a local pretender, and Ottoman power appeared to be destroyed. The Circassian Mamlukes had been humiliated by their failure to defend Damascus, and recurring waves of the plague kept them weaker than their Qipchaq predecessors.

The Mongol conquests, it should be remembered, were only the latest wave of violence and suffering to afflict the Muslim world. On the other hand, they were so destructive that they caused mass migrations of peasants, nomads, craftsmen, intellectuals, and merchants to areas not under the immediate threat of Mongol attack. One important consequence was that the ethnic composition of many parts of the Muslim world would be changed for centuries to come. Moreover, regions which up to that time had been peripheral to mainstream developments in the Dar al-Islam now became thriving centers of commerce and culture due to the influx of refugees from the Mongol advance.

The period 1260–1405 represents a major watershed in Muslim history. It witnessed a degree of destruction and suffering that can hardly be imagined, and yet the thoroughness of the changes that took place created the conditions for new societies to assert themselves. A comparable period in western European history would be that of the Frankish conquests and the Norsemen's raids, or from the sixth through the late tenth centuries. The cumulative effect of this period was that, by the beginning of the fifteenth century, the political structures of the central and eastern sections of the Dar al-Islam had been so shaken that a contemporary outside observer could be forgiven for wondering if Islamic civilization had a future. As it turned out, that civilization was about to rise, phoenixlike, and become the most dominant force in the world for several centuries.

FURTHER READING

The Mongol Khanates

Adshead, S.A.M. *Central Asia in World History*. New York: St. Martin's Press, 1993.

Kwanten, Luc. *Imperial Nomads: A History of Central Asia, 500–1500*. Philadelphia: University of Pennsylvania Press, 1979.

Morgan, David. *The Mongols*. Oxford: Basil Blackwell, 1986.

Vernadsky, George. *The Mongols and Russia*. New Haven, Connecticut: Yale University Press, 1953.

New Centers of Islamic Culture

Ahmed, Aziz. *Studies in Islamic Culture in the Indian Environment*. Oxford: Oxford University Press, 1962.

Ayalon, David. *Islam and the Abode of War*. London: Variorum, 1994.

———. *Outsiders in the Lands of Islam: Mamluks, Mongols and Eunuchs*. London: Variorum Reprints, 1988.

Cahen, Claude. *The Formation of Turkey*. Translated and edited by P. M. Holt. Harlow, U.K.: Longman, 2001.

Canfield, Robert L., ed. *Turko–Persia in Historical Perspective*. Cambridge, U.K.: Cambridge University Press, 1991.

Ikram, S.M. *Muslim Civilization in India*. Edited by Ainslie T. Embree. New York and London: Columbia University Press, 1964.

Inalcik, Halil. *The Ottoman Empire: The Classical Age, 1300–1600.* Translated by Norman Itzkowitz and Colin Imber. New York and Washington: Praeger Publishers, 1973.

Kafadar, Cemal. *Between Two Worlds: The Construction of the Ottoman State.* Berkeley, California: The University of California Press, 1995.

Irwin, R. *The Middle East in the Middle Ages: The Early Mamluk Sultanate (1250–1382).* Carbondale, Illinois: Southern Illinois University Press, 1986.

Jackson, Peter. *The Delhi Sultanate.* Cambridge and New York: Cambridge University Press, 1999.

McCarthy, Justin. *The Ottoman Turks: An Introductory History to 1923.* London and New York: Longman, 1997.

Scourges

Adshead, S.A.M. *Central Asia in World History.* New York: St. Martin's Press, 1993.

Dols, Michael. *The Black Death in the Middle East.* Princeton, New Jersey: Princeton University Press, 1977.

Manz, Beatrice Forbes. *The Rise and Rule of Tamerlane.* Cambridge, U.K.: Cambridge University Press, 1989.

CHAPTER 11

Unity and Diversity in Islamic Traditions

In 1325, a young Moroccan named Ibn Battuta embarked upon the hajj. Others from his hometown who had traveled to Mecca before him had usually been away for two to three years. Thus, he knew that he would be gone for an extended period, but it is doubtful that he had any idea at the time just how long it would be before he saw home again. In fact, after he had completed the rituals of the pilgrimage, he decided to travel the extent of the Muslim world. He sailed along the coast of East Africa, ventured into the realm of the Horde in southern Russia, lived for seven years in India, and may even have sailed through the straits of Southeast Asia on his way to China. He did not return home until 1349. His return trip was fraught with numerous perils, for he had to make his way through the collapsing states of the mid-fourteenth century as well as avoid becoming a victim of the plague, which was ravaging much of the world at the time.

Ibn Battuta's career opens a window upon Muslim cultures of the fourteenth century. Muslim states, as a rule, proved ephemeral in the face of the cataclysms of the thirteenth and fourteenth centuries. More impressive was the strength of the ideas and institutions that had evolved within the Muslim world over the previous several centuries. Scholars in many disciplines had not ceased producing original work, and Ibn Battuta visited many whose fame was spread all across the Dar al-Islam. The Shari'a, or Islamic law, provided cultural continuity when states failed, and Ibn Battuta financed his travels by serving as an itinerant qadi: Everywhere he went, his credentials qualified him to adjudicate disputes according to Islamic law, and local Muslims paid handsomely for his services. By the mid-fourteenth century, Sufi lodges and orders were widespread throughout the Muslim world. Ibn Battuta visited many different Sufi masters, enjoyed the hospitality of numerous Sufi lodges, and marveled at the variety of Sufi expression wherever he went.

Intellectual Life in the Fourteenth Century

In previous chapters, we have seen that the development of Islamic civilization took place in the context of widespread and repeated violence. The era of Mongol hegemony was the climax of that remarkable period. The stunning gains of the Reconquista, the widespread elimination of Muslim states by the Mongols, the collapse of the newly Islamized Mongol regimes themselves, the catastrophe of the plague, and the utter ruthlessness of Timur were spectacularly destructive and severely demoralizing. Many European historians of the nineteenth and twentieth centuries, viewing the Muslim experience of the thirteenth and fourteenth centuries through the prism of the subsequent rise of Europe to world dominance, found it easy to assume that Islamic civilization had been shattered and left moribund. That view can no longer be defended.

The End of the "Golden Age"?

Unlike early medieval western Europe after the collapse of Roman administration, the Muslim world never suffered from a cessation of its cultural life. As had happened earlier during times of great turmoil, Islamic law continued to function, precisely because it was not dependent upon the stability of any particular regime. Also as before, the new states, even the transitory ones, attempted to gain legitimacy for themselves by patronizing scholars and artists who exemplified the best of Islamic civilization.

Even though Islamic civilization did not collapse in the fourteenth century, a shift in the locus of cultural creativity did slowly occur. Until the thirteenth century, the level of intellectual production in the Muslim world had been vastly superior to that of Europe. With the work of scholars such as Albertus Magnus, Robert Grosseteste, and Roger Bacon (all of whom were inspired by translations of Arabic manuscripts), however, European thought began to value mathematical and experimental methods in the practice of natural science. The twelfth- and thirteenth-century translation of Arabic versions of Greek texts prompted a desire to read the Greek originals, and in the process of searching for them, scholars discovered previously unknown texts by Plato, Aristotle, and other intellectuals. Although philosophy remained largely within the framework set by the Church for two more centuries, numerous new currents in philosophy emerged, laying the foundation for humanism and other secular developments of the fifteenth and sixteenth centuries.

These changes did not take place overnight. Cultural production in the Muslim world continued to flourish in many quarters, and the visual arts were about to enter their most creative phase. In the fields of pure mathematics and astronomy, as well, the Muslim world continued to eclipse Europe until the mid-sixteenth century, when Copernicus made his breakthrough. Even in the field of astronomy we must remember that the Copernican thesis was not readily accepted in Europe. The rejection of the geocentric theory flew in the face of the everyday experience of everyone, but also seemed heretical to both Protestants and Catholics. Since the Bible contains several passages that refer to the sun's movement around the earth and never mentions a possible revolution of the earth around the sun, most Christians were reluctant even to consider the new theory. Not until the late seventeenth century was the geocentric view decisively discredited in scientific circles, and the Catholic Church had so much institutional prestige invested in it that it continued to adhere officially to the notion until 1860. In science and mathematics, therefore, we can say that Protestant Europe began to move beyond Muslim achievements by the late seventeenth century. It was also during this period that European universities finally began to discard Ibn Sina's seven-hundred-year-old book of medicine in favor of the new European discoveries in physiology, based upon the work of Vesalius and Harvey.

The reversal of fortunes in the scientific and philosophical productivity of Europe and the Muslim world has given rise to much speculation about "what went wrong" for the Dar al-Islam. Often forgotten in the discussion is the fact that Europe's subsequent development was unique and unpredictable. Its science and technology eventually dwarfed that of all other regions of the globe, not just the predominantly Muslim regions. The cultural systems of China, India, Southeast Asia, and the Americas all contained elements that had been more sophisticated than their European counterparts, but by the late eighteenth century, their technological prowess was eclipsed. The European aberration is actually the topic that needs explanation, and we still cannot provide an adequate one. Much of the speculation has been based on misplaced assumptions about historical inevitability and progress, rather than on a careful analysis of how history actually takes place.

The contrasting trajectories of the intellectual history of Europe and the Muslim world are of particular interest due to their common heritage. They shared many features: Their monotheistic traditions were remarkably parallel, and they enjoyed the same access to the Greco–Roman traditions of architecture, philosophy, engineering, medicine, and political thought. The advantages the Muslim world enjoyed were a more direct access to the creative traditions of China and India and not having to overcome the disastrous collapse of Roman administration that western Europe suffered after the fourth century. A major advantage for western Europe was that it no longer suffered from outside invasions after the mid-tenth century, and subsequently enjoyed a period of economic growth that resulted in political centralization and cultural sophistication. The Muslim world, by contrast, began suffering from sustained violence from the same, mid-tenth century, period.

Muslim religious scholars became increasingly intolerant of speculative thought. Innovation (*bid'a*) in religious affairs had always been frowned upon due to the perceived obligation to act strictly in accord with the Qur'an and the Prophet's own behavior, but the charge of "bid'a" was increasingly effective in limiting the scope of intellectual inquiry. By the thirteenth century, when Muslims felt hemmed in by aggressive Christian enemies to the west and ruthless pagan Mongol enemies to the east, philosophical speculation had practically ceased.

At this time, it is as impossible to explain the growing conservatism of Muslim intellectuals as it is to explain the increasing creativity of European intellectuals. A multitude of factors played a part, and it is possible that we will never be able to discover many of the most important ones. It does, however, seem useful to keep in mind two elements of the Muslim experience. One is the conjunction between the sense of collective insecurity, on the one hand, and the growing reluctance to allow challenges to established religious doctrine, on the other. A confident society is likely to allow more scope to intellectual inquiry than one that fears for its future.

The other element is the fact that Muslim philosopher–scientists required the patronage of ruling families for their economic support, whereas, by the twelfth century, European scholars were beginning to organize autonomous universities. European scientists and philosophers enjoyed legal protection as communities of scholars. They benefitted from the exchange of ideas and the criticism that came from belonging to a faculty, and they could respond to threats to their livelihood by going to court. Muslim scholars, however were attached individually to the palaces of ruling dynasties. They shared ideas with fellow scholars, but at a distance. If their ideas were criticized by local religious leaders or by public opinion, the patron usually found it expedient to dismiss them. Under those conditions, it was next to impossible for a school of thought to develop based on an original idea.

Thus, it is possible to say that the period of Mongol hegemony represents a period during which Muslim philosophical thought practically disappeared except as an adjunct to theology and law. The fields of prose, poetry, the sciences, and mathematics, however, continued to boast the work of outstanding talents, and the visual arts were entering their most spectacular period. Scientists and mathematicians continued to make important revisions to existing knowledge, but their isolation from each other and their dependence on the good will of a ruler limited the scope of their work. Their plight was similar to that of the vast majority of intellectuals in the world at the time.

Against All Odds

A remarkable feature of the period of the Mongols and of Timur is the vibrancy of the religious, artistic, and intellectual life of the Muslim world. The cultural and intellectual life of the Dar al-Islam showed that it had securely established itself across a wide area, and even the hammer blows of the fourteenth century could not destroy it. As we have seen, even the Mamluke Empire, which may have experienced the worst effects of the plague of any region in the world, made contributions to art and architecture which are still regarded with awe. The intellectual life of Muslims, too, continued to flourish. Philosophy continued to be suspect because of its association with challenges to the authority of revelation, but the use of disciplined reason was highly valued in most theological and legal circles. Historical and scientific studies also continued to flourish wherever manuscripts survived or were copied and where patronage made scholarship possible. Sometimes these conditions made vibrant scholarship possible in the most unlikely of settings.

Ibn Taymiya

One of the greatest Muslim religious scholars of the fourteenth century was Ibn Taymiya (1262–1327). He was born in 1262 in the city of Harran, located near today's border between Syria and Turkey. Fearing the effects of the onset of Hulagu's rule, his family moved to Damascus while Ibn Taymiya was a small child. For the rest of his life, he lived under Mamluke rule. Through a combination of formal education and independent study, he mastered the disciplines that focused on the study of the Qur'an, Hadith, jurisprudence, rational theology, philosophy, and Sufi metaphysics. His keen intellect, his deep knowledge of the religious sciences, and his forceful personality combined to create one of the most influential thinkers in Islamic history.

Ibn Taymiya's career was committed to the cause of Islamic reform. He was convinced that certain doctrines and practices had arisen that were not sanctioned by the legitimate sources of the faith, and he became a tireless advocate of the need to return to what he regarded as the purity of early Islamic history. He argued that the two sources of all religious truth are the Qur'an and the Hadith as interpreted by the first generation of Muslim scholars. As a member of the Hanbali school of law, he believed that whatever is commanded in those sources must be obeyed, and whatever is not mentioned in them must not be required. Although he was proficient in the methods of philosophy and rational theology, he was bitterly critical of the conclusions that philosophers and theologians drew from them.

He was particularly critical of philosophers who asserted that scripture had been deliberately couched in metaphors and pictorial images so that common people could understand it. He also found fault with certain features of Sufism, although he was not opposed to Sufism as such. He did, however, object to common Sufi practices such as the pilgrimages that were made to the tombs of saints, and he rejected the monism of Ibn al-'Arabi. One of his greatest contributions to subsequent Islamic history was his criticism of fellow jurists for accepting without question the decisions of jurists of previous generations. He was convinced that scholars of the Shari'a had an obligation to continue interpreting the will of God as it applied to contemporary society, provided that all such decisions were firmly grounded in the two major sources of law, extended where necessary by analogical reasoning.

Ibn Taymiya was what today we would call a "public intellectual." He brought his passionate concerns to the attention of both the public and the authorities, not just to the small group of his fellow intellectuals. Because some of his criticism threatened other intellectuals, popular religious leaders, and the interests of government officials, he became the center of controversy and conflict. From at least 1298 until his death in 1327, he was repeatedly brought before the courts on various charges—"anthropomorphism," his attacks on rituals at saints' shrines, and his support of a revision to the Shari'a that would make it more difficult for a man to divorce his wife, among others—and was jailed several times for a total of at least five years for his "offenses." His funeral attracted thousands of admirers, many of whom he had criticized for un-Islamic practices, but who respected him for his courage, brilliance, and integrity.

Ibn Taymiya's moral courage and his uncompromising dedication to truth as he understood it has made him a role model for many Islamic reformers to the present day. He is particularly remembered today for his evaluation of Ghazan, the Il-khan ruler whose army occupied Damascus for a year after defeating the Mamlukes in 1300. Ghazan, as we have seen, was a professed Muslim, but Ibn Taymiya never forgot that the Mongols had destroyed much of the civilization of the Islamic world and had frightened his family out of their home in Harran. He led an opposition group to the Mongol occupation of his adopted city, and afterward he wrote extensively on the duty of believers to oppose rulers who professed to be Muslim and performed the basic rites, but who in fact failed to apply the Shari'a. As a result, he is revered today by Muslim activists who challenge the oppressive and corrupt governments of their countries and advocate the creation of an Islamic state.

Ibn al-Shatir

Until the late twentieth century, the focus of historians of astronomy on the Copernican tradition caused them to ignore the original work of Muslim astronomers. In fact, from the tenth century on, a large number of Muslim astronomers recorded important observations and made significant contributions to astronomical theory. Some of the most important Muslim astronomers lived during the period from the thirteenth to the sixteenth centuries, an era when many western historians assumed that Islamic scholarship had died. One of the most important astronomers in history was Ibn al-Shatir of Damascus (1306–1375), whose career spanned the last, turbulent decades of the Qipchaq period of Mamluke rule. He was a young man in Damascus when Ibn Taymiya died there. Ibn al-Shatir was the *muwaqqit*, or timekeeper for the congregational mosque of Damascus, and he was chief of the mosque's muezzins. He designed and constructed his own versions of several observational and computing instruments, including the quadrant and sundial. His large sundial for the congregational mosque of Damascus still stands, and a portable one is preserved in the Aleppo Museum.

Even more impressive is Ibn al-Shatir's work in astronomy. He stands in the tradition of what has come to be known as the "Maragha school" of astronomy. As we have seen, Hulagu's observatory at Maragha attracted scientists from China to Andalus. The astronomers at Maragha engaged in much observational work, but are best known for their revision of existing astronomical theory. Ibn al-Shatir, although not at Maragha itself, continued in this tradition. At the center of the debate was the work of Ptolemy, the great second-century geographer and astronomer. In addition to having established the basis for determining latitudes on earth, he proposed a geocentric (earth-centered) model of the universe that incorporated the important observations and theories up to his time in a brilliant synthesis. It rapidly became the paradigm that explained the structure of the universe as seen from earth. Its basic features remained unchallenged until the sixteenth century, when Copernicus proposed his heliocentric (sun-centered) theory.

The Muslim astronomers did not offer a heliocentric theory, for, at the time, such a theory was contrary to the evidence of the senses as well as unnecessary, since the Ptolemaic theory was highly accurate in predicting eclipses and other celestial events. What concerned them was the inconsistency between Ptolemy's model and the mechanics that he proposed to explain how it worked. A major problem was that Ptolemy assumed for philosophical purposes that celestial orbits were perfectly circular, but actual observations demonstrated that they acted in an elliptical fashion. He had attempted to explain the discrepancy by proposing that the spherical orbits moved uniformly around an axis that did not pass through the center of the sphere (an "eccentric" circle, rather than a "concentric" one).

Another problem was that, over the centuries, astronomers found that the assumption of the perfect uniformity of the velocity of planets ran counter to their observations. Planets appeared to wander in random patterns and to speed up or slow down. Rather than abandoning the Ptolemaic model, however, astronomers proposed that a given planet actually moves in a small circular orbit (an "epicycle"), which is itself centered on the rim of an orbit around the earth. This corollary seemed adequate until so many epicycles had to be proposed that the entire model became

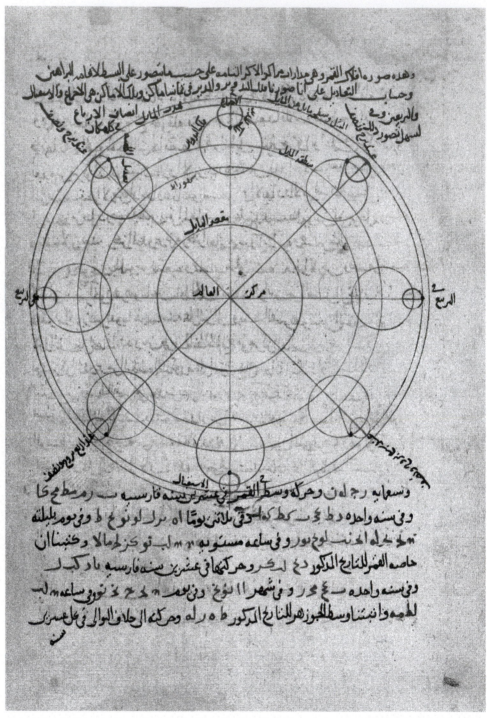

A solution proposed by Ibn al-Shatir to the problem of the moon's orbit around the earth.

unwieldy. When the dozens of epicycles were combined with the eccentric orbits, the Ptolemaic model was beginning to look like a Rube Goldberg machine. The Copernican "revolution" was provoked in part because Copernicus could not believe that God had designed such an awkward instrument.

Ibn al-Shatir, too, was concerned with the problems of the eccentrics and the epicycles. Like all other astronomers of the fourteenth century, he saw no need to challenge Ptolemy's basic model, but rather to make it internally consistent. Starting with the assumption that celestial orbits are the result of a succession of uniform circular motions, he developed models of orbits of the moon and the planets that did not require eccentrics. His highly sophisticated geometry allowed him to accomplish what the master Ptolemy could not. His geometric models, which assume a geocentric universe, show up in a revised form two hundred years later in the heliocentric model of Copernicus. Since the late 1950s, when Ibn al-Shatir's manuscripts were first discovered by European scholars, historians of science have been wrestling with the remarkable similarity of the models of Ibn al-Shatir and of Copernicus. They are aware that just because Ibn al-Shatir came up with such models prior to Copernicus does not mean that someone else could not devise them, but two considerations cause them to think that they must have been transmitted in some form to central Europe, where Copernicus could have had access to them. One reason is that no such models existed in the European tradition from which Copernicus could borrow. The other is that it is inconceivable that Copernicus would come up with the models himself, since they cause, rather than solve, problems for his theory. The lack of a theory of gravity in the Copernican model renders Ibn al-Shatir's models problematic in a heliocentric context: Without gravity, Copernicus has no explanation for why celestial bodies orbit the sun, whereas the Ptolemaic model utilized the Aristotelian theory that planets and moon "desire" the earth. The discovery of a "missing link" between Ibn al-Shatir and Copernicus would provide a fascinating glimpse of late medieval intellectual history.

Ibn Khaldun

Ibn Khaldun (1332–1406) was descended from one of the great families of Seville. His great-grandparents fled the city just before its fall to Castile in 1248 and settled in Tunis, where Ibn Khaldun was born. As the scion of a wealthy and powerful family, he received the best education possible, but was forced to migrate west in 1352 after the plague epidemic took the lives of his parents and teachers. For most of the rest of his life he served as a government minister. He found advisory positions in the Marinid capital of Fez, and then at Granada and several small principalities in modern Morocco and Algeria. Life as a government minister in that era was notoriously unpredictable and dangerous, but Ibn Khaldun seems to have had a knack for making enemies that made his own career even more unpredictable and dangerous than most: In every position that he held, he was either jailed or forced to leave town. Perhaps seeking a more stable career line, he sailed for Egypt in 1382, the same year that Sultan Barquq seized power and inaugurated the Circassian period in Mamluke history. Barquq recognized Ibn Khaldun's achievement as a scholar and a jurist, so he appointed him professor of Maliki law and then to be the senior Maliki qadi of Egypt.

Even in Egypt, Ibn Khaldun encountered political problems and temporarily lost his posts. Because he was so adept at establishing contacts with important patrons, however, he always regained his positions.

Soon after Barquq's death in 1400, Timur began his invasion of Syria. The new Mamluke sultan insisted that Ibn Khaldun join his entourage as he went to Damascus to repel the attack. When the sultan returned in haste to Cairo, however, and his army straggled after him, he left Ibn Khaldun behind in the defenseless city. Timur asked to see him. Ibn Khaldun was thereupon lowered over the city's walls by ropes in a scene strikingly evocative of an episode in the life of the Christian theologian and missionary Paul fourteen centuries earlier. He spent five weeks in Timur's camp, serving as "scholar in residence." Ibn Khaldun recorded his experiences in the camp in a remarkably informal style. (See the extract in Chapter 10.) Timur wanted detailed knowledge of the Maghrib, and Ibn Khaldun presented enormous quantities of oral and written information, but in a way that portrayed the area as strong and united, rather than as the weak and divided region that it actually was. Whether the information he provided had anything to do with the fact that Timur did not venture south of Damascus is a matter of conjecture. Ibn Khaldun managed to obtain a safe conduct for himself and several of his friends, but witnessed the murderous sack of the city and the burning of the great congregational mosque for which Ibn al-Shatir had served as timekeeper. Ibn Khaldun died in Egypt in 1406, a year after Timur.

Ibn Khaldun is best known for the *Muqaddima,* or "Introduction," to his history of the Arabs and Berbers. In 1374, after a particularly exhausting period of government service in North Africa, Ibn Khaldun had sought refuge with a Berber tribe in what is now Algeria. He stayed with them for four years, and it was during this time that he wrote the *Muqaddima,* a massive introduction (the English translation is in three large volumes) to an even larger work of history. Its originality and profundity have had a major influence on Egyptian historians of the fifteenth century, Ottoman historians, and social scientists and philosophers of our own time. Many consider it to be the first work of genuine social science. While it is too complex to be summarized in a few dozen words, mention can be made of its most famous features. It includes a survey of the full range of Islamic learning, but concentrates on the dynamics of historical change. Ibn Khaldun's positivism is revealed in his blistering critique of the metaphysics of philosophy and is expressed again in his theory of history, which he believes to be governed by rational or natural laws. He stresses the role of climate, geography, economics, and ecology in creating the distinctive characteristics of given societies.

Most famously, Ibn Khaldun proposes a theory of historical change based on his understanding of North African history: An aggressive and simple nomadic community conquers an existing state and then develops a dynamic community characterized by ethnic, religious, or lineal solidarity. As the nomads become assimilated to the urban society they have conquered, however, the second generation becomes corrupted by the vices of urban civilization, and in particular tends to reject the loyalty-based political authority that had made the state possible in the first place. The third and final generation loses both its solidarity and its martial spirit, and becomes the easy prey of yet another vigorous nomadic community. Ibn Khaldun offered numerous examples from the time of the Arab conquests through the Berber dynasties of the Almoravids, Almohads, and Marinids to support his theory. The destructive campaigns of Timur, coming after he had written his book, could only reinforce his conclusions.

Hafez

The rebirth of Persian literature that began in the ninth century produced numerous talented poets. The epic poet Ferdowsi (ca. 940–1020) and the mystical poets Farid al-Din 'Attar (ca. 1120–ca. 1220), Sa'di (ca. 1193–1292), and Jamal al-Din al-Rumi (1207–1273) are still revered in Iran. Speakers of Persian, literate and illiterate alike, can recite from memory numerous verses of their poetry, and can harmonize Ferdowsi's celebration of pre-Islamic Iran with the religious themes of the others. As beloved as these poets are, however, the favorite poet of many Iranians is Hafez (ca. 1325–ca. 1390). Widely regarded as the greatest lyric poet in Persian, Hafez honed his craft in the midst of the chaos of the immediate post-Il-khanid era.

Hafez lived almost his entire life in Shiraz. When he was about ten years old, the Il-khanid ruler Abu Sa'id was poisoned, and the Il-khanid regime disintegrated. Various chieftains throughout the former empire seized power in the provinces. In Shiraz and western Iran, the Muzaffarid dynasty proved to be dominant until Timur conquered the area in 1387. Local revolts continued throughout Hafez's life, however, and Shiraz changed hands several times. Hafez's family was not prominent in the community, but he managed to acquire a deep knowledge of the Islamic sciences, Arabic, and Persian literature. He is said to have written several commentaries on religious texts and to have taught the Qur'an. (His name is actually an honorific, deriving from the Arabic word *hafiz*, which literally means "memorizer," specifically one who has memorized the entire Qur'an.)

Hafez was a deeply spiritual Sufi, but he did not possess an ascetic nature. He saw no contradiction between a love for God and a robust delight in the pleasures of the senses, and he composed poetry celebrating both. He became so renowned in Shiraz for his verses that he became a court poet for the Muzaffarids, although he fell out of favor with them in 1368. His sensual lifestyle and love of wine provoked the ulama to criticize him, and at his death, some of them did not even want him buried in a regular cemetery.

Hafez specialized in the type of poetry known as the *ghazal*, a lyric poem of six to fifteen couplets. By the fourteenth century, Arabic and Persian poetry had developed certain conventions that were beginning to make poetry stilted and formal. Hafez deliberately chose to write about everyday experience in simple and colloquial language, avoiding artificial display. The listener detects a remarkably humane and honest spirit in the poet. Unlike most court poets, he wrote few panegyrics, and even when he satirized hypocrites, he did not use the insults commonly hurled by other poets.

Hafez continued the Persian Sufi tradition of allusive images. His poetry contains many references to lovers (both male and female), wine, idols, mosques, birds, flowers, and other potent symbols. On the other hand, even at its most materialistic, it is often couched in Islamic terminology. Western students of his poetry have often wondered whether his language is allegorical and needs to be "decoded" for its spiritual message, or whether it is simply the sly musings of a profligate. Neither approach is adequate for the great Persian poets. Ambiguity of meaning is intrinsic

The People's Poet

The poetry of Hafez, like that of many of the great Persian poets, can be read on at least two levels. Its literal meaning expresses the values of the secular sophisticate, but its words can be interpreted as metaphors for Sufi mystical theology. After Hafez's death, his poetry became popular even in the Ottoman Empire and in Muslim India, where Persian literature benefitted from court patronage. On the level of popular culture, many people used his poems for divination: They would open a copy of his collection of poetry, the Diwan, at random and place their finger on a poem, expecting it to give them guidance for the day.

THE BODY'S CUP

Last night I saw angels knocking at the tavern door;
they shaped and cast a winecup from Adam's clay,

and I was drunk with potent wine poured
by ascetic angels who dwell behind the sacred veil.

The sky couldn't bear that burden of love along,
so they cast the dice and my poor name came up.

Seventy-two sects bicker over fairy tales;
forgive them, they don't know the truth.

Thank you God for making peace with me;
the Sufis dance and raise their cups to you.

The candle laughs flame, but the true fire
harvests bodies of countless ecstatic moths.

The brides of poetry have combed my hair.
Only Hafiz has ripped the veil from wisdom's face.

SOURCE: Willis Barnstone and Tony Barnstone, eds. *Literatures of the Middle East.* Upper Saddle River, New Jersey: Prentice Hall, 2003. Translation ©2003 by Tony Barnstone. Reprinted by arrangement with Prentice Hall.

and essential to their poetry. The cultivation of ambiguity was born in the midst of political and religious tension. Iranians chafed under the political dominance first of Arabs, and then of Turks and Mongols. Iran was a religious cauldron, as well. Both Zoroastrianism and Manichaeism (a religion that arose in third-century Iran and was severely persecuted by both Christians and Muslims over the next millennium) contained elements that still appealed to some Iranians. As a result, literally minded interpreters of the Qur'an bitterly criticized Muslims who were philosophically or mystically inclined, out of suspicion that they were being seduced by the older religions. In this political and religious hothouse, poets with serious themes learned to express themselves through double entendre, symbol, and metaphor. Everyday experience became inextricably entwined with the mystic's hunger for union with God.

Ibn Battuta

Ibn Taymiya, Ibn al-Shatir, Ibn Khaldun, and Hafez were intellectuals of the first order whose work is still the object of scholarly inquiry. Other intellectuals of similar stature could be treated here who worked in the natural sciences, historical studies, and religious studies. It seems appropriate to close this section, however, with Ibn Battuta (1304–1368), who was a minor intellectual but whose career, as suggested at the beginning of this chapter, demonstrates the scope and depth achieved by Islamic civilization by the fourteenth century. Ibn Battuta may have qualified as the most widely traveled individual prior to modern times. Born in 1304 in Tangier, he had the typical education of a young man who was preparing for a career as a qadi. Like many other young scholars, after his preparatory training he was ready to seek certificates from the more celebrated ulama in the great centers of Islamic studies. Thus, he embarked upon the hajj in 1325, planning to combine the fulfillment of that religious duty with the experience of studying with some of the more famous scholars of the two Holy Cities and of the Mamluke Empire. By the time he had completed the hajj, however, he had developed a passion for seeing the world. Over the next two decades, he became a citizen of the world, and before returning to Morocco in 1349, he had traveled at least 60,000—and perhaps as many as 75,000—miles.

Ibn Battuta could not have timed his travels better if he had had the hindsight of history and returned in a time machine. He passed through Cairo during the third reign of the Mamluke al-Nasir Muhammad, and thus saw Egypt and Syria at their most prosperous and stable period for centuries before or after that time. He sailed south along the African coast as far as modern Tanzania. Later, he was introduced to Orhan, the Ottoman leader; to Abu Sa'id, the last of the Il-khan rulers; and to Uzbeg, the great khan of the Golden Horde. (He even accompanied one of Uzbeg's wives—a Byzantine princess—to Constantinople so that she could give birth to her child in her father's palace.) He took advantage of Muhammad ibn Tughluq's generosity to foreign scholars and served the Delhi Sultanate as a qadi and administrator of a huge mausoleum complex. After serving the sultan for seven years, he spent several months as a qadi in the Maldive Islands and may have traveled as far east as China, although features of the account of his trip to Sumatra and Beijing cause some scholars to think that this section was composed by the editor of his book.

On his way back to Morocco from the Indian Ocean basin, Ibn Battuta began to see evidence of the problems that would have made his trip impossible had he begun it later. As he came through Iran and Iraq, he had to dodge the chaos and anarchy that followed the death of Abu Sa'id, and in Syria he witnessed the devastation of the plague. By the time he reached Cairo, it, too, was reeling from the epidemic, as well as from the violence that had begun to diminish the quality of life there since the death of al-Nasir Muhammad seven years earlier. He returned home to Morocco in 1349, but his travels were not over. During the remaining twenty years of his life, he visited both Granada and Mali.

The significance of Ibn Battuta's career goes well beyond the actual number of miles that he traveled. A contrast with the extensive travels of Marco Polo, which had taken place some fifty years earlier, is instructive: Whereas Polo's travels took place almost entirely in strange and alien cultures, Ibn Battuta always found a Muslim community in which his skills were valued. Polo could not possibly have traveled as extensively as he did had he remained within a Christian, Latin, or Greek culture. By contrast, Ibn Battuta found mosques, schools, Sufi communities, and the recognition of the Shari'a as the legal norm in an uninterrupted zone from Morocco to the steppes of Russia and Central Asia, and all around the rim of the Indian Ocean basin. Everywhere he went, he found that his mastery of the Arabic language was useful to him, either as a lingua franca or as a skill that qualified him for remunerative positions as a religious specialist. He found the areas on the periphery of the Islamic heartland to be the most rewarding, for there he was invariably given a lavish welcome, including money, robes, horses, and wives. In those areas, the members of the Muslim community were eager to have a religious authority who could advise them on how to follow the Shari'a, and the local rulers were eager to have their own authority legitimized by their patronage of specialists in the Islamic sciences. Ibn Battuta's career reveals in strikingly personal and concrete detail that, despite the catastrophes of the thirteenth and fourteenth centuries, the Islamic world had become the largest cultural continuum in the world.

Law

The most honored intellectual activity in the Muslim world was jurisprudence, or *fiqh*. This valuation was justified: Not only did Muslims consider Islamic law to reflect God's will, but, as we have seen repeatedly, the independence of Islamic law from any given regime enabled societies to continue even when their governments were destroyed. Thus, the Shari'a was one of the most important elements in the "glue" that held Islamic civilization together. As the law books proliferated, however, many jurists began to question what their role was. If they did not make the law, but only inferred from the sources what God's will was, would there come a time when they had no more original work to do?

The Queen of the Sciences

The delineation of Islamic law had begun at the initiative of private scholars, and it continued to be elaborated in the same, unofficial manner. Qadis, it is true, were appointed by specific regimes, and their jobs depended upon the good will of those regimes. But the existence and perpetuation of the law itself was totally independent of the patronage of governments. A myriad of "schools," or traditions of interpretation, arose in the eighth century, but most of them failed to attract a sizable following and disappeared. The number of viable schools continued to decline, and by the end of the tenth century a consensus had been established that no new schools could emerge. The appearance of a new school, after all, would imply a rejection of the methods of fiqh that had been used up to that time.

By the fourteenth century, the Sunni community had consolidated into four main traditions. Until the thirteenth century, it was not uncommon to hear of riots between the followers of two competing law schools, but thereafter such clashes were less likely to happen. Despite the differences among them, their adherents came to recognize the legitimacy of the others. Ibn Battuta's experience was typical in this regard. He was trained in the Maliki school of North Africa, and yet his services were welcomed in communities in which the Hanafi, Hanbali, or Shafi'i traditions predominated.

Members of the public accorded high respect to a scholar who engaged in fiqh (a *faqih*). Since scholarship of any kind was regarded to be a form of worship of God, the study of jurisprudence was considered one of the highest acts of piety. The faqih was also respected for his intelligence and perseverance: One was accepted as a faqih only after a long and rigorous course of study. He had to demonstrate that he could derive a legal ruling from the Qur'an or Hadith, know when to stress the literal rather than the metaphorical meaning of a text, realize whether a general rule fit a specific case, and refer to the entire corpus of his school's literature in order to cite a precedent.

Despite the insistence of all the schools that their work was not original, but rather was the methodical deduction of the will of God from the Qur'an and Hadith, all the schools tacitly admitted that the process of fiqh involved at least some degree of *ijtihad*, the "effort" or "exercise" of one's judgment or reasoning. Everyone acknowledged that such judgment had to be employed when interpreting texts or assessing the authenticity of Hadith, and the jurists who defended its use in fiqh argued that it had to be exercised when extending the principles established by the Qur'an and Sunna to problems not directly addressed by those texts. These faqihs had been careful to point out that they advocated the use of reasoning only when it was subordinate to the dictates of divine revelation. Some early faqihs, notably in the Hanbali school, campaigned vigorously against analogical reasoning. By the twelfth century, however, even the members of the Hanbali school (as we have seen in the case of thirteenth-century Ibn Taymiya) had come to realize that the practice of finding analogies between cases was unavoidable and that the logic and good sense of the faqih had to come into play.

The period of the most original work in fiqh was the eighth through the twelfth centuries. Most of the problems of ritual, family law, and criminal law had been identified during the first three centuries, but the eleventh and twelfth centuries witnessed an increased sophistication of legal concepts, as well as a growing precision in the use of language. As the issues to be addressed declined in number, and the actual work of the faqih became that of framing the legal issues with more clarity and subtlety, it was becoming clear that some faqihs were more original than others. Some were able to recast an issue in a new light, while others were more comfortable simply applying the results of a precedent to a current case.

The "Closing of the Gate of Ijtihad"?

During the twelfth century, the fact that fewer faqihs were doing original work led some Sunni scholars to voice the opinion that the era of engaging in ijtihad was now past. In the rhythmic and rhyming style so popular in Arabic prose, this sentiment was often expressed in the phrase "*insidad bab al-ijtihad*," or the "closing (blocking) of the gate (door) of ijtihad." Those who expressed this opinion regarded the earlier members of their legal schools to have been intellectual and spiritual giants and felt that it was disrespectful and even impious to think that further ijtihad could be exercised. This sentiment was expressed most frequently by members of the Hanafi and Maliki schools and by some members of the Shafi'i school.

Other legal scholars insisted that the exercise of juristic judgment was a continuing need. They argued that there was no reason to think that intellectual abilities and spiritual qualities had declined over the generations. Moreover, since there was now more legal knowledge available to scholars precisely because of the work of those past generations of jurists, there was more opportunity to make wise judgments than ever before, assuming that jurists made the effort to apply sound reasoning to their decisions. Most members of the Shafi'i school took this position. More surprising, in light of the antirationalist origins of the Hanbali school, the Hanbalis after the twelfth century were the most adamant in their insistence on the necessity of practicing ijtihad.

The issue of the closing of the gate of ijtihad slowly grew more controversial within the Sunni community. In the thirteenth century, some scholars began ranking each other in terms of their proficiency in exercising original judgment. Some rankings included up to seven grades of proficiency, ranging from very original to extremely imitative. The rankings provided ammunition to some scholars to argue that the number of genuine *mujtahid*s (practitioners of ijtihad) was decreasing, that the day would soon come when no qualified scholars would be alive, and that ijtihad could no longer be practiced. The Hanbalis were contemptuous of this position and argued that ijtihad was an obligation imposed on the totality of Muslim scholars and that to stop exercising it would be a sin. This was the position of Ibn Taymiya, and his differences with other faqihs over this issue was a major irritant for many of his critics.

By the second half of the fourteenth century, the majority of Sunni scholars had come to agree that ijtihad was no longer an option for faqihs. They argued that *taqlid* ("imitation" of previous scholars) was the only option for "modern" jurists. Taqlid came to be understood as the unquestioning acceptance of a previous decision or doctrine without inquiring into the reasons and evidence that were the basis for them. Most Hanbalis and a few Shafi'is continued to claim the right to practice ijtihad, but they were in a conspicuous minority. Many Hanafis considered them heretical for doing so.

The sentiment that led to the near consensus to terminate ijtihad can be appreciated in light of a conservative understanding of Islamic law. Most jurists would have agreed that the Shari'a, as God's law, is ultimately unknowable. Fiqh, they would argue, represents the efforts of the jurists to discover God's law, and thus the jurists' writings are works of jurisprudence rather than statements of God's law. In daily life, however, with concrete decisions having to be made, it was easy to slip into the habit of referring to the statements of the jurists as the Shari'a: The jurists needed to feel that what they were doing was worthwhile, and the community needed to have confidence in the rules they were accepting. A Hadith that quoted the Prophet as saying that his community would never agree upon error reassured them that they in fact had approximated God's will. Since God's will does not change, one did not have to worry about revising laws; besides, revisions would smack of human agency rather than divine decree.

In practice, ijtihad could not stop. Legal experts, even Hanafis, continued to employ it, but few faqihs admitted that they were doing so, and those who witnessed it pretended not to see it. New problems continued to arise that needed ijtihad in order to be solved. Jurists who were active in solving those problems understood their work in a different light from that of the outspoken advocates of taqlid. They believed that the work of all jurists throughout Islamic history had been approximate and had been achieved within a specific time and region. Circumstances, they knew, change from time to time and from society to society, and therefore ijtihad was necessary. Their work can be seen most vividly in the careers of the most preeminent jurists in Muslim societies, who were called upon to give rulings (*fatwas*) on vexing questions that other jurists could not provide. Such a legal authority, usually known as a *shaykh al-islam* or *mufti*, could issue thousands of fatwas on a wide variety of issues during his career.

The very fact that fatwas from muftis were necessary because other jurists could not agree on an issue seems to the eyes of the twenty-first century to be evidence that ijtihad continued. Nevertheless, taqlid became the official practice of the period after the fourteenth century. As a result, the fundamentals of the law did not change for centuries. The legal concepts that had developed during the creative eleventh and twelfth centuries remained unchanged until the nineteenth century. Discussions among jurists tended to be over hypothetical cases or even over issues that had once been important, but were no longer relevant. The occasional mujtahid did make revisions in practice when necessary, and sometimes a mufti's defense of his novel decision entered into the corpus of juristic tradition. On the whole, however, jurists understood that their primary mission was not to codify the law and to make the process of adjudication more streamlined and efficient. They continued to learn the body of decisions that had been recorded in the legal books and tried to apply them to their own circumstances with as little innovation as possible.

Twelver Shi'ite law faced similar issues, but underwent a different evolution. The Shi'ite jurists who advocated ijtihad won a tenth-century victory over those who opposed the exercise of reason. The opponents of ijtihad would have to wait until the late seventeenth century to (temporarily) close the "gate." The advocates of the use of reason continued to develop more sophisticated arguments for its employment. During the fourteenth century, when the Sunnis were achieving a near consensus on agreeing that ijtihad was no longer possible, the great Shi'ite jurist 'Allama al-Hilli was reorganizing jurisprudence so as to make reasoning its central feature.

The practical results of the apparent contrast between Sunni and Shi'ite jurisprudence were not as great as one might think, however. The actual Shi'ite experience after the fourteenth century was the mirror image of that of the Sunnis: Whereas the Sunnis claimed that ijtihad was no longer acceptable, but found to their embarrassment that they continued to practice it, the Shi'ites claimed to practice it, but found that the scope within which reason could be exercised was quite limited. Shi'ite jurists understood that they must exercise what they called "prudence and caution" in their decisions, so as not to stray from the path of the Imams. This self-censorship limited the number of original initiatives that a jurist might make.

The Varieties of Religious Expression

The members of any major religion exhibit a wide variety in their patterns of ritual behaviors and beliefs. Protestants, Catholics and Orthodox Christians all belong to the same religion, and yet differ considerably from each other. Even within

Protestantism or Catholicism, the range of expression is great: If a Catholic bishop from Paris were to spend a month in the home of fellow Catholics in a village in Haiti, he might well experience moments when he would wonder what religion his hosts practiced, after all. Muslims are equally diverse in their beliefs and practices. Muslims from North Africa, Central Asia, and the littoral of the Indian Ocean inevitably received the Islamic tradition through the filter of their respective cultural heritages. The remarkable fact about Islam is that it has a common identity at all. Unlike most monotheistic traditions, it has no institution with the authority to enforce orthodoxy. During the period of Mongol hegemony, many of the myriad expressions of Islam were becoming organized into institutional form and would be prepared to affect history in profound ways over the following centuries.

"Orthodoxy" and "Heterodoxy"

Throughout history, the various Christian denominations have enforced orthodox doctrines and practices within their respective churches. Persons who claim to be within a particular tradition, but who preach or teach contrary to orthodoxy ("correct doctrine") and engage in other than orthopraxy ("correct practice") are labeled "heretics." In earlier centuries, heretics were severely disciplined, often by execution. Since the Enlightenment, the typical response of the officials of the Church in question has been to exclude the person from membership. Islam does not have the equivalent of a pope or patriarch who can enforce conformity. Several individuals have claimed such a role, to be sure: During the first two centuries of Islamic history, some of the Umayyad and Abbasid caliphs attempted to enforce correct religious practices; the Imams of the various Shi'ite groups served such a function; and subsequent caliphs of many splinter groups all over the globe claimed such authority. In every case, however, the actual authority of a given leader extended over a limited territory or period of time. The majority of Muslims were unaffected.

Islamic history has witnessed many instances in which the charge of *kufr* ("unbelief," the equivalent of "heresy") has been leveled at various individuals and groups who claimed to be Muslim. The seventh-century Kharijites stimulated one of the most intense of these crises, for they regarded all Muslims who disagreed with them to be outside the pale, while other Muslims considered that attitude itself to be un-Islamic. This conflict gradually resolved itself over the next couple of centuries as the extreme Kharijites died out in the battles they provoked, and the surviving Ibadi Kharijites of North Africa and Oman were known primarily for their puritanism and reluctance to interact with outsiders, rather than for their aggression.

Early Shi'ites who elevated 'Ali (or other personages) to the status of a divinity were regarded as having compromised the monotheistic status of Islam. The extremist Shi'ites were gradually marginalized when the major Shi'ite groups officially denied deifying 'Ali or anyone else. Two important groups that were excluded from the Muslim Umma in this fashion still play important roles in the countries of the eastern Mediterranean. The Druze, who deified al-Hakim, the eleventh-century Fatimid caliph, were forced by popular pressure to seek refuge in the mountains of Lebanon and southern Syria. Farther north, the Nusayris sought refuge in the mountains of the Lataqiya province of western Syria. The Nusayris were the followers of the ninth-century figure Ibn Nusayr, who had preached the divinity of the eleventh Imam, and thus split from the group that subsequently became the Twelver Shi'ites. His group came to be associated with a divine trinity of 'Ali, Muhammad, and Salman the Iranian, in which 'Ali takes precedence as the God of the Qur'an. Because of this worship of 'Ali, the Nusayris are often called Alawis. The Nusayris worship in homes instead of mosques, do not observe Ramadan or the hajj, drink wine at religious services, and hold to the doctrine of transmigration of souls. For these reasons, Muslims have frequently persecuted Nusayris as heretics, although in the 1970s, the Nusayri ruler of Syria, Hafez al-Asad, obtained a ruling from Syrian Sunni ulama that declared him to be a Muslim.

Early Sufis who claimed to have experienced union with God during their mystical experiences were also ostracized. Once again, the central issue at stake was the compromising of the doctrine of the unity of God, which to most scholars also entailed a radical distinction between the Creator and his creatures. Al-Hallaj, the most famous of the extreme Sufis, was even executed by the state in 922 as a threat to public peace. Sufi leaders then began working toward a consensus on the doctrine that union with God was not a legitimate claim for the mystical experience.

With the exception of the execution of al-Hallaj, these examples of spiritual disciplining were largely collective affairs in which private religious scholars managed to win a consensus among other scholars and influential men of affairs to exclude (and even persecute) groups that had violated basic Islamic tenets. The key to understanding the continuity of Sunni Islam is an appreciation of the insistence upon fidelity to the text of the Qur'an and to the Sunna ("practice") of the Prophet as revealed in the Hadith. The various schools of Islamic law insisted upon the centrality of those two sources; theologians condemned the practice of philosophical speculation not limited by the truths of revelation; and Sufi orders developed traditions that reputedly linked their practice to the practice of the Prophet. The Sunni tradition was one of self-censorship. It was inevitably conservative and traditional in spirit, leading to the withering of an independent philosophical tradition and the closing of the gate of ijtihad.

In order to maintain a consensus across the vast Muslim world, scholars corresponded frequently with each other about their own work. They went on journeys to study with scholars greater than themselves. Most importantly, the practice of the hajj ensured that scholars would travel from every part of the Muslim world to Mecca, where they would be kept up to date on current thinking on theology and practice. Meccan scholars served as the touchstone for piety. They had absolutely no authority to enforce any doctrine or practice on anyone in any region, but pilgrims who came to Mecca seeking to study under such scholars for a period of time could learn whether their home community practiced a version of Islam that reflected the Meccan standard. Many pilgrims throughout history returned to their homes to begin reform movements, jolted by their experience on the hajj. Their reform movements could be campaigns of persuasion or of force.

This Sunni tradition of self-censorship was somewhat different from the attainment of a consensus within the various Kharijite and Shi'ite traditions. The Kharijites (Ibadis) comprised a relatively small number of Muslims, but they were scattered from Iran to North Africa. They maintained a high level of scholarly activity, and they maintained communications over vast distances in order to stay current with each other. Their political leaders were religious authorities, as well, and they maintained an effective discipline within their oases.

The Shi'ite communities that had the good fortune of being led by a "visible" Imam had direct access to the keeper of the consensus, for the Imam by definition possessed the authority to define truth. He could enforce any doctrine and maintain tight discipline. The communities that had a "hidden" Imam were a step removed from that sense of certainty, but still had confidence that the Hidden Imam maintained at least indirect communication with their religious scholars. As we have seen, the dominant school of religious scholars within the Twelver Shi'ite community did not share the opinion of most Sunnis that the gate of ijtihad ever closed. When they were left without a visible Imam, they were confident that pious, consecrated reason was capable of determining the will of the Hidden Imam. They developed the doctrine that the Hidden Imam would never allow his community to be misled by an erroneous ruling. If it should ever happen that (1) two jurists' rulings be in opposition, (2) one be totally wrong, and (3) the methods of jurisprudence not be able to detect the error, the Hidden Imam would intervene in person. Since he has never intervened, the members of the Twelver community can be confident that no rulings have ever been in error.

Thus, Islam had no Vatican, synod, or rabbinate to determine orthodoxy or orthopraxy. The scholarly consensus served as a remarkably effective method for obtaining cohesion among large groups of Muslims across a vast swath of the planet. The achievement is all the more impressive when one remembers that the vast majority of Muslims were illiterate. Just as it is impossible to appreciate Luther's accomplishments in the years after 1517 without realizing that most contemporary Europeans were illiterate and lightly Christianized, one cannot appreciate the fact that "Islam" exists today without understanding the far-flung, multiethnic, decentralized, and largely illiterate society in which the small group of private scholars labored to conserve the heritage of the Prophet.

Cohesion and a common sense of identity did not mean homogeneity, of course: Muslims developed distinctive differences in the expression of their faith. Sunnis, Shi'ites, and Kharijites formed three quite distinct groupings. Subsects formed within each of these traditions, and yet were regarded to be within the bounds of acceptable doctrine and practice. Some Muslims were persuaded that a scrupulous performance of ritual was the height of piety; others felt that ritual had to be balanced by a spiritual communion with God; and yet others regarded ritual as the mere outward expression of piety, placing emphasis on a mystical experience. The Qur'an and the Hadith (Sunni or Shi'ite) remained central, however.

The Proliferation of Sufi Groups

Historians assume a linkage between the upheavals of the twelfth and early thirteenth centuries on the one hand and the rise of Sufi lodges and orders during those centuries, on the other. In the face of the sufferings and uncertainties of the period, the small communities established by Sufis provided spiritual and material support, as well as the possibility of common defense. The subsequent disasters of the Mongol era from the mid-thirteenth century to the end of the fourteenth century were accompanied by a rapid increase in the number of Sufi organizations and an even larger increase in the percentage of Muslims who identified with Sufism. Once again, it appears that

Sufism responded to a deep need. In damaged and leaderless societies, the new Sufi orders (tariqas) satisfied social and religious needs that were not being met in any other way. The lodges (variously known as ribats, zawiyas, khanaqas, and tekkes), became centers of local worship, teaching and healing, and politics.

Sufism Triumphant

Sufism first appeared in the Muslim East (Iraq and Iran) in the eighth century. By the beginning of the tenth century, it was established in Andalus, and a century later it had secured a foothold in Morocco. By the fourteenth century, Sufism had become integrated into the everyday religious life of many—if not most—Muslims. Believers performed the ritual and moral duties of the Shari'a obediently and willingly and understood these to be the public expression of their faith and commitment. The Sufi dimension was the inner, emotional, personal relationship that they sought with their Creator God. "Sufism" could assume a wide range of expressions: Some adherents lived permanently in a lodge following the teachings of the founder of the order, and others were wandering mendicants, but most lived ordinary lives at home with their families and occasionally attended meetings of the local chapter of an order in order to recite mystical litanies.

Along with the work of intellectuals and artists and the consensus of the Shari'a, Sufism was one of the critical universal features that held the Umma together in the absence of a central authority. Each order had its own distinct devotional practices and ethical system that were used in lodges and mosques wherever the order was found. A given order's common tradition, authoritative texts, network of lodges, and distinctive lifestyle became elements that the culturally and ethnically diverse societies of Islam shared in common.

Sufism was also important because it provided women an acceptable avenue of both religious expression and religious leadership. Over the centuries, mosques had practically become preserves of males. The increasing exclusion of women from urban public spaces, coupled with the requirements of modesty during the ritual of the prescribed prayers, resulted in a consensus in most parts of the Muslim world that the community was better served if women performed their prayers at home. The expression of women's religious needs therefore frequently took the form of maintaining folk cults and performing pilgrimages to local shrines. Certain pious women themselves became the objects of intense veneration: In Cairo, both al-Sayyida Nafisa (great-granddaughter of Hasan, celebrated for her learning and piety) and al-Sayyida Zaynab (daughter of Ali) are revered in magnificent tomb–mosques. (*Sayyida* is an Arabic word normally meaning "lady" or "Mrs"; here, it implies both lineal descent from the Prophet and the status of sainthood.)

Sufism did not shatter any gender barriers, but in most locales it did encourage women's participation in Islamic rituals. Some Sufi preachers ministered primarily to women; a few lodges that served a largely male clientele were staffed primarily by women; women held their own Sufi meetings; some women became preachers; and other women were accorded the status of saint. It is clear that a number of women were initiated into Sufi orders. One young fourteenth-century male even received from his grandmother a *khirqa*, the robe that a Sufi novice received from his mentor.

Sufi masters—the heads of lodges and the teachers of the mystical path—rarely limited their services to their formal disciples. Usually known as *shaykh* in the Arabic-speaking communities and *pir* in Persian-speaking regions, they served the entire community, whether it be urban or rural. They provided spiritual guidance, mediation, and medical cures. Their primary function was to serve as a religious specialist, teaching their students how to achieve the mystical experience. For local residents, however, they also served as spiritual counselors, led prayers in mosques, and helped as needed at times of special rites, such as circumcision, marriage, and funerals. Some of the shaykhs, particularly in Morocco, were well versed in the Shari'a, and were able to give definitive rulings on legal matters and trought.

Sufi shaykhs also mediated disputes. They provided arbitration in disputes among local residents and between local residents and the conquerors who came and went with dizzying frequency. Their zawiyas would become busy centers where disciples would live and learn; local inhabitants would come for religious services, spiritual counsel, and food; and local tribesmen would come to settle conflicts. The lodge would often be located at an intersection of trade routes or near water sources, making the site easily accessible to as many people in the area as possible. In rural areas it was usually fortified, in order to provide a refuge for local residents from raiders.

Religious specialists throughout history have often been called upon to provide aid to those in need of medical attention, since they are believed to be able to intercede with God. That was particularly true in the premodern period, when modern medicines were not available. Sufi shaykhs were believed to have the power to heal persons and animals and to bestow blessings that enabled petitioners to become prosperous, bear children, and restore affection in a marriage relationship.

A Sufi shaykh with outstanding spiritual gifts might become revered as a "saint." The status of saint, or "friend of God," was accorded to notable martyrs, Shi'ite Imams, companions of the Prophet, and noteworthy ascetics. Sufi shaykhs achieved the distinction by their combination of exceptional piety, ecstatic states, the power of intercession, and extraordinary miracles. Most saints were credited with the gifts of clairvoyance and telepathy. Some were said to be able to fly, to be in two places at once, to ride rainbows, and to end droughts.

People far and near sought out saints in order to share in the power of their spiritual gifts. Their authority was enhanced even further when they combined evidence of spiritual power with an esteemed genealogical descent, either from a notable local family or, especially, from the Prophet's family. Saints were thus in a good position to provide an alternative source of authority in the absence of a strong central government. By virtue of their personal qualities and, perhaps, their family lineage, they possessed an authority that enabled them to keep the peace within an impressive radius of their zawiya, intercede for the poor with the wealthy landowner, and assure that travelers could enjoy both hospitality and safety.

A saint's service to his community did not end with his death. He was usually buried at the site of his zawiya, and his tomb would typically become the object of pilgrimages, as individuals continued to look to him as a source of aid. The shrine was regarded to be the repository of the spiritual power (*baraka*) that inhered in the saint in death as in life. Pilgrims came to shrines to ask for healing and the other blessings that the saint had provided during his lifetime. There they touched or kissed the

A Sufi saint's tomb in Morocco.

tomb, made small gifts or sacrifices, attached written requests to the shrine, celebrated the major religious festivals of the year, and observed the death day of the saint.

After the saint's death, the zawiya complex might actually increase in importance, for it boasted the attraction of the shrine in addition to the services of the saint's successor and his disciples. Its influence would typically spread into an even wider radius, providing the services of a market, religious education, the settling of tribal disputes, and the distribution of food to the poor. Over time, the shrine would typically become the recipient of gifts from grateful local residents and develop a wealthy endowment, able to exercise power at the spiritual, political, and economic levels.

Sufism as Social Critique

The practice of pilgrimage to shrines did not attract much controversy before the eighteenth century. The veneration of holy men and women—or of sacred places and objects—is a phenomenon common to all the major religious traditions and should be seen as a normal aspect of premodern Islam. It was the Muslim parallel to the contemporary Western Christian traffic in relics and visits to shrines such as Canterbury, Santiago de Compostela, and Jerusalem. The practice was validated by mainstream Sufism and sanctioned by most jurists, who cited passages from the Qur'an and the Hadith supporting the doctrine that some individuals have superior spiritual power. A handful of religious scholars opposed the veneration of saints, however: Ibn Taymiya vehemently attacked the practice as a flagrant violation of the Shari'a. The great Hanbali scholar practiced Sufi meditation techniques himself and did not oppose Sufi spirituality. On the other hand, he regarded shrine visits to be a remnant of pre-Islamic idolatry, and he accused supplicants at shrines of being "grave worshipers." His diatribes had no impact on the practice, and only landed him in jail. The masses, the majority of religious scholars, and government officials (throughout the Muslim world, not just the Mamlukes) agreed that the veneration of living and dead saints was a valid Islamic practice.

The veneration of saints drew the ire of Ibn Taymiya because he thought it compromised features of Islamic monotheism. Other critics of Sufism focused on the fact that some of the movement's features had taken on the trappings of a fully mature social institution. Indeed, the more elaborate shrines were eloquent testimony to the power, wealth, and systematization that had come to characterize much of the Sufi experience by the thirteenth and fourteenth centuries. This development was criticized by some individuals who were aware that Sufism had begun as a critique of the material and institutional elements of society, and that ascetic tendencies were always latent within the movement. In the thirteenth century, a rejection of mainstream Sufism appeared in the form of "Sufi deviancy." It was characterized by mendicancy, celibacy, asceticism, and the deliberate tweaking of what today would be called middle class sensibilities.

Forms of deviancy had manifested themselves throughout most of Sufi history. From at least as early as the tenth century, individuals known as the *malamatiya* ("those who draw blame upon themselves") were Sufis who were so concerned not to parade their virtue that they deliberately invited the contempt of their neighbors by committing unseemly, and even unlawful, acts. Most other Sufis, however, recognized that, while the malamatiya might be overzealous and overly conscientious in obeying the precept to avoid trying to impress the world of one's purity, they were sincere and pure of heart.

During the thirteenth century, Sufi deviancy became a much larger movement and was viewed with hostility by much of society. Several groups emerged, including the Qalandars, Haydaris, Abdals, Bektashis, and Madaris. Their individual members were usually called "dervishes." "Dervish" is the Turkish pronunciation of the Persian word "darvish," which suggests "wandering mendicant." Dervishes first appeared in Syria and Egypt in the thirteenth century, but soon became more characteristic of the region that includes Anatolia, Iran, and India.

In some ways, the life styles of dervishes suggest parallels with the Cynics, who became notorious in the Hellenistic world of the eastern Mediterranean beginning in the fourth century B.C.E. Typically, dervishes showed their contempt for social conventions by rejecting family life and choosing celibacy; rarely bathing; wearing unusual clothing (such as turbans with horns) or abandoning clothing altogether and going nude; shaving all bodily and facial hair (a practice that went contrary to the Shari'a); and using forbidden hallucinogens and intoxicants.

Beyond the obvious characteristics shared by many of the dervishes lay differences in their attitudes toward communal life. Some were solitary mendicants, who tended to exhibit the more extreme of the unconventional traits we have described. It is these individuals that European travelers and novelists of the nineteenth century made famous as "wild-eyed dervishes." Others also wandered across the countryside, but did so as a group of disciples who followed their shaykh. Still others maintained a permanent community, but their lodge was distinctively decorated and they themselves were clearly marked off from their fellow townsmen by their clothing and behavior.

The cultural elite of Muslim societies consistently identified the dervishes as the riffraff of society, and frequently accused them of being impostors and frauds. In fact, a considerable number of the dervishes were the sons of the elite. They rejected the comfortable and staid world of their fathers, and engaged in behavior that scandalized and disappointed their families. Like the Cynics (and hippies), they were engaged in a countercultural critique of dominant social norms. Unlike those two groups, most of the dervishes were also sincerely seeking a close spiritual relationship with God. They thought that establishing a relationship with God required severing their ties with the world of conventional morality.

Sufism, Syncretism, and Shi'ism

During the Mongol period, Sufi deviancy was most likely to be found in Anatolia, northern Iran, and northern India. The arc that stretched from Anatolia across northern Iran was also the primary setting for the rise of some Sufi groups that would exercise much more influence on subsequent Muslim history than did the Sufi deviants. Their story is the result of the Turkish migrations into the era.

During the century of Mongol rule of Iran, the composition of the population underwent a significant change. Under the Il-khanate, Iran was opened to the migration of large numbers of Turkish and Mongol peoples. Many of them made the long journey all the way into western Anatolia, where they played important roles in the early history of the Ottoman Sultanate. Most of those who entered the Iranian cultural area, however, settled in Transoxiana and in the region that comprises both Azerbaijan and eastern Anatolia. In both Transoxiana and Azerbaijan/eastern Anatolia, the Turkish-speaking peoples gradually came to outnumber the speakers of Persian. One result of this change in the ethnic composition of the area was a significant modification of the economy. Because many of the Turkish immigrants continued their nomadic existence, large areas of Iran, Azerbaijan, and eastern Anatolia were converted from agriculture into grazing areas for the service of a pastoral economy. In order to adjust, many erstwhile villagers began to practice semipastoralism: They cultivated the valleys that remained under cultivation and took herds of sheep into the mountain highlands during the summer for grazing. Other than the short-lived reforms of Ghazan (1295–1304), the agricultural economy of the region from the Amu Darya River to the headwaters of the Euphrates River suffered alternate bouts of destruction and neglect for several centuries.

The decline of urban life and the long-term absence of state security institutions also encouraged the development of new forms of social and religious organization in the region. With the decline of central governments in the region, the traditional social organization that the Turks brought with them from Central Asia remained important for purposes of security. This structure was based on what has been called a household state: A chief ruled over a large group of people related by kinship ties or alliances. He was aided by his family and by lesser chiefs and their followers, whose support was won by leadership ability and martial skills. The system was financed by raiding and by extorting revenues from nomads, peasants, and towns under its control. It was very unstable, however, for the authority of the chief was constantly challenged by ambitious subordinates. Rebellions were common, and the ensuing violence wreaked havoc among defenseless subject populations.

It was within this unstable and violent environment that Sufism began making inroads. As early as the twelfth century, Sufis had been working among the Turks of Transoxiana. The most revered of these was Ahmad Yasavi (d. 1166). Yasavi met with considerable success due to his technique of setting religious and moral education to music, using the lute as an accompaniment. From the mid-thirteenth to mid-fourteenth centuries, several other Sufi-led movements appeared among both peasant and nomadic communities from Transoxiana into rural Anatolia. There, shaykhs served the functions mentioned earlier: They were healers, mediators, and religious guides, and they resisted the oppression and exploitation of the poor by the household states.

Given the insecurity and oppression that characterized the era, it is understandable that the doctrines that flourished in the Sufi communities stressed deliverance and rewards. Popular religious figures included those of the Mahdi, who would come at the end of time to create a just order; the Qutb, the figure in Sufi circles who served as the axis for the world and a haven for oppressed peoples; and 'Ali, Muhammad's closest companion, cousin, and son-in-law, whose combination of religious piety and martial valor provided a role model for serious young men. 'Ali was particularly popular among Sufis of this era, and many of the newly emerging Sufi orders constructed *silsilas*, or spiritual genealogies, that traced their teachings back to him. For some groups, 'Ali became as prominent as Muhammad, although the groups seem not to have viewed themselves as Shi'ite. Unlike the urban Sunni and Shi'ite scholars, distinctions such as "Sunni" and "Shi'ite" do not seem to have been important to them.

Of the many Sufi groups that emerged at this time among the primarily Turkish-speaking peoples, four are particularly worthy of notice because of their subsequent historical importance. The Naqshbandi order, attributed to Baha al-Din Naqshband (1318–1398) of Bukhara, later became highly influential in Central Asia and India. One of its distinguishing characteristics was the teaching of a "silent <u>dh</u>ikr": Whereas most orders practiced a communal, vocal <u>dh</u>ikr, the silent <u>dh</u>ikr enabled an individual to engage in it mentally and thus under practically any circumstance and at any time. The order arose in the highly sophisticated atmosphere of Bukhara, and despite its subsequent dissemination among the rural population of the Ottoman realm, Central Asia, and India, it was always characterized by a careful attention to normative ritual and doctrine.

By contrast, several groups that emerged at this time exhibited syncretistic qualities that reflected their origins in the multireligious and multiethnic rural area between central Anatolia and Azerbaijan. After the battle of Kose Dagh in 1243, when Batu defeated the Sultanate of Rum, the region's cities went into decline. With Hulagu's creation of the Il-khanate in 1259, the region was inundated by Turkish and Mongol immigrants. The influence of the Shari'a-minded ulama was no longer as strong as it had been. In contrast to the strict adherence to the Shari'a practiced by the Naqshbandi order and the rural shaykhs of Morocco, Sufi leaders of eastern Anatolia and Azerbaijan tended to stress the universal aspects of Islam in their preaching. They relaxed their ritual requirements, making it easier for shamanistic Turks and local Christian peasants alike to make the transition into their communities.

One example of this trend was the career of Hajji Bektash. Scholars have traditionally thought that Bektash lived until 1337, but recent research suggests that he died in the last quarter of the thirteenth century. He was a learned Sufi shaykh who emphasized the importance of the mystical way and taught his followers that the details of the Shari'a, including the daily prayers, were not important. As a result, his original movement is regarded as an example of Sufi deviancy. Over the next two centuries, as the Bektashi movement developed in the melting pot of Anatolia and Azerbaijan, it acquired many doctrines and practices that, had it not been so secretive, would almost certainly have caused it to be ostracized or even persecuted. Nevertheless, it became highly popular all across Anatolia and eventually in the Balkans.

Similarities between the mature Bektashi order and the Nusayri sect are striking. Its members considered many elements of Islamic ritual and worship, such as performance of the salat and observing the fast during the month of Ramadan, to be unimportant. Bektashis did not attend mosques, but rather held a communal weekly prayer in a private home. Ostensibly Sunni, the Bektashis revered the Twelve Shi'ite Imams, but scandalized the Twelver Shi'ites by their extremist practice of worshiping 'Ali as the center of a trinity of 'Ali, Muhammad, and "God." They denied the doctrine of the resurrection of the body and taught instead that souls are reincarnated into other bodies. They initiated new members with a reception of wine, bread, and cheese, a practice that seems to have been borrowed from a heretical Christian group of Anatolia called the Paulicians.

The Bektashis were usually found in towns and cities, and they were tightly organized under their leader. The Alevi (the Turkish spelling of "Alawi") movement was closely related to it and seems to have been the result of a schism in the historical development of Hajji Bektash's group. The Alevis tended to be rural, located in central and eastern Anatolia, and less educated than their urban counterparts. Their practices and doctrines were almost identical to those of the Bektashis, however. Because they were scattered among farming villages and nomadic tribes, they were not as cohesive as the Bektashis, who looked down upon them for their rustic ways.

Of the other Sufi groups that emerged at this time, one stands out for its role in creating an empire. Shaykh Safi al-Din (1252–1334) created a Sufi community in Ardabil, near the southwestern shore of the Caspian Sea. In acknowledgment of his founding role, his organization has come to be known as the Safavid movement. During the fourteenth century, the order developed schools and residences in Ardabil and expanded its missionary activities among the Turkish-speaking populations of Anatolia and Azerbaijan. In the fifteenth and early sixteenth centuries, the Safavids and Alevis shared a wide range of doctrines and practices and were almost indistinguishable. At the beginning of the sixteenth century, the Safavids caught the attention of the world when they created an empire in what is now Iran.

Conclusion

By the end of the fourteenth century, the majority of the population from Morocco to eastern Iran were Muslim. Numerous new clusters of Muslims were beginning to form all around the Indian Ocean and south of the Sahara Desert. Their mosques, Shari'a courts, schools, and fraternal organizations provided networks of support that proved to be decisive for surviving crises. In the areas that the Mongols captured, those institutions proved to be strong enough to survive the severest of challenges, confirming the work of centuries of laborious effort on the part of pious scholars and activists. Individual Muslims were able to maintain their identities and ways of life precisely because the major Islamic institutions were independent of government control. The destruction of a given regime, therefore, did not entail the destruction of the judicial, educational, or religious traditions of the society in question. In areas recently settled by Muslims, their institutions served to buttress their faith and to attract new converts.

Muslim societies survived the era of Mongol hegemony, from 1260 to 1405. They were more conservative and cautious at the end of it than they had been at the beginning, but they also had more reason to be confident that, having survived the fourteenth century, they could survive anything. In fact, Islam was about to enter upon a period of dynamic expansion into Africa, Central Asia, and Southeast Asia, when a group of Muslim states were among the superpowers of the world.

FURTHER READING

Intellectual Life in the Fourteenth Century

Dunn, Ross E. *The Adventures of Ibn Battuta: A Muslim Traveler of the 14*[th] *Century.* Berkeley and Los Angeles: University of California Press, 1986.

Ibn Khaldun. *The Muqaddimah: an Introduction to History.* Tr. Franz Rosenthal, Vol. 3 2d ed. London: Routledge and Kegan Paul, 1967.

Kennedy, E.S. and Imad Ghanem, eds. *The Life & Work of Ibn al-Shātir.* Aleppo, Syria: The University of Aleppo, 1976.

Laoust, Henri. "Ibn Taymiyya," in *Encyclopedia of Islam, New Edition.* III. Edited by Bernard Lewis, et al. Leiden: E.J. Brill; London: Luzac & Co., 1971.

Mahdi, Muhsin. *Ibn Khaldūn's Philosophy of History.* Chicago and London: University of Chicago Press, 1957.

Saliba, George. *A History of Arabic Astronomy: Planetary Theories During the Golden Age of Islam.* New York University Studies in Near Eastern Civilization. New York and London: New York University Press, 1994.

Law

Hallaq, Wael B. "Was the Gate of Ijtihad Closed?", *IJMES,* Vol. 16, No. 1 (March 1984), pp. 3–41.

Imber, Colin. *Ebu's-Su'ud: The Islamic Legal Tradition.* Stanford, California: Stanford University Press, 1997.

Stewart, Devin J. *Islamic Legal Orthodoxy: Twelver Shiite Responses to the Sunni Legal System.* Salt Lake City, Utah: The University of Utah Press, 1998.

The Varieties of Religious Expression

Cornell, Vincent J. *Realm of the Saint: Power and Authority in Moroccan Sufism.* Austin, Texas: University of Texas Press, 1998.

Karamustafa, Ahmet T. "Early Sufism in Eastern Anatolia." In *Classical Persian Sufism: From its Origins to Rumi,* ed. Leonard Lewisohn, pp. 175–198. London and New York: Khaniqahi Nimatullahi Publications, 1993.

Karamustafa, Ahmet T. *God's Unruly Friends: Dervish Groups in the Islamic Later Middle Period, 1200–1550.* Salt Lake City, Utah: The University of Utah Press, 1994.

Knysh, Alexander. *Islamic Mysticism: A Short History.* Leiden, Boston, Koln: Brill, 2000.

Moosa, Matti. *Extremist Shiites: The Ghulāt Sects.* Syracuse, New York: Syracuse University Press, 1988.

Glossary

'abd: Arabic term meaning "slave" or "servant." In conjunction with the name of God or one of his attributes, the word is a component of many Muslim names: 'Abd Allah (or 'Abdullah) 'Abd al-Rahman, 'Abd al-Karim, etc. (It is worth noting that "Abdul" ("'Abd al-") is not a name, despite popular representations of it in English; it must be followed by the name of God or one of his attributes.)

abu: Arabic term meaning "father." Many Arab men often consider it a point of pride to be called the father of their firstborn son. Hence, Abu Hasan is a nickname for someone who was born with a name such as Mahmud until his son Hasan was born, at which time he became known as Abu Hasan.

A.H.: Abbreviation of the Latin phrase *anno hejirae*, referring to the dating system based on the Islamic calendar. Muslims decided to use the year of the Hijra (622 C.E.) to begin their calendar and to use a lunar, rather than a solar, calculation, resulting in a calendar of 354 days rather than 365/6 days. As a result, it gains a year on the Gregorian calendar approximately every thirty-three years. Thus, the year A.H. 100 did not correspond, as one might think, with 722 C.E., but rather extended from August 718 through July 719.

ahl: Arabic term meaning "family," "household," or "people." *Ahl al-kitab* means "People of the Book," referring to the Jews and Christians; *Ahl al-sunna* are those who follow the Prophet's example.

Alid: Lineal descendant of 'Ali.

amir: Arabic term connoting "military commander" or "ruler." The caliph's title was frequently *amir al-mu'minin*, or "commander of the faithful."

Anatolia: Asia Minor, or the section of western Asia that juts westward between the Black Sea and the Mediterranean Sea. Anatolia comprises the bulk of modern Turkey.

Andalus: Muslim-occupied portion of the Iberian Peninsula. Its frontier with the Christian kingdoms to the north fluctuated over time.

Ashura: Islamic holy day, observed on the tenth day of Muharram, the first month of the Islamic calendar. Muhammad had designated Ashura to be a day of voluntary fasting, but it became most celebrated when Husayn, the elder son of 'Ali by

Fatima, was killed at Karbala. Because of this tragedy, Ashura became the major religious day of the year among Shi'ites. Many of them dedicate the first ten days of the month to fasting, reading from the Qur'an, prayers, and reenactments of the martyrdom. Many Sunnis also observe Ashura, but on a more subdued note, and normally only on the tenth day.

baraka Arabic term for the spiritual power of a holy man. It can be "tapped" by a supplicant whether the holy man is living or dead.

baqa': Arabic term used by Sufis to suggest the "survival" of personal identify in the material world during the mystical experience; is paired with *fana'*.

batin: Arabic term for the inner, hidden, or esoteric meaning of a text. Contrasts with *zahir*.

bayt: Arabic term for "house." Often used metaphorically, as in Bayt al-Hikma ("house of wisdom"), the institute created by the Abbasid caliph al-Ma'mun (813–833) to translate scientific and philosophical texts into Arabic.

bid'a: Arabic term for "innovation." In religious usage, the term came to imply "heresy," since nothing should be added to Islam that is not found in the Qur'an or Hadith.

Central Asia: The inland part of Asia. The term usually designates the region from the Caspian Sea in the west to northwestern China and Mongolia in the east, and from southern Siberia in the north to northern Iran and Afghanistan in the south.

Cyrenaica: Area of Libya lying east of the Gulf of Sidra.

dar: Arabic term meaning "abode" or "dwelling." Often used metaphorically, as in Dar al-Hikma ("Abode of Wisdom"), the institute of higher learning in the Fatimid caliphate; Dar al-Islam, the term used for the lands under Muslim rule; and Dar al-Kufr ("Abode of Unbelief") and Dar al-Harb ("Abode of War"), terms used for the lands not yet under Muslim rule.

dervish: Turkish variant of Persian "*darvish*," literally meaning "poor" (*faqir* in Arabic). Sometimes used as a synonym for "Sufi," sometimes used to designate a wandering, mendicant spiritualist.

devshirme: Turkish term for the levy of young Christian boys that was begun in the late fourteenth century to staff the infantry and higher civil administration in the Ottoman realm.

dhikr: Arabic term for "recollection" or memory, sometimes rendered *zikr*. The term is used for Sufi devotional practices intended to accentuate the awareness of the presence of God. In later Sufi history, the various *tariqas* were differentiated in part by their distinctive *dhikrs*.

dhimmi: Arabic term for a free non-Muslim subject living in a Muslim country who, in return for paying a head tax, was granted protection and safety.

fana': Arabic term used by Sufis to express the "passing away" or "annihilation" of personal identity during the mystical experience; is paired with *baqa'*.

fatwa: Arabic term for a ruling made by a very high government-appointed authority on the Shari'a (*mufti*) on a point of Islamic law; became important in the Muslim empires that emerged in the fifteenth and sixteenth centuries.

Fertile Crescent: A term popularized by the American archaeologist James Henry Breasted for the crescent-shaped area that extends from the Persian Gulf up almost to the headwaters of the Tigris and Euphrates rivers, and then westward through Syria to the Mediterranean and southward to southern Palestine. Sometimes the Nile valley of Egypt is included as a further extension of the area.

fiqh: Arabic term for Islamic jurisprudence, or the method of determining the Shari'a. The jurist who follows the method is called a *faqih.*

ghazi: Arabic term for "raider" (Turkicized as *gazi*). After the Arab conquests and the frontiers with the Dar al-Harb were relatively stabilized, the term connoted a "warrior for the faith" who raided non-Muslim territories, particularly in Anatolia. In this sense, it was usually synonymous with *mujahid,* "one who engages in *jihad.*"

Ghadir Khumm: Shi'ite festival instituted by the Buyids in the tenth century. It derives its name from the Pool (*ghadir*) of Khumm, located between Mecca and Medina, where Shi'ites believe that Muhammad formally designated 'Ali to be his successor as spiritual and political leader of the Umma.

ghulat: Arabic term meaning "exaggerators," or "those who go beyond the proper bounds." Usually applied to certain Shi'ites who have claimed a divine status for 'Ali, believed in metempsychosis, and engaged in rituals that seemed to other Muslims to violate Islamic norms.

hadith: Arabic term for a "report" of something that takes place. When applied to a saying or action of the Prophet and his companions, it became a "tradition" that was passed down from generation to generation. The Hadith became a source of religious authority second only to the Qur'an.

hajj: Annual pilgrimage to Mecca. One of the Five Pillars of Islam, it is to be performed at least once in a lifetime if possible, during the month of Dhu al-Hijja. It is distinguished from *'umra,* which is a pilgrimage to Mecca at any other time of the year.

Hanafi: Referring to the *madhhab* attributed to Abu Hanifa (699–767).

Hanbali: Referring to the *madhhab* attributed to Ahmad ibn Hanbal (780–855).

Hijra: Muhammad's trek from Mecca to Medina in 622. This marks the beginning of the Muslim calendar.

Iberian Peninsula: European peninsula comprising the modern countries of Spain and Portugal.

ibn: Arabic term for "son." Just as Arab men often are known to their friends as the "Father of So-and-So," their sons are often known as the "Son of So-and-So" rather than by their personal name. Many famous figures in Muslim history are known this way: Ibn Sina, Ibn Khaldun, Ibn Battuta, etc. Often abbreviated, as in Ahmad b. Hanbal.

Ifriqiya: Area roughly corresponding to present-day Tunisia and eastern Algeria.

ijaza: Arabic term indicating an authorization or license to teach a certain book on the grounds that the recipient of the *ijaza* has shown that he or she fully understands it.

ijtihad: Arabic term meaning, in the context of *fiqh,* independent judgment to establish a ruling upon a given point. One who exercises *ijtihad* is a *mujtahid.* Contrasts with *taqlid.*

imam: Cognate of the Arabic preposition meaning "before" or "in front of." Among Sunni Muslims the term has been applied to (1) the prayer leader at a mosque, since he stands in front of the congregation, (2) the caliph, and (3) an outstanding religious scholar, especially the founder of a *madhhab.* Among Shi'ite Muslims the imam (rendered in this book as Imam) is the legitimate leader of the Muslim world. Shi'ite sects have defined the characteristics of their Imams in different ways over the centuries, but generally the Imam is understood not to have prophetic status. He does, however, provide indispensable religious guidance, and he is the rightful head of the entire Muslim community. Some Shi'ite groups consider their Imam to be "hidden" or "invisible," because they do not know where he is, whereas other groups have a "visible" Imam who lives among them and from whom they can obtain direct guidance.

iqta': Arabic term for a grant of land or of its revenues by a government to a military officer or civil official in lieu of direct cash payment for services.

isnad: Arabic term for the chain of names of the transmitters of a Hadith, cited to guarantee its validity.

jami': Cognate of the Arabic word connoting "to gather, unite, combine." It is the term used for the large, officially designated congregational mosque in a large city that usually combines the functions of worship, education, and information.

jihad: Arabic term for "struggle" or "battle." The Prophet said that the Greater Jihad was the struggle against spiritual impurity, and the Lesser Jihad was the war against unbelievers. One who engages in *jihad* is a *mujahid.*

kalam: Arabic term literally meaning "speech," "discussion," or "discourse." As *'ilm al-kalam,* or the science of discourse, it refers approximately to what is called theology in Christianity.

khan: Turkish term for "ruler." Can also mean "hostel" for merchants or students.

khanaqa: Persian term for a lodge that Sufis visit or live in, in order to pursue the mystical way.

khirqa: Arabic term for a cloak or frock (usually patched or showing signs of age) that a Sufi *shaykh/pir* bestowed upon a *murid.* Supposedly the shaykh's own cloak, its bestowal signified the shaykh's recognition of the murid's high level of spiritual approval; it also suggested that the murid would be able to acquire some of the shaykh's *baraka* while wearing it.

Khorasan: Region in northeastern Iran whose area has been defined differently over the centuries, but prior to the demarcation of modern national boundaries it approximated the area bounded on the west by the Dasht-e Kavir desert, on the south by the Dasht-e Lut desert, and on the north by the Amu Darya River, and it comprised the western quarter of modern Afghanistan.

khutba: Arabic term for the sermon delivered at the noon Friday worship service in the mosque. It contained prayers for the caliph as a declaration of his sovereignty.

Khwarazm: Region on lower Amu Darya River, on the shore of the Aral Sea.

Kurds: Members of an ethnic group located primarily in the mountains and highlands of western Iran, northeastern Iraq, and eastern Turkey who speak languages belonging to the Indo–European linguistic family. Their languages are closely related to Farsi (Persian).

kuttab: Cognate of the Arabic root word for "book" and "read"; connotes a primary school whose primary function is to teach the memorization of the Qur'an. Also *maktab.*

madhhab: Arabic term indicating a formalized, traditional system or method of determining *fiqh,* often translated as "school of law."

madrasa: Cognate of the Arabic word to "study," it connotes a school for the study of Islamic jurisprudence, Qur'an interpretation, Hadith, biographies of great Muslims, and dialectic.

Maghrib: Literally, "West." In general, it denotes North Africa west of central Libya (the Gulf of Sidra), but some commentators denote by it all of North Africa west of Egypt, and still others use it to identify the area comprising Tunisia, Algeria, and Morocco, and even Andalus.

mahdi: Arabic term meaning "guided one," an eschatological figure who is first mentioned in the literature of Islam's first century. He is usually considered to be a Muslim leader who will be sent by God at the end of history to bring an end to the corruption and injustice of a wicked world and to implement God's will. Within Shi'ism the use of the term is usually understood to mean the (hidden) Imam.

Maliki: Referring to the *ma<u>dhh</u>ab* attributed to Malik ibn Anas (715–797).

mamluk: Arabic term meaning "owned," usually connoting a slave soldier, most often of Turkish origin.

Mamlukes: Regime that ruled Egypt from 1250 to 1517, composed of *mamluks*. (Also rendered "Mamluks.")

masjid: Arabic term meaning "place of prostration." The word from which "mosque" is derived, connoting an edifice designed for the performance of the *salah*.

mihrab: Arabic term for the niche or recess in an interior wall of a mosque that designates the *qibla*.

mudejar: Spanish rendering of the Arabic word *mudajjan*, meaning "permitted to remain," or "domesticated." In the Iberian Peninsula, the term denoted a Muslim who was a subject of a Christian ruler in the aftermath of the Reconquista.

Muharram: First month of the Islamic calendar.

muhtasib: Arabic term used for the inspector of the market and enforcer of public morality.

murabit: Arabic term meaning "one who lives in a ribat." In some locales at certain periods of time, the term meant "a soldier who defended the frontier." At other times and places, it could connote a pious individual who spread the message of Islam among rural people. The word "Almoravid" is a corruption of *al-murabit*.

murid: Arabic term denoting a Sufi aspirant or disciple who follows a *shaykh* or *pir*.

muwallad: Term used in al-Andalus for a Hispano–Roman convert to Islam.

nabi: Arabic term for "prophet," applied to the Hebrew prophets and Jesus as well as to Muhammad.

Oghuz: (also "Ghuzz") A Turkish confederation that, during the tenth century, roamed the area north of the Aral Sea and Syr Darya River. The Saljuq family was the most famous group from this confederation.

Palestine: Term used for the first several centuries of Muslim history to refer to southern Syria, or roughly the territory occupied today by Jordan and Israel.

pir: Persian term for a Sufi master who leads disciples on the mystical way.

Punjab: (also "Panjab") A geographical region deriving its name from the words *punj* meaning "five," and *aab* meaning "waters," referring to five rivers that are tributaries of the Indus River: the Sutlej, Beas, Ravi, Chenab and Jhelum rivers. Today, the Punjab is divided between Pakistan and India.

pro-Alid: Muslim who believed that only an Alid could be the legitimate caliph.

qadi: Arabic term for a member of the ulama who sits in a Shari'a court and rules on cases, using as his reference the body of jurisprudence (*fiqh*) worked up by scholars over the centuries.

qanun: Arabic variant of Roman "canon" law. Connotes secular government statutes and laws, in contrast to the Shari'a.

Qara-khanid: Dynasty from the Qarluq group of Turks who invaded Transoxiana during the last decade of the tenth century. Although the members of the dynasty were not able to maintain control over the entire region for long, they ruled in many of the individual oases for the next three centuries.

Qara-khitai: Mongol group that dominated the area north and east of the Syr Darya river in the twelfth and early thirteenth centuries before Chinggis Khan defeated them.

Qarluq: Turkish confederation which, in the tenth century, roamed north of the Syr Darya river. Its leading dynasty, the Qara-khanid, invaded Transoxiana on the eve of the eleventh century.

qibla: Arabic term indicating the correct direction in which to perform the salah (facing the Ka'ba) from a given point on earth.

Qipchaq: Turkish confederation that dominated the so-called Qipchaq steppe north of the Black Sea. They were the primary source for the ruling elite of the Mamluke Empire from 1260 to 1382 and became the dominant cultural and demographic element within the Golden Horde.

Ramadan: Ninth month of the Islamic calendar.

rasul: Arabic term for "messenger" or "apostle." The most common title for Muhammad, as a channel for revelation from God.

Reconquista: Spanish term literally meaning "reconquest" that was applied to the process by which the Christian kingdoms of the northern Iberian Peninsula conquered Andalus over a period of four centuries.

ribat: Cognate of an Arabic word suggesting to "tie up" or "hitch." The word is used to refer to the forts that guarded frontier areas in North Africa, Andalus, and Anatolia. A ribat in this sense served as a garrison for what was (usually) a volunteer force that served at least in part out of religious commitment and thus became associated with religious devotionals as well as with the idea of a garrison. When conditions changed and a ribat was no longer needed for defensive purposes, it might become a Sufi lodge. In North Africa, Sufi lodges were typically called ribats whether they had originally been used as forts or built new for specifically devotional purposes.

Rum: Name Arabs and Turks used to designate Byzantine territories (from "Rome").

salat: Arabic term for the worship service of congregational prayer, performed five times daily. One of the Five Pillars of Islam. The call to prayer (*adhan*) is made by a *mu'adhdhan* (muezzin) from a *manara* (minaret).

Saljuq: Dynasty from the Oghuz Turkish confederation that conquered huge areas of the Muslim world in the eleventh century.

sawm: Arabic term for "abstinence" or "fasting." Fasting from dawn until sundown during the month of Ramadan is one of the Five Pillars of Islam.

Shafi'i: Referring to the *madhhab* attributed to al-Shafi'i (767–820).

shahada: Arabic term referring to the declaration that there is no god but God and Muhammad is his prophet. One of the Five Pillars of Islam.

shari'a: Arabic word originally connoting "the approach to a watering hole" in the desert; later identified with Islamic law, derived from the Qur'an, Hadith, analogy, and consensus.

shaykh: Arabic term connoting "elderly man" or "venerable gentleman." It is also used to denote a chieftain or a Sufi leader.

silsila: Arabic term for "chain," used for the "spiritual family tree" that linked the teachings of the founder of a Sufi order to the teachings of the Prophet himself.

Sind: Region of the lower Indus River.

South Asia: Term usually applied to the region between the Hindu Kush mountains and the Himalayas on the north and the Indian Ocean on the south.

Sufism: Most common expression of the mystical life in Islam, organized into *tariqas* and focused on meetings in *khanaqas*.

Sultan: From the Arabic word "*sulta,*" meaning "power" or "authority." Buyid and Saljuq military rulers assumed the title to distinguish their actual power from the nominal authority of the Abbasid caliph; in later centuries it became the typical term for the sovereign of a Muslim state.

sunna: Arabic term meaning "customary practice." It came to mean the ritual and ethical practice of (1) the Companions of the Prophet or (2) the Prophet himself.

sura: Arabic term used to indicate a chapter in the Qur'an. Individual verses are called *ayat*.

Syria: Historically, the area from the Taurus Mountains in the north to the Gulf of Aqaba in the south.

taqiya: Doctrine within the Shi'ite community that allows a believer who is being persecuted to dissimulate, or deny his or her beliefs.

taqlid: Arabic word meaning "uncritical, unquestioning acceptance." Used as a contrast to *ijtihad* in the debate over how much latitude a Muslim jurist had to exercise his own judgment.

tariqa: Arabic term literally meaning "path" or "route," it technically applies to the method of spiritual growth that the eponymous founder of a particular Sufi order reputedly taught.

tekke: Turkish term for a lodge that Sufis visit or live in, in order to pursue the mystical way.

Transoxiana: (also "Transoxania") The area known by the Arabs as *ma wara an-nahr,* or "that which lies beyond the (Oxus) river." Usually the term refers to the area between the Oxus (Amu Darya) and Jaxartes (Syr Darya) rivers, but sometimes connotes areas north of the Syr Darya, as well.

Turkmen/Turcomans: Term often used to denote nomadic Turkish-speaking Muslims, to distinguish them from urban or settled Turkish-speaking Muslims and from pagan Turks.

'ulama': Arabic word literally meaning "scholars," it usually denotes the specialists in Qur'an, Hadith, and religious law. Rendered "ulama" in this book.

umma: Arabic term for "nation" or "people," came to be applied to the Muslim community as a whole.

vizier: English transliteration of the Turkish variant of *wazir*.

wali: Arabic word used in Sufism that is usually translated "saint."

waqf: Arabic word meaning "religious endowment." The Shari'a allowed a person to allocated part or all of his or her estate to an endowment that would provide funds to build and maintain mosques, schools, fountains, orphanages, hospitals, etc.

wazir: Arabic word denoting the chief administrative officer to the head of state (caliph or sultan) in a premodern Muslim state. In the modern era, the term usually denotes the head of a ministry or department within the national government.

zahir: Arabic term for the apparent, external, surface meaning of a text. Contrasts with *batin*.

zakat: Arabic word denoting the contribution that Muslims are expected to make as a tax to support charity and governmental services. One of the Five Pillars of Islam.

zawiya: Arabic term for a lodge that Sufis visit or live in, in order to pursue the mystical way.

Credits

Index